Black Women and Social Justice Education

SUNY series, Praxis: Theory in Action

Nancy A. Naples, editor

# Black Women and Social Justice Education

*Legacies and Lessons*

Edited by
Stephanie Y. Evans, Andrea D. Domingue,
and Tania D. Mitchell

**SUNY** PRESS

Cover image courtesy of Francis Mead. Reproduced with permission of the artist.

Published by State University of New York Press, Albany

© 2019 State University of New York

Chapter 20 "The Dialectic of Radical Black Feminism" © Keeanga-Yamahtta Taylor

All rights reserved

Printed in the United States of America

No part of this book may be used or reproduced in any manner whatsoever without written permission. No part of this book may be stored in a retrieval system or transmitted in any form or by any means including electronic, electrostatic, magnetic tape, mechanical, photocopying, recording, or otherwise without the prior permission in writing of the publisher.

For information, contact State University of New York Press, Albany, NY
www.sunypress.edu

## Library of Congress Cataloging-in-Publication Data

Names: Evans, Stephanie Y., editor. | Domingue, Andrea D., 1981– editor. | Mitchell, Tania D., 1974– editor.
Title: Black women and social justice education : legacies and lessons / edited by Stephanie Y. Evans, Andrea D. Domingue, Tania D. Mitchell.
Description: Albany : State University of New York Press, [2019] | Series: SUNY series, praxis: theory in action | Includes bibliographical references and index.
Identifiers: LCCN 2018013692 | ISBN 9781438472959 (hardcover : alk. paper) | ISBN 9781438472966 (ebook) | ISBN 9781438472942 (pbk. : alk. paper)
Subjects: LCSH: African American women—History. | Women in education—United States—History. | African American women college teachers—United States—History. | African American social reformers—United States—History. | Discrimination—United States—History. | Social justice—Study and teaching—United States—History.
Classification: LCC E185.86 .B54165 2019 | DDC 305.48/896073—dc23
LC record available at https://lccn.loc.gov/2018013692

10 9 8 7 6 5 4 3 2 1

# Contents

ACKNOWLEDGMENTS ix

FOREWORD
Black Women Rising: Jumping Double-Dutch with a Liberatory
Consciousness xi
   *Barbara J. Love and Valerie D. Jiggetts*

INTRODUCTION
Black Women's Educational Philosophies and Social Justice Values
of the 94 Percent 1
   *Stephanie Y. Evans, Andrea D. Domingue, and Tania D. Mitchell*

## PART I
### EXAMINING IDENTITY AND THEORY

CHAPTER 1
Gone Missin': The Absence of Black Women's Praxis in
Social Justice Theory 23
   *Tania D. Mitchell*

CHAPTER 2
Social Justice Education and Luxocracy 43
   *Layli Maparyan*

CHAPTER 3
When Intersections Collide: Young Black Women Combat Sexism,
Racism, and Ageism in Higher Education 55
   *Jaymee Lewis-Flenaugh, Eboni N. Turnbow, and Sharee L. Myricks*

## Chapter 4
Standing Outside of the Circle: The Politics of Identity and
Leadership in the Life of a Black Lesbian Professor — 67
*Judy A. Alston*

## Chapter 5
Black Feminist Thought: A Response to White Fragility — 75
*Michele D. Smith and Maia Niguel Moore*

## Chapter 6
The Reproduction of the Anti-Black Misogynist Apparatus in U.S.
and Latin American Pop Culture — 91
*Natasha Howard*

# PART II
# EVALUATING FOUNDATIONS AND GENERATIONS

## Chapter 7
A Seat at the Table: Mary McLeod Bethune's Call for the Inclusion
of Black Women During World War II — 105
*Ashley Robertson Preston*

## Chapter 8
The Life of Dovey Johnson Roundtree (1914–2018): A Centenarian
Lesson in Social Justice and Regenerative Power — 121
*Katie McCabe and Stephanie Y. Evans*

## Chapter 9
This Ain't Yo' Mama's Revolution—Or Maybe It Is: #TakeBackTheFlag
and the New Student Activism — 141
*Shennette Garrett-Scott and Dominique Garrett-Scott*

## Chapter 10
We Got a Lot to Be Mad About: A Seat at Solange's Table — 165
*Bettina L. Love and Sarah Abdelaziz*

# PART III
# POSITING PEDAGOGY

## Chapter 11
Black, Female, and Teaching Social Justice: Transformative Pedagogy
for Challenging Times — 183
*Robin Brooks*

CHAPTER 12
Moments in the Danger Zone: Encountering "Non-Racist,"
"Non-Racial," and "Non-Color-Seeing" Do-Gooders 201
    *Michelle R. Dunlap, Christina D. Burrell, and*
    *Penney Jade Beaubrun*

CHAPTER 13
And the Tree is NOT ALWAYS Happy!: A Black Woman
Authentically Leading and Teaching Social Justice in
Higher Education 219
    *Colette M. Taylor*

CHAPTER 14
Effectively Teaching the One Course on Race and Culture:
Critical Explorations from a Black Woman Social Justice
Teacher Educator 231
    *Keffrelyn D. Brown*

CHAPTER 15
Social Conceptions and the Angst of Mentoring Women of
Diverse Backgrounds in Higher Education 245
    *Brenda L. H. Marina*

## PART IV
### REINFORCING ACTIVISM AND COMMUNITY BUILDING

CHAPTER 16
Navigating the Complexities of Race-Based Activism 261
    *Cherjanét D. Lenzy*

CHAPTER 17
Storytelling: Advising Black Women Student Leaders in White Spaces 275
    *Lydia Washington*

CHAPTER 18
Reflections on Moving Theory to Praxis: Dialectical Engagements of
Black Women Faculty in an Urban High School Space 285
    *Chrystal A. George Mwangi and Keisha L. Green*

CHAPTER 19
Scholarly Personal Narrative of an Inaugural Chief Diversity Officer:
A Primer for Municipality Leaders 305
    *Malika Carter*

## PART V
## AFTER WORDS

CHAPTER 20
The Dialectic of Radical Black Feminism                        319
    Keeanga-Yamahtta Taylor

CHAPTER 21
For Black Women Who Educate for Social Justice and Put Their
Time, Lives, and Spirits on the Line                           327
    Rhonda Y. Williams

CONCLUDING THOUGHTS
Black Women Educators, Healing History, and Developing a
Sustainable Social Justice Practice                            341
    Andrea D. Domingue and Stephanie Y. Evans

Contributors                                                   353

Index                                                          363

# Acknowledgments

**Stephanie Y. Evans:** Thank you to "Dr. Dre" Domingue and my longtime UMass friend Tania Mitchell, scholars with both intellectual and practical expertise in social justice education. Without you two, this book would not be as clear or complete. Special thanks to authors who contributed their minds and hearts to this volume. We gather in the spirit of collectives like the Combahee River Collective, *But Some of Us are Brave* editors, Spelman College scholar collaboratives, *Presumed Incompetent* editors, Crunk Feminist Collective, and so many other scholar-activist sister circles. Thanks to campuses and organizations that encourage, facilitate, or institutionalize social justice education work. The progress of our world depends on this pedagogy and praxis. I am especially grateful to my ancestors who learned and taught despite personal, social, and structural violence. This book is dedicated to the millions of Black women educators across continents who not only teach but inspire. And I offer gratitude for my life partner in love and justice, Dr. Curtis D. Byrd.

**Andrea D. Domingue:** First, and most important, I dedicate this work to my late parents, Lois M. Domingue and Claude J. Domingue. Both parents were my earliest role models and biggest supporters. They believed in me and my ability to lead, educate, and strive for social change before I believed in myself. I would like to express deep gratitude to Dr. Stephanie Y. Evans and Dr. Tania D. Mitchell. I am continually humbled that I was considered and invited to co-edit this pivotal text. I consider you both my possibility models; I appreciate your patience and flexibility during our process, and it has been an honor to learn from the two of you. I also hold appreciation for my dissertation advisor, Dr. Maurianne Adams. Her exceptional mentorship was vital in my personal development as an educator and writer; she always encouraged me to use my authentic voice. I would like to thank my colleagues in the UMass Social Justice Education concentration for the mentorship, expertise, resources, and insights that supported my work over the last 10 years. A few in particular stand out: Dr. Ximena Zuniga as an early advisor who continually guides me in my work on critical pedagogy and facilitation, and my beloved community of collaborators, whom I depend on for co-facilitation, design considerations, and exchange of resources—Molly Keehn, Dave Neely, Chase Catalano, Rachel Wagner, Mike Funk, Rani Varghese, and Safire DeJong. Successful completion of this book is also attributed to my dearest friends and community. Words cannot adequately express how sincerely appreciative I am for each of you who cared for me throughout my writing process and believed in me when I needed it most. A special thank you to the coaches and members of Pioneer Valley Crossfit who demonstrated the power of community and showed me that no obstacle is too great to overcome. I appreciate the check-ins about my progress and taking the time to help me talk through ideas. Last, but certainly not least, I would like to thank Prince for his unquestionable companionship.

**Tania D. Mitchell:** This project would not have been possible without the amazing contributors who shared their knowledge, experiences, and passion in this volume. I also want to appreciate Stephanie Evans and Dre Domingue for inviting me into this experience and for their leadership and care throughout the process. A book titled *Black Women and Social Justice Education* requires gratitude and appreciation for the Black women who have mentored me, mothered me, befriended me, and inspired me throughout my lifetime. To Harriet Tubman, Sojourner Truth, Dorothy Height, Ella Baker, Barbara Jordan, Audre Lorde, Ruby Dee, Octavia Butler, and so many more—thank you. To my grandmothers Alice Lynch, O'telia Mitchell, and Hilda Pierre, and to my mother, Sharon Mitchell-Pierre, who laid the foundation, made the bricks, and fashioned the mortar—I am so grateful. I dedicate this effort to Ellison Pier Hans who came into the world as this book was coming together and gave me every motivation to make sure it was finished. May the legacies and lessons compiled in this volume give its readers the knowledge, strength, and courage to work for the world she deserves.

# Foreword

*Black Women Rising: Jumping Double-Dutch with a Liberatory Consciousness*

BARBARA J. LOVE AND VALERIE D. JIGGETTS

> You Black, you poor, you a woman.
> You ain't nobody at all.
>
> —Mister, *The Color Purple*

To survive—and even to prosper—has been the goal, the challenge, and the legacy of Black women in the academy, Black women in community engagement, and Black women in nonprofit work. Mister's assessment of the Black woman as "nobody at all" reflects a sentiment that Black women encounter daily in the academy, in the community, and in nonprofit work, and with which she must contend and overcome. To survive, prosper, and maneuver above the harm that falls her way, a steady tool has been the development and application of a liberatory consciousness. This consciousness includes perspectives about social justice rooted in the historical experience of colonialism, genocide, enforced involuntary servitude, dislocation due to immigration, and forced migration. These perspectives provide important parameters and guidelines for survival and flourishing.

## Double Jeopardy: Difficulties Faced by Black Women in Institutional Settings

The hazards of racism and sexism, in both their direct and internalized forms, are basics (givens) for Black women in most institutional and community settings. First, most current institutional settings in the Western world were developed by white people to serve the interests, values, and needs of white people. These institutions have opened in recent periods to accommodate People of the Global Majority. We use the term People of the Global Majority—PGM—to replace the more familiar term People of Color in order to avoid the ambiguities inherent in the term People of Color. Finding a term to appropriately refer to the peoples of African, Asian, Latino/a, and Native American heritages is complex. The one thing that is true of these groups of people is that they are the majority of the people on the globe. We like the term PGM because it nuances the political usage of terms like minority to refer to members of this group, and clarifies that the language is less about numbers and more about power. There is a certain power reflected in acknowledging that your people are a global majority that is not reflected in stating that your people are "of color."

While these institutions have been opened to PGM, Black women are still less often represented in positions of power and decision making. For instance, in the fall of 2013, out of 1.5 million faculty at degree-granting institutions of higher education in the United States, a mere 3% were Black females, and only 2% were full professors.[1] The number of Black female college presidents can be counted on fingers rather than in percentages.[2] The same is true for Black female bank presidents, CEOs of Fortune 500 companies, governors, and other representations of participation in the mainstream. Besides numerical indices of inclusion and participation, there are similarly few indications of changes in institutional values and programs that would prioritize the ambitions and goals of Black women.

Second, institutions developed on the basis of ideologies of white supremacy by people who advocated for and encouraged the development of policies, procedures, norms, and rules that reflect the ideology of white supremacy are not easily responsive to the needs of Black women. Since much of institutional functioning operates below the level of conscious awareness, the ways that institutions deflect, misdirect, and interfere with social justice goals and objectives often goes undetected, unremarked, and in many cases, denied.

Jumping double-dutch, facing and managing the challenges and difficulties of racism and sexism has been the experience of Black women. In institutional settings, these challenges and difficulties are usually and generally viewed by decision makers, and often by Black women themselves, as matters of private problems, personal shortcomings, and individual limitations.

To survive, and to flourish, Black women have been required to hold a vision of themselves as belonging, of institutions as capable of supporting their participation, and institutional members as capable of supporting their inclusion, all the while confronting and transforming the daily instances when that vision was shortchanged by the double hazards of racism and sexism. A sustainable vision of inclusion and participation, in the frequent absence of material evidence supporting such a vision, and the more frequent requirement that they jump double-dutch, has depended on the development of a liberatory consciousness.

## Developing a Liberatory Consciousness

Freire, hooks, and many others have discussed elements and uses of a liberatory consciousness.[3] A liberatory consciousness has enabled Black women not only to stand against the double hazards of racism and sexism, but to simultaneously work toward liberatory spaces, language, and relationships. Liberatory consciousness has enabled them to work toward creating systems and organizations characterized by greater equity and social justice. It has enabled Black women to live and function with awareness and intentionality within oppressive institutions and communities that direct the twin hazards of racism and sexism toward them daily. This awareness and intentionality enables Black women to squarely face these imposters, without allowing them to debilitate, disrupt, dehumanize, or immobilize.

Four elements are noted in the development of a liberatory consciousness: awareness, analysis, action, and accountability/allyship. The labeling of these four elements of a liberatory consciousness is meant to serve as a reminder in our daily lives that, while necessary, a liberatory consciousness is neither static nor fixed. Nor is it something that some special few have that is not available to others. A liberatory consciousness is practiced daily, each time a situation occurs that would impose racism or sexism, either directly or in their internalized forms. These labels remind us that everyone can acquire the skill to become liberation workers in our organizations and communities, as is illustrated in many of the chapters in the current volume.

The first element of a liberatory consciousness, awareness, includes practicing the capacity to notice what is happening in the world around you. The second includes analyzing what you observe from a critical perspective. Element three includes deciding, on the basis of one's awareness of what is happening and critical analysis of that observation, what needs to be done, and seeing to it that appropriate action is undertaken. Accountability, the fourth part of liberatory consciousness, requires the individual to accept accountability to self and community for the consequences of the action that has been taken or not taken.

With a liberatory consciousness, every individual gets a chance to theorize about issues of equity and social justice, to analyze events and activities from an equity and social justice perspective, and to act in responsive ways to transform institutions and society to accomplish goals of fairness, justice, and equity.

## Awareness

The awareness component of a liberatory consciousness involves developing the capacity to notice, to give attention to our daily lives, our language, our behavior, and even our thoughts. It means making the decision to live our lives from a waking position. It means giving up numbness, dullness, and lack of awareness, or even dysconscious living, whether intentional or unintentional. It means facing the ways that the mind has been colonized by growing up and living in a society where white is right and everything and everyone is understood in relationship and proximity to whiteness. Awareness means following Ngugi Wa Thiongo's notion of decolonizing our minds, and taking back our capacity for observing and naming our own experiences.[4] It means creating the theoretical contexts that frame our observations of our world, and choosing the language with which we name our world within those user-created theoretical contexts. For instance, we might decide that we will no longer use the term "fair" to describe light skin because of the way this usage supports and perpetuates notions of white supremacy. Fair means that which is right, good, or just. If light or white skin is that which is right, good, or representing justice, then dark or Black skin would therefore mean that which is not right, not good, and not just. Continued usage of such terminology helps to cement and reinforce notions of the rightness of whiteness in our own minds.

With awareness rooted in a historical perspective, we might decide to avoid using the term "slave" to refer to Africans who were sold into slavery. Slavery is a condition or a state, not an identity. Africans sold into slavery were forced upon pain of dismemberment and death to give up their identity as African. They were forbidden to use African names, speak African languages, or practice African religious forms. This was part of the process of reducing Africans from human to the status of property. The term "slave" refers to property, and as Chief Justice Taney opined in the Dred Scott Supreme Court Decision, slaves "have no rights that a white man need respect."[5] Continued use of the term "slave" reinforces and perpetuates the notion of Africans as property removed from their humanity, an identity passed along to their descendants. Awareness means noticing what is happening in the world around us and framing that understanding in an historical perspective.

## Analysis

A liberatory consciousness requires Black women not only to think about what is going on in the world around them, but also to theorize about those events and circumstances. They must develop their own explanation for what is happening, why it is happening, and what needs to be done about it. The analysis element of a liberatory consciousness includes the activity of thinking about what needs to be done in a given situation. Every human has the capacity to examine any situation in order to determine what seems to be true about that situation. The analysis of that situation becomes the basis for determining whether change is required, and if so, the nature of the change that is needed.

If what we observed about a given situation seems consistent with our values of an equitable society, then the analysis will conclude that the situation is fine exactly as is. On the other hand, if the observation and analysis lead to the conclusion that the situation is unjust, then a determination is made that the situation needs to be changed.

Analysis will reveal a range of possible courses of action. Each possibility will be examined to determine what results are likely to be produced. Some possible activities will produce results that are consistent with our goals of justice and fairness, while some will not. Analysis means considering the range of possible activities and the results that each of them is likely to produce.

A Black female faculty member, serving on the College Personnel committee, noted that the files of Black faculty under review seemed to receive a different level of scrutiny using different criteria than their white colleagues. Having determined that an intervention was needed, this faculty member made a flow chart of all decisions that had been made by the committee, showing each faculty member reviewed, the criteria used, and the outcome, or the vote of the committee. She presented this to the committee for their review and their analysis. A clear pattern of white faculty with scanty files receiving positive recommendations and Black faculty with more robust files receiving negative committee votes emerged. She then asked the committee, "what can we do about what we have observed here?" This led to a discussion among committee members about the role of unaware and unconscious bias and how this can unawarely affect the voting of individual committee members. The committee decided to construct a rubric to organize review and discussion of all future cases as a way to overcome the effect of this unaware bias.

Proceeding from the elements of a liberatory consciousness, this Black woman initiated change in the way that an institutional process impacted the lives and careers of her Black colleagues. Rather than being angry or frustrated about what was happening on the committee, or suffering in powerlessness, a range of alternatives were considered, and the one that she felt would make the most significant difference was selected for action.

## Action

The action element of a liberatory consciousness proceeds from recognition that awareness and analysis alone are not enough. There can be no division between those who think and those who put thinking into action. The action component of a liberatory consciousness is based on the assumption that the participation of each of us in the liberation project provides the best possibility of gaining liberation for any of us.

The action component of a liberatory consciousness includes deciding what needs to be done, and then seeing to it that action is taken. Sometimes it means taking individual initiative to follow a course of action. Sometimes it means encouraging others to take action. Sometimes it means organizing and supporting other people to feel empowered to take the action that the situation requires. At times, locating the resources that empower another person to act with agency is required. On occasion, the action required will be to remind others that they are the right person for the task, that they know enough and are powerful enough to take on the challenge of seeing that the task is completed. In any event, liberatory consciousness requires each human to take some action in every situation that presents an opportunity to transform the society and move toward a more just world.

## Accountability/Allyship

The socialization to which we have been subjected results in our thinking and behaving in very role-specific ways. Socialization into roles of dominant and subordinant limits our vision of possibilities for change.[6] The roles we have been assigned shapes and provides boundaries to our vision of what is possible. Liberatory consciousness requires a recognition of the need for collaboration and mutual support across and within these roles to be able to take the actions that are needed to transform society.

Many white people flounder in their efforts to extricate themselves from racist conditioning. Their socialization to the role of dominant provides very little opportunity to understand what life might be like outside that role. Many become stuck while working on racism. Black women will often have a perspective or window of understanding about racism that is not available to a white person because of the latter's socialization into whiteness. Left alone in their struggle, some white people do eventually figure out the difficulty and develop many good skills in interrupting whiteness and white supremacy. Many others do not. When a Black woman chooses to share her window of understanding with a white person, the growth and development of that white person away from racist conditioning can be significantly enhanced and quickened.

Similarly, a Black woman can become stuck in patterns of internalized racism and left alone to struggle. A white person can hold a perspective that is outside the socialization into racial subordination that, when shared, can boost the efforts of that Black woman to step outside patterns of internalized racism and engage the world in a different way.

Mary Jackson was keenly interested in engineering and worked as a human computer in the NASA Space Program. She declined to apply for the NASA engineering program, fearing rejection based on the history of racial apartheid in the United States, and specifically in Virginia. Kazimierz Czarnecki, a white Jewish engineer, encouraged her to step outside her fear. She applied to the program, graduated with honors, and became the first Black female engineer at NASA. Czarnecki's allyship made a difference for Mary Jackson, and many Black women who came through NASA after her.[7]

People raised on one end of patterns of gender, race, and class subordination or domination can provide a different perspective for people raised on the other end of the pattern. At the same time, people within role groups can assist other members of their own role group to recognize and eliminate those patterns of thought and behavior that originate in internalized subordination or domination. For example, Black women can help each other better understand the ways that our automatic responses help to perpetuate and maintain our own oppression.

The accountability element of a liberatory consciousness is concerned with how we understand and manage this opportunity and possibility for perspective sharing as allyship in liberation work. Individuals engaged in liberation work can have confidence that, left to their own struggles, others will eventually figure out what they need to know to disentangle thought and behavior patterns originating in internalized oppression, either internalized domination or internalized subordination. Working in connection and collaboration with each other, across and within role groups, we can make progress in ways that are not apparent when working in isolation and in separate communities.

## Conclusion: Liberation Work

In our liberation work, many of us have taken the position that it is not the responsibility of Black women to teach or help to educate members of the dominant group. This is a reasonable and essentially "righteous" position. Those people who bear the brunt of the oppression should not be required to also take responsibility for eliminating it. At the same time, it is self-evident that people in the subordinant group can take the lead in setting the world right, and have a perspective that make them ideal to lead this change. For one thing, if people in the dominant group had access to and were able to hold a liberatory perspective that allows them to change systems and patterns of domination, they would have done so already. Black women can wait for members of the dominant group to recognize that their language or behavior is oppressive, or they can share their perspective in every place where it could make a difference, including in the lives of members of the dominant group. In the end, it is in their best interest to do so.

This does not mean that Black women should focus their attention outward on the dominant group, or that members of dominant groups should be focused on Black women. It is to suggest that when the perspective of the other group can serve as the critical energy to move things forward, liberation will be hampered if we hold our thinking and perspective back from each other. It is of paramount importance that Black women offer their perspective to other Black women in the effort to move forward.

As liberation workers, it is axiomatic that we will make mistakes. Rather than self-condemnation or blame from others, it will be important to have the opportunity and the openness to hear an analysis from others that allows us to reevaluate problematic behaviors or positions. If a Black person notices another Black person acting out of internalized racism, a liberatory consciousness requires considering the usefulness of sharing a viewpoint that enables that person to explore the implications of internalized racism for their own behavior. While we do not take responsibility for another's thinking or behavior, accountability means that we support each other to learn more about the ways that the internalized domination and internalized subordination manifest in our lives and agree with each other that we will act to interrupt it.

Accepting accountability to self and community for the consequences of actions taken or not taken can be an elusive concept for a people steeped in the ideology of individualism. Multiplicities of experiences and points of view contribute to problematizing the concept of accountability as well. None of us can claim for ourselves the right to tell another that her analysis is retrogressive. Discussions of political correctness can also prove troubling in the effort to grasp the idea of accountability and make it a workable concept.

There will be no easy answers here. The significance of a liberatory consciousness is that Black women will always question, explore, and interrogate ourselves about possibilities for supporting each other in the effort to come to grips with our conditioning into oppression, and give each other a hand to move outside of the assigned role of subordinant. The accountability element of a liberatory consciousness requires us to develop new agreements regarding our interactions with each other. As a beginning we get to decide the extent to which we will make ourselves available to interrupt language and behavior patterns that, in our best analysis, originate in an internalization of the ideology of white supremacy and patriarchy.

In the end, institutions and systems respond to the initiatives of individuals and groups of individuals. Systems do not perpetuate themselves; they are supported, maintained, and perpetuated by the actions of people and groups of people who typically act automatically on the basis of their socialization.

In communities and organizational settings, Black women represent transformational readiness. The strength and agility required to jump double-dutch is rooted in our development and display of a liberatory consciousness. This has allowed us to more and more frequently reclaim choice in our values and attitudes, and consequently in our response patterns. It has enabled us to move from automatic response systems grounded in socialization for subordination to the capacity to act on a range of responses based on our own awareness, analysis, and decision making, and the opportunities we have to learn from our colleagues and others who are themselves embarked on a journey to liberation.

## Notes

1. National Center for Education Statistics.

2. Sandra Jackson and Sandra Harris, 2007, "African American Female College and University Presidents: Experiences and Perceptions of Barriers to the Presidency."

3. Paulo Freire, 1973, *Education for Critical Consciousness*; bell hooks, 1994, *Feminist Theory: From Margin to Center*.

4. Ngugi Wa Thiongo, 1986. *Decolonising the Mind: The Politics of Language in African Studies*.

5. Many argue that enslaved more accurately reflects their condition. Library of Congress, Primary Documents. Dred Scott v. Sandford.

6. I use the term "subordinant" instead of the more common "subordinate" to parallel the term "dominant." In systems of oppression, dominants have agency, whereas to subordinate is to have something done unto that person. I prefer using language that disrupts patterns of oppression rather than language that reflects, supports, and perpetuates the oppression.

7. Mary Jackson at NASA Langley.

## References

Freire, P. (1973). *Education for critical consciousness*. New York: Seabury Press.

hooks, b. (1994). *Feminist theory: From margin to center*. Boston: South End Press.

Jackson, S., & Harris, S. (2007). African American female college and university presidents: Experiences and perceptions of barriers to the presidency. *Journal of Women in Educational Leadership*. https://digitalcommons.unl.edu/jwel/7. Retrieved February 18, 2017.

Library of Congress, Primary Documents. *Dred Scott v. Sandford*. https://www.loc.gov/rr/program/bib/ourdocs/DredScott.html. Retrieved February 18, 2017.

Mary Jackson at NASA Langley. https://www.nasa.gov/image-feature/mary-jackson-at-nasa-langley-1. Retrieved February 18, 2017.

National Center for Education Statistics. https://nces.ed.gov/fastfacts/display.asp?id=61. Retrieved February 17, 2017.

Thiongo, N. W. (1986). *Decolonising the mind: The politics of language in African studies*. Portsmouth, NH: Heinemann.

# Introduction

*Black Women's Educational Philosophies and Social Justice Values of the 94 Percent*

STEPHANIE Y. EVANS, ANDREA D. DOMINGUE, AND TANIA D. MITCHELL

Black women's intellectual history is inextricably linked to peace studies. As outlined in *Black Women in the Ivory Tower, 1850–1954: An Intellectual History* (2007), Black women's scholarship and pedagogies exemplify empowerment education and represent four central characteristics: applied research, cultural standpoint, critical epistemology, and moral existentialism. In the 1800s and 1900s, women like Maria Stewart, Frances E. W. Harper, Nannie Helen Burroughs, and Anna Julia Cooper wrote that the disadvantaged position of Black women based on race and sex was one that allowed for and required Black women activists to lead the country into the true possibilities inherent in liberal, progressive, and radical ideals of democracy.[1]

Noted scholar Anna Julia Cooper argued that African American women have a peculiar perspective, as we reside at the intersection of racial and gender oppression. In the foreword to this book, Love and Jiggetts reimagine this social location as jumping double-dutch. This edited volume synthesizes critical discussion of justice and education from our unique, intersectional, racial, and gendered position. Authors define experiences of justice, injustice, and scholar-activism from an insider perspective of a demographic most often sequestered on the bottom rung of society.

Our work exemplifies action toward a more perfect union and resistance to the status quo. There is a reason that CNN exit polls after the November 2016 Presidential election estimated that 94% of Black women voted for Hillary

Clinton as an alternative to the Republican candidate. This phenomenon of Black women forming an unmatched progressive voting block was replicated in the December 2017 election of Doug Jones over the Republican candidate in the Alabama Senate. However, as soon as Jones claimed victory, he indicated he was on board with conservative agendas—turning his back on the body of voters that got him elected. Black women love American democracy, but American democracy does not seem to love us back.

In February 2017, a cartoonist equated protesters barring school entry to billionaire Secretary of Education Betsy DeVos with racists barring school entry to 6-year-old Ruby Bridges attempting to desegregate a New Orleans elementary school in 1960. This false equivalency illustrates the glaring misunderstanding of race and equality in educational access. Monique Morris's *Push Out: The Criminalization of Black Girls in Schools* (2015) demonstrated the conditions that must be changed if education in the United States is to reach its fullest potential. Evidence abounds regarding the lack of social justice knowledge, values, and practices in school systems from K–12 to higher education that readily contribute to "conservative" and essentially regressive social policies.

Moreover, policies at national and state levels are bolstered by a vapid curriculum that teaches hatred of anyone deemed other than White, male, heterosexual, Christian, and born in the United States. Education that does not include fundamental investigation of inclusive democracy and that reinforces exclusivity is miseducation. This collection of authors serves as corrective measures to discuss historical and contemporary issues in education as they relate to achieving goals of justice.

Foundational texts in social justice education such as *Teaching for Diversity and Social Justice* (*TDSJ*) analyze and synthesize identity within educational contexts. In a closing chapter of *TDSJ* titled "Knowing Ourselves as Social Justice Educators," Bell, Love, Washington, and Weinstein discuss the imperative to be mindful of cultural differences that might exist between the facilitator-educators and students in the classroom (Adams & Bell, 1997, 382). The collection of chapters in *Black Women and Social Justice Education* offers an expansion of educational discussions by centering Black women's identity in order to broaden extant curriculum. By decentering maleness and whiteness, questions of justice at once solidify intersectional analyses and moves discussion out of locations traditionally represented as normative. When difference is taught as divisiveness and diversity devalued, the result is often deadly, as can be seen with incidences as personal as bullying to events as globally impactful as World War II.

The United Nations Universal Declaration of Human Rights (UDHR) set a benchmark in world history. Drafted by a representative leadership team

Introduction

from nine nations, the United Nations General Assembly formalized the UDHR in Paris on December 10, 1948.[2] The Second World War created conditions of unprecedented destruction, and the Declaration became a pact to ensure the devastation was not repeated.[3] Eventually, however, the United Nations realized rights were not sufficient to ensure peace, and a document in 2006 acknowledged the need to actively advocate social justice implementation as supplemental to human rights language.[4] The committee conceded:

> The concept of *social justice* and its relevance and application within the present context require a more detailed explanation. . . . The concept first surfaced in Western thought and political language in the wake of the industrial revolution and the parallel development of the socialist doctrine. It emerged as an expression of protest against what was perceived as the capitalist exploitation of labour and as a focal point for the development of measures to improve the human condition. It was born as a revolutionary slogan embodying the ideals of progress and fraternity. Following the revolutions that shook Europe in the mid-1800s, social justice became a rallying cry for progressive thinkers and political activists. (11–12)

A decade before this embrace of social justice with human rights within the United Nations, *Teaching for Diversity and Social Justice* (1997) was published, grounding a pioneer program in social justice and higher education at the University of Massachusetts-Amherst. All of these resources are important to bring to bear in order to facilitate a full understanding of the breadth of contribution that Black women's narratives can bring to human rights and social justice literature and to reinforce foundational concepts such as inclusion, oppression, privilege, and power. Black women authors and educators show that all human beings have what Anna Julia Cooper called a "right to grow," and a close reading of writing from theory and policy to memoirs and pedagogical praxis reveals legacies, lessons, and guides for social regeneration.[5]

Like social justice, the term social regeneration also originated in the Progressive Era, based in Reconstruction-era demands for public healing that foreshadowed post–world war language of reconciliation. W. E. B. Du Bois argued the concept of social regeneration was a fundamental goal of Black education. Black women's educational philosophies and pedagogical values provide primary source material to advance education about social justice, human rights, and civil rights that can be useful inside and out of the classroom. In 1892, Anna Julia Cooper used the terms "regeneration" and "progress" to identify the need to look backward to find wisdom, to look inward to find strength, and to look forward with hope. Both Cooper and Du Bois recognized injustice based on economic, gendered, racial, and cultural identity. As Tania Mitchell explicates in the following chapter, these scholars recognized justice as a process, equitable recognition, and access to resources. In the tradition of Cooper and Du Bois, we define this collaborative body of work to fight for justice as a project in social regeneration.[6]

As with regenerative medicine, Black women's writing can be used to restore, repair, and replace failing or unhealthy aspects of society. Regenerative writing combines the past, present, and future tense to facilitate growth. Growth can include spiritual, individual, communal, social, political, or global health. In the late 20th century, researchers developed regenerative medicine. Medical doctors are now pushing boundaries of exploration in order to repair cells, tissues, and organs and to restore functionality to bodies. Much advancement, such as in the case of Henrietta Lacks, has been at the unethical expense of Black bodies. Still, Black women's traditions of purposeful healing proves all-the-more indispensable, particularly when we are primarily concerned with healing ourselves.[7] Similarly, we argue Black women's regenerative writing serves to repair, replace, restore, and regenerate health in individual lives, communities, educational institutions, societies, and nations.

In *Black Women in the Ivory Tower*, Evans observed, "Anna Cooper, Mary Bethune, and their contemporaries articulated educational philosophies that had four central themes: demand for applied learning; recognition of the importance of social standpoint and cultural identity in scholarship; a critical epistemology that both supported and resisted mainstream American ideals; and moral existentialism grounded in a sense of communal responsibility" (Evans, 2007, 8). *Black Women and Social Justice Education* builds on the legacies of Black women who articulate educational values that investigate identity and demand moral accountability in ways that directly upset and undermine systems of inequality. This effort simultaneously deconstructs systems of oppression and constructs liberatory pedagogical principals. These principles should be taught, studied, and institutionalized.

Many Black women authors have taken the time to collect their life stories, posit frameworks for education, and share reflections from the far reaches of their souls and intellects. Only a small number are represented in this edited volume, but the collection of narratives, theories, case studies, and paradigms adequately demonstrates we have only begun to tap available resources in this area.

First, reading Black women's intellectual history and educational philosophy demonstrates potential gains if we study history not only to identify the seeds of oppression, but that we also appreciate historic educators and their insights into the "process and goals" of how to solve social problems.

Second, by looking at the intersection of race and gender, educators can visualize conversion and diversion of experience useful when learning and teaching about diversity and social justice.

Historical and contemporary Black women's educational writing provides insights from which to teach the matrix of individual, social, and institutional oppression. This body of work offers a deeper inquiry into questions of instruction, solutions to curricular challenges, and opportunities for strength-based assessments of oppressed communities—identifying effective practices by marginalized groups. Studying Black women's writing expands our understanding of how to better comprehend identity, society, oppression, and equity, the four major themes in social justice education.[8]

## Democratic Praxis as Social Justice Education

A focus on activism and democratic engagement are central to Black women's contributions to social justice education. Definitions of social justice often emphasize full participation of all (and especially those most marginalized); therefore, Black women's work to enact more just conditions are often centered on engagement in and with communities. Work for social justice begins with acknowledgment and recognition of inequitable conditions. Efforts to remedy these conditions, then, become pivotal to the work. As social justice is comprised of both process and goal orientations (Bell, 2007), it is not surprising that social justice education often combines consciousness-raising work that makes plain the realities of oppression with engaged action that seeks to bring this nation closer to a democratic ideal.[9]

We can trace this legacy of awareness and action to Sojourner Truth, who named herself as she traveled the union states speaking in support of abolition and women's rights. Her truth aimed to educate the masses about the worth of Black women and the evils of slavery. Simultaneously, Sojourner Truth recruited Black soldiers for the union army and rode street cars in Washington, DC, to force their desegregation (*The Sojourner Truth Biography*, n.d.). As a public speaker, Truth, like Harriet Tubman, was a public educator. Anna Julia Cooper integrated her roles as high school teacher and university professor with that of activist: "[S]he co-founded and assumed significant leadership roles in community improvement organizations and 'racial uplift' advocacies" focused on the advancement and empowerment of Black communities.[10] Their work made transparent that social justice education comprises both work to build knowledge and work to build action.[11]

Barbara Ransby (2003) in her biography of activist and educator Ella Baker describes Baker's service as a "patchwork quilt." She notes Ella Baker's teaching style as more facilitative than conventional. She sought to build and advance knowledge by recognizing examples and experiences that already existed in the group. Recognizing democracy as a process of participation and inclusion, her praxis required "tapping oppressed communities for their own knowledge, strength, and leadership in constructing models for social change." In this quilting fashion, Ransby describes Baker's activism as one that "saw enormous beauty and potential" in those who were discarded, dismissed, and considered inconsequential and that she worked collectively to bring and hold those individuals together in working on a movement for change.[12]

Baker's recognition that root causes of injustice must be revealed and transformed in order to bring about justice is an underlying contention that shapes much current social justice education practice. Mitchell's (2008) operationalizing of a critical service learning pedagogy reflects this process and goal orientation of social justice by bringing attention to social change, working to redistribute power, and developing authentic relationships. Baker's attention to root causes is reflected in Mitchell's contention that community engagement must "investigate and understand the root causes of social problems and the courses of action necessary to challenge and change the structures that perpetuate those problems."[13]

Cohen's (2011) work to queer ethnic studies brings forward Cooper's contention of education as an "equalizing tool"[14] with Baker's focus on those most oppressed and marginalized. Cohen's queer politics "grounds our work squarely in the lives of folks of color who are clearly not subjectless, but instead are subjected to the post-identity veneer of white supremacy" (131). She insists on efforts that interrogate how power is structured along axes of identity and what that means for our efforts to transform society. This work, Cohen maintains, reaches "beyond the academy" and requires "creating and protecting spaces where liberatory thought, discourse, and action can be explored and rehearsed."[15]

We concur that, in the tradition of Baker in the Civil Rights Movement and educators like Septima Clark, our work must go "beyond the academy" to engage those most marginalized. In collective efforts to build knowledge and transform structures of injustice, we recognize social justice education as democratic praxis.

## Black Women's Narratives and Social Justice Education

Since the 1773 publication of Phillis Wheatley's *Poems on Various Subjects, Religious and Moral*, Black women artists, activists, and intellectuals have provided critical insight into issues of national and global importance. Shaped by lives lived at the crossroads of race, gender, and justice, their ideas have been distinctive but often ignored.[16]

Social justice education is a core part of Black women's educational philosophy. Educators such as Fanny Jackson Coppin, Anna Julia Cooper, Mary McLeod Bethune, and Septima Clark, who were all engaged in community work in their capacity as administrative leaders, clearly articulated educational philosophies that presumed a goal of justice. It is no coincidence that their writing was highly reflective, as their understanding of injustice was grounded in personal experience of enslavement (Coppin and Cooper), unequal access (Bethune), and political persecution (Clark).[17]

Searching the online library Africana Memoirs (a comprehensive database of over 500 Black women's autobiographies), several narratives expose ample opportunities to connect Black women's intellectual history to social justice education. This encourages a deeper consideration of both form and function of teaching and learning.[18] Over 118 Black women's narratives in the Africana Memoirs database mention social justice (about half of the searchable books). Within this group, there is significant overlap of terms. Beyond this larger set of social justice narratives, 25 solely reference human rights and 18 mention civil rights. Thus, neither human rights nor civil rights as terms were referenced as often as "social justice," which is most likely a function of the timing of the terms: "social justice" was in use as an early 20th-century term, whereas "human rights" came into wide use after World War II and "civil rights" most notably in the 1950s and 1960s. Further, the term "human rights" was found in more international settings, whereas "civil rights" was largely in reference to a movement in the United States. Search terms, included from all three areas, appear in 161 Black women's memoirs that reference "social justice, human rights, and civil rights." Clearly, these values are central to Black women's lives, which explains the pervasive presence in educational philosophies that are embedded in personal narratives.[19]

As scholar-activist Dr. Cooper argued, service must go beyond social change—it must advance social justice. Without understanding African American history and acknowledging Black presence, oppression, and creative resistance, justice work in America will be incomplete, and education will fail to be "higher" in significant ways. It is no wonder, then, that numerous chapters in this collection carry on the tradition of educational memoir.[20]

Life writing is a radical act of self-care; through penning stories of struggle and growth, Africana authors have resisted invisibility, dehumanization, and injustice. This body of work about how to instill knowledge, skills, beliefs, and competencies into American educational systems reflects Black women's intellectual history of looking back, inside, and forward to demand both inner peace and social justice.[21]

Empowerment is a central part of educational philosophies. Defining empowerment is a task that can impact evaluation and assessment of objectives inside institutions, be they college classrooms, after-school programs, or community agencies. Investing in a deeper understanding of Black women's philosophies, values, and educational imperatives is the foundation of community-based research and collaborative knowledge production for social justice.[22] Below are five examples from a century of educators—from Fanny Jackson Coppin, who began teaching in the 1860s, to Angela Davis, who began teaching in the 1960s—who locate social justice at the center of their life's work.[23]

*Fannie Jackson Coppin (1913, Reminiscences of School Life and Hints on Teaching)*

Therefore we feel that resolutely and in unmistakable language, yet in the dignity of moderation, we should strive to make known to all men the **justice** of our claims to the same employments as other men under the same conditions. We do not ask that any one of our people shall be put into a position because he is a colored person, but we do most emphatically ask that he shall not be kept out of a position because he is a colored person.

*Anna Julia Cooper (1930, The Voice of Anna Julia Cooper)*

For, after all, **Social Justice,** the desired goal, is not to be reached through any panacea by mass production. . . . As I see it then, the patient persistence of the individual, working as Browning has it, "mouth wise and pen-wise" in whatever station and with whatever talent God has given, in truth and loyalty to serve the whole, will come as near as any other to proving worthwhile.

*Mary McLeod Bethune (1935, Building a Better World)*

And with this happiness comes humble gratitude for the distinguished approval of this organization [NAACP] dedicated to the cause of **social justice** and human welfare. To be worthy of being included in the illustrious group of Spingarn medalists, who by their intelligence, courage, devotion, faith, and work have helped to shape and build a better world, one must respond to the stimulus of this occasion with a spirit of rededication to service, of reconsecration to the needs of the people.

*Septima Poinsette Clark (1962, Echo in My Soul)*

I was director of the Highlander workshops, I am Septima Clark, a Negro school teacher on Johns Island off the coast of my native Charleston, South Carolina. Forty years later my contract with the Charleston city schools was not renewed due, I think, to my activities and work for my own people for **social justice**. [Describing a 1959 raid on Highlander in Monteagle, Tennessee.]

*Angela Davis (1994, "Black Women in the Academy")*

. . . [I]f the presence of increasing numbers of Black women within the academy is to have a transformative impact both on the academy and on communities beyond the academy, we have to think seriously about linkages between research and activism, about cross-racial and transnational coalitional strategies, and about the importance of linking our work to **radical social agendas**.

༄

Political philosopher Joy James, who edited the *Angela Davis Reader* (1998), pointed out that Davis's article, "Black Women in the Academy," presented a treatise of challenges for the 1994 conference In Defense of Ourselves, after the political persecution of Anita Hill. James wrote that the essay "raises the issues of women's political work, responsibilities, and rights in connection with representation and education for social justice" (87). Angela Davis published her autobiography in 1974, after winning her freedom from being a political prisoner while she was a faculty member at UCLA. Her persistence and consistency of message can be seen in her 2017 National Women's March speech, which shared the themes of critical thinking, intersectional activism, and solidarity for all justice movements.

Between the historical accounts and contemporary educators lie the Civil Rights and Women's Rights Movements, chock-full of manuscripts worthy of discussion and instruction. Black women educators and scholars have written about social justice long before and long after the much-cited Paulo Freire's *Pedagogy of the Oppressed* (1970). Recent narratives on the 20th century and beyond written by Black women university professors offer a highly visual syllabus for race, gender, and justice in higher education:

1. Trudier Harris, University of Alabama. *Summer Snow: Reflections from a Black Daughter of the South* (2007).

2. Saidiya Hartman, Columbia University. *Lose Your Mother: A Journey Along the Atlantic Slave Route* (2008).

3. Lani Guinier, Harvard Law School. *Lift Every Voice: Turning a Civil Rights Setback into a New Vision of Social Justice* (1998).

4. Nikki Giovanni, Virginia Technical University. *Racism 101* (1995).

5. Toi Derricotte, University of Pittsburgh. *The Black Notebooks: An Interior Journey* (1999).

6. Marita Golden, Fairfield University. *Migrations of the Heart: An Autobiography* (2005)

7. Carole Boyce Davies, Cornell University. *Caribbean Spaces: Escapes from Twilight* Zone (2013).

8. Angela Davis, University of California-Santa Cruz. *Angela Davis: An Autobiography* (1974; 2013).

9. Dolores Cross, Chicago State University President, Morris Brown College President. *Beyond the Wall: A Memoir* (2010).

10. Lorene Cary, University of Pennsylvania. *Black Ice* (1988).

11. Theresa Cameron, Arizona State University. *Foster Care Odyssey: A Black Girl's Story* (2002).

12. Yvonne Bobb-Smith, University of West Indies. *I Know Who I Am: A Caribbean Woman's Identity in Canada* (2003).

13. Dr. Bertice Berry, Kent State University. *I'm on My Way but Your Foot Is on My Head: A Black Woman's Story of Getting Over Life's Hurdles* (1997).

14. Elizabeth Alexander, Yale University. *The Light of the World: A Memoir* (2015).

15. Jan Willis, Wesleyan University. *Dreaming Me: Black, Baptist, and Buddhist—One Woman's Spiritual Journey* (2012).

16. Patricia J. Williams, Columbia University Law. *Open House: Of Family, Friends, Food, Piano Lessons, and the Search for a Room of My Own* (2005) and *Alchemy of Race and Rights: Diary of a Law Professor* (1992).

17. Jesmyn Ward, Tulane University. *Men We Reaped: A Memoir* (2011).

18. Gloria Wade-Gayles, Spelman College. *Rooted Against the Win* (1996).
19. Claudia Lynn Thomas, Johns Hopkins University Medical School, *God Spare Life* (2007).
20. Judy Scales-Trent, SUNY–Buffalo School of Law. *Notes of a White Black Woman: Race, Color, Community* (2001).
21. Elaine Richardson, The Ohio State University Literacy Studies. *PHD to Ph.D.: How Education Saved My Life* (2013).
22. Condoleezza Rice, Stanford University Business, Public Policy, and Political Science. *A Memoir of My Extraordinary, Ordinary Family and Me* (2010) and *No Higher Honor: A Memoir of My Years in Washington* (2011).
23. Gayle Pemberton, Wesleyan University. *The Hottest Water in Chicago: Notes of a Native Daughter* (1998).
24. Kitty Oliver, Florida Atlantic University Race and Change Initiative. *Multicolored Memories of a Black Southern Girl* (2004).
25. Colleen McElroy, University of Washington English. *A Long Way from St. Louie* (1997).
26. Jamaica Kincaid, Harvard University English. *A Small Place* (1988).
27. Layli Maparyan, Wellesley College Women's Studies. *The Womanist Idea* (2012).
28. Estella Conwill Majozo, University of Louisville English. *Come Out the Wilderness: Memoir of a Black Woman Artist* (2000).
29. Sara Lawrence-Lightfoot, Harvard University. *Balm in Gilead: Journey of a Healer* (1995).
30. Carole Ione, University of Wisconsin Theatre. *Pride of Family: Four Generations of American Women of Color* (2007).

This representative list is a powerful collection of voices to begin to unpack issues of epistemology and instruction.

Black women are not a monolith . . . there is no universal agreement on ideological or political issues, which offers an even more compelling case for collective study. However, even Condoleezza Rice, far right on the political spectrum of most educators mentioned in this chapter, touted the value of social justice in her memoir, *No Higher Honor*, which chronicled her political career as National Security Advisor and Secretary of State to George W. Bush. On one hand, Rice derided social justice as a tactic of those who sided with those whom she viewed as radical, such as Hugo Chavez, Former President of Venezuela; on the other hand, she stated social justice was inherently connected to democracy: "When people choose their leaders they tend to expect more of them in terms of economic prosperity and social justice. That is why support for democracy must be accompanied by support for development. . . . Ultimately, good leaders will free their economies and their markets and attract private investment. . . ."[24] While advancing a wildly conservative and destructive definition of social justice based on "free markets," even Rice nonetheless wrote in the tradition of positioning justice as a central value and aim of social and governmental institutions.

Notably, approximately 30 contemporary educators have penned memoirs featured in the database. Of this group, 14 mention social justice in their book title or main theme: Angela Davis, Carole Boyce, Yvonne Bobb-Smith, Jan Willis, Judy Scales-Trent, Layli Maparyan, Sara Lawrence-Lightfoot, Lani Guinier, Betty Brown-Chapelle, Janet Cheatham Bell, Adele Logan Alexander, Yvonne Shorter Brown, Endesha Ida Mae Holland, and Paula C. Johnson. As a primary example, Lani Guinier's *Lift Every Voice: Turning a Civil Rights Setback into a New Vision of Social Justice* underscores the fundamental shift needed in those who shape American institutions, "This book is not an effort to settle scores. It's a story of people whose voices are too often missing from public debate about issues on which they are expert" (17). Black women are expert educators, and social justice must make an increased, proactive role in educational agendas.

Clearly, Black women academics have been doing intellectual social justice work for several generations and are current leaders in the area. In addition to memoirs serving as mentors to Black women in an array of professions, educators at all levels can benefit from this body of work. Regenerative writing can directly contribute to conceptions of regenerative education recently established in many K–12 schools. In 2008, Ashley Nielson pioneered the philosophy of regenerative education in a dissertation that used terms such as "living schools," and "holistic education" to outline parameters of educative practice dedicated to developing "self and systems."[25] Theoretical approaches such as this provide a frame for the substance of narratives to be read as valuable curricular guides.

While not all chapters in this book are autobiographical, many are. Those that foreground history or theory do so from an informed and experiential perspective where there is a commitment to equality on racial and gender terms. In order to realize "justice for all," in a society, all voices must be heard in framing, shaping, and implementing justice models in education.

## Framework: Teaching Values in Higher Education

Toni Morrison's "How Can Values Be Taught in the University" provides the editorial framework used to ground this volume (*What Moves at the Margin: Selected Non-Fiction*, edited by Carolyn Denard, 2008). We argue for the need to teach social justice values in higher education, and the authors each provide fundamental contributions toward this goal. An excerpt from Morrison's essay is provided below to give a sense of how social justice as an educational value contributes to prior discussions about the goals of a university. Understanding that teachers are trained in schools of education, universities are the focal point. Re-evaluating subjectivity in educational philosophy is one of our main contributions to the theoretical framework/methodologies of social justice education in particular and higher education in general. Morrison writes:

> Certain disciplines pride themselves on the value-free nature of their intellectual inquiries, and the pursuit of "objectivity" is at the heart of their claims, claims which are understood to place the stature of these disciplines far above interpretive ones. Nevertheless, explicitly or implicitly, the university has always taught (by which I mean examined, evaluated, posited, reinforced) values, and I should think it will always follow or circle the track of its origins. . . . What I think and do I already inscribed on my teaching, my work. And so should it be. We teach values by having them. . . . If the university does not take seriously and rigorously its role as guardian of wider civic freedoms, as interrogators of more and more complex ethical problems, as servant and preserver of deeper democratic practices, then some other regime or *ménage* of regimes will do it for us, in spite of us, and without us. (191–197)

This volume examines, evaluates, posits, and reinforces Black women's values of social justice in education at all levels. Grounded in Black feminist and womanist texts, this work advances educational philosophy by engaging foundational theorists in Black women's studies. To call the names of our predecessors, let it suffice to say chapters in this book share investigation and testimony of *The Black Woman* (Cade) and our *Brave* and creative survival (Smith, Bell-Scott, and Hull), to share *Words of Fire* (Guy-Sheftall) about our

*Black Feminist Thought* (Collins) and our *Womanist Ideas* (Maparyan). Authors in this volume consciously cite, celebrate, question, and commemorate the work of those who have written before us in the area of SJE, and we purposefully build on foremothers in social justice education literature, most notably the double-dutch professor herself, Dr. Barbara Love.

We read, write, and teach in order to pass on wisdom to the next generation of educators, students, and scholar-activists. We write to teach, guard, service, and preserve the values of social justice. As Dr. Love outlines in the foreword to this volume, "Four elements are noted in the development of a liberatory consciousness: awareness, analysis, action, and accountability/allyship." Thus, in a text dedicated to centering Black women's voices, Black women offer the theoretical frame (Morrison), philosophical underpinnings (Cade, Guy-Sheftall, Smith, Bell-Scott, Hull, Collins, Maparyan), as well as guidelines for practical application of these values (Love).

## Organization

Part I emphasizes theory and identity as key tenets of social justice education. The authors' contributions in this section explore Black women in the academy and our responsibility to ourselves and others as people committed to social justice. It begins with Tania Mitchell's exploration of the dominant paradigms of social justice theory and the elevation of white men and women's voices as the primary architects of theorizing about social justice. The marginalization of Black women's theorizing and practice is invoked to recognize the contributions of Black women to the redistribution, recognition, and procedural paradigms of social justice theory. In Chapter 2, Layli Maparyan introduces Luxocracy as a social justice framework that allows one to recognize the "Divine Light as reflected in all people by virtue of human connection." Recognition of this Divine Light encourages us to see ourselves as "responsible for shepherding humanity toward well-being" and, therefore, step into our roles as educators to create opportunities and accountability structures that might bring us closer to social justice.

In Chapter 3, Eboni Turnbow, Sharee Myricks, and Jaymee Lewis-Flenaugh explore the multiple marginalizations of Black women under age 30 in student affairs roles in higher education. They emphasize the importance of recognizing the intersections of racism, ageism, and sexism in higher education as an impediment to Black women's progression to senior student affairs roles. Judy Alston's narrative of self as "outsider-within" in Chapter 4 provides insight into her journeys as an academic simultaneously holding identities of privilege and marginalization. Her work toward an authentic presentation of self encourages reflection on our own identities to understand how we might position ourselves outside and within to be reciprocal and responsible leaders. To that end, in Chapter 5, Michele Smith and Maia Moore encourage persistence among Black women in the academy, naming how our opportunities toward self-definition are to be found in family and community. They position Black feminist thought as a response to white fragility and the white racial frame that often dominate our interactions with white students and faculty in higher education settings. In short, they interrupt reactionary responses to oppression.

Part I concludes with Natasha Howard bringing forward the global phenomena of anti-Black misogyny (what Dr. Moya Bailey termed "misogynoir"), as she explores the degradation and humiliation of Black women in popular film and music. Using examples from the United States and Brazil as primary examples of misogynoir in practice, Howard reveals "gratuitous humiliation" as a "pillar of oppression" in Black women's experiences. Advancing a transnational feminism in which women can assert their humanity becomes a central feature of Howard's social justice education practice.

In Part II, narratives connect historical accounts of activists who fought for desegregation to millennial continuation of those struggles and in culture. "Evaluating Foundations and Generations" offers four chapters in which readers can witness the evolution of discussions about equal access to spaces of power, equal opportunity to use resources from transportation to education, as well as rights of expression to caption the next generation of struggle. The opening and closing chapters in this section both engage Solange Knowles's song "A Seat at the Table" as a pathway to understanding justice as access.

In Chapter 7, "A Seat at the Table: Mary McLeod Bethune's Call for the Inclusion of Black Women during World War II," Ashley Robertson Preston outlines how educator Mary McLeod Bethune worked at the forefront of Franklin Roosevelt's administration to create visibility and opportunity for Black women in military labor and recognition of war-time contributions. The next chapter, "The Life of Dovey Johnson Roundtree: A Centenarian Lesson in Social Justice and Regenerative Power" by Katie McCabe and Stephanie Evans, builds on Bethune's legacy and presents the life story of Roundtree who was, coincidently, a mentee of Bethune. Roundtree's work as a lawyer contributed to freedom for individuals in cases such as the murder case of Ray Crump; she also impacted the nation as a head lawyer in the transportation desegregation case that overturned the precedent of *Plessy v. Ferguson*, used to make segregation legal. Roundtree's role as minister also provides a compelling example of community-based education.

Desegregation may have ended by law in 1955, but Shennette Garrett-Scott and Dominique Scott discuss in Chapter 9 how it has yet to end in custom. "This Ain't Yo' Mama's Revolution—Or Maybe It Is: #TakeBackTheFlag and the New Student Activism" chronicles Garrett-Scott's participation in the battle to remove the Confederate flag from the University of Mississippi campus. This chapter exemplifies the connection of scholarship to coalition activism that Angela Davis deemed a unique contribution Black women educators can make. Garrett-Scott and Scott show how we are still contending with the likes of the Ku Klux Klan, and how this is not simply a theoretical problem that must be addressed. Closing Part II, in Chapter 10 Bettina Love and Sarah Abdelaziz present "We Got a Lot to Be Mad About: A Seat at Solange's Table," which demonstrates the complexities of intersectionality in Knowles's album's lyrics. They make plain not only "what Black women teach us," but through a dialogue with the artist they demonstrate the communal, interactive, and sisterly process in which Black women engage when learning from each other.

Part II reveals the continuity of thought and action Black women scholars offer, from the Civil Rights Movement to #BlackLivesMatter and #SayHerName, including cultural reshaping of our image and reclaiming rights to democratic participation. These chapters certainly advance our understanding of what Tania Mitchell identifies as three types of justice: distributive (equity of material resources), recognition (equity based on perceived difference), and procedural (the process of gaining equity).

Part III, "Positing Pedagogy," focuses on educational approaches and facilitation of social justice content in an emerging politically charged climate. This section brings attention to the positionality of Black women as educators and how these social identities inform approaches to teaching and leadership. The first four chapters offer deeply reflective narratives by Black women educators in college classroom and campuses, while the fifth chapter provides highlights from a research study on mentorship needs among diverse higher education professionals.

In Chapter 11, "Black, Female, and Teaching Social Justice: Transformative Pedagogy for Challenging Times," Robin Brooks shares her evolution of pedagogical choices teaching in literary studies courses during a time of increasing racial tensions in the United States. Through media, personal dress, storytelling, and intentional facilitation, the author discusses how these strategies contribute to changed worldviews among students. In Chapter 12, "Moments in the Danger Zone: Encountering Non-Racist, Non-Racial, Non-Color-Seeing Do-Gooders," Michelle Dunlap, Christina Burrell, and Penney Jade Beaubrun's recall past encounters with colorblind ideology and White privileges as women of color educators. Through attention to identity development theory, these authors offer Black women educators strategies to help navigate these complex interpersonal dynamics.

The next two chapters bring attention to the pedagogical challenges and strategies of introducing social change ideas to contemporary college students.

Colette Taylor's chapter, "And the Tree is NOT ALWAYS Happy!: A Black Woman Authentically Leading and Teaching Social Justice in Higher Education" narrates her personal journey exploring ways to intersect authenticity as Black women leader more effectively educate college students on her campus. She uses Shel Silverstein's *The Giving Tree* as a tool for developing personal resilience and incorporating mindfulness as a social justice practitioner. In Chapter 14, "Effectively Teaching the One Course on Race and Culture: Critical Explorations from a Black, Woman Social Justice Teacher Educator," Keffrelyn Brown highlights the all-too-common scenario of a Black woman instructor teaching the sole course on race in an academic program consisting of predominantly White college students. This chapter highlights how Brown uses moments of resistance as opportunities to reevaluate assignments, readings, and discussion facilitation choices to more effectively prepare teacher education candidates on social justice issues.

This section's concluding chapter by Brenda Marina examines mentorship dynamics of Black women higher education professionals. Chapter 15, "Social Conceptions and the Angst of Mentoring Women of Diverse Backgrounds in Higher Education," discusses how mentoring differs across diverse social groups and suggests that Black women must have specific needs often addressed to better support their success as educators.

In sum, Part III highlights the unique pedagogical challenges that Black women educators face in an emerging and ever-complex U.S. political climate. Through personal awareness, analysis of oppression dynamics, and strategies for action and accountability, the authors illustrate the possibility of social change while providing contemporary examples of Barbara Love's liberatory consciousness framework.

Part IV, "Reinforcing Activism and Community Building," reflects the work of Black women as social justice educators and the ways these commitments are actualized. The authors have taken care to relate their experiences as people engaged in this work, and also to share the possibilities and opportunities so that diverse populations reading this volume might benefit from their experiences.

In Chapter 16, "Navigating the Complexities of Race-Based Activism" Cherjanét Lenzy shares an excerpt from her qualitative research: one woman's story extracted from a larger study that explores experiences of college-aged Black women engaged in race-based activism. Lenzy reveals how Nilta engages activism as a space where identity is shaped and affirmed. In the following chapter, "Storytelling: Advising Black Women Student Leaders in White Spaces," Lydia Washington builds on student narratives by focusing on her role as an advisor to Black women student leaders. She offers an advising model based on three elements of storytelling and encourages an approach that honors racial identity and creates place for learning and development that recognizes Black women's leadership styles.

Chapter 18, Chrystal A. George Mwangi and Keisha L. Green's "Reflections on Moving Theory to Praxis: Dialectical Engagements of Black Women Faculty in Urban High School Space," fuses higher education with secondary education by reflecting on experiences of two faculty attempting to bridge several gaps—between theory and practice; between school campuses; between cultural identities of Puerto Rican students and school educators or curricula; and between expectations and project outcomes.

In Chapter 19, "Scholarly Personal Narrative of an Inaugural Chief Diversity Officer: A Primer for Municipality Leaders," Malika Carter demonstrates the power of storytelling through scholarly professional narrative (SPN). Carter recounts her experiences as the first chief diversity officer of a local municipality and affirms that social justice education happens in multiple contexts. Carter's work underscores Washington's narrative to demonstrate how Black women's physical, emotional, and intellectual labor is all too often unappreciated but absolutely necessary to realizing a more just world.

In Part V, "After Words," the concluding section of the book, authors offer two different perspectives of liberatory consciousness: one personal, one communal. In her chapter, Rhonda Williams, founder and inaugural director of the Social Justice Institute at Case Western Reserve University, offers a creative interpretation of the mindfulness that must be present for Black women's SJ work to be sustainable. In the preceding chapter, Keeanga-Yamahtta Taylor, who personifies front-line scholar-activism in her work as professor of African American Studies at Princeton University, provides a view of collective liberation in the tradition of the Combahee River Collective. Williams channels creative history and Taylor engages critical history; both harken to Black women elders as means to their liberatory pedagogies. The section closes with final reflections from Stephanie Evans and Andrea Domingue—editors who offer a Coda as we look backward, inside, and forward to Black women's educational legacies and lessons.

Reading this cohort of Black women educators provides insight via two avenues: our writing provides case studies of how intersectionality operates, while our voices offer valuable historical and cultural context to problem-solving education. In closing, we restate the practical, cultural, critical, and moral imperative to amplify Black women's voices in order to counteract violence and oppression through improved education. If the passing on of human knowledge ignores the life writing of Black women, we miss a vital opportunity to ensure that the values of social justice are communicated to future generations.

## Notes

1. In Stephanie Evans (2007), *Black Women in the Ivory Tower, 1850–1965: An Intellectual History.* University Press of Florida.
2. United Nations Universal Declaration of Human Rights http://www.un.org/en/universal-declaration-human-rights/ (1948).
3. United Nations Universal Declaration of Human Rights, "History of the Document" http://www.un.org/en/sections/universal-declaration/history-document/index.html
4. UN International Forum for Social Development, Social Justice in an Open World: The Role of the United Nations. Department of Economic and Social Affairs, Division for Social Policy and Development. New York, 2006. http://www.un.org/esa/socdev/documents/ifsd/SocialJustice.pdf
5. In Adams and Bell (1997), *Teaching for Diversity and Social Justice: A Sourcebook.* New York: Routledge.
6. W. E. B. Du Bois: "The function of the Negro college, then, is clear: it must maintain the standards of popular education, it must seek the social regeneration of the Negro, and it must help in the solution of problems of race contact and cooperation. And finally, beyond all this, it must develop men." From Du Bois, "Of the Training of Black Men" in *The Souls of Black Folk* ([1903] 1997), edited by D. W. Blight and R. G. Williams. Boston: Bedford Books.
7. Coletti, Teodori, Lin, Beranudin, and Adamo (2013), "Restoration versus Reconstruction: Cellular Mechanisms of Skin, Nerve and Muscle Regeneration Compared." *Regenerative Medicine Research* 1(4) https://www.researchgate.net/publication/274367643_Restoration_versus_reconstruction_cellular_mechanisms_of_skin_nerve_and_muscle_regeneration_compared; Steve Bauer (2014, August), "Stem Cell Therapy: FDA Regulatory Science Aims to Facilitate Development of Safe and Effective Regenerative Medicine." Accessed at FDA Voice: blogs.fda.gov/fdavoice/index.php/2014/08/stem-cell-therapy-fda-regulatory-science-aims-to-facilitate-development-of-safe-and-effective-regenerative-medicine-products
8. Adams, M., Blumenfeld, W., Castaneda, R., Hackman, H., Peters, M., and Zuniga, X. (2000). *Readings for Diversity and Social Justice: An Anthology on Racism, Antisemitism, Sexism, Heterosexism, Ableism, and Classism.* New York: Routledge. For the seven core concepts see Adams and Bell (Eds.) (2016), *Teaching for Diversity and Social Justice*, 3rd edition. New York: Routledge, pp. 95–96.
9. Bell (2007). "Theoretical Foundations for Social Justice Education." In M. Adams, L. A. Bell, & P. Griffin (Eds.) *Teaching for diversity and social justice*, 2nd edition. New York: Routledge, pp. 1–14.
10. Johnson, K. A. (2009). "Gender and Race: Exploring Anna Julia Cooper's Thoughts for Socially Just Educational Opportunities." *Philosophia Africana*, 12(1), 67–82, p. 68.
11. *The Sojourner Truth Biography* (n.d.). Sojourner's amazing life . . . and beyond. Retrieved from http://www.sojournertruth.org/History/Biography/BC.htm

12. Ransby, B. (2003). *Ella Baker and the Black Freedom Movement: A Radical Democratic Vision*. Chapel Hill: University of North Carolina Press, pp. 373–374.

13. Mitchell, T. D. (2008). "Traditional vs. Critical Service-Learning: Engaging the Literature to Differentiate Two Models." *Michigan Journal of Community Service Learning*, 14(2), 50–65; quote on p. 53.

14. Johnson (2009), p. 73.

15. Cohen, C. (2011). "Death and Rebirth of a Movement: Queering Critical Ethnic Studies." *Social Justice*, 37(4), 126–132; quote on p. 131.

16. "Introduction." *Toward an Intellectual History of Black Women* (The John Hope Franklin Series in African American History and Culture). Chapel Hill: University of North Carolina Press.

17. See Evans (2003), "Living Legacies: Black Women, Educational Philosophies, and Community Service, 1865–1965," and (2007), *Black Women in the Ivory Tower*.

18. Franklin, V. P. (1995). *Living Our Stories, Telling Our Truths: Autobiography and the Making of the African-American Intellectual Tradition*. New York: Scribner's; Thompson, A. (2001), *African-American Histories, Biographies, and Fictionalized Biographies for Children and Young Adults: A Bibliography* http://www.pauahtun.org/aakidlit.html; Henry Louis Gates Jr. and Evelyn Higginbotham (2004), *African American Lives*. Oxford University Press; Stephanie Evans (2014), *Black Passports: Travel Memoirs as a Tool for Youth Empowerment*. Albany, NY: SUNY Press.

19. For full bibliography, visit online library at AfricanaMemoirs.net database, www.africanamemoir.net. Only those electronically searchable were included in the sample.

20. Evans, S. Y. (2009). *African Americans and Community Engagement*. Albany, NY: SUNY Press, pp. xxi–xxii.

21. See Evans (2017) in *Black Women's Mental Health: Balancing Strength and Vulnerability*, Albany, NY: SUNY Press.

22. Evans (2017). "From Worthless to Wellness: Self-Worth and Personal Power," in *Black Women's Mental Health*, Albany, NY: SUNY Press.

23. Coppin, F. J. (1913). *Reminiscences of School Life, and Hints on Teaching*. Philadelphia: A.M.E. Book Concern.

24. Rice, C. (2011). *No Higher Honor*. New York: Crown, p. 732.

25. Nielsen, A. "The Philosophy of Regenerative Education and Living Schools." PhD dissertation, Saybrook University, 2008. Abstract excerpt: "Building from this foundational review of the holistic education movement, the philosophy of regenerative education was developed, comprising four types of education: understanding-based, self-revealing, systems, and spiritual education. . . . In a regenerative education learning environment, students engage in self-actualization, self-realization, system-actualization, and system-realization growth processes. This dissertation also provides a framework for bringing the philosophy of regenerative education to life: the living school."

# Part I

# EXAMINING IDENTITY AND THEORY

Chapter 1

# Gone Missin'

*The Absence of Black Women's Praxis in Social Justice Theory*

TANIA D. MITCHELL

Social justice is a contested concept that has eluded concrete definition. Nieto and Bode (2012) discuss social justice as a term that is "frequently invoked but rarely defined" (12). Rather than trying to bound social justice with a limiting definition, it is often referenced and highlighted as if universal understanding can be assumed. Chapman and Hobbel (2010) contend that social justice, when defined by scholars, is comported to be "convenient to their arguments rather than comprehensive across contexts of inquiry" (3).

In social justice education, definitions focus on practice and ideal conditions, but rarely invoke theories of social justice. Bell (2007) wrote:

> . . . social justice is both a process and a goal. The goal of social justice is the full and equal participation of all groups in a society that is mutually shaped to meet their needs. [It] includes a vision of society in which the distribution of resources is equitable and all members are physically and psychologically safe and secure. . . . [A] society in which individuals are both self-determining (able to develop their full capacities) and interdependent (capable of interacting democratically with others). Social justice involves social actors who have a sense of their capabilities as well as a sense of social responsibility toward and with others, their society, and the broader world in which we live. (1–2)

These process and goal aims of social justice are not always jointly presented as in Bell's definition. Warren (1998), for example, defines social justice as "intentional steps that move society in the direction of equality, support for diversity, economic justice, participatory democracy, environmental harmony, and resolution of conflicts nonviolently" (134). While Nieto and Bode (2008) explain social justice as "*a philosophy, an approach, and actions that embody treating all people with fairness, respect, dignity, and generosity*" (12; emphasis in original). Foos (1998), by contrast, offers, "A just society is one in which one would be content to live, and whose laws and institutions one would be willing to embrace, no matter what segment of society one occupied or what disadvantages one suffered" (16). These three definitions of social justice demonstrate how diverse understandings of this concept can be. Whether defined as paths to an ideal society (Warren), a process for dignified treatment (Nieto & Bode), or an end result (Foos), our understanding of social justice is a philosophized notion of what could be or how things should be. It is a creation of imagination that becomes concretized through the articulation of possibilities to attaining social justice.

The recognition of the stratification of people across social and economic lines, as well as hope and possibility that something more and better is attainable, generates much of the theory on social justice. While our understanding of social justice continues to evolve in theory and practice as the world and circumstances change, relationships and community (the notion of connection to others in society) remains central to social justice theorizing in Western political thought. Social justice is a concept centered in our relationships to one another. It is a concept that forces us to compare and contrast our existence and experience in society to that of another. That which we identify as unjust or in need of justice is most often based on an understanding of "better" life options available to some. The differences (and almost inevitably the inequality) uncovered become the central text for our theory. Social justice theory asks, what must occur in order for circumstances to be different from how they are now? Unfortunately, the answer is seldom simple. It is a question with many potential answers that have been articulated by philosophers and political theorists for centuries. The absence of Black women's voices, perspectives, and praxis in the formal articulations of social justice theory remains a slight to the intellectual contributions and actions of Black women. This chapter aims to remedy that omission through exploration of contemporary theorists (specifically Western philosophers from 1971 to the present) most often invoked to understand more recent conceptions of social justice in the United States and adds exposition of how Black women's work has informed and influenced social justice theory.

Theorizing on social justice has been categorized by tradition (Fraser, 1997; Wendorf, Alexander, & Firestone, 2002). Following a review of the literature, I have divided contemporary social justice theory into three paradigms: (re)distribution, recognition, and procedural. These paradigms are centrally the theorists' notion for how social justice will (or can) be attained. They are organized according to these notions, with the theorists' requirements for people and institutions determining where in the traditions the theory fits.

In what follows I review each of the paradigms and the major constructs of the chief theorists in each of these areas. The questions guiding this review are: How is social justice defined or understood? What are the key arguments to support this view of justice? How is social justice codified (or what are the constructs of justice) under this theoretical paradigm? Following the review of the theoretical paradigms in social justice theory, in my conclusion I look at how these theoretical conceptions might intersect and overlap to guide action toward a just society and Black women's contributions in theory and practice that I believe have informed our understandings of social justice.

## (Re)distribution

The first paradigm of social justice theory in Western philosophy is the distributive paradigm (Young, 1990). The concept of (re)distribution, allocating resources, benefits, and advantages in a method deemed fair or just, is the dominant form of theorizing social justice. Resources, in this paradigm, are primarily material, but access to resources that lead to material wealth (e.g., education) are sometimes included. In many theories, social and distributive justice are terms used interchangeably to indicate that they are indeed the same concept (Barry, 1980, 1989; Hayek, 1976; Mill, 2000; Miller, 1976, 1999). In the distributive paradigm, social justice is almost always theorized as solely an aspect of economic or material position in society. The role of social justice in the distributive paradigm is to correct the injustice (seen as the inequality that results from material inequity) by redistributing the resources, benefits, and advantages in a manner that would "fix" the prevailing system of stratification.

The terms of redistribution may vary, and the circumstances for theorizing redistribution are often abstract and hypothetical. Rawls (1971/1999), for example, makes certain to inform readers that his distributive theory is hypothetical and only applicable in democratic nation-states. Barry (1980) critiques the distributive paradigm, questioning all of the theories concocted in the hypothetical. Social justice theories cannot rely on actual examples (societies where there is justice) to demonstrate the value of redistribution.

Distributive theorizing has the tendency to feel isolating or ignorant of the experiences of people, the realities of culture and social groups (Barry, 1980; Fraser, 1997; Okin, 1989; Young, 1990). This paradigm requires a centering of socioeconomic class (Fraser, 1997; Young, 1990). Because distributive justice is focused on the allocation of goods and resources for economic opportunity, wealth becomes central to the understanding of justice advanced in this paradigm. Socioeconomic equality is paramount, and our moral responsibility under redistribution is to institute structural change that allows for fair access and opportunity to the material wealth, jobs, and resources available in society. Social justice "entails a right to the basic opportunities necessary for the satisfaction of one's basic needs" (Sterba, 1995, 11). Distributive theories of justice hold not only that we center our understanding of injustice and inequality on the stratification of social classes, but that all other terms of injustice can be collapsed and somehow understood as concerns of distribution (Young, 1990). John Rawls (1971/1999) offers "self-respect" as a good to be distributed under his theory of justice, as if self-respect can somehow be controlled or monitored in a way to be allocated. Theories of justice centered in distribution require color-blind, gender-neutral societies blind to sociocultural difference in order to attain justice, because the redistribution of material wealth and resources is seen as the solution to conditions of injustice (Fraser, 1997; Okin, 1989; Sterba, 1995; Young, 1990). Miller (1999) looks to distributive justice not only to resolve class inequalities but to address issues of injustice on account of race, ethnicity, and sexual orientation. The categories in which injustice is found (e.g., race, gender, sexual orientation, ability, religion, first language, etc.) are viewed in terms of the material inequality that results instead of considering the other ways in which these groups might experience injustice (Fraser, 1997; Miller, 1999).

Under the distributive paradigm, most often the principles for attaining social justice are applied universally to all people in society. Although in most theories, the language of justice assumes recipients are white, male, and heterosexual. Barry (1980), Butler (1997), Fraser (1997), Okin (1989), and Sterba (1995) critique these assumptions. The assumptions in redistribution theories often fail to reverse the conditions of stratification because they are developed with ideal visions of society in which the people suffer no injustice outside of those controlled in political-economic contexts (Barry, 1989; Fraser, 1997; Hayek, 1976). Conditions of power and authority are given no weight in distributive theories because they are not considered relevant to understanding social justice (Miller, 1976). Distributive theorists, particularly Miller (1976, 1999) and Barry (1989) do not question the possibilities of dominance inherent in redistribution. Who controls the allocation of resources should be as important as who is receiving said resources. I question the capacity for justice in a society where power and dominance are not relevant, especially given the importance of this concept to theories of justice in the other paradigms presented in this chapter. It is believed that providing "equal" application, access, and opportunity to the benefits and burdens of society will somehow result in an outcome that will be received as fair or just. Too often, however, the stratification under redistribution continues to widen without the considerations of power and authority.

Recognizing the widening gaps and the maintenance of socioeconomic class stratification perpetuated under distributive theories of justice, John Rawls (1971/1999) re-ignited theorizing on social justice by employing a twist to the universal applications of social justice theory. "While the distribution of wealth and income need not be equal, it must be to everyone's advantage, and at the same time, positions of authority and responsibility must be accessible to all" (Rawls, 1971/1999, 53). In this way, social justice does not require equality, but that all people benefit from the method in which resources are distributed. In his "justice as fairness" theory, Rawls (1971/1999) introduced the "difference principle" acknowledging that issues of social position and sociocultural difference must be considered in distributive theories. He contends that distribution of all "primary goods" (i.e., material wealth and resources, access to the resources of economic opportunity, self-respect) must be equal unless an unequal distribution of these goods would benefit the least advantaged in society.

> Thus the principle holds that in order to treat all persons equally, to provide genuine equality of opportunity, society must give more attention to those with fewer native assets and to those born into the less favorable social positions. The idea is to redress the bias of contingencies in the direction of equality. (Rawls, 1971/1999, 86)

With the assertion of the difference principle, the conditions of social justice then also changed. Rawls's (1971/1999) principle acknowledged that conditions in society privileged some above others and that society was responsible for changing those structures of privilege. The goal could no longer be absolute equality, because justice as fairness mandates inequality in the favor of the least advantaged (Miller, 1976). If goods are distributed using the difference principle, they will not be allocated equally. The greatest portion will serve the least advantaged, meaning that others will receive resources according to their comparable need.

Yet, some worry that the distributive paradigm and Rawls's difference principle puts too much emphasis on income and wealth and therefore leaves some social identity groups behind that cannot attribute the inequity they experience to issues of economic position (Butler, 1997; Nussbaum, 2001). Martha Nussbaum (2001) used the example of gays and lesbians in society to demonstrate her concern:

> One might argue . . . that gays and lesbians in our own society, while not the least well off with regard to income and wealth, are very badly off with regard to the social bases of self-respect in that such fundamental social institutions as the structure of marriage deny their equal worth. But Rawls's difference principle would not recognize them as a group in need of special attention to remove the inequalities that they suffer. (B9)

While *Obergefell v. Hodges* (2015) responds to the concerns Nussbaum raises regarding marriage, enduring inequalities such as the lack of federal protections barring employment discrimination for those who are lesbian, gay, bisexual, transgender, or queer ensures that the LGBTQ community does indeed experience injustice and inequalities with regard to income and wealth that cannot and should not be ignored in considerations of distribution.

Critics of the difference principle are concerned that redistribution advantageous to the least favored requires structural changes not only in access to the free market, but to the outcome as well (Hayek, 1976). It is argued that conditions of good fortune or luck, natural intelligence or upbringing, which all impact material position, cannot be legislated or governed through distributive mechanisms of social justice (Hayek, 1976; Miller, 1976). To further impede on individual liberty by claiming that people do not deserve what they have earned because others have not earned as much creates more injustice than the distributive properties enforced attempt to rectify (Hayek, 1976).

Hayek (1976), as a critic of social justice, believes that society should play a role in assuring that all people have their basic needs met. "There is no reason why in a free society government should not assure to all protection against severe deprivation in the form of an assured minimum income, or a floor below which nobody need to descend" (Hayek, 1976, 87). Instead, he is concerned that the requirements of distributive justice interrupt with the free market system, denying individuals the opportunity to develop (and earn) at their full capacity. This interruption, Hayek (1976) claims, is not social justice but rather the attempts of those seeking to alleviate injustice at the expense of those pursuing individual liberty.

Social justice in the distributive paradigm works to rectify conditions of inequality by redressing and redistributing the material resources of and access to economic opportunity in a given society. (Re)distribution requires a centering of the economic concerns of injustice usually at the expense of the other ways injustice manifests. While opportunities for economic wealth and participation are expanded, there are no controls for or attempts to rectify the other conditions whereby people experience injustice. (Re)distribution assumes that providing the financial means for life to all people will meet the demands of justice.

## Recognition

Social justice in the recognition paradigm seeks to remedy the injustice experienced by members of various social groups because of difference or perceived difference. Recognition theories of justice are based on a theory of oppression. To work for social justice, then, is to work toward the elimination of oppression. Oppression fuses "institutional and systemic discrimination, personal bias, bigotry, and social prejudice in a complex web of relationships and structures that saturate most aspects of life in our society" (Bell, 2007, 3). Recognition theorists argue that dominant culture is the locus of oppression and that in order to attain social justice in society we must acknowledge group difference and the oppression that results and take action to challenge the structures of dominance that propagate those differences (Fraser, 1997; Harvey, 1996; Okin, 1989; Young, 1990). "Misrecognition shows not just a lack of due respect. It can inflict a grievous wound, saddling its victims with a crippling self-hatred. Due recognition is not just a courtesy we owe people. It is a vital human need" (Taylor, 1992, 26).

The recognition paradigm of social justice theorizing seems focused on counteracting three major tenets of social justice theory in the distributive paradigm: first, that social justice is merely a responsibility of institutional structures; second, that social justice is a matter of equal (or equitable) distribution; and third, that issues of injustice result from difference solely in political-economic contexts.

The distributive paradigm views social justice as a tangible entity that can be doled out by some central authority (Barry, 1980; Hayek, 1976). A just society is the product of the government that makes it so. Recognition does not hold government solely responsible for change, as in distributive theories, because of the role government has played in oppression. Instead, recognition relies on the perspective that oppression is wrong and that the dynamics created by oppression in society must be dismantled for social justice to occur. In recognition theories, action is necessary to bring about justice, and the actions necessary to create social justice are institutional, community-based, and individual. The recognition paradigm names specifically the conditions and circumstances that must change for social justice to be realized. Ending oppression requires commitments and changes at all levels: through individuals challenging myths of superiority, questioning their place in society, and taking action to interrupt oppression (and to interrupt their own actions that perpetuate oppression); by communities demonstrating respect and appreciation for all of the cultures, identities, and experiences of the people it serves; and by institutions removing barriers (or providing support) to allow society members the safety, security, and necessary provisions for full participation in society (Young, 1990). Social justice, in this paradigm, belongs to all and is forged by all. It is an understanding of justice as the providence of all who work to create it.

Rawls's (1971/1999) difference principle in the distributive paradigm attempted to widen the responsibility of social justice past the distribution of wealth and resources to other dimensions of social goods, such as self-respect. This ascension of self-respect to a primary good that all members should possess in a just society also brings recognition to structures of injustice and inequality based on social group membership, although Rawls himself does not acknowledge this. The identification of race and gender as locations of the inequitable "distribution" of self-respect opens up theorizing on social justice beyond the distributive paradigm and beyond dimensions of socioeconomic class. The recognition paradigm concentrates on the locations within and outside of class where injustice manifests.

Young (1990) argues that the focus on distributive mechanisms for social justice give "primacy to having" (8). This attention to issues of class in social justice theory has the tendency to ignore the experiences of other groups because it does not acknowledge that differences exist in terms of access, opportunity, and participation for groups based in categories such as race, gender, sex, sexual orientation, citizenship status, religion, body norm and ability, as well as class. "Group identity supplants class interest as the chief medium of political mobilization" (Fraser, 1997, 11). Recognition theorists demand that we recognize that injustice manifests in more ways than class inequality and that those manifestations impact different groups differently. Social justice struggles characterized by recognition seek respect and recognition for group difference and the identities of individuals in these social groups, acknowledgment of the institutional and individual actions that perpetuate the "othering" of members of these groups, and representation in decision-making structures and structures of society that are responsible for cultural production (Fraser, 1997; Sterba, 1998; Young, 1990). The goal is to deconstruct notions of dominance through a cultural revolution that views deviation from a singular norm as variations of possibility, thus protecting and affirming different ways of being.

Understanding the goals of recognition theorists requires understanding the various manifestations of oppression and how these outcomes produce injustice in mechanisms that cannot be solved solely through the distribution of material goods and resources. Iris Marion Young (1990) demonstrates her vision of oppression by describing five "faces" through which capacity is inhibited: exploitation, marginalization, powerlessness, cultural imperialism, and violence. Young (1990) separates exploitation, marginalization, and powerlessness as aspects of the social and economic divisions of labor and sees cultural imperialism and violence as social practice outside of economic structures. "Cultural imperialism involves the paradox of experiencing oneself as invisible at the same time that one is marked out as different" (Young, 1990, 60). Violence is viewed not only as the systematic practice of bringing physical and psychological harm on individuals because of social group membership but also the condition of fear that results from knowing that you could face attack because of affiliation with a particular social group.

The alleviation of oppression in the economic structure, Young (1990) argues, requires a restructuring of the decision-making processes and the value of certain types of work over others. The reparation of oppression expressed through cultural imperialism and violence require a restructuring of education and communication systems so that a dominant paradigm is not centered and valued above that of other cultural expressions employed by different social groups (Bell, 1997; Young, 1990). "Public recognition of our identity requires a politics that leaves room for us to deliberate publicly about those aspects of our identities that we share, or potentially share, with other citizens" (Gutmann, 1992, 7). It also requires greater representation of difference in cultural production.

Critics of the recognition paradigm are concerned that recognition focuses too much on individual differences in a manner prohibitive to the attainment of justice. David Miller (1999) contends:

> People become less concerned about inequalities in wealth and income and more concerned about the way in which certain cultural identities are acknowledged and promoted by the state and others sidelined. . . . Thus the problem is not merely one of trying to reach a consensus about social justice; the problem is that social justice itself, in the traditional sense[,] becomes an issue of declining importance to groups whose main purpose is the struggle for cultural recognition. (253)

Miller (1976, 1999) believes that the "traditional sense of social justice" is based in the distributive paradigm. He concedes that issues of recognition are justice in "the broader sense" (Miller, 1999, 253), but that the purview of social justice is limited to the distribution of material wealth and resources.

Miller's (1999) critique of recognition is based on his concern that the focus on differences that recognition requires makes it more difficult to reach consensus about a conception of social justice for all people. He fears that groups will be so wrapped up in their own self-interest that the goals of social justice are neglected for the particular wants of individual groups (Miller, 1999). Recognition theories do seek to address the particular ways that different groups experience injustice, but they also seek to dismantle the conditions that oppress all groups addressing not only issues of oppression based in race, gender, religion, ability, or sexual orientation (for example), but also that oppression experienced because of socioeconomic class. The recognition paradigm seeks to achieve justice by attending to all of the different ways a group experiences injustice in society. Recognition theories do not address the multiplicity of identity (How do we alleviate injustice for a person that experiences oppression across categories of identity?), but the paradigm is singular in viewing oppression as a location for social injustice.

Theorists in the recognition paradigm seek to acknowledge injustice outside of the dimension of class. Often, struggles for recognition are dismissed as "identity politics" or "merely cultural," marking struggles whose experience of injustice does not hold its primacy in issues of material wealth as illegitimate or secondary (Butler, 1997; Walker, 2001). Recognition theories bring the dismantling of oppression as central to the concept of social justice (Young, 1990). Recognizing that injustice and oppression manifest in a number of ways that impact life economically, physically, and psychologically, the recognition paradigm requires actions that challenge both institutional structures and individual attitudes and actions in order to achieve social justice.

## Procedural

"Two types of justice judgments matter: assessments of the fairness of allocations (distributive justice) and evaluations of the fairness of processes (procedural justice)" (T. R. Tyler, 2001, 345). This distinction between outcomes and process is important to the way that many theorists conceptualize social justice. The perspective Young (1990) stipulates—that is, "Democracy is both an element and a condition of social justice" (91)—reminds us that social justice does not solely entail end results and outcomes related to fair distribution, participation, or respectful recognition, but is also driven by a process (Bell, 2007; Rawls, 1971/1999; Wendorf et al., 2002; Young, 1990).

In contemporary social justice theory, there is frequently discussion about the end-result (i.e., should social justice be a reality, society would operate or look like this) and the manner in which justice is achieved (i.e., in order for justice to occur, people or organizations would operate like this). The manner in which justice is achieved, or procedural justice, negates the issue of distributive outcomes. Rather, if fair methods and procedures are used, the outcome is just regardless (Miller, 1976). Distributive justice is frequently critiqued as being limited in its ability to address the central social justice concerns of most people (Miller, 1999; T. R. Tyler, 2001; Young, 1990). "People's dissatisfactions . . . are not typically linked to issues of reward allocation. Instead, people more often complain about the manner in which they are treated" (T. R. Tyler, 2001, 345). Indeed, as Wendorf and colleagues (2002) argue, justice judgments tend to center most often on conditions of "personal relevance or involvement (i.e., 'was I treated fairly?')" rather than the objective standards redistribution theory aims to define (21–22). Procedural justice theorists encourage us to look more closely and critically at the process in order to understand social justice. This focus advances the primacy of relationships between people.

The paradigm of procedural justice looks at relationships between people and institutions and people's connections to one another (Noddings, 1999a; T. Tyler, Degoey, & Smith, 2001). It is a vision of "society as a fair system of cooperation" (Rawls, 2000, 344). The goal through this paradigm of justice is to alleviate conditions that create injustice by placing emphasis on the manner in which people are treated and by challenging people toward empathy and care in their interactions with others.

John Rawls's (1971/1999) conception of procedural justice is contingent on "the original position." The original position is part of Rawls's contract theory "justice as fairness," the distributive theory that introduced the difference principle. Justice as fairness requires that representatives make decisions regarding the distribution of goods and resources. Representatives from society are selected and brought together to determine how the material wealth and opportunity of a society will be distributed amongst its members. These selected representatives are also mandated to take the original position. The original position is a theoretical condition of ignorance in which the individuals are completely unaware of their place in society. Those in the original position strip themselves of social roles, having no knowledge of their race, gender, economic status, religious identity, or any other factor that might sway their judgment to the benefit of individuals in a particular position (Douvan, 1988). The original position seeks to create representatives who can make decisions justly or fairly because their ignorance brings them to the table without allegiances or affiliations to particular communities. Through this position, it is believed that the process for attaining justice will be "pure," as no person has knowledge of any condition that could bias the outcome (Miller, 1976; Rawls, 1971/1999).

Susan Moller Okin (1989) praises this contingency:

> This significance of Rawls's central, brilliant idea, the original position, is that it forces one to question and consider traditions, customs, and institutions from all points of view, and ensures that the principles of justice will be acceptable to everyone, regardless of what position "he" ends up in. (101)

The notion of absolute fairness that follows the original position seems crucial to the process of social justice. Theorists who follow Rawls's (1971/1999) idea believe that the original position develops empathy and care for differing viewpoints that leads those persons to imagine themselves in the position of the least advantaged or the perspective of every person, and thus choosing a process fair to all (Douvan, 1988; Miller, 1976; Okin, 1989; T. R. Tyler, 2001). The original position ensures that all parties are given equal concern and respect, resulting in a fair process for social justice (Dworkin, 2000).

Theorists in the recognition paradigm are most frequently at odds with Rawls's (1971/1999) idea of the original position. Notions of difference and dealing with difference are central to these paradigms (Douvan, 1988; Young, 1990). The veil of ignorance Rawls (1971/1999) imposes seems to deny the history of privilege and the realities of sociocultural difference by demanding those in the original position relinquish their experiences of dominance or subordination. In this way, the process continues to be unjust as the realities and conditions of all members of society are silenced (not considered) in attempts to create a fair process. Awareness and understanding are central to the process of social justice for recognition theorists.

Procedural justice concerns the knowledge and attitudes that inform and impact relationships. Feelings for how one person (or group of people) feels that another treats, respects, or interacts with him or her are a marker of whether or not the process is just. Tyler, Degoey, and Smith (2001) name three aspects of procedural justice that are important considerations for determining fairness:

> The first, *neutrality*, involves assessments of the degree to which decision-making procedures are unbiased, honest and promote decisions based on evidence. The second, *trustworthiness*, involves assessments of the motives of authorities—judgments about their benevolence and concern for the needs of those with whom they deal. The third, *status recognition*, involves assessments of polite-

ness, treatment with dignity, and respect for rights and entitlements due to every group member. (206; emphasis in original)

With the dimensions of trustworthiness and status recognition, the theorists affirm the attitudes of concern and respect that are important aspects of relationship. The dimension of neutrality promotes the idea of unbiased decision making similar to Rawls's (1971/1999) original position. However, the decree of Tyler and colleagues (2001), that these decisions "be based on evidence," appears to grant those making the decisions access to information regarding sociocultural difference that would foster decisions that do not negate the realities of dominance and subordination in society.

Social justice is a moral theory based on human relations (Gilligan, 1993; Wendorf et al., 2002). In theorizing how people should best interact and relate and what would represent fair treatment in relationships, a notable split attributed to gender has developed in procedural justice theories (Douvan, 1988; Gilligan, 1993; Noddings, 1999a; Okin, 1989; Strike, 1999). This split is often labeled along two orientations. The justice orientation is most frequently credited to men and advances a focus on objectivity, detachment, and rights (Gilligan, 1993; Strike, 1999), while the care orientation, ascribed to women, advances empathy, concern, and the well-being of others:

> Justice insists on general rules. It has a concept of the self that reduces everyone to a thin moral sameness and that denigrates the importance of particularities and relationships. Caring, in contrast, is context sensitive, has a situated self, and is fundamentally concerned for relationships. (Strike, 1999, 22)

This statement by Kenneth Strike (1999) reinforces the dichotomous relationship of care and justice, yet other theorists do not consider the rift between the orientations to be that extensive. Okin (1989) believes that

> [t]he distinction between an ethic of justice and an ethic of care has been overdrawn. The best theorizing about justice, I argue, has integral to it the notions of care and empathy, of thinking of the interests and well-being of others who may be very different from ourselves. It is, therefore, misleading to draw a dichotomy as though they were two contrasting ethics. The best theorizing about justice is not some abstract "view from nowhere," but results from the carefully attentive consideration of *everyone's* point of view. This means, of course, that the best theorizing about justice

is not good enough if it does not, or cannot readily be adapted to, include women and their points of view as fully as men and their points of view. (15; emphasis in original)

Nel Noddings (1999b) encourages us to think of care and justice not as dichotomous ethics, but as different pieces to the same puzzle. "I think now that care and justice often apply to different moments in immoral episodes" (Noddings, 1999b, 4). She uses an example of policy development and implementation to explain this view. Policies are frequently written as objective and unbiased, seeking to address and resolve an issue. The development of that policy reflects justice. The implementation of that policy requires care in order to ensure that its application has fulfilled its purpose without causing harm or introducing new inequities (Noddings, 1999b). Noddings's (1999b) perspective affirms the procedural elements of neutrality, trustworthiness, and status recognition offered by Tyler and colleagues (2001). Objectivity and impartiality alongside care, concern, and respect are all essential elements of procedural justice.

University practices such as "avoiding discrimination in hiring promotion [and] ensuring that researchers do not conduct experiments on human subjects without informing them of the risks" are evidence of procedural justice (Katz, 2002, B7-B8). The emphasis of procedural theories on fair treatment for all people brings closer the possibility of justice, but procedural theories do not remedy injustice already present. The process of justice in the procedural paradigm does not look at conditions and circumstances that have established inequality or injustice; instead, the paradigm works to ensure that further injustice does not occur. This focus on process instead of outcome allows for the possibility of justice (or something closer to it) to be realized through our daily interactions. Unfortunately, without the attention to outcomes or current injustices, it is difficult to imagine social justice fully realized under the procedural paradigm. Conditions may not be worsened, but they also might not improve.

Theories of procedural justice encourage us to look at the relationships between people to understand social justice. It is a reminder that indicators of social justice are not just assessed by who has and has not, but by the way people are treated and our concern for the well-being of others. "Relationship requires connection" (Gilligan, 1993, xix). A vision of social justice based in relationships requires members of a society to learn about and from one another in order to develop care, empathy, and concern. Procedural justice asks that we open ourselves to the perspectives and experiences of others, that we work to make decisions cooperatively, and that we make those decisions with respect and concern for all people involved.

## Black Women's Praxis

The omission of Black women from social justice theorizing is unmistakable and remarkable given their intellectual and activist contributions to work for social justice. Fannie Jackson Coppin's (1913) aim "to make known to all men the justice of our claims to the same employments as other men under the same conditions" incites the distributive paradigm nearly 60 years before Rawls's *Theory of Justice* was first published (p. 37). Similarly, Audre Lorde's (1984/2007) critique of feminist movements for ignoring the realities of racism and homophobia were undoubtedly instrumental in the recognition paradigm and initiating conversations about the remediation of oppression as central to our understanding of social justice. Sojourner Truth's cry of "ain't I a woman" may have been one of the earliest claims for recognition in seeking justice, and Crenshaw's (1993) work to "map the margins" was an incredible contribution that brought intersectionality to our recognition of oppression. "Through an awareness of intersectionality," Crenshaw explains, "we can better acknowledge and ground the differences among us and negotiate the means by which these differences will find expression in constructing group politics" (1299). In particular, her analysis of the unique experiences of women of color and how our experiences of violence are simultaneously shaped by race and gender revealed the realities of multiple marginalizations and encouraged shifts in policy, practice, and organizing, thereby shaping procedural paradigms.

Anna Julia Cooper's aim to use education as an equalizing tool "to assist in the overall Black liberation battle for justice and social transformation" brought Black women's intellectual contributions on social justice from theory to practice (Johnson, 2009, 74). Black women's contributions to social justice persist beyond changing our understanding to the ways we organize and strategize to bring forth a more just society. The legislative and political contributions of Black women such as Shirley Chisholm and Barbara Jordan stand alongside civic leaders such as Fannie Lou Hamer and Dorothy Height. Ella Baker's democratic and egalitarian practice in civil rights organizing provided alternative structures from the "normative presence of many undemocratic traditions" limiting the full exercise of humanity of Blacks (Ransby, 2003, 364). Her praxis emphasized "interaction, discussion, debate, and consensus building" relegating "voting, lobbying the corridors of power and getting favored candidates elected [as] secondary concerns" (370).

Baker's search for alternative structures for democratic and reciprocal engagement are reminders of Lorde's (1984/2007) edict that "the master's tools will never dismantle the master's house." Black women's focus away from the traditional mechanisms for changemaking served to widen the "parameters of change" and our visions for what is "possible and allowable" (Lorde, 1984/2007,

110). Baker's praxis exemplifies the process and goal orientations of social justice articulated in Bell's definition of social justice. Ransby (2003) explains:

> Ella Baker understood that laws, structures, and institutions had to change in order to correct injustice and oppression, but part of the process had to involve oppressed people, ordinary people, infusing new meanings into the concept of democracy and finding their own individual and collective power to determine their lives and shape the direction of history. (1)

This emphasis on self-determination reflects current work for social justice as exemplified by the efforts of the #BlackLivesMatter movement. In articulating the "herstory" of Black Lives Matter, Garza (2014) does not singularly advance a recognition argument but simultaneously invokes distributive and procedural aims. The demand for acknowledgment of the material conditions of Black lives can be remedied only through a redistribution. The centering of Black lives in prison, Black lives who are undocumented, Black queer and trans lives, Black lives living with disabilities, and Black lives otherwise marginalized seeks recognition for the criminalization and oppression that shapes our lives. The naming of these realities as "state violence" suggests that different processes are needed to bring justice to Black lives (Garza, 2014, para. 12). "When we are able to end hyper-criminalization and sexualization of Black people and end the poverty, control, and surveillance of Black people, every single person in this world has a better shot at getting and staying free" (Garza, 2014, para. 13).

## Conclusion

Social justice entails a vision for society. A precise definition or single conception of social justice may always elude us, as understandings of social justice are based on individual notions, values, and beliefs. My desire, vision, or understanding of social justice will never meet every person's needs. One person's vision of social justice is likely to be in conflict with another's, and likely to not represent the concerns and values of every person. The theoretical paradigms of social justice I have described and discussed in this chapter—(re)distribution, recognition, and procedural justice—represent some of the ways social justice is conceptualized in the Western world. While each paradigm is unique, we can acknowledge that:

> Underpinning the theories of social justice are implicit assumptions about the meaning, the significance of difference(s): how we will

view difference, what we think needs to be done to integrate difference into a theory of social justice, how difference or diversity relates to concepts of the just society. (Douvan, 1988, 10)

Social justice is about how society should function. In developing the process and structures to implement social justice, who people are—their experiences, beliefs, and values—and how society will work to ensure that differences will not be tools of subjugation are important to social justice theorizing.

While I have taken care to present three distinct paradigms of social justice theory (see table 1.1), it is important to recognize that most theories of justice do not fit neatly into one paradigm. Each maintains a primary aim for society in order to realize justice, but this is often tempered with requirements based on other theoretical paradigms. For example, Rawls (1971/1999) utilizes distributive and procedural justice in outlining his vision for social justice. Young (1990) details distributive measures and recognition as necessary to realize her vision for justice. I have come to believe that in order for social justice to be fully realized as a "society in which the distribution of resources is equitable and all members are physically and psychologically safe and secure . . . [where] individuals are both self-determining (able to develop their full capacities), and interdependent (capable of interacting democratically with others)," we will need to employ multiple theories (Bell, 2007, 2). Grant and Gibson's (2010) articulation of social justice concurs: "Justice is not simply the redistribution of material resources but also the recognition

Table 1.1. Theoretical Paradigms of Social Justice

| Paradigm | Vision of Social Justice | Responsibility Change |
| --- | --- | --- |
| (Re)distribution | To correct the inequality resulting from material inequity by redistributing the resources, benefits, and advantages in a manner that fixes the prevailing system of stratification | Structures of Governance (Institutions) |
| Recognition | To work toward the elimination of oppression and the various ways it manifests in society | Individual, Community, and Institutions |
| Procedural | "society as a fair system of cooperation" (Rawls, 2000, 344) | Individual, Community, and Institutions |

and acceptance of diversity" (27). This understanding invokes redistribution, recognition, and procedure (i.e., "acceptance") to realize social justice.

(Re)distributive justice is necessary to change institutional structures that guard access to material resources. Recognition strategies must be employed to actively combat oppression and to radically transform our understanding of identity so that hierarchies of difference do not occur. Finally, procedural justice is essential to social justice. Through fairness and cooperation, care, empathy, and understanding, relationships are developed and individuals and groups feel respected. Each of these paradigms must interact and overlap for social justice to be realized.

Black women's intellectual history and activism have been omitted from social justice theory, and this chapter has sought to reintegrate those missing voices into the primary paradigms of this theoretical tradition. Doing this now feels especially relevant, as Garza (2014) insists: "It is appropriate and necessary for us to acknowledge the critical role that Black lives and struggles for Black liberation have played in inspiring and anchoring, through practice and theory, social movements for the liberation of all people" (para. 14).

## References

Barry, B. (1980). Is social justice a myth? In L. O. Ericsson, H. Ofstad & G. Pontara (Eds.), *Justice, social and global* (pp. 9–19). Stockholm, Sweden: Akademilitteratur.
Barry, B. (1989). *Theories of justice*. Berkeley: University of California Press.
Bell, L. A. (2007). Theoretical foundations for social justice education. In M. Adams, L. A. Bell, & P. Griffin (Eds.) *Teaching for diversity and social justice* (2nd ed., pp. 1–14). New York: Routledge.
Butler, J. (1997). Merely cultural. *Social Text 52/53, 15*(3/4), 265–277.
Chapman, T. K., & Hobbel, N. (2010). Introduction: Conversations, problems, and action. In T. K. Chapman & N. Hobbel (Eds.), *Social justice pedagogy across the curriculum* (pp. 1–5). New York: Routledge.
Coppin, F. J. (1913). *Reminiscences of school life, and hints on teaching*. Philadelphia: A.M.E. Book Concern.
Crenshaw, K. (1993). Mapping the margins: Intersectionality, identity politics, and violence against women of color. *Stanford Law Review, 43*, 1241–1299.
Douvan, E. (1988). *Difference and social justice: A feminist perspective*. Unpublished manuscript, University of Michigan, Ann Arbor, MI.
Dworkin, R. (2000). "Justice and Hypothetical Agreements," from "The Original Position" (1973). In R. C. Solomon & M. C. Murphy (Eds.), *What is justice? Classic and contemporary readings* (2nd ed., pp. 288–295). New York: Oxford University Press.

Foos, C. L. (1998). The "different voice" of service. *Michigan Journal of Community Service Learning, 5,* 14–21.

Fraser, N. (1997). *Justice interruptus: Critical reflections on the "postsocialist" condition.* New York: Routledge.

Garza, A. (2014, October 7). A herstory of the #BlackLivesMatter movement. *The Feminist Wire.* Retrieved from http://www.thefeministwire.com/2014/10/Blacklivesmatter-2

Gilligan, C. (1993). *In a different voice: Psychological theory and women's development.* Cambridge, MA: Harvard University Press.

Grant, C. A., & Gibson, M. L. (2010). "These are revolutionary times": Human rights, social justice, and popular protest. In T. K. Chapman & N. Hobbel (Eds.), *Social justice pedagogy across the curriculum* (pp. 9–35). New York, NY: Routledge.

Gutmann, A. (1992). Introduction. In A. Gutmann (Ed.), *Multiculturalism and "the politics of recognition"* (pp. 3–24). Princeton, NJ: Princeton University Press.

Hayek, F. A. (1976). *Law, legislation, and liberty: The mirage of social justice* (Vol. 2). Chicago: University of Chicago Press.

Johnson, K. A. (2009). Gender and race: Exploring Anna Julia Cooper's thoughts for socially just educational opportunities. *Philosophia Africana, 12*(1), 67–82.

Katz, S. N. (2002, May 17). Choosing justice over excellence. *The Chronicle of Higher Education, XLVIII,* B7–B9.

Lorde, A. (1984/2007). *Sister outsider: Essays and speeches.* Berkeley, CA: Crossing Press.

Mill, J. S. (2000). "Social Justice and Utility," from Utilitarianism (1861). In R. C. Solomon & M. C. Murphy (Eds.), *What is justice? Classic and contemporary readings* (2nd ed., pp. 166–174). New York: Oxford University Press.

Miller, D. (1976). *Social justice.* London: Oxford University Press.

Miller, D. (1999). *Principles of social justice.* Cambridge, MA: Harvard University Press.

Nieto, S., & Bode, P. (2012). *Affirming diversity: The sociopolitical context of multicultural education* (6th ed.). Boston, MA: Allyn & Bacon.

Noddings, N. (1999a). Care, justice, and equity. In M. S. Katz, N. Noddings, & K. A. Strike (Eds.), *Justice and caring: The search for common ground in education* (pp. 7–20). New York, NY: Teachers College Press.

Noddings, N. (1999b). Introduction. In M. S. Katz, N. Noddings, & K. A. Strike (Eds.), *Justice and caring: The search for common ground in education* (pp. 1–4). New York: Teachers College Press.

Nussbaum, M. (2001, July 20). The enduring significance of John Rawls. *The Chronicle of Higher Education, XLVII,* B7–B9.

Okin, S. M. (1989). *Justice, gender, and the family.* New York: Basic Books.

Ransby, B. (2003). *Ella Baker and the Black freedom movement: A radical democratic vision.* Chapel Hill: University of North Carolina Press.

Rawls, J. (1971/1999). *A Theory of Justice.* Cambridge, MA: Harvard University Press.

Sterba, J. P. (1995). Reconciling conceptions of justice. In J. P. Sterba, T. R. Machan, A. M. Jaggar, W. A. Galston, C. C. Gould, M. Fisk, & R. C. Solomon (Eds.), *Morality and social justice: Point/counterpoint* (pp. 1–57). Lanham, MD: Rowman & Littlefield.

Strike, K. A. (1999). Justice, caring, and universality: In defense of moral pluralism. In M. S. Katz, N. Noddings, & K. A. Strike (Eds.), *Justice and caring: The search for common ground in education* (pp. 21–36). New York: Teachers College Press.

Taylor, C. (1992). The politics of recognition. In A. Gutmann (Ed.), *Multiculturalism and "the politics of recognition"* (pp. 25–73). Princeton, NJ: Princeton University Press.

Tyler, T., Degoey, P., & Smith, H. (2001). Understanding why the justice of group procedures matters: A test of the psychological dynamics of the group-value model. In M. A. Hogg & D. Abrams (Eds.), *Intergroup relations: Essential readings* (pp. 205–228). Philadelphia: Psychology Press.

Tyler, T. R. (2001). Social justice. In R. Brown & S. L. Gaertner (Eds.), *Blackwell handbook of social psychology: Intergroup processes* (pp. 344–364). Malden, MA: Blackwell Publishers.

Walker, L. (2001). *Looking like what you are: Sexual style, race, and lesbian identity.* New York: New York University Press.

Warren, K. (1998). Educating students for social justice in service learning. *The Journal of Experiential Education, 21*(3), 134–139.

Wendorf, C. A., Alexander, S., & Firestone, I. J. (2002). Social justice and moral reasoning: An empirical integration of two paradigms in psychological research. *Social Justice Research, 15*(1), 19–39.

Young, I. M. (1990). *Justice and the politics of difference.* Princeton, NJ: Princeton University Press.

Chapter 2

# Social Justice Education and Luxocracy

LAYLI MAPARYAN

Since the surprising election results of November 2016, I have been deep in reflection about how best to move in the world as a person who desires profound transformation of the human condition. Since childhood, participation in this process of transformation has been central to my sense of self and purpose, manifesting in different ways during different eras of my life. Yet, over the years, there have been a few major moments, like this one, that have stopped me in my tracks and forced reassessment of myself and the situation around me. I have had to stop and ask myself: What is truly going on? Am I being effective? What should I do to make sure that we continue to move in a direction that is vitalizing for the human race and the planet? These questions have continued in months succeeding the election, as the conditions precipitating them have only seemingly worsened day by day.

I know that I am not alone; many others who care about the same things I do have retreated into places where they can focus on self-care, re-centering, re-strategizing, and restoration of their energies. For some, these places are solitary; for others, these places are social. For all of us, these are places where we can reconnect with truth and retool ourselves for fulfilling the purpose of our lives: to shepherd the collective toward peace and freedom, justice and well-being. We are a particular tribe—one among many—and we know who we are.

The night before I wrote this essay, I was jolted to wakefulness by the thought that I should write about social justice education and Luxocracy. Luxocracy means "rule by Light," and it refers to the inherent capacity of human beings to continually move toward that which is highest and best, based on the universal Divine[1] nature of humans. As I wrote in *The Womanist Idea*, "Light in this instance refers to the Inner Light, the Higher Self, the Soul, the

God Within—what I will hereafter refer to as Innate Divinity—as described by mystics and others across cultures, across faiths, and across the centuries, if not millennia."[2] In this manifesto on Luxocracy, I argued that humanity is in the process of evolving toward global society and planetary identity, that this evolution is both individual and collective, and that critical mass in this phase shift toward a new form of social organization is rapidly building.

At present, such assertions seem laughably counterintuitive. What happened in 2016 in terms of the elections feels like a setback. And maybe it is. But when I asked myself whether I still believed in—and am guided by—the core premises of Luxocracy, the answer came back as yes. In this essay, I will write about why, and I will develop Luxocracy as a social justice framework, exploring in particular its relevance to education as a tool of social justice. I will also highlight an influence on my own thinking that I have not previously written on at length, namely, the Baha'i Faith,[3] the religion in which I was reared, from which I took a 20-year hiatus, only to return with new eyes in middle age. My mother, a Black woman, and my father, a White man, both became Baha'is in college—my mother at Spelman College, an historically Black college where she learned about the Faith from international students from Africa, and my father at the University of Wisconsin, where he learned about the Faith from a Japanese classmate whose family had been Baha'i for three generations. My parents, who met at a Baha'i conference and married in 1962, were featured in the April 1965 issue of *Ebony* magazine in an article about the Baha'i Faith and its global message. It is in this Baha'i environment that I grew up and became a Black woman deeply committed to social justice, service to humanity, and spirituality.

I recognize and respect in this writing that not all of my readers and not all of the members of "the tribe" are as religious or spiritually or mystically oriented as I am, and at the same time, that many, often quite quietly, are as powered by religion or spirit as I am. I write this in the interest of our being in conversation together and doing our best work together on behalf of the planet and humanity that we all love.

Let me get something out of the way. I do not think that politics can save us. As I wrote in *The Womanist Idea*,

> [i]n today's world, many people look towards politics for liberation. Politics or political activism is assumed to be the answer to human misery, strife, and injustice. Yet, the limitations of this strategy are rendered invisible by belief systems that, at best, separate the material world from the spiritual realm or, at worst, negate the spiritual realm altogether. The political is earthbound. If politics

is not undergirded by a sense of the spiritual, the sacred, it is a dead end. This is equally true of politics on the right and politics on the left. Politics as it is understood and enacted today is incapable of delivering humanity to its own potentiality. Yet, outside politics, this potentiality is gaining expression and momentum in the larger global society among people from all walks of life who are awakening to the power and reality of their own spirituality as well as the spirituality of others and the spirituality of the world around them. As people come to apprehend their own Innate Divinity directly, as well as the Innate Divinity of others, Earth, and all aspects of Creation, they think, speak, and act differently; they expect different things from their world, and they begin to live in a different reality altogether, regardless of what is going on around them.[4]

It is important to clarify that I am not talking about religious government here, that is, theocracy of any kind. We have seen the dangers of theocracies throughout recent and past history. What we have not seen clearly is the influence of government informed by a universal understanding that human beings are sacred, that all creation is sacred, and, by association, government should serve the highest and best interests of humans and creation. We have not seen this; we have not tried this. Most people probably do not even think that this is possible, but I do. Yet, we are a ways from it, generations probably. Therefore, we have to begin where we are, which is a place where people can self-organize "outside" government and enact ways of being in the world wherever they find themselves—in their neighborhoods, their workplaces, their schools, and all the places they move throughout the day. Change is as important in these spaces as it is in the government. Are we working hard enough to be transformative in the spaces where we find ourselves every day?

One space where many of us reading this volume find ourselves is the area of education. We are educators, educational administrators, educational policymakers, and education enthusiasts of different kinds. We are here because we believe in the transformative power of education for individuals and society. We are here because we love children, youth, and adults enough to help them develop optimally. We are here because we are questers after knowledge—researchers, scientists, scholars of all kinds—who document our findings for humanity. We are people who put blood, sweat, and tears into making educational institutions run effectively, despite not enough resources and many competing social, political, economic, cultural, and moral interests. We are people with a particular angle of vision on how social injustice plays out in education and academia. For many of us, this view is informed by our cultural rootedness—in Blackness, Africanity, or another ethnic or cultural lineage that has been socially and politically marginalized, yet is the source of profound knowledge and liberatory educational praxis.[5] Thus, we have access to a particular space of healing, of rectification, of transformation. Based on our cultural positionalities and their associated worldviews—communalistic, holistic, vitalistic—many of us, without ever saying so, already see and revolve our lifework around the sacredness of human beings. But could we do this more explicitly?

> Man is the supreme Talisman. Lack of a proper education hath, however, deprived him of that which he doth inherently possess. Through a word proceeding out of the mouth of God he was called into being; by one word more he was guided to recognize the Source of his education; by yet another word his station and destiny were safeguarded. The Great Being saith: Regard man as a mine rich in gems of inestimable value. Education can, alone, cause it to reveal its treasures, and enable mankind to benefit therefrom. If any man were to meditate on that which the Scriptures, send down from the heaven of God's holy Will, have revealed, he would readily recognize that their purpose is that all men shall be regarded as one soul, so that the seal bearing the words "The Kingdom shall be God's" may be stamped on every heart, and the light of Divine bounty, of grace, and mercy may envelop all mankind. The one true God, exalted be His glory, hath wished nothing for Himself. The allegiance of mankind profiteth Him not, neither doth its perversity harm Him. The Bird of the Realm of Utterance voiceth continually this call: "All things have I willed for thee, and thee, too, for thine own sake." If the learned and worldly-wise men of this age were to allow mankind to inhale the fragrance of fellowship and love, every understanding heart would apprehend the meaning of true liberty, and discover the secret of undisturbed peace and absolute composure. Were the earth to attain this station and be illumined with its light it could then be truly said of it "Thou shall see in it no hollows or rising hills." (Bahá'u'lláh, *Gleanings from the Writings of Bahá'u'lláh* [1990, pp. 259–260])[6]

This quote is one of my all-time favorite passages from the entire corpus of sacred writings by Bahá'u'lláh, the Prophet Founder of the Baha'i Faith. I think it speaks to me because I am an educator, but also because I believe to the very core of my being that the key to transforming society—away from injustice, violence, oppression, discrimination, prejudice, hatred, and all related ills and toward peace, justice, freedom, and well-being—is education built on recognition of the sacred and Divine nature of humans. I would like to share my close reading of this quote, which has guided my life since early adulthood.

The first thing that stands out is the use of the curious word "Talisman." Generally, talisman means something akin to a good luck charm. However, etymological research reveals that the word arose from *telesma*, the Greek word for completion or religious rite, which in turn emerged from the word *telein* (complete, perform a rite), and ultimately from the word *telos* (result or end). "Telos" is a word used in Greek philosophy to refer to a future end state that acts as a cause in the present. In other words, it refers to something not unlike "becoming" or "destiny." Thus, one could read closely in the opening statement, "Man is the supreme Talisman," that human beings are the ultimate "becoming thing" or "thing in formation." In other words, there is something special about what human beings are capable of becoming.

We see some reference to this in the three-stage process outlined in the next sentence, which indicates that human beings were Divinely created, then invested with the faculty to recognize their Creator, and finally set on a course toward realization of their "station and destiny." It is as though a profound gestational process was set in motion.

What has deprived us from becoming all that we are ultimately capable of becoming? The second line lets us know, in no uncertain terms: "Lack of a proper education" has deprived us. And what is a "proper education"? Again, I turn to etymology, where education, broken down, means to "lead something out from" (e = out from; duc[are] = to lead, in Latin). What is it we are "leading out"? Reading a few lines further, we find that the Great Being says, "Regard man as a mine rich in gems of inestimable value. Education can, alone, cause it to reveal its treasures, and enable mankind to benefit therefrom." Thus, it is the gems that are hidden within us, the gems that need to be brought out. What are these gems? The passage doesn't specify, but we can speculate: These gems are all forms of human excellence, including the unique talents invested in each person—those very elements that we as teachers seek to nurture and cultivate in our students when we are at our very best. Anyone who knows gemstones knows that they are typically hidden within very ordinary looking stones, which often must be cracked open to reveal their treasures. We also know that gemstones often have a wonderful quality of refracting the light in beautiful ways. Returning to the concept of Luxocracy, which refers to Divine Light as reflected in all people by virtue of the human connection, we can imagine these hidden gemstones refracting the Divine Light in very beautiful—indeed, splendid—ways, if revealed.

After this commentary on education, the passage shifts topically to a distillation of the message of Sacred Writings, insofar as the purpose of all of them is "that all men should be regarded as one soul." This is, in my view, the missing piece of our current "political" discourse, insofar as it is not structured in a way to facilitate our seeing ourselves as "one soul." This "one soul" idea is not unlike Thich Nhat Hanh's notion of "interbeing"—We "inter-are."[7] It is a radical concept of interconnectedness, not just of humans, but also of humans with all created things, a kind of existential interpenetration, interdependence, and co-construction that is always in motion and always in effect. When we set up—indeed, reify—lines of division, lines in the sand, enemy lines, we undermine our ability to see, benefit from, and leverage a notion of human oneness. Oneness does not, in this context, refer to uniformity, sameness, or lack of appreciation of and respect for difference, diversity, and distinction; rather, it is an understanding in which all people and created things are mutually constitutive, for better or worse. It is an understanding that, when one part of "the Folk" is ailing, "the Folk" as a whole is ailing, and there's no getting around that.[8] It is a recognition of Ubuntu: "I am because we are, and because we are, I am."[9] It is a recognition of ntulogy: "All sets are interrelated through human and spiritual networks."[10]

From a Baha'i perspective, this oneness already exists—it is the foundational condition of human beingness, the ontological reality, *not* something to be created or achieved—yet we veil ourselves from it through a variety of means, including ego, materialism, undue focus on appetitiveness, and, importantly, lack of a "proper education." Education helps us to unveil our own faculties, to develop moderation over our appetites, to see beyond ourselves and our own interests, and to delve into the mysteries—that is, to explore what is beyond materialism and a purely material reality. This process prepares us for Justice—as spelled out in another verse penned by Bahá'u'lláh, which states: "O SON OF SPIRIT! The best beloved of all things in My sight is Justice; turn not away therefrom if thou desirest Me, and neglect it not that I may confide in thee. By its aid, thou shalt see with thine own eyes and not through the eyes of others, and shalt know of thine own knowledge and not through the knowledge of thy neighbor. Ponder this in thy heart; how it behooveth thee to be. Very justice is My gift to thee and the sign of My loving-kindness. Set it then before thine eyes."[11]

I digress here to show the links between education, sight, and justice. Education aids the development of clear sight, which, in turn, prepares people to be able to enact justice. Additionally, for justice to be fully realized, people must develop the ability to control their behavior ("how it behooveth thee to be"), a discipline also aided by "proper education."

Returning to the earlier Baha'i passage on education, we see a logical syllogism (which could, of course, be empirically tested) that suggests that our recognition that human beings are one soul will be followed by social transformation ("Divine bounty, . . . grace, and mercy may envelop all mankind"). These are the goods of relief to human suffering.

The balance of the passage reiterates the idea that God has given these gifts—talismanic power, education, Scripture and Divine guidance, gems, treasures—to humankind strictly for the benefit of humankind. God is independent; God is beyond the conditions, good or ill, of humankind. God has conferred upon humanity all that it needs to prosper, to realize its own highest and best good. As the passage states, "All things have I willed for thee, and thee, too, for thine own sake." This places tremendous responsibility on us to reach for and achieve our own great destiny, our own ultimate nobility, and all the social goods—justice, peace, freedom, well-being—that go with it. This connects the passage to the notion of Luxocracy—"rule by Light"—because it speaks to the realization of our Divine natures in ways that enable the best of society also to emerge—not because we have been forced into good through law or government, but because we have autonomously chosen to form society in ways that reinforce our goodness.

In my estimation, the penultimate sentence summarizes the relationship between sacredness, education, and social justice, with an admonition to the very kinds of people who challenge our faith in humanity in times such as these: "If the learned and worldly-wise men of this age were to allow mankind to inhale the fragrance of fellowship and love, every understanding heart would apprehend the meaning of true liberty, and discover the secret of undisturbed peace and absolute composure." This assertion speaks to the fact that those in power, those whom we uphold (perhaps falsely) as the leaders and guardians of society, are holding us back from the very simple things that would ensure our liberation and healing, namely, fellowship and love. There are active inimical forces keeping us separated from the keys that would release us from this cage, this prison of suboptimal human development, expression, and experience.

One of the challenges of this point of view that I am advocating is to see all people—even those whom we dislike strongly, those whom we view as "anti-," those we deem as "bad"—through the lens of sacredness. How can we keep everyone in the fold while still acknowledging and addressing the evils, harms, and injustices that undermine human peace, freedom, and well-being? One way to do this is by tracing causal pathways and by understanding that a chain of factors and influences that, over time, caused an innocent baby to become an agent of harm in the larger collective. Do we truly understand that chain of factors? We must remember that, anytime we demonize anyone, we are recreating the pattern of drawing lines that separate people. Yet, how can we hold people accountable without demonizing them?

Anything that is caused can be uncaused or prevented, particularly in a future scenario. "Lack of a proper education" is often one factor that allows evil to arise unchecked, whether in individuals or in swaths of people. We must take more care—particularly those of us of this tribe responsible for shepherding humanity toward well-being—to explicitly trace, document, and attend to factors that entrench people in patterns of thinking, feeling, or behaving that are unjust, evil, or harmful so that we can develop interventions—individual and collective—that interrupt and re-route these patterns. Social scientists play an important role here, as do clinicians, therapists, and healers. All of us must collaborate.

The institutions of society are responsible for establishing safeguards for the development of people's goodness across the lifespan, but collectively we have lost site of this responsibility of institutions. The recursive loop of influence linking individuals and institutions has broken down in favor of institutions serving the bad at least as often as the good, to our peril. Stated differently, these institutions are serving interests other than human well-being—often, interests that aren't even human at all—and thus short-shrifting humans. Although it will be a gradual process to reclaim and retrain our social institutions, we must keep this goal in mind. In the meantime, we begin with something relatively simple—education, where we can have direct influence on many people right away. How can we right things in the educational sphere?

For starters, as social justice educators, we can begin each day with the remembrance that everyone is sacred. By sacred, I mean noble, of Divine origin, blessed and a blessing, inspiring awe and gratitude, worthy of reverence and respect at our core. We are sacred, our students are sacred, our colleagues are sacred, parents are sacred, even the people we are teaching about are sacred. Additionally, our earth is sacred, our cosmos is sacred—from our desks and chalkboard to our books and computers to the critters crawling around and beyond. See with the sacred eye, and teach students to see with the sacred eye. Then watch what happens. Does justice come more easily when we are creating a community of sacred beings? How do we interrupt problems in the classroom from a sacred starting point? How do we initiate discussions about historical or contemporary injustice from a sacred starting point? How do we encourage one another to keep up these practices despite a steady stream of stressors as well as invitations to do otherwise? While it is beyond the scope of this essay to provide in-depth answers to these questions, it is my hope to spur wider dialogue along such lines among educators, educational administrators, educational policymakers, and the general public, as well as to support educational programs that are already based on notions of human sacredness.[12]

Education is the most powerful, accessible means of social change at our disposal. It is global, it is established, it is peopled, and it is malleable. The greatest intervention on education itself at this time in line with Luxocracy would be to universalize the notion of the sacredness of human beings and creation. It is an emotional transformation that doesn't require anyone to be religious or even to characterize themselves as spiritual. We all can access those feelings of awe and reverence that accompany the recognition of sacredness in a person or thing and bootstrap from this shared affective experience. In fact, it would be counterproductive to situate this practice inside religions or spiritual traditions because that would risk initiating a process of drawing lines in the sand. However, that does not mean we can't access the energy from deep without our souls or the universe if that is our inclination. Wherever we find inspiration—which is, in itself, a form of power—that is where we begin.

Sometimes I find my ASÉ in Audre Lorde or Barbara Smith.[13] Sometimes I find my ASÉ in Shirley Chisholm. Sometimes I find my ASÉ in Oshun, Oya, Yemaya, Mammywata, or Obatala. Sometimes I find my ASÉ in my sister scholars who are doing the same work (you know who you are), or different work (you, too, know who you are). Or in my beloved brother scholars (ASÉ-O, Brothers—you know who you are). Sometimes I find my ASÉ in the Báb or Bahá'u'lláh, Jesus Christ or Muhammad (peace be upon Him), Moses or Buddha, the Rishis or Thich Nhat Hanh. Sometimes I find it in teachers I have had along the way, such as Mary Wilson in 7th grade or Beverly Guy-Sheftall in college or Pregs Govender at the international feminist pedagogy workshop in South Africa. Sometimes I find my ASÉ in unknown beautiful-spirited people who serendipitously cross my path, blessings all. Sometimes I find it in Hip Hop or classical music or the marvelous sound of the kora. Sometimes I find my ASÉ in my father, my mother, my sisters or sisters-in-law, my children, or the love of my life, my husband Seboe. Or in my Ancestors, my grandmother, my daughter. Sometimes I find my ASÉ in my books or in a library or online. Sometimes I find it in my own head when I meditate or watch a sunrise or sunset or the stars or walk through a forest, sit by the ocean, or stand in the wind. It is always there, always available, always a source of power, of connection to Source. I give these many examples just to show how ubiquitous inspiration is for our work and how important it is to connect—also to remind ourselves to help our students and colleagues discover this Source.

Social justice education from a Luxocratic perspective begins when, fortified in this power, we step into our institutions, our classrooms, and our offices, knowing when to close the door and *really teach* and when to open the door to widen the circle. It requires us to check in with our own power to transform institutions from within by our own participation in highly intentional ways, as well as our power to counteract the ways in which institutions are failing by engaging in social justice–oriented and Divine Light–connecting practices outside institutions. It requires us to think beyond rote definitions of justice or social justice work and really expand the vocabulary of social justice activity, remaining humble and open in this process of discovery. It requires us to remember that there are no shortcuts and that we must strive to be impeccable internally and externally. We must challenge ourselves to love harder and, at the same time, exact accountability with more consistency and resolve. Most important, we must support one another as trailblazers in the doing of this work.

## Notes

1. The word "Divine" is capitalized here and elsewhere out of reverence for the Creator.

2. Maparyan, L. (2012). *The Womanist Idea*. New York: Routledge, p. 3.

3. "Founded in Iran in 1844, the Baha'i Faith is the youngest of the world's independent, monotheistic religions, with more than 5 million adherents in 236 countries and territories. Baha'is come from nearly every national, ethnic, and religious background, making the Baha'i Faith the second most widespread religion in the world, after Christianity, according to the *Encyclopedia Britannica*. Baha'is view the world's major religions as part of a single, progressive process through which God reveals His will to humanity. Baha'u'llah (1817–1892), the Founder of the Baha'i Faith, is recognized by Baha'is as the most recent in a line of Divine Messengers that includes Abraham, Krishna, Moses, the Buddha, Zoroaster, Jesus Christ, and Muhammad. The central theme of Baha'u'llah's message is that humanity is one single race and that it is imperative, for the security and prosperity of all, that it resolve to move toward a united, global civilization. Baha'is believe in the harmony of science and religion, the equality of women and men, the elimination of the extremes of wealth and poverty, the common origin and unity of all world religions, and the elimination of all forms of prejudice." (Baha'i Office of Public Affairs, (n.d.), retrieved from publicaffairs.bahai.us/who-we-are/ourvision)

4. Ibid., p. 4.

5. See, for example, Vanessa Sheared's "Giving Voice: An Inclusive Model of Instruction—A Womanist Perspective" and Tamara Beauboeuf-Lafontant's "A Womanist Experience of Caring: Understanding the Pedagogy of Exemplary Black Women Teachers," both anthologized in Phillips, L. (2006). *The Womanist Reader*. New York: Routledge (pp. 269–279 and 280–295, respectively).

6. In this passage, the words "he," "him," "man," "men," and "mankind" are to be regarded as referring to people of all genders.

7. Thich Nhat Hanh (1987). *Interbeing: Fourteen Guidelines for Engaged Buddhism*. Berkeley, CA: Parallax Press.

8. The reference here is to "the Folk" mentioned by Alice Walker in her 1983 definition of "womanist," where she wrote that a womanist "Loves the Folk." See Alice Walker (1983), Preface. *In Search of Our Mothers' Gardens: Womanist Prose*. San Francisco: Harcourt Brace Jovanovich.

9. Ifeanye Menkiti. (1984). "Person and Community in African Traditional Thought." In *African Philosophy: An Introduction*, edited by Richard Wright. Lanham, MD: University Press of America.

10. Linda James Myers. (1988). *Understanding an Afrocentric World View: Introduction to an Optimal Psychology*, Dubuque, IA: Kendall/Hunt.

11. Bahá'u'lláh. (1985). *Hidden Words of Bahá'u'lláh*, Wilmette, IL: Baha'i Publishing Trust, pp. 3–4.

12. Two Baha'i-inspired examples would be *The Virtues Project* by Linda Kavelin Popov, Dan Popov, and John Kavelin and *Raising Peacemakers* curriculum by Somava Saha Stout, MD. A Buddhist example can be observed in the book *It's Always Possible* by Kiran Bedi or the film *Doing Time, Doing Vipassana*. A Christian and ecowomanist example can be seen in Wangari Maathai's Green Belt Movement, as well as the film *Taking Root*.

13. ASÉ is a Yoruba word that refers to both the power to make things happen or change and power, authority, and command in relation to this energy. SOURCE: https://en.wikipedia.org/wiki/Ase_(Yoruba)

Chapter 3

# When Intersections Collide

*Young Black Women Combat Sexism, Racism, and Ageism in Higher Education*

Jaymee Lewis-Flenaugh, Eboni N. Turnbow,
and Sharee L. Myricks

Despite anti-discrimination legislation and societal progress, institutions, organizations, and places of employment continue to make decisions that perpetuate discriminatory practices that negatively impact those with multiple marginalizations (Jyrkinen & McKie, 2011). Like other workplaces, the glass ceiling—barriers that prevent women and other minorities from career advancement, particularly to senior management—exists in the academy as well (Moore, 1997). Although white women encounter sexist barriers in higher education, racial identity presents an additional sociopolitical challenge in self-perception and advancement for women of color. Research regarding the double oppression of Black women has illustrated the erasure of histories and the contemporary contexts in which they impact work organization's gender and racial bias (Crenshaw, 1989). Thus, young Black women continually navigate intersectional inequalities in order to thrive within their careers. Currently, a gap remains among senior level positions between men and women, and is exacerbated when race/ethnicity are incorporated (Catalyst, 2004b). Challenging work organizations through an anti-racist and Black feminist perspective aims to maneuver current work environments toward change.

The purpose of this chapter is to examine the intersections of gender, race, and age for young Black women working in higher education. Crenshaw's *Black Feminist Theory* (1989) frames the view in which the intersections of gender, race, and age demonstrate a need for ongoing interventions that combat challenging workplace cultures that unconsciously impede growth for Black women in the academy. This framework addresses the shortage of young Black women in upper-management positions and explores the "outsider within" notion. Black feminism explores three primary endeavors: (1) to explicate experiences of Black women regardless of previously documented accounts; (2) to acknowledge women's personal experiences while simultaneously categorizing their similarities; and (3) to aggregate the similarities and differences as these experiences enrich the entire group (Collins, 1991).

Our focus is concentrated on young Black women professionals, defined as women who identify as African American, under 30 years of age, and/or who have less than 7 years of professional experience working in higher education. The experiences of young Black professional women are significant to advancing social justice education in the academy. While the vast majority of people are not entirely privileged or entirely subordinated (Davis & Harrison, 2013), intersecting identities help illustrate the need to view experiences from a social justice perspective. To advance toward a more socially just organization, it would involve critiquing the workplace and its established structures. Social justice becomes the equitable process and outcome of efforts to close the gap between stated and enacted missions. The history of social justice in higher education is a direct reflection of the larger American context, which places hierarchical oppression at the forefront (Davis & Harrison, 2013). Whether providing alternate perspectives through lived experiences or challenging gendered age norms, young Black women positively impact an organization's growth. Often, there are practical and social implications for Black women when positively influencing institutions from challenging the status quo, shattering glass ceilings, and addressing unjust practices in which racism, ageism, and sexism manifest in higher education.

Social justice education must permeate existing workspaces with an eye toward critical policy review that promotes equality. What follows is a summary of literature on women in the workplace. We provide a generational analysis via research to expose the unique challenges sexism, racism, and ageism present for young Black women in higher education. After, we provide tangible strategies that can be utilized to overcome intersectional inequalities for career advancement for young Black women.

## Challenges of Black Women on Gender, Race, and Age

Our failure to attend to ways in which intersectionality has grown beyond double oppression has limited our ability to see where the theory can go as it relates to social justice in the workplace (Carbado, Crenshaw, Mays, &

Tomlinson, 2013). Gender, race, and age as social identities all impact lived experiences that need to be explored further to improve institutional cultures. Gender provides its own set of challenges for women in higher education. According to the Institute for Women's Policy Research (2015) and Costello and Hegewisch (2016), today's professional women still make less than their male counterparts: 80 cents to the dollar. Black women experience an augmented wage gap at 68 cents to a man's dollar, which is a larger gap than their White and Asian women peers (DuMonthier & Hegewisch, 2016). Yet, Claypool and colleagues (2017) report that women who negotiate their salaries in academia are less successful than their male counterparts. This asserts economic disparities that are affected by age, gender, and race while raising a concern for young Black women professionals regarding negotiation techniques and the consequences they can incur.

Academic institutional cultures are not immensely supportive with career interruptions for women, which aid in elongated career trajectories. Women commonly experience career interruptions due to familial and life conflicts (Catalyst, 2004b). For instance, after establishing a family, young Black women may work part-time or exit the institution temporarily to focus on their children. However, when re-entering the academy, Black women are likely to experience hardship seeking advanced positions. In a study by Motaung, Bussin, and Joseph (2017), 90% of Black women participants agreed maternity leave negatively affected their career progression in middle management and leadership opportunities.

For women who decide to remain in the workplace after having children, they must find a balance between work and personal life (McClinton, 2012). Black women often serve as the primary caregiver in the traditional home setting or situated within a nontraditional family arrangement, such as single motherhood (Catalyst, 2004a). One challenge presented to young Black women is the receptiveness to the request for flexible work arrangements with their supervisor or the adjustment of their work schedules in its entirety (McClinton, 2012). If this is not a workplace practice or policy, young Black women must determine their best route in balancing work and family. Due to factors such as these, Black women may feel conflicted between career success and prioritizing family commitments, as confirmed by the study of Motaung and colleagues (2017). When this happens, young Black women might bypass opportunities to climb the ladder in higher education and focus on positions that require less time and restraint; thus, it is no surprise that young Black women report experiencing a decline in organizational advancement for senior-level positions (Catalyst, 2004b). As a social justice tenet, the exploration of intersecting identities as it relates to womanhood allows for the creation of policies that speak to the needs of all employees.

Black feminists would argue how these personal narratives directly expose a direct barrier for Black women advancing in academia via institutionalized unequal organizational logic.

Race also has its own challenges for women in higher education. Blacks have historically endured systematic oppression in higher education, including an unequal distribution of power and societal resources (Bivens, 1995). American racial inequality was evidenced by a Black person's inability to gain admission into institutions of higher education prior to the Civil War (Allen & Jewell, 2002). This barrier has been specifically troubling for Black women; however, after the Civil War and the subsequent women's suffrage movement, societal structures began to shift (Nieto-Gómez, 1997). Despite increased presence, Black women remain 3 decades behind some of their peers and the victims of negative barriers and pressures, including but not limited to segregation and criticism from male and white female peers (Harper, Patton, & Wooden, 2009; Hayden Glover, 2012).

Black women have struggled not only to obtain college degrees but also to serve as faculty and administrators through tenure and promotion practices (Matthew, 2016). Even with Federal legislation, such as Title IX of the Civil Rights Act of 1964 and the Title IX Education Act of 1972, challenging gender and racial discriminatory practices, the day-to-day barriers and microaggressions Black women encounter are far from being eliminated (Hayden Glover, 2012). For example, Mena (2016) argues that Black women face challenges of professional credibility and competence via overt and covert oppressive encounters in higher education. Black women confront the double-jeopardy dilemma of their gender and racial identities in the workplace. Yet, it is oppressive behaviors that make the deciphering of these multiple identities even more challenging (Howard-Hamilton & Logan Patitu, 2012).

As examining identity is a core indicator of social justice work, incorporating its concept is important to push workplaces toward becoming socially just organizations. In order to appreciate the need for and practice of social justice, it is essential to understand that the self is multidimensional and identity is intersectional (Davis & Harrison, 2013). Exposing the unique challenges that race poses on young Black women individually makes work organizations and colleagues more cognizant of the hardships the intersections create. For instance, young Black women experience challenges such as a lack of institutional support based strictly on negative stereotypes (Catalyst, 2004a). A major stereotype that plagues Black women is being perceived as the "angry Black woman"—aggressive, defensive, and impossible to work with. Young Black professional women in higher education also suffer from being placed into stereotypical oppressive categories due to assumptions of being inexperienced because of their age. Negative stereotypes perceived by supervisors and colleagues serve as a roadblock to young Black women aspiring to enhance professional skill sets. It is the simultaneous colliding of race and gender that compound a problem in higher education.

In addition to discriminatory practices, Black women battle narrow advancement opportunity in higher education (Mena, 2016). Professional development is essential, yet costly, for career growth in academia, which disadvantages young Black women as their support in entry- and mid-level positions are much less than senior-level positions. For example, many entry-level administrative positions do not include the scope of supervision over professional staff that is required to become a senior student affairs officer (SSAO). SSAOs are senior and chief level administrators within the nonacademic divisions of administration in higher education. Young Black women, therefore, must strategically and deliberately find ways to incorporate supervising or leading professional staff to satisfy this competency. Race is embedded within institutional cultures in the academy and continues to negatively affect the overall success for young Black professional women in the field.

Ageism is a recent component researchers have identified as a challenge to women in the workplace. Ageism is the systematic stereotyping, discrimination, and institutionalized forms of prejudice against someone due to their age (Butler, 1969; Cuddy & Fiske, 2002). This is important, as young Black women in higher education may suffer from being placed into oppressive categories due to assumptions of experience based on age. Research focused on young Black women concluded that "age emerged as an additional identity operating with race, ethnicity, and gender" (Mena, 2016, 203). The discussion of the intersection of sexism, racism, and ageism was scarce prior to this study. The Centre for Research on Families and Relationships suggest gendered ageism "takes different forms at early, midlife, and later stages of careers" (Jyrkinen & McKie, 2011, 56). However, the experiences of young women surrounding ageism and its effects on their career opportunities are often overlooked in the literature, notably in higher education. Within business, some researchers have begun to uncover challenges age and gender have on young professional women, including disparities in pay, benefits, and career advancement, as well as unfair treatment from seasoned women counterparts (Duncan & Loretto, 2004; Ransom, 2013).

Young Black women encounter challenges regarding age discrimination in higher education, such as the feeling of suppression or imperfection as they experience a lack of opportunities to exhibit their leadership skills or experience less favorable treatment at work (Duncan & Loretto, 2004). On the contrary, young women who seek advanced opportunities early in their careers are frequently met with elements of sexism from male colleagues and ageism from female colleagues (Turnbow & Myricks Williamson, 2015). A participant in a qualitative study conducted by Jyrkinen and McKie (2011) indicated that she is rarely taken seriously due to being a woman, or sometimes because she is young, and other times a combination of the two.

Women in work organizations often serve as prominent barriers to other women in regards to age discrimination. Research has found that gendered bullying is a common element among younger women and older women working in the same environment. According to a study by the Workplace Bullying Institute (Namie, 2007), 71% of women target, and are less likely to support, other women who are outside their age range due to feeling threatened within their position. Many of these behaviors are implicit biases that create unnecessary challenges for young professional women and have long-lasting effects on their careers. When women do not support and empower other women in the workforce, they undermine their talent and the progression of gender inequality as an entirety (Ransom, 2013).

Studies have shown that sexism, racism, and ageism independently all have adverse effects on women, yet the gap in literature calls for more in-depth research and discussion on how to challenge the development and retention of young Black women in higher education. Lampman's (2012) study reinforces that young minority female professionals in higher education face multiple challenges, as discussed above, but also face a significant risk for receiving more incivility, bullying, and aggression than their white counterparts. Essed (1991) coined the concept of gendered racism, which is a feeling of double jeopardy Black women experience when racism and sexism intersect. This concept asserts racism and sexism combine to create racialized gender-based stereotypes, which serves as its own form of oppression uniquely associated with Black women (Williams, 2015). However, even this notion of gendered racism has rarely been studied, and therefore the incorporation of ageism into the already oppressive equation complicates accurately deciphering the experiences of young Black women in higher education. If obstacles such as these are not considered from the standpoint of civility, along with insight on how to successfully navigate these inequalities, higher education could lose talented young Black women professionals (Turnbow & Myricks Williamson, 2015). As institutions begin to acknowledge structural inequities and awareness of power dynamics, they become more socially just and begin dismantling structures of oppression (Adams, 2016).

## Action Strategies

African American women within an unequal structure are not viable to challenge the culture of subordination in the workplace alone (Crenshaw, 1989).

The value employers place on diversifying and supporting young Black women puts a focus on creating environments where the stated mission can become the enacted mission. It is the latter where the academy falls short. Disclosing the daily realities of young Black women professionals in higher education is an important step in creating change in environments that produce and maintain microaggressions in the workplace. Modifications must begin structurally by intentionally instilling transformation in organizational culture. Transforming the culture thereby begins to include young Black women's voices and embeds them as intricate pieces to the operation of the institution.

To avoid the erasure of young Black women's voices at work, work organizations must encourage self-efficacy. For example, implementing a flexible work culture strategy that focuses on hours worked versus in-office hours that targets both genders regardless of parental status allows for young Black women to feel supported. Kelly and colleagues (2010) document the *Results Only Work Environment* (ROWE) initiative at the Best Buy headquarters as an alternative to standard flexible work policies. ROWE encourages work organizations to reexamine what productivity looks like, and emphasizes changes with regard to long work hours, visible busyness, and response to unexpected work (Kelly, Ammons, Chermack, & Moen, 2010). These three areas are all impeding barriers that young Black professional women in higher education experience. Changing institutional culture by shedding traditional work schedules, decreasing the necessity to attend countless meetings, and establishing innovative expectations of what productivity looks like are all examples of ways to change structural systems to level the playing field for women to advance their careers.

Simultaneously, an outcome of self-efficacy calls for Black women to combat these negative occurrences in order to maintain mental health as well as career progression. One strategy to dealing with the intersection of racism, sexism, and ageism is to establish an even balance of role flexing. Taking ownership of an experience is a forward-thinking action and coping mechanism to handling racial oppression, while role flexing is an indirect mechanism that addresses sexist inequalities (Shorter-Gooden, 2004). Time and place is important in this instance to avoid stereotypes, as young Black women may borrow what society deems as masculine traits—confidence, experience, strength, and avoidance of emotion (Shorter-Gooden, 2004). A conscious effort of gender, age, and/or race performance in the workplace is a step Black women can take to begin transformation of more equitable work environments.

Another strategy for work organizations is to be diligent about supporting professional development for career advancement to combat ageism, sexism, and racism. The competence of Black women to be able to significantly contribute to work institutions is consistently questioned; demystifying the competence of Black women by being proficient in one's area helps eliminate bias among colleagues (Ridgeway, 1997). It is important to stay current on new trends and research in the field, particularly for younger women, as this serves as an opportunity to enhance professional skills over time. Likewise, work institutions can implement continuous training processes for employees, therefore providing young Black women an opportunity to articulate their goals toward advancement in higher education. Funds are also needed from institutions for professional conferences and training, as these help retain professional staff and grow the organization. Other considerations include mindfulness in cross-cultural supervision, flexible professional development plans, increased exposure to SSAOs, and opportunity to supervise full-time professionals.

Visibility has also been identified as a structural barrier to work competency, as minority women are not as visible in senior-level roles (Kalev, 2009). A way to take personal ownership in becoming more visible is to ask directly for advanced opportunities. McGinn and Tempest (2010) contend that young women display a lack of confidence in their early years, which impacts their ambition and can even halt their careers. Low confidence levels can also lead to microaggressions concerning ageism and lack of experience. Young Black women are encouraged to work with a mentor to enhance their confidence to navigate through institutional barriers of advancement as well as to develop a progressive career blueprint with a mentor in which seeking opportunities for aggressive advancement is focused.

Last, cultivating the ability to value one's self is a helpful strategy for individuals in navigating oppressive barriers. Shorter-Gooden (2004) asserts that when Black women value themselves, negative perceptions of Black women are challenged, reinforcing positive self-image. She explains: "[F]or some women, the emphasis here was on loving oneself, feeling good about oneself, respecting oneself, and working hard to not take in the negative stereotypes or damaging views of Black women that are perpetuated in the larger society" (Shorter-Gooden, 2004, 417). By enhancing self-care and focusing on the positive attributes brought to the table, young Black women naturally embrace what Williams (2015) classifies as gendered racial identity. The more central a young Black woman's gender racial identity is to her daily infrastructure, the more positive her view about being a Black woman; simultaneously, a reduction occurs in the ability for negative experiences from oppressive inequalities to impact her well-being (Williams, 2015). Employing a self-determined outlook can empower young Black women to advocate for themselves in the workplace.

The recommended strategies for battling the three intersections of racism, sexism, and ageism include empowering self-efficacy, work organizations supporting their staff professionally, and instilling value in oneself. Though a challenge to implement, these strategies can give rise to young Black women feeling empowered in the workplace to share their voices toward equitable partnerships in the creation of workplace culture.

## Conclusion and Future Research

Black feminism and intersectionality work has begun to speak for the needed discourse on intersectional approaches to work organizations. More work is needed to account for the intersecting oppressions that gender, race, and age present. For years, Black women have battled racism and sexism in higher education. Recent research highlights how ageism contributes to Black women's inability to break through glass ceilings in higher education. Continued research should extend the work of this chapter not only by demonstrating how racism, sexism, and ageism independently affect Black women, but also engaging in research to explore the impact of the three oppressions directly. Black women are left to analyze oppressive behaviors and interactions in the workplace to determine if they are consequences of their race, gender, or age. This creates a dynamic of continually working and living in isolation. As prior research has shown, mastering the art of role-flexing, being deliberate about professional development opportunities, valuing one's self, and building a broad network of mentors are all approaches that aid in combating racism, sexism, and ageism. However, this alone is not enough. Higher educational institutions must also begin to create policies that are more flexible, infuse more supportive environments, and strategically incorporate a social just framework into their institutional logic in order to combat oppressive work environments.

For success in progressing through barriers on a larger scale, women collectively must be able to relate with one another within their inequality (Lorde, 1995). All women must acknowledge and recognize their differences, see one another as equals, and then establish ways to use one another's difference to enhance the vision and struggles of their experiences (Lorde, 1995). It is under this micro-level unification that macro-level changes can begin to infiltrate structural shifts to alleviate sexism, racism, and ageism that impact so many women in society. This is where the exposure of the challenges of young Black women in higher education seeks to positively impact social justice education of colleagues and superiors. In order for unification to occur, Black women must be included, and not be treated as outsiders in the workplace. In promotion of social justice, white colleagues must critically reflect on how to invest in social justice work to move past cognitive investment into active engagement with personal narratives. Such depth would make higher education a leader in advancing opportunities for young Black women.

## References

Adams, M. (2016). Pedagogical foundations for social justice education. In M. Adams & L. A. Bell (Eds.), *Teaching for diversity and social justice* (pp. 27–42). Howick Place, London: Routledge.

Allen, W. R., & Jewell, J. O. (2002). A backward glance forward: past, present and future perspectives on historically Black colleges and universities. *The Review of Higher Education, 25*(3), 241–261. doi: 10.1353/rhe.2002.0007

Bivens, D. (1995). Internalized racism: A definition. *Women's Theological Center.* Retrieved from www.thewtc.org/Internalized_Racism.pdf

Butler, R. (1969). Age-ism: Another form of bigotry. *The Gerontologist, 9*, 243–246.

Catalyst. (2004a). *Advancing African American women in the workforce: What managers need to know.* New York: Catalyst. Retrieved from www.catalyst.org/system/files/Advancing_African_American_Women_in_the_Workplace_What_Managers_Need_to_Know.pdf

Catalyst. (2004b). *Women and men in U.S. corporate leadership: Same workplace, different realities?* New York: Catalyst. Retrieved from www.catalyst.org/system/files/Women%20and_Men_in_U.S._corporate_Leadership_Same_Workplace_Different_Realities.pdf

Carbado, D. W., Crenshaw, K. W., Mays, V. M., & Tomlinson, B. (2013). Intersectionality. *Du Bois review: Social science research on race, 10*(2), 303–312. doi.org/10.1017/S1742058X13000349

Collins, P. H. (1991). *Black feminist thought: Knowledge, consciousness, and politics of empowerment.* New York: Routledge.

Claypool, V. H., Janssen, B. D., Kim, D., & Mitchell, S. M. (2017). Determinants of salary dispersion among political science faculty: The differential effects of where you work (institutional characteristics) and what you do (negotiate and publish). *PS: Political Science & Politics, 50*(1), 146–156. doi.org/10.1017/S104909651600233X

Costello, C. B., & Hegewisch, A. (2016). *The gender wage gap and public policy* (Policy brief 507). Institute for Women's Policy Research. Retrieved from www.iwpr.org/initiatives/pay-equity-and-discrimination

Crenshaw, K. (1989). Demarginalizing the Intersection of Race and Sex: Black Feminist Critique of Antidiscrimination Doctrine, Feminist Theory and Antiracist Politics. University of Chicago Legal Forum 1989, 139–168. Chicago.

Cuddy, A. J. C., & Fiske, S. T. (2002). Doddering but dear: Process, content, and function in stereotyping of older persons. In T. D. Nelson (Ed.) *Ageism: Stereotyping and prejudice against older persons* (pp. 3–26). Cambridge, MA: MIT Press.

Davis, T., & Harrison, L. M. (2013). *Advancing social justice: Tools, pedagogies, and strategies to transform your campus.* Hoboken, NJ: Jossey Bass.

DuMonthier, A., & Hegewisch, A. (2016). The gender wage gap: 2015; Annual earnings differences by gender, race, and ethnicity. *Institute for Women's Policy Research.* Retrieved from www.iwpr.org/publications/pubs/the-gender-wage-gap-2015-annual-earnings-differences-by-gender-race-and-ethnicity#sthash.H8udEBhQ.dpuf

Duncan, C., & Loretto, W. (2004). Never the right age? Gender and age-based discrimination in employment. *Gender, Work & Organization, 11,* 95–115. doi: 10.1111/j.1468-0432.2004.00222.x

Essed, P. (1991). *Understanding everyday racism: An interdisciplinary theory.* Newbury Park, CA: Sage.

Harper, S. R., Patton, L. D., & Wooden, O. S. (2009). Access and equity for African American students in higher education: A critical race historical analysis of policy efforts. *The Journal of Higher Education, 80*(4), 389–414. doi.org/10.1080/00221546.2009.11779022

Hayden Glover, M. (2012). Existing pathways: A historical overview of Black women in higher education administration. In T. Jones, L. Dawkins, M. McClinton, M. Glover, & J. Brazzell (Eds.), *Pathways to higher education administration for African American women* (pp. 4–17). Sterling, VA: Stylus.

Howard-Hamilton, M., & Logan Patitu, C. (2012). Decision to make (or not) along the careerpath. In T. Jones, L. Dawkins, M. McClinton, M. Glover, & J. Brazzell (Eds.), *Pathways to higher education administration for African American women* (pp. 85–102). Sterling, VA: Stylus.

Institute for Women's Policy Research (2015). *Pay equity & discrimination.* Retrieved from www.iwpr.org/initiatives/pay-equity-and-discrimination

Jyrkinen, M., & McKie, L. (2011). Women in management: Gender, age and working lives. (Policy brief 56). Centre for Research on Families and Relationships. Retrieved from https://www.era.lib.ed.ac.uk/bitstream/handle/1842/6679/Briefing%2056.pdf?sequence=1&isAllowed=y

Kalev, A. (2009). Cracking the glass cages? Restructuring and ascriptive inequality at work. *American Journal of Sociology, 114*(6), 1591–1643. doi.org/10.1086/597175

Kelly, E. L., Ammons, S. K., Chermack, K., & Moen, P. (2010). Gendered challenge, gendered response: Confronting the ideal worker norm in a white-collar organization. *Gender & Society, 24,* 281–303. doi.org/10.1177/0891243210372073

Lampman, C. (2012). Women faculty at risk: U.S. professors report on their experiences with student incivility, bullying, aggression, and sexual attention. *NASPA Journal About Women in Higher Education, 5,* 184–208.

Lorde, A. (1995). Age, race, class, and sex: Women redefining difference. In B. Guy-Sheftal (Ed.), *Words of fire: An anthology of African American feminist thought* (pp. 284–291). New York: The New Press.

Matthew, P. A. (2016). *Written/unwritten: Diversity and the hidden truths of tenure.* Chapel Hill: University of North Carolina Press.

McClinton, M. M. (2012). Leveling the pathway: Balancing work and family. In T. Jones & J. C. Brazzell (2012). *Pathways to higher education administration for African American women.* Sterling, VA: Stylus.

McGinn, K. L., & Tempest, N. (2010). *Heide roizen*. HBS No. 800-228. Boston: Harvard Business School Publishing.

Mena, J. A. (2016). "I Love My Work, but This Is Not My Life": Women of Color in the Academy. *NASPA Journal About Women in Higher Education, 9*(2), 190–207. doi.org/10.1080/19407882.2016.1195274

Moore, D. P. (1997). *Women entrepreneurs: Moving beyond the glass ceiling*. Thousand Oaks, CA: Sage Publications.

Motaung, L. L., Bussin, M. H., & Joseph, R. M. (2017). Maternity and paternity leave and career progression of Black African women in dual-career couples. *SA Journal of Human Resource Management, 15*. doi: 10.4102/sajhrm.v15i0.902

Turnbow, E., & Myricks Williamson, S. L. (2015). In her own words: New professionals' battle ageism and sexism in career success. *Women in Higher Education, 24*(4), 16–17. doi: 10.1002/whe.20192

Namie, G. (2007). U.S. workplace bullying survey. *Workplace bullying institute and zogby International*. Retrieved from http://bullyinginstitute.org/wbi-zogby2.html

Nieto-Gómez, A. (1997). Sexism in the movimiento. In A. M. Garcia (Ed.), *Chicana feminist thought: The basic historical writings* (pp. 97–100). London: Routledge.

Ridegway, C. (1997). Interaction and the conservation of gender inequality: Considering employment. *American Sociological Review, 62*, 218–235. Retrieved from www.jstor.org/stable/2657301

Shorter-Gooden, K. (2004). Multiple resistance strategies: How African American women cope with racism and sexism. *Journal of Black Psychology, 30*(3), 406–425.

Williams, J. L. (2015). *Gendered racism and the moderating influence of racial identity: implications for African American women's well-being* (Unpublished doctoral dissertation). Georgia State University, Atlanta, GA. Retrieved from scholarworks.gsu.edu/psych_diss/136

Chapter 4

# Standing Outside of the Circle

*The Politics of Identity and Leadership in the Life of a Black Lesbian Professor*

JUDY A. ALSTON

Those of us who stand outside the circle of this society's definition of acceptable women; those of us who have been forged in the crucibles of difference—those of us who are poor, who are lesbians, who are Black, who are older—know that survival is not an academic skill. It is learning how to stand alone, unpopular and sometimes reviled, and how to make common cause with those others identified as outside the structures in order to define and seek a world in which we can all flourish. It is learning how to take our differences and make them strengths. For the master's tools will never dismantle the master's house. They may allow us temporarily to beat him at his own game, but they will never enable us to bring about genuine change. And this fact is only threatening to those women who still define the master's house as their only source of support. (Lorde, 1984, 112)

Standing outside of the circle . . . I am one who stands outside of the circle of acceptable women because I hold these identities: Black, lesbian, soft stud (masculine-of-center), ordained Reverend. Yet I can sometimes stand inside of the circle because of other parts of my identity: upper middle class, degreed, full professor, author, sorority girl, former debutante. "These 'axes of identity,' public and private, create the intersections of my selfhood and give me a particular set of truths that are not checked at any door, particularly the door of academia in my leadership position and as a professor in the courses that I teach" (Alston, 2011, 35).

It's the way that I walk, the way that I dress, the way that I talk, and the way that I carry myself. It is my authenticity that while in theory should make me acceptable is what really puts me on the outside looking in, even while I am inside. However, I refuse to not be authentic. Brown (2010) noted that "authenticity is a collection of choices that we have to make every day. It's about the choice to show up and be real. The choice to be honest. The choice to let our true selves be seen" (49). I consciously choose to be authentic both inside and outside of the academy. I consciously choose to show up in the world just as I am. This can, however, be problematic and have adverse effects for me sometimes. In this chapter I will examine the position of "standing outside" via the lenses of the invisibility syndrome, reciprocity, and leadership as a lifestyle.

## Standing Alone, Unpopular, and Sometimes Reviled

"Some achieve greatness through people who lift them higher. Others find it when they have to stand alone."

—R. Hamilton

"When he was reviled, he did not revile in return . . ."

—1 Peter 2:23, ESV

### Invisibility Syndrome

How does one stand in the world when you are an African American, masculine-of-center lesbian? Oftimes you are either overlooked, side-eyed, or simply ignored, as if you are invisible. Franklin and Franklin (2000) noted that the invisibility syndrome is a "conceptual model for understanding the inner evaluative processes and adaptive behavior of African Americans in managing experiences of racism" (33).

Yet, there can be power in invisibility. In Ellison's (1952) *Invisible Man*, the author noted that to be invisible means to be construed by others as a collection of general stereotypes rather than an actual, individual person. Stolyarov (2014) observed of the notion of invisibility in *Invisible Man*: "[W]hen people of the dominant society think of the narrator, states he, 'they see only my surroundings, themselves, or figments of their imagination—indeed, everything except me'" (para. 1).

The power in invisibility can lead to establishing influence and status within the larger context. It is here that an application of Hill Collins's (2000) concept of "outsider within," a place of marginality that "stimulated a distinctive Black women's perspective" (11) serves this analysis well. As she stated:

> For Black women who are agents of knowledge, the marginality that accompanies outsider-within status can be the source of both frustration and creativity. In an attempt to minimize the differences between the cultural context of African-American communities and the expectations of social institutions, some women dichotomize their behavior and become two different people. Over time, the strain of doing this can be enormous. Others reject their cultural context and work against their own best interests by enforcing the dominant group's specialized thought. Still others manage to inhabit both contexts but do so critically, using their outsider-within perspectives as a source of insights and ideas. (Hill Collins, 1990, 238)

It is precisely this "outsider-within" invisible space that breeds and develops the tempered radical persona: the one who is the subversive, behind-the-scenes change agent. This tempered radical is as Debra Myerson stated in a 2005 interview:

> . . . a way of being, a stance toward a dominant culture, organization, or profession. It's being both an insider and an outsider, working to fit into what is currently acceptable and working to change norms of acceptability. It's about rocking the boat, but not so hard that you fall out of it. (Sparks, 2005, 21)

So, while invisible, I stand outside of and within the circle to gain power, knowledge, and ultimately to press toward the goal of change. As a tempered radical, I want to fit in and yet want to retain what makes me different (Meyerson & Scully, 1995). Thus, it is from this particular standpoint that I as the Black, lesbian, soft stud (masculine-of-center), Reverend, upper middle class, degreed, full professor, author, sorority girl, and former debutante share and produce what Hill Collins (1986) called a "distinctive analysis of race, class, and gender" (S15).

*Reciprocity*

From my identity and perspective as an ordained Disciples of Christ (Christian Church) minister, when I consider reciprocity, I immediately recall the biblical verse Matthew 7:12 (NASB), also known as the "Golden Rule": "In everything, therefore, treat people the same way you want them to treat you, for this is the Law and the Prophets." How is this operationalized in the life of the one who stands on the out(side)? According to Falk and Fischbacher (2009), reciprocity is a "behavioral response to perceived kindness and unkindness, where kindness comprises both distributional fairness as well as fairness intentions" (294). How should I do unto others as they have done unto me?

The truth of the matter is that it is difficult to abide by the Golden Rule, particularly in light of the results of the 2016 U.S. presidential election. We are *seemingly* a more intolerant society than ever before. According to Eversley (2016), the surge of hate crimes in this country is worse than post-9/11, and has risen since the November 2016 elections.

What is real-life reciprocity for those of us who "stand alone, unpopular, and sometimes reviled"? How do we make sense of/respond to questions about our ability to teach a course or whether or not the information we are imparting is correct? (Do they do this to our white colleagues?) How do we make sense of/respond to aggressive behavior by white males toward us in our classes, departments, and office spaces? How do we make sense of/respond to white students who simply walk out because they disagree with the historically proven facts? How do we respond to white colleagues who simply "just don't get it" and don't intend to get it? Why is it that it seems to be the responsibility of those of us who are outside the circle to always do the work of educating, mending fences, or acting with kindness to the degradation, dehumanization, and discrimination we often face?

For me, it is about using the tools with which I have been trained during my 30 years in education—the tools that I obtained at predominantly white institutions of higher learning as well as the foundation that I received in my African American home, church, and social communities in which I was raised. These tools and training have led me to a particular meaning-making that guides me to think, interrogate, analyze, critique, and react. It is within this positionality that my ethic of responsibility has been formed, and thus my recognition that since I have been given and earned much, I am required to do more for others like me as well as for those who are completely different. It is the foundation for who I am as a leader: Black, lesbian, soft stud (masculine-of-center), Reverend, upper middle class, degreed, full professor, author, sorority girl, former debutante.

## Using the Master's Tools: Leadership as a Lifestyle

Mathis (n.d.) noted:

> Souls work is the process of bringing the essential self—the soul—out of hiding. It's a fundamental shift away from occupying the constructed self, and toward the art of living from our soul.
>
> Soul work begins with the knowledge that the soul is always trying to move us toward wholeness. When we learn the movements of the soul we can begin to deconstruct the habits of the self-we-became-instead and yield to the profound joy and wisdom of who-we-could-have-been-all-along. This is a profound shift, one that affects every aspect of our lives—our relationships, our work, our beliefs, and our bodies. (para. 6–7)

Leadership for me is soul work. It is a part of my DNA, who I am at my nucleus, who I was created to be. As Giovanni (1988) stated, "the purpose of any leadership is to build more leadership. The purpose of being a spokesperson is to speak until the people gain a voice" (135). Thus, while the master's tools may not be able to dismantle the master's house, I can do my own version of renovations using the tools. These are the tools that have been used to promote racist, sexist, and homophobic patriarchy that have ruled and resided in our culture from the beginning of time. The tools of revolution and oppression themselves are not evil; it is merely how they have been wielded. The challenge is to refashion the use of tools that are already there and utilize them for our own good and advancement. In my life, both professionally and personally, this refashioning and reshaping of the tools in leadership looks like what bell hooks (1994) calls "enactment"—the lived practice of interacting in nondominating ways, making evident to all observers that we are acting in ways that suggest, for example, care, respect, and affirmation of others.

### Identity of Authenticity

> "Let me live my life out loud. Don't dial it back, don't dilute it, don't apologize for it. It speaks for itself."
>
> —M. Obama, 2016

The longer that I am alive, the more that I understand, experience, and embody what my Grandma Janie used to always say to the grandchildren when we questioned things that we didn't understand; she would simply say "just live." In other words, as long as the good Lord blesses me to live, I will have the opportunity to experience all (good and bad) that life has to offer, including those things that made no sense to me when I was younger. In my more recent years, I have also understood that phrase to mean that

I should be who I am, who God created me to be—that is, be authentic. In this authenticity, I bring it all to the table. The living and leading is my soul work that I do in a parrhesiatic voice that is grounded in authenticity. As Taylor (1991) stated:

> There is a certain way of being human that is my way. I am called upon to live my life in this way, and not in imitation of anyone else's. But this gives a new importance to being true to myself. If I am not, I miss the point of my life, I miss what being human is for me. [. . .] Being true to myself means being true to my own originality, and that is something only I can articulate and discover. In articulating it, I am also defining myself. I am realizing a potentiality that is properly my own. (28–29)

This is leadership as a lifestyle, a way of life. Whether inside or outside of the circle, I am called to be my true self. My identity in authentic leadership embodies the experiences and social factors that have shaped my beliefs. It is this connection to my soul work that causes me to behave and lead in ways that are congruent with my values, goals, and beliefs. As Polonius advises his son Laertes in Shakespeare's (1987) *Hamlet*: "This above all, to thine own self be true, and it must follow, as the night the day, Thou canst not be false to any man" (3).

This authentic leadership works while standing outside of and within the circle. In my life, it works because it is a part of my self-care as a leader; I must be who I am and not who or what the world says that I should be or preconditioned me to be. While in the midst of the double consciousness (Du Bois, 1903), the code-switching tactics, and biculturalism, it is the growth over my lifetime and understanding of who I am authentically that has allowed me to see the value of this way of leadership, this way of being. Palmer (2000) noted that the power of authentic leadership resides in the human heart. That is the center for control and life—it is the soul.

*Identity of Responsibility*

This identity of responsibility looks like me being one of a very small number of out lesbian Black full professors in the country. It is my soul work to interact, admonish, praise, and teach those around me who sometimes do not see the full array of this rainbow of human beings. As a leader and a teacher of leaders, I want to "reflect important aspects of leadership that are absent in the more traditional portraits" (Meyerson, 2001, 171).

This identity of responsibility looks like me being the only one many times in spaces that are soaked with the majority. It is being the first and still only Black woman to ever be promoted (in 2010) to full professor in an institution that first opened in 1878. It is being that same Black woman who is also an out lesbian at the same very conservative and far-right-leaning institution of higher education. It is being that same Black, lesbian full professor who served as a department chair for 8 years. It is being the only Black faculty member at the 2016 Winter Commencement in a group of more than 40 faculty in attendance. My responsibility is to those few Black, brown, and other historically marginalized students who attend the institution and those very few who graduated in the ceremony. That responsibility is so much more than me. It is the "lift as we climb" responsibility. It is the "I am because you (we) are"—UBUNTU. For me, no matter if I am outside of the circle or not, this responsibility of my soul requires that as one who is placed in a position of power, I have the responsibility to do the work and bring others along.

## Conclusion

So, here I am back to the beginning—I am one who stands outside of the circle of acceptable women because I hold these identities: Black, lesbian, soft stud (masculine-of-center), Reverend. Yet I am also inside the circle because I am upper middle class, degreed, full professor, author, sorority girl, former debutante. I am only because so many others came before me, and I am dedicated to making sure that those who follow will be educated, cared for, treated fairly, and loved as I continue to pass it on (Alston, 2015).

In a holistic view of all that I am, I connect to that which I believe to be my purpose in life, my soul work of leadership. It is my standing both outside of and within the circle that I am more powerful, more effective, and am guided to leave a legacy for those to come.

## References

Alston, J. A. (2011). An ethic of responsibility: A Black lesbian scholar ponders the intersections of racism and heterosexism in educational leadership. In R. Johnson & S. Jackson (Eds.) *The Black professoriate: Negotiating a habitable space* (pp. 32–45). New York: Peter Lang.

Alston, J. A. (2015). Leadership as soul work: Living, leading, and loving the work. In C. Boske & A. Osanloo (Eds.) *Living the work: Promoting social justice and equity in schools around the world* (pp. 395–404). Bingley, UK: Emerald Books.

Brown, B. (2010). *The gifts of imperfection: Let go of who you're supposed to be and embrace who you are.* Center City, MO: Hazeldon.

Du Bois, W. E. B. (1903). *The souls of Black folk.* New York: A. C. McClurg & Co.

Ellison, R. (1952). *Invisible man.* New York: Random House.

Eversley, M. (2016, November 14). Post-election spate of hate crimes worse than post-9/11 experts say. *USA Today.* Retrieved from www.usatoday.com

Falk, A., & Fischbacher, U. (2006). A theory of reciprocity. *Games and Economic Behavior, 54,* 293–315.

Franklin, A. J., & Boyd-Franklin, N. (2000). Invisibility syndrome: A clinical model of the effects of racism on African-American males. *American Journal of Orthopsychiatry, 70*(1), 33–41.

Giovanni, N. (1988). *Sacred cows . . . and other edibles.* New York: Quill/William Morrow.

Hamilton, R. (n.d.). Quotable quote. Retrieved from http://www.goodreads.com/quotes/1447261-some-achieve-greatness-through-people-who-lift-them-higher-others

Hill Collins, P. (1986). Learning from the outsider within: The sociological significance of Black feminist thought. *Social Problems, 33*(6), S14–S32.

Hill Collins, P. (1990). *Black feminist thought: Knowledge, consciousness, and the politics of empowerment.* Boston: Unwin Hyman.

Hill Collins, P. (2000). *Black feminist thought: Knowledge, consciousness, and the politics of empowerment.* (2nd Ed.). New York: Routledge.

hooks, b. (1994). *Teaching to transgress: Education as the practice of freedom.* New York: Routledge.

Lorde, A. (Ed.) (1984). *Sister outsider: Essays and speeches.* Berkeley, CA: Crossing Press.

Mathis, P. (n.d.) What is soul work? Retrieved from http://www.phyllismathis.com/what-is-soul-work

Meyerson, D. (2001). *Tempered radicals: How people use difference to inspire change at work.* Boston: Harvard Business School Press.

Meyerson, D. E., & Scully, M. A. (1995). Tempered radicalism and the politics of ambivalence and change. *Organization Science, 6,* 585–600.

Obama, M. (2016, December 19). *First Lady Michelle Obama says farewell to the White House—An Oprah Winfrey special interview.* New York: CBS.

Palmer, P. J. (2000). *Let your life speak: Listening for the voice of vocation.* San Francisco: Jossey Bass.

Shakespeare, W. (1987). *The tragedy of Hamlet, Prince of Denmark.* Edited by E. Hubler. New York: Penguin Books.

Sparks, D. (2005). Tempered radicals speak courageously to inspire change (interview with Debra Meyerson). *National Staff Development Council, 26*(1), 20–23.

Stolyarov II, G. (2014, July 28). The meaning of invisibility in Ralph Ellison's *Invisible Man* (2005). Retrieved from http://rationalargumentator.com/InvisibleMan.html

Taylor, C. (1991). *The ethics of authenticity.* Cambridge, MA: Harvard University Press.

Chapter 5

# Black Feminist Thought

## *A Response to White Fragility*

MICHELE D. SMITH AND MAIA NIGUEL MOORE

Though the number of diverse faculty is growing (Walesby, 2013), whether or not university structures, policies, and procedures have grown in parallel to support them is questionable. Faculty of color remain vulnerable to continued tokenization (Ortega-Liston & Soto, 2014) and salary disparities in comparison to white faculty. There have been significant accomplishments in the education of Blacks since the landmark *Brown v. Board of Education* decision more than 60 years ago that ended legal segregation of schools. However, disturbing trends point to the continuing underrepresentation, marginalization, and in some cases reversal of accomplishments in the education of racial and ethnic minorities in the United States.

This is especially true for Black women in higher education (Abdul-Raheem, 2016; Dade, Tartakov, Hargrave, & Leigh, 2016; Shillingford & Butler, 2012). Many Black female faculty in academe report experiencing feelings related to alienation, confusion, and marginalization due to being both Black and woman (Abdul-Raheem, 2016; Shillingford, 2012). Dade et al. (2016) describe being a Black woman in the academy as a "burden" that intersects both race and gender within a system that has been built to privilege white men. As a result, underrepresented faculty members may feel only symbolically hired, stigmatized, or out of place in the academy (Thompson & Dey, 1998). Sometimes a single person of color represents "diversity." The result is that in many predominantly and historically white institutions (PWIs), Black faculty are still treated in stereotypic and racist ways (Frazier, 2011).

Consequently, this chapter will explore the experiences of Black women working in higher education through expanding Joe Feagin's (2013) "white racial frame" to include Robin Di Angelo's (2011) concept of white fragility. Specifically, the purpose of this chapter is to provide a thorough discussion of current literature that examines many of the unique challenges that Black women in academia face, including addressing white fragility, challenging whiteness as a construct, providing corrective feedback on racist behavior, white privilege, and racial arrogance. We will then conclude the chapter by providing examples of how Black feminist thought can be used to empower Black women working in the academy to help address these challenges through the acquisition of knowledge, finding sisterhood, and developing and maintaining a strong definition of self.

## Current Landscape

Faculty of color often believe tenure is required in order to be viewed as an equal by their peers (Abdul-Raheem, 2016). The desire to earn tenure to feel valued is problematic when investigating many of the environments Black female faculty must navigate to earn tenure. Black women in academe often face additional barriers and challenges in higher education compared to their colleagues (Agyepong, 2011; Shillingford & Butler, 2012). Fewer faculty of color are in associate professor ranks; they are often paid less and are unable to persist in the professoriate for lack of success in tenure and journal review processes (Smith, Turner, Osei-Kofi, & Richards, 2004). In 2006, 31% of female faculty earned tenure compared to 69% of men, and 24% of full professors were women compared to 76% of men (The American Association of University Professors, 2006). In a study examining promotion and race in higher education, it was found that 10 of 43 minority faculty who applied for tenure were denied, while 100% of white faculty were approved (Abdul-Raheem, 2016).

Factors that may impact earning tenure include experiences with isolation; course overload; excessive committee work; racial, gender, and language biases; and minimal guidance or mentoring relating to promotion, tenure, and reappointment (Harvey, 1994; Jayakuma, Howard, Allen, & Han, 2009; Johnson & Pichon, 2007; Laden & Hagedorn, 2000). More often than documented, Black women faculty function under routine racially hostile conditions that exist both in society and in the "ivory towers" of academia. In fact, Lynn and Adams (2002) contend that the educational establishment is a key arena "where the impact of racism is felt most" (87).

## The White Racial Frame

Joe Feagin (2013) coined the white racial frame (WRF) to examine systemic racism as a structure that has been maintained and propagated by whites and accepted by people of color. Feagin argues that WRF is broadly encompassing and deeply held within U.S. cultural norms, shaping behaviors through stereotypes, images, and racialized understandings that facilitate in maintaining systems of privilege and oppression (Feagin, 2013). Whiteness is a construct that preserves systems of racism by making whiteness itself a nonracialized norm, which in juxtaposition places persons of color as racialized others who live outside of the norm (Di Angelo, 2011).

Consequently, whiteness also functions as a social location that places whites in closer proximity to structural advantages (Di Angelo, 2011). White privilege is a corollary to the concept of whiteness. McIntosh (1988) argues that white privilege is like "an invisible package of unearned assets" that white people can use to their advantage—and are conditioned to not acknowledge (109). Jayakumar et al. (2009) write that white privilege within higher education institutions is the translation of whiteness as the normative standard into "systematic advantages afforded to the dominant racial group" (555). Though the use of privilege by whites may be unintentionally oppressive, it nevertheless perpetuates inequitable power dynamics and social conditions (McIntosh, 1988). Thus, a white person will attribute markers of difference to a person who is unlike her (e.g., skin color, hair texture) rather than conceiving that she is different. The white person sets herself as the norm, which creates an un-like, unequal other (Leonardo, 2013).

## White Fragility

Robin Di Angelo (2011) defines white fragility as "a state in which even a minimum amount of racial stress becomes intolerable for Whites, triggering a range of defensive moves" (55). Examples of defensive moves include fear, anger, guilt, avoidance, and silence. These behaviors ultimately restore in what Di Angelo refers to as "white racial equilibrium" (2). These responses help to restore feelings of comfort and privilege.

> Whiteness accrues privilege and status; gets itself surrounded by protective pillows of resources and/or benefits of the doubt this is how Whiteness repels gossip and voyeurism and instead demands dignity. Whites are rarely without these protective pillows, and

when they are, it is usually temporary and by choice. This insulated environment of racial privilege builds white expectations for racial comfort while at the same time lowering the ability to tolerate racial stress. (Di Angelo, 2011, 55)

When this insulated environment is interrupted with conversations about race, responses are triggered as a result of a lack of "racial stamina" (Di Angelo, 2011, 56). As we further examine the ways in which some Black female faculty are impacted by whiteness and white fragility in the academy, we will refer to the following instances in which levels of racial stress can increase among white faculty (Di Angelo, 2011):

- *Challenging whiteness and objectivity*: Others challenge white racial norms by sharing their racial views.

- *Corrective feedback on racist behavior*: Receiving feedback that behavior was influenced by racist ideology or had a racist impact on a person of color.

- *Challenging individualism and addressing white privilege*: Receiving feedback that challenges individualism and addresses how whites benefit from the oppression of people of color.

- *Challenges with authority*: The responses of whites to a person of color in an authoritative position.

## Challenging Whiteness and Objectivity: Invisibility and Stereotypes

Many Black women in the academy feel they represent an Affirmative Action quota because their institution views diversity as a mandate and not as an asset. The lack of value some institutions place on diversity can cause Black female faculty to be viewed as a racialized other who is invisible and out of place (Agyepong, 2011; Dade et al., 2016). Some Black women experience what Witherspoon-Arnold, Crawford, and Muhammad (2016) refer to as "entrapment." Entrapment is characterized by Black female faculty being faced with various negative and limiting stereotypes about their abilities, leadership, and the expectation that they will behave "nicely" when faced with discrimination or else be perceived as "angry" (23). Howard-Baptiste and Harris (2014) argue, "[a]s racial and gender hierarchies are historically embedded and culturally rooted in stereotypical notions and representations of Black women, such is often transferred to Black female faculty causing a misunderstanding about them" (12). For example, a Black female faculty shared,

> No matter how many successes we experience as Black women, it is hard to escape the "imposter syndrome." In our country . . . all Black folks are doomed to be intellectually inferior to all white folks. Thus, the last image that many Americans would have of an African American woman is that of an intellectual, an academic, a college president, a person of the academy. (Cole, 1997)

Due to some of the images in popular culture that portray Black women as angry, many Black female faculty are fearful to be expressive about their encounters with discrimination to avoid offending their white colleagues and fulfilling debilitating stereotypes.

Sharing direct experiences with white faculty about discrimination can also increase racial stress among whites. Labeling a Black female faculty as angry is an example of what Di Angelo (2011) would call a defensive move. That is, to avoid feeling racial stress and emotions that might accompany a conversation about discrimination, it becomes preferable to blame and label a Black female colleague as angry (Di Angelo, 2011; Johnson, 2006). This approach to addressing discrimination that many Black women in higher education encounter causes some white faculty to view challenges that Black women experience as not indicative of a larger systemic issue within the institution and society at large, but rather a characteristic of Black women, their ability, and their work ethic (Agyepong, 2011). To that end, Black women in the academy also often feel pressure to outperform their white male and female colleagues in order to dispel stereotyped images of Black women (Agyepong, 2011; Howard-Baptiste & Harris, 2014).

Historically, Black female faculty have reported being excluded from professional development opportunities that many white faculty take for granted, such as attending conferences, being asked to participate in research, and even receiving timely evaluations on their performance; this leaves many Black women in the academy feeling hopeless, marginalized, and alienated (Shillingford & Butler, 2012). Segregation is a primary factor that inculcates white fragility and creates an environment in higher education conducive for white faculty to dismiss their Black female colleagues (Di Angelo, 2011). The presence of modern segregation between whites and Blacks manifests both in how whites experience the world and in what they learn about race and diversity (Di Angelo, 2011).

Because we live in a world that is dominated by whiteness, very little accurate information is shared within white communities about issues related to racial difference (Di Angelo, 2011). In fact, many whites are taught to not feel loss over the lack of presence of Blacks in their lives (Di Angelo, 2011). More disheartening, the absence of Blacks often creates a framework for the criteria of what is perceived to be a "good neighborhood" (Di Angelo, 2011). Good schools and good neighborhoods then become "coded" language for "white" (Di Angelo, 2011; Johnson & Shapiro, 2003). Contemporary examples of segregation are integral factors to consider when conceptualizing white fragility and the invisibility of Black women in academe, as many colleges and universities are microcosms of the values and norms that govern our society, and in many cases, uphold whiteness (Bertrand-Jones, Wilder, Lampkin, 2013; Fisher & Houseworth, 2012).

## Corrective Feedback on Racist Behavior and Universalism: Is it Worth it?

For most Black women in the academy, providing white faculty with corrective feedback about racist behavior is far from an option (Agyepong, 2011; Shallcross, & Butler, 2012). Many Black female faculty members fear possible consequences associated with confronting racism and racist behaviors experienced in the academy (Agyepong, 2011; Shallcross & Butler 2012). Others feel that efforts used toward confrontation are futile and often fall onto deaf ears.

An example is illustrated by a Black full professor who shared an experience she had with a group of students:

> I learned later that prejudgments about my abilities had been conveyed to them by several senior scholars, particularly those who had opposed my hiring. My reaction was to first recognize the racism that was virtually explicit in their behavior. They would not have treated a white professor in this manner. They had not been accustomed to having a Black professor and their negative reaction was bolstered by the attitudes of some senior professors. I recognized this as a "no-win" situation and decided it useless to say anything and not to teach the introductory anthropology course again. (Smedly & Hutchinson, 2012, 58)

An assistant professor shared similar feelings:

> After each session, I was sickened and disheartened by the reality and nature of racism and prejudice in the university. I was

comforted by the resilience of my colleagues but troubled by the lack of ownership and accountability on the part of the university administration. Yet I was left feeling as though there was nothing I could do. Who would listen to me? And if I were heard what price would I have to pay? (Dade et al., 2015, 142)

Because many whites have become accustomed to a certain level of racial comfort, receiving feedback about racist behaviors can lead to an increase in racial stress (Di Angelo, 2011). "When racial discomfort arises, whites typically blame the person or event that triggered the discomfort. This blame results in a socially-sanctioned array of counter-moves against the perceived source of the discomfort" (Di Angelo, 2011, 61).

White fragility is rooted in the philosophies found throughout various colleges and universities and shared and perpetuated among its faculty. The rise of post-racial liberalism and the concept of universalism were formally introduced in the late 1970s (Wise, 2010). Universalism and what is now referred to as colorblindness essentially argues that there is no race outside of the human race (Di Angelo, 2011; Wise, 2010). Because whites view their perceptions as objective, some whites view their experiences and perspectives as universal norms for all humans (Di Angelo, 2011; Johnson, 2006). The idea of universalism becomes problematic when white faculty apply this philosophy to race because it does not take into consideration the unique experiences of Black women and assumes that Black female faculty share the same experiences as their white counterparts.

## Challenging Individualism and White Privilege: The Blame Game

While universalism is a significant factor that inoculates white fragility within the halls of the academy, individualism is a contrasting yet equally significant factor that is at the heart of white fragility. Whites are taught to view themselves as individuals opposed to being a part of a larger population (Di Angelo, 2011; Johnson, 2006). Because whites are not a member of a racialized group, they are better able to separate themselves from other whites compared to people of color (Di Angelo, 2011; Johnson, 2006), thus making it easier for whites to detach themselves from the behaviors of members from their racial group and "demand to be given the benefit of the doubt" (Di Angelo, 2011, 65).

Individualistic thinking in academe can be problematic when confronted with issues related to race. White faculty members might respond defensively as a result of not wanting to be associated with an event or group of people who are being criticized (Di Angelo, 2011, 2012). Despite the good intentions of many white faculty who would wish otherwise, white faculty, be it directly or indirectly, automatically receive certain benefits that are a result of the oppression of Black women in the academy (Howard-Baptiste & Harris, 2014). For example, Black female faculty are often viewed as authorities on Black culture, thereby placing the brunt of the responsibility of mentoring students of color on them. Black women in the academy also have had to meet increased expectations advising students overall and are often asked to take on increased service responsibilities such as sitting on committees and community involvement compared to their white counterparts. Yet, most Black women in academe are not presented with as many opportunities to collaborate with their peers on research compared with their non-Black colleagues (Howard-Baptiste & Harris, 2014).

Di Angelo (2011) asserts that the racial stamina of some whites is not strong enough to carry the burden of accepting that they participate in and benefit from white privileges that protect them from various challenges while presenting unique barriers for people of color. "Many whites believe their financial and professional successes are the result of their own efforts while ignoring the fact of white privilege" (Di Angelo, 2011, 66). Blaming Black women is an easier way for some white faculty to conceptualize the challenges Black women in higher education face because it implies that there are not issues related to white privilege that need to be addressed (Johnson, 2006). This would also suggest they are not benefitting from the inequities that their Black female colleagues are experiencing, relieving them of possible feelings of guilt and shame (Di Angelo, 2011).

## Challenges with Authority: Racial Arrogance, White Faculty, and the Students Too?

The self-concept of many whites has been shaped by constant positive images of whiteness both in the media and in popular culture (Di Angelo, 2011). Conversely, negative images are regularly associated with racial others, which often results in a more entitled and racially arrogant self-concept (Di Angelo, 2011). Some whites remain misinformed about historical racism and discrimination Blacks have experienced, confusing their lack of knowledge with not agreeing (Di Angelo, 2011).

Research has documented challenges that Black women in the academy have encountered with whites who have taken exception to their position of authority as faculty members (Agyepong, 2011; Dade et al., 2015; Shallcrosss & Butler 2012). Not only have Black women in higher education encountered this type of racial arrogance from white faculty, but many Black women have also experienced similar encounters with white students (Pittman, 2010; Shallcross and Butler, 2012). We can refer to the earlier example in the chapter of the Black full professor who was challenged by her class about her approach to teaching and later discovered that some of her white colleagues played a role in instigating the confrontation.

Similarly, a study surveying 46 Black female professors found that the women experienced difficulties almost exclusively with their white male students (Pittman, 2010). Participants from the same study reported their white male students displayed behaviors that they felt were intimidating or threatening (Pittman, 2010). One of the participants from the study said,

> White males will open my door to my office without knocking. . . . Why, again only white males, choose to just open my door. No one else just opens up my door. They're snide, they'll sit with their arms crossed and they doodle and they sit right up in the front[,] so that is definite passive aggressive behavior. The tone sometimes in the e-mails they send . . . it's the kind of things you don't even know how to express to other people. But you're like, if I was a white male you wouldn't dare write to me in that tone. (188)

The double minority status of being a Black woman places Black female faculty in a vulnerable position not only among white faculty but among white students as well.

## A Move Toward Black Feminist Thought/Theory

Black women intellectuals have long explored the private, hidden space of Black women's consciousness, the "inside" ideas that allow Black women to cope with and, in most cases, transcend the confines of race, class, and gender oppression. How have Black women as a group found the strength to oppose our objectification as "de mule uh de world?" How do we account for the voices of resistance of Audre Lorde, Ella Surrey, Maria Stewart, Fannie Barrier Williams, and Marita Bonner? What foundation sustained Sojourner Truth so that she could ask, "aint I a woman?" The voices of these Black women are not those of victims but of survivors. Their ideas and actions suggest that not only does a self-defined, articulated Black woman's standpoint exist, but its presence has been essential to Black women's survival (Hill Collins, 2000). Black women's lives are a series of negotiations that aim to reconcile the contradictions separating our own internally defined images of self as Black women with our objectification as the other. The struggle of living two lives, one for "them and one for ourselves" (Gwaltney, 1980, 240), creates a peculiar tension. Audre Lorde (1984) observes that "within this country where racial difference creates a constant, if unspoken, distortion of vision, Black women have on the one hand always been highly visible, and so, on the other hand, have been rendered invisible through the depersonalization of racism" (42). Lorde also points out that the "visibility which makes us more vulnerable" that accompanies being Black "is that which is also the source of our greatest strength" (42). This category of "Black women" makes all Black women especially visible and open to the objectification afforded Black women as a category. This group treatment renders each Black woman invisible as a fully human individual (Lorde, 1984).

Racist stereotypes of the strong, superhuman Black woman are operative myths in the minds of many white women, allowing them to ignore the extent to which Black women are likely to be victimized in this society, and the role white women may play in the maintenance and perpetuation of that victimization. Privileged feminists have largely been unable to speak to, with, and for diverse groups of women because they either do not understand fully the interrelatedness of sex, race, and class oppression or refuse to take this interrelatedness seriously (hooks, 2000). One can say that it is significantly easier for women who do not have to contend with or experience race or class oppression to focus exclusively on gender. In some respects, socialist feminists who focus on class and gender tend to sometimes dismiss race, or they make a point of acknowledging that race is important and then proceed to offer an analysis in which race is not considered (hooks, 2000).

Black feminist thought provides a keen exploration of oppression by extending beyond the limitations of traditional feminist theory to confront the interconnectedness of race, gender, and class and how these interlocking systems shape a specific and unique experience for Black women. For many, this experience is fraught with oppression, discrimination, and bias. Black feminist thought thereby conceptualizes Black women through their evolving power as agents of knowledge, a distinctive feature of Black feminist thought (Collins, 1990). The theory insists on the intentional and deliberate change of racial and cultural consciousness among individuals and emphasizes the importance for "social transformation of political and economic institutions that constitute essential ingredients for social change" (Collins, 1990, 34). Consequently, the theory is driven by its mandate that Black women become and remain knowledgeable about the world in which they live in, find sisterhood with other Black women, and create and maintain a healthy image and definition of one's self that acknowledges her power.

*Knowledge is Power*

For many in higher education, being knowledgeable about one's position, field, study in academia, and even the overall political structure of the institution is critical. This is especially true for Black women in the academy. Because Black women are often discriminated against, held to higher standards, and isolated, knowledge takes on a much more significant and detrimental role to the survival and ultimate success and happiness of Black women. Knowledge about one's social location to power and privilege also becomes critical, as many colleges and universities function as a microcosm of the larger outside world.

Patricia Hill Collins argues that "knowledge is a vitally important part of the social relations of domination and resistance" (1990, 23). Further, the objectification of Black women and the "recasting of our experiences to serve the interests of elite white men, much of the Eurocentric masculinist worldview, fosters Black women's subordination." (1990, 23) However, by centering the experience of Black women as a focal part of analysis, inquisition, and discussion, historical and current systems of oppression within and outside of higher education are conceptualized by more culturally and racially appropriate concepts, paradigms, and epistemologies through the lens of feminist and Afrocentric critiques. Becoming and remaining informed about ourselves, our histories, and the world around us is a powerful and liberating tool that can be used to better understand and address some of the challenges many Black women in academia face with white privilege, providing corrective feedback about racism, and challenges with authority.

*Finding Sisterhood*

Many Black women find themselves as either one of the very few Black women or the only Black woman working within their office, program, department, or in some cases, the entire university or college. For many, the isolation they experience might feel tangible, overwhelming, and impossible to overcome. However, there can be immense value in finding sisterhood. The issue of Black women being the ones who really listen to one another is an important one, particularly given the importance of voice in Black women's lives (hooks, 2000). Audre Lorde describes the importance of voice in self-affirmation: "Of course I am afraid, because the transformation of silence into language and action is an act of self-revelation, and that always seems fraught with danger" (1984, 42).

For Black women, the listener most able to move beyond invisibility created by objectification as the Other in order to see and hear the fully human Black woman, is another Black woman. This process of trusting one another can seem dangerous because only Black women know what it means to be a Black woman. But if we will not listen to one another, then who will? (Hill Collins, 2000). Consequently, Black women working in higher education might find comfort, support, and solace by making it a priority to actively build relationships with other Black women working in higher education with whom they can draw strength. This might include networking and building relationships with other Black women at their institution, through professional email list-serve communities, at professional development seminars, or during conferences. Regardless of how one chooses to get connected, the key is to find sisterhood.

*Finding Power in Self*

Challenges that many Black women in the academy face, such as addressing white privilege, isolation, heightened expectations, questioned credibility, and addressing racist behaviors, can take a significant and a detrimental toll on self-image. If we are constantly treated less than, not good enough, and invisible to respect, accolades, and support, and yet hypervisible to criticism and skepticism, how do Black women in higher education keep themselves intact and remain sane? How do we find some semblance of peace and happiness while working within the confines of the ivory towers?

Given the physical limitations on Black women's mobility, the conceptualization of self that is part of Black women's self-definition is distinctive. Self is not defined as the increased autonomy gained by separating oneself from others. Instead, self is found in the context of family and community (Hill Collins, 2000). Poet Nikki Giovanni cautions that we should "[k]now who's playing the music before you dance" (1971, 126). Her advice is especially germane for Black women. Giovanni suggests that Black women are the only group that derives their identity from themselves. She states: "I think it's been rather unconscious but we measure ourselves by ourselves, and I think that's a practice we can ill afford to lose" (144). Black women's survival is at stake, and creating self-definitions, reflection, and independent Afrocentric feminist consciousness is an essential part of that survival.

Hill Collins states: "While self-definition speaks to the power dynamics involved in rejecting externally defined, controlling images of Back womanhood, the theme of Black women's self-definition addresses the actual content of these self-definitions" (2000, 107). Through relationships with one another, Black women create self-valuations that challenge externally defined notions of Black womanhood. Many of the controlling images applied to Black women are actually distorted renderings of those aspects of our behavior that threaten existing power arrangements (Gilkes, 1983). Patricia Hill Collins has written that the significance of "self-valuation is illustrated through the emphasis that Black feminist thinkers place on respect. In a society in which no one is obligated to respect Black women, we have long admonished one another to have self-respect and to demand the respect of others" (1991, 107). As Black women listen to and observe direct and indirect negative messages about Black women and their ability that their colleagues, supervisors, students, and society might perpetuate, it is critical that we take care not to internalize these messages and instead develop and maintain healthy and positive images of self—definitions of self that lead to finding and living in our power.

Persistence is a fundamental requirement during the journey of Black women from silence to language to action. Black women's persistence is fostered by the strong belief that to be Black and female is valuable and worthy of respect (Hill Collins, 2000). Actions to bring about change, whether the struggle for an Afrocentric feminist consciousness or the persistence needed for institutional transformation, empower Black women. Because our actions change the world from one in which we merely exist to one over which we have some control, they enable us to see everyday life as a process and thus amenable to change. By persisting in the journey toward self-definition, we are changed, and this change empowers us. Perhaps this is why so many Black women have managed to persist and "make a way out of no way" (Hill Collins, 2000, 113). Robin Di Angelo (2011) might argue that we see this persistence among Black women faculty who work in the confines of colleges and universities in which individualism is a luxury assigned to white faculty and universalism is a convoluted and hypocritical concept that yields to the benefit of whites but works to the detriment and sometimes to the oppression of Black women. Yet, she, her, I, we must be careful and cautious to not damage or offend the fragility of the privileged white nonracialized conscious. This is the persistence of Black women that has been so eloquently sung in songs by Black women, such as Aretha Franklin's "A Change is Gonna' Come" (1967), India Arie's "I am not my Hair" (2005), Destiny's Child's "Survivor" (2009), and Beyoncé's "Run the World (Girls)" (2011). Perhaps these women knew, and know, the power of self-definition.

## References

Abdul-Raheem, J. (2016). Faculty diversity and tenure in higher education. *Journal of Cultural Diversity*, *23*(2), 53–57.
Agyepong, R. (2011). Spirituality and the empowerment of Black women in the academy. *Canadian Women Studies*, *29*(1), 176–182.

American Association of University Professors. (2006). AAUP faculty gender equity indicators 2006. Retrieved from www.aaup.org/NR/rdonlyres/63396944-44BE-4ABA-9815-5792D93856F1/0/AAUPGenderEquityIndicators2006.pdf

Bertrand-Jones, T., Wilder, J., & Osbourne-Lampkin, L. (2013). Employing Black feminist approach to doctoral advising: Preparing Black women for the professorate. *The Journal of Negro Education, 82*(3), 326–338.

Cole, J. B. (1997). *Ten years at Spelman: Reflections on a special journey.* Keynote address presented at Otelia Cromwell Day Symposium at Smith College, Northampton, MA.

Dade, K., Tartakov, C., Hargrave, C., & Leigh, P. (2015). Assessing the impact of racism on Black faculty in White Academe: A collective case study of African American female faculty. *The Western Journal of Black Studies, 39*(2), 134–147.

Di Angelo, R. (2011). White fragility. *The Journal of Critical Pedagogy, 3*(3), 54–70.

Di Angelo, R. (2012). *What does it mean to be white: Developing white racial literacy.* New York: Peter Lang Publishing.

Feagin, J. R. (2013). *The white racial frame: Centuries of racial framing and counter-framing.* New York: Routledge.

Fisher, J. D., & Houseworth, C. A. (2012). The reverse wage gap among educated white and Black women. *Journal of Economic Inequality, 10*(4), 449–470.

Frazier, K. N. (2011). Academic bullying: A barrier to tenure and promotion for African American faculty. *Florida Journal of Educational Administration & Policy, 5*(1), 1–13.

Gilkes, C. T. (1983). From slavery to social welfare: Racism and the control of Black women. In A. Swerdlow, H. Lessinger, & J. Lessinger (Eds.), *Class, race, and sex: The dynamics of control* (pp. 288–300). Boston: G. K. Hall.

Giovanni, N. (1971). *Gemini.* New York: Penguin.

Gwaltney, J. L. (1980). *Drylongso: A self portrait of Black America.* Toronto: Random House.

Harvey, W. B., & Valadez, J. (Eds.) (1994). Creating and maintaining a diverse faculty. *New Directions for Community Colleges, 22*(3). Retrieved from www.eric.ed.gov/ERICDocs/data/ericdocs2sql/content_storage_01/0000019b/80/13/72/82.pdf

Hill Collins, P. (1991). *Black feminist thought: Knowledge consciousness, and the politics of empowerment.* New York: Routledge.

Hines, M. T. (2016). The embeddedness of white fragility within white pre-service principals' reflections on white privilege. *Critical Questions in Education, 7*(2), 130–145.

hooks, b. (2000). *Feminist theory: From margin to center.* London: Pluto Press.

Howard-Baptiste, S. H., & Harris, J. C. (2014). Teaching then and now: Black female scholars and the mission to move beyond the borders. *The Negro Educational Review, 65*(1), 5–22.

Jayakumar, U. M., Howard, T. C., Allen, W. R., & Han, J. C. (2009). Racial privilege in the professoriate: An exploration of campus climate, retention, and satisfaction. *The Journal of Higher Education, 80*(5), 538–563.

Johnson, A. G. (2006). *Privilege, power, and difference.* New York: McGraw-Hill.

Johnson, B. J., & Pichon, H. (2007). The status of African American faculty in the academy: Where do we go from here? In J.F.L. Jackson (Ed.) *Strengthening the*

*African American educational pipeline: Informing research, policy, and practice* (pp. 97–114). Albany: State University of New York Press.

Johnson, H. B., & Shapiro, T. M. (2003). Good neighborhoods, good schools: Race and the "good choices" of white families. In A. W. Doane & E. Bonilla-Silva (Eds). *White out: The continuing significance of racism* (pp. 173–187). New York: Routledge.

Laden, B., & Hagedorn, L. (2000*).* Job satisfaction among faculty of color in academe: Individual survivors or institutional transformers. *New Directions for Institutional Research, 105,* 57–66.

Leonardo, Z. (2013). *Race frameworks: A multidimensional theory of racism and education.* New York: Teachers College Press.

Lorde, A. (1984). *Sister outsider.* New York: Ten Speed Press.

Lynn, M., & Adams, M. (2002). Introductory overview to the special issue Critical Race Theory and education: Recent developments in the field. *Equity and Excellence in Education, 35*(2), 87–92.

McIntosh, P. (1988). *White privilege and male privilege: A personal account of coming to see correspondences through work in women's studies.* Wellesley, MA: Wellesley College, Center for Research on Women, *189.*

Pittman, C. T. (2010). Race and gender oppression in the classroom: The experiences of women faculty of color with white male students. *American Sociological Association, 38*(3), 183–196.

Ortega-Liston, R., & Soto, I. R. (2014). Challenges, choices, and decisions of women in higher education: A discourse on the future of Hispanic, Black, and Asian members of the professoriate. *Journal of Hispanic Higher Education, 13*(4), 285–302.

Shillingford, M.A., Trice-Black, S., & Butler, K. (2012). Wellness of minority female counselor educators. *Counselor Education and Supervision, 52,* 255–269.

Smeldy, A., & Hutchinson, J. F. (2012). *Racism in the academy: The new millennium.* Retrieved from s3.amazonaws.com/rdcms-aaa/files/production/public/File Downloads/pdfs/cmtes/commissions/upload/CRR_reportF ULL.pdf

Smith, D. G., Turner, C.S.V., Osei-Kofi, N., & Richards, S. (2004). Interrupting the usual: Successful strategies for hiring faculty of color. *The Journal of Higher Education, 75*(2), 133–160.

Thompson, C. J., & Dey, E. L. (1998). Pushed to the margins: Sources of stress for African American college and university faculty. *The Journal of Higher Education, 69*(3), 324–345.

Walesby, A. (2013). *Future hiring trends in higher education: What institutions can do to thrive and succeed in challenging times?* Retrieved from https://www.higheredjobs.com/articles/articleDisplay.cfm?ID=466

Wise, T. (2010). *Color blind: The rise of post-racial politics and the retreat from racial equity.* San Francisco: City Light Books.

Witherspoon-Arnold, N., Crawford, E. R., Muhammad, K. (2016). Psychological heuristics and faculty of Color: Racial battle fatigue and tenure/promotion. *The Journal of Higher Education, 87*(6), 890–920.

Chapter 6

# The Reproduction of the Anti-Black Misogynist Apparatus in U.S. and Latin American Pop Culture

Natasha Howard

> The new places, the new experiences I had expected to discover through travel turned out to be the same old places, the same old experiences with a common message of struggle.
>
> —Angela Davis: *An Autobiography*

The above quote from Angela Davis highlights the interrelationship between global systems of oppression that work against Black women. This chapter challenges the politics of deconstruction that seek to draw boundaries between Black women globally and instead argues for a politics of interrelatedness to understand how race, class, gender, and sexuality cooperate transnationally to marginalize Black women in U.S. and Latin American contexts. Though this conversation can be situated quite broadly, I will focus on one particular pillar of oppression that I believe define Black women's transnational oppression: dehumanization through relentless public humiliation. I argue that this pillar is persistent in both U.S. and Latin American contexts, making it a transnational anti-Black misogynistic apparatus that has historically persevered.[1] Rather than defining social phenomena as unique to particular contexts, this pillar of oppression unveils the transnational, yet commonplace, ways Black women are targeted for misogynist violence. Because anti-Black misogyny is a global phenomenon, it is important to consider how the development of a transnational Black feminist educational project can challenge its perseverance.

## Romanticizing Deconstruction

Some time ago it became quite fashionable in academia to deconstruct everything, lest we become guilty of essentialism. The notion that deconstruction was a more powerful point of departure led to the diminishing of larger group identity politics. We were to believe that by focusing on smaller group specificities and even individual experiences we would be drawn to better solutions to disrupt oppressive power structures. Of course, some of this is true. For example, much research has been produced that examines how Black women experience patriarchy uniquely from White women (Davis, 1983; Hill Collins, 2008; hooks, 1981). Race, as well as class, sexual identity, and even nationality complicate how women experience patriarchy (Guillard-Limonta, 2016). We discovered that feminism and its attempt to paint a broad stroke on female lives could be oppressive, especially when White women did not attend to their racialized social privileges and the ways they have often engaged in both passive and even overt racial oppression of Black women (Lorde, 1984). At some point, however, we decided that the politics of deconstruction should also be useful in the dismantling of Blackness as an all-consuming category. The attempts to deconstruct Blackness gained traction as some scholars challenged the idea of a universal Black experience (Hintzen & Rahier, 2003). This of course would suggest that a collective Black identity could be insubstantial. Accordingly, a more productive approach might be to examine the many spaces of Black experience. This movement has been largely led by scholars concerned about how a foreign-born African-descent population has been ascribed an African American Black identity (Waters, 1994, 1999). This scholarship has suggested that the Black experience has come to be narrowly defined as the African American experience. This ignores Afro-descendants who do not identity with the same historical experiences of U.S.-born African Americans. It is as though foreign-born African-descendant people may be poised to usher in a third radical space of identity that is somehow more complicated than the African American one (Butterfield, 2004).

I want to depart for a moment from the principles of deconstructionism, mostly because I find its politics also often align with divide-and-conquer tactics. And while it is true that one does not want to become guilty of essentialism, it is also true that similar tactics to oppress Black women exist across diverse contexts. We must acknowledge the transnationalism of not only people, but also the transnational character of anti-Black misogyny. In this next section I discuss one pillar that has been harnessed to uphold the manifestation of anti-Black misogyny in the United States and Latin America. Though anti-Black misogyny occurs in many domains, I will focus on the domain of degradation through public humiliation in the production of popular film and music.

## Public Humiliation of Black Women as Good Entertainment

In 2009, comedian and actor Chris Rock produced and narrated a documentary, *Good Hair*, which tells the social story of Black women's hair. The film received critical acclaim, including a special award at the highly regarded Sundance Film Festival. *Good Hair* has been heralded as a film that takes seriously the politics of hair for Black American women but through a more light-hearted, entertaining, and comedic lens. Like many, before I saw the film I had hoped that Rock, who at times has delivered scathing critiques of white supremacy, might set aside entertainment value in order to produce a more serious account of the relationship between white supremacy and beauty aesthetics. In several interviews, Rock has said that what he hoped to achieve with this film is the stimulation of a deeper dialogue. Yet, he is rather imprecise about who he hoped would be part of this dialogue and how this would contribute to a broader dialogue on social issues confronting Black women. While the film supposedly empowers Black women by giving voice to their hair experiences, it views more like an indictment of Black women and their attitudes about their physical appearance.

The inclusion of interviews with Black female celebrities alongside everyday working class Black women who spend significant amounts of money and time on achieving a more European hair aesthetic appears to be produced for a strategic purpose. First, that so many Black women, both celebrity and noncelebrity, appear overly focused on a European hair aesthetic suggests a widespread problem among Black women in general. We see women who reportedly spend hundreds, potentially thousands, of dollars on hair weaves and who willingly endanger themselves with the application of dangerous chemicals to straighten their naturally coiled hair. That this happens among a broad spectrum of Black women is an important element for building the argument for a sort of universal senselessness among Black women when it comes to aesthetics.

The second message, and perhaps a more important element in the acclaimed film, is its focus on working-class Black women, whom Rock asserts spend as much as 20% of their income on hair weaves or extensions to make their hair appear long and flowing. Rock goes to great lengths to drive this point home and has mentioned it in interviews promoting the film. We are to believe that rather than investing in more important things in life, Black women are wasting money on their hair. It should be noted that in the same year that Rock's documentary received a Sundance Film award, another film—*Precious*, directed by Lee Daniels—also received special recognition at the 2009 Sundance Film festival. One striking similarity between the two films, besides their mass popularity, is in each one's targeting of Black women in a way that coincides with what Patricia Hill Collins (2000) refers to as "controlling images."

While the film *Precious* more openly reproduces the image of the Black welfare queen, Rock's documentary is a subtler repackaging of this image that represents Black women as abusers of money and selfishly spending for things that really do not matter. Of course, we do not have any sense as to whether the Black women interviewed by Rock are receiving any sort of government income assistance. The fact is, however, many Americans believe that Black women are indeed welfare queens and gold diggers (another image made popular in hip hop music). In the minds of many, the women whom Rock interviews at the beauty salon are the same gold diggers and welfare queens that have come to be familiar and authentic representations of all Black women. The attention given to the amount of money that flows through the hair care industry juxtaposed against images of everyday Black women who are paying for hair—sometimes going so far as to purchase expensive human hair on layaway plans—carries the message that Black women are wasteful. Black women become the brunt of a joke that imagines them as thoughtlessly spending money that they likely received through government support.

This point of Black women as desperate for beauty is only buttressed when Rock travels to India to seek out authentically "good hair" and jokingly tells an Indian woman, "If you see a Black woman, run in the other direction"—underscoring that the Indian woman possesses something of value that Black women are willing to do anything to acquire. The other clear purpose of the trip to India presented in the film is to demonstrate how even poor women from India are more enlightened as they demonstrate much less vanity about their hair, unlike Black women who are desperate about hair they have not even inherited naturally. Rock includes a part in the film in which a point is made about Black women's addiction to the "creamy crack." This of course is racially coded discourse since crack cocaine is most often associated with Black Americans. In the film, the discussion on Black women's addiction to creamy crack is presented as funny; however, these sort of representations are not just lighthearted satire—they become one of the many platforms working to regularly reproduce and circulate controlling images of Black women.

The film includes the sexual humiliation of Black women through soft pornographic talk. Hypersexualizing the Black body is part of a long history of racist ideology. It is through the sexual degradation of the Black female body that White women achieve sexual purity and inherent value. Racist imagery often includes juxtapositions that identify that which is to represent good and pure through the opposing image of that which represents the defiled and impure. Even the way sex becomes play in the film alludes to the "dirty" nature of Black women. Audience viewers are told that Black women have to stay on top for sexual play because they do not want to mess up their hair. In the case of *Good Hair*, the sexual consumption of the Black female body is ever-present—in fact, it would be odd if it were not present. Rock poses the question, how do Black women have sex, given the complicatedness of their hair situation. If the viewer had not up to that point thought about sex, they were carefully led toward imagining what it is like to have sex with a Black woman. It is true that Black women's voices are included in responding to this question, but, not surprisingly, the sex dialogue is actually centered on barbershop talk from Black men, laughing about what would happen if you dared touch a Black woman's hair during sex. Mind you, the film is marketed as PG-13. Why include this imagery for anyone, let alone a potentially younger audience?

When Rock was asked why he wanted to make the film, his explanation is that one day his younger daughter asked why she did not have good hair. He questioned how she came up with that idea. The way the film approaches answering this question leads back to Black women themselves as self-sabotaging and then teaching this to other young Black girls. It is as though all of this privileging of a white aesthetic originates in the minds of Black women with no social foundation grounded in the history of white supremacy. This sort of rationalizing in the film contributes to the perception of Black women as irrational. It makes light or completely ignores how White aesthetics are often contributing factors in determining Black women's career opportunities, Black children's interactions at school, and how people respond when Black women enter a room. In other words, the politics of hair is not only about how one feels about the hair they were born with; it is not simply internal—we must recognize that there are real tangible consequences to Black women's physical aesthetics that are external to her.

The history of an anti-Black misogynist apparatus includes Black women being told that they are physically unacceptable, ugly, and undesirable. More important, Black women have found real ramifications relating to their physical appearance. For example, it is doubtful that the Black female celebrities Rock interviews in his documentary would even be employable in the industry if they did not wear long straight hair weaves that mimic a white women's hair. Noncelebrity Black women have confronted this same dilemma for as long as they have had to interview for jobs in white spaces. For Black women, hair is political, just as our very phenotype is political, and it is not because Black women are too inept to love their God-given physical attributes. It is because aesthetics are also part of the machinery that drives racism, patriarchy, and misogyny in this world. Yet, this is little explored in the documentary.

In the post–Civil Rights era, U.S. racial ideology has experienced a shift from very overt Jim Crow–like racial schema to a more coded colorblind racial schema. Accompanying discourse has also shifted over time. What has not changed is the evolution of a racialized misogynistic social structure that abuses Black women, employing various tools to do so—including gratuitous humiliation.[2] One of the symptoms of colorblind racial ideology is that it upsets how we historicize social issues. In the book *The Miner's Canary*, Lani Guinier and Gerald Torres (2002) write that one of the rules of the colorblind universe is that "the individual has no historical antecedents, no important social relationship, and no political commitments" (38). Accordingly, anti-Black racism has no history, at least not one that is relevant for us today. In other words, the horrible things done to Black women happened in the past, have not occurred since, and therefore we have no business dredging up what is purportedly no longer consistent with our lives today. Another rule in the colorblind universe is that anti-Black racism exists only in the personal sphere and is rooted solely in biologically racist discourse. One of the ways that *Good Hair* attempts to escape accusations of anti-Black racism is that it is produced and narrated by Chris Rock, an African American man.

The film also predominantly includes Black people, both male and female, discussing Black women's hair issues. The Internet Movie Database (IMDb) says, "Chris Rock explores the wonders of African American hairstyles." This description is interesting because it evokes the idea of personal choice rather than the history and politics of Black women's hair. It suggests that this is all about personal choice, and given the representations in the film we are left wondering why Black women are making such questionable choices. In the post-racial era it is all about personal choices and, pursuant to that, personal responsibility for one's choices. History is unimportant in the context of personal choices.

One unfortunate legacy we inherited in the culmination of the 1960s Civil Rights Movement was the development of colorblind racism. We have seen the persistence of a racialized social structure despite the claims by many that racism is no longer a significant problem (Bonilla-Silva, 2003). The prevailing colorblind apparatus asks that we ignore anti-Black misogyny because it is not overtly packaged in problematic language or ostentatious imagery. Because Chris Rock is a Black man, we are expected to ignore how his film treats Black women. Because Chris Rock is a comedian and approaches the topic through comedy, we are supposed to get that it is meant to solicit a laugh. We are asked to ignore the difference between humor and gratuitous humiliation. The consequence of this film is that Black women are humiliated while being told to absorb the lie that this is all just good-hearted fun that makes them actually think. But who is the audience? I doubt if the film would be made if it were produced to cater to only Black women. The film has been marketed largely to a much broader non-Black audience.

## Public Humiliation of Black Women in Latin America

To underscore that Black women's degradation is a vital part of an active global anti-Black misogynist apparatus, and how this hinges on Black women's bodies, it is important to highlight the transnational character of this pillar. In Kia Caldwell's (2007) book *Negras in Brazil*, she examines the ridicule and degradation of Black women's bodies in Brazilian popular culture. Though racial ideology in Brazil, as in most of Latin America, has developed uniquely from the United States, an anti-Black misogynist apparatus still allows for satiric violence against Black women. Caldwell highlights the popularity of a song in Brazil, *Veja os cabelos dela* (*Look at Her Hair*). The song refers to Black women's hair in derogatory terms but also goes on to comment that Black women smell like skunks. Caldwell describes the controversy that later ensued as Sony Records confronted charges from Black Brazilian organizations challenging the racist content of the song. Many were adamant that the song was not racist, since racism does not exist in Brazil. Those who defended the song argued that it was lighthearted comedy, for entertainment purposes only, and not a serious commentary about Black women's hair or body.

At present, the song is available on YouTube. A number of people have uploaded the song. One presentation on YouTube includes a photo montage of Black women, and even young Black girls, wearing their natural afro-like hair. That the video includes photos of young Black children should be surprising but really is not given that the onslaught of racist misogynistic imagery begins at the earliest age. The consequence is that any young girl who hears the song and views the imagery will quickly be able to identify herself and understand where she belongs in society. In order for the anti-Black misogynist apparatus to function, young girls must experience this ridicule at an early age. The imagery has important psychological functioning for both Black and non-Blacks. The YouTube comments section offers up very interesting social science data. It is a peek into how people perceive the song in relationship to actual Black women and whether they see the song as merely humor with no connection to real women.

Many comments support the song, noting that it is funny. Still others question if all the women represented in the photos are really as ugly as the song describes, since many in the video are lighter-skinned mulata (mixed race) women who are beautiful with nice hair and perhaps should not be included alongside other browner-skinned and more obviously Negra (Black) women who do in fact represent the statements made in the song. Though it is a Brazilian song, the photos include both African American and Brazilian women—notably, African American and loc-wearing singer Lauryn Hill is among the photos presented.

Latin American nations such as Brazil have long been identified as racial democracies (Winddance-Twine, 1998). This does not mean they are entirely free of racial thinking or forms of discrimination. When racist sentiment becomes evident, it is thought to be isolated, unusual, and not representative of the culture or the people. Given that just about everyone identifies as mixed race, racism could not possibly exist. There is a strong denial of the existence of anti-Black racial discrimination, even when other forms of discrimination, such as class and even sexist discrimination, are acknowledged (Hernandez, 2012).

In an ethnography on sex tourism in Brazil, Erica Williams (2013) notes a general assumption in Brazil that Black women are engaged in prostitution. Black women may find they are more often approached in public places for casual sex. This sort of misrepresentation of Black women is also dominant in other parts of Latin America. In my travels throughout the Dominican Republic, I have also found a general perception that darker-skinned women—Negras—are more promiscuous and sexually available. This narrative is reproduced in popular culture, especially music, but also through jokes. One frequently hears songs that imagine sexual play with Black women. And while some would say this speaks to the sexual openness of Latin American culture and perhaps should be applauded, the focus is almost exclusively on Black women. The consequences are that Black women's bodies become sites of violent public sexual consumption that they have little agency over. One will often hear that Black women are for domestic work and wild sex. The tangible consequences for Black women who must daily confront these distortions are real.

The consequences for phenotype are more overt in Brazil and other parts of Latin America, where there is still the practice of requiring "boa aparência" (good appearance) when applying for a job. Many Black Brazilians have commented that this is code talk for white appearance. It is a way to openly discriminate against qualified Black Brazilian applicants, yet subverts any charge of anti-Black racism because the language is coded and does not assert a racial preference. This sort of racial practices emerge against the backdrop of racial democracy discourse (DeWitt & Stepan, 2002).

## The Power of a Transnational Black feminism

This chapter has analyzed how gratuitous humiliation is deployed in the global anti-Black misogynistic apparatus. Globally, Black women experience this pillar of oppression. Black feminism responds to this apparatus by, first, challenging deconstructionist ideas that promote thinking only about local uniqueness. This does not mean that Black feminism's approach is essentialist, because Black feminism asks that we look at both the specificities of a local context, as in the condition of Black women in the United States, but also requires us to do the work of examining how Black women in other parts of the world confront similar challenges.

When I teach my Black feminism class, students are sometimes surprised to hear that Black women in Latin America are also struggling to assert their humanity, similar to Black women in the United States. The very same tools used against U.S. Black women are also manipulated to suppress Black Latin American women. As U.S. Black women are hypersexualized, so too are Black Latin American women. As U.S. Black women face public humiliation, so to do Black Latin American women. A history of slavery in the United States, as well as a long history of slavery in Latin America, has similarly appropriated and abused Black women's bodies. While slavery and its consequences developed uniquely to fit the particular contexts, it is also true that the apparatus has always worked toward the same end—the slow and steady oppression of Black women. The apparatus has always deployed many agents to do this. Popular culture, including music and film, has proven to be an important element in sustaining anti-Black misogyny.

Music and film are important media because of their power to transport ideology globally. Now more than ever, as a result of the internet, people access popular culture from all over the world. Representations through film and music become the vehicles through which many people have come to (mis) recognize Black women (hooks, 1992). Images inherently include ideology that crafts how people respond to the organization of the social structure. This means that many people interact regularly with Black women through a distorted imagination. Additionally, the continuous reproduction and marketing of these representations over time means that Black women too may become susceptible to them. Black feminism counters these false representations of Black women by capturing how they uphold anti-Black misogyny. Black feminism demands that we seek out more thoughtful images of Black women in all of their complexities. This is a crucial step toward what Patricia Hill Collins (2000) has referred to as the power of self-definition.

Black feminism draws our attention to what bell hooks (1992) calls the inner-workings of power. It is significant that we understand the global tentacles of power. The emergence of post-racial colorblind ideology in the United States closely mirrors racial democracy ideology in Latin America. We gain a more valuable perspective through our examination of what is similar about the global deployment of anti-Black misogyny than we do by focusing solely on deconstructing in search of difference.

Finally, Black feminism challenges us to search for those spaces that are seemingly benign. Anti-Black misogyny happens through the realm of comedic play. It has often been thought that comedy opens up dialogue about social issues. Supposedly, when we can laugh about something, we take away its power to oppress us. As we have seen, however, comedy can also become a tool to support the apparatus of oppression, resulting in palpable consequences for all Black women. As Black feminists, our goal is to look for ways to collectively construct our experiences and tell our stories together. As Black feminist educators, our responsibility is to cultivate critical-mindfulness within our students. I believe in Black feminism's ability to challenge oppressive structures; therefore, my classroom is a space organized from a Black feminist worldview. Toni Morrison (2008) points to the ways universities inherently teach values. Black feminist thought disrupts the idea that classrooms are nonpolitical, neutral spaces. Given that educators are always political actors, we must ask ourselves what values we want our students to learn. While we want to avoid essentialist theorizing, we also do not want our fear of being labeled essentialist to hinder us from acknowledging what links us together. The anti-Black misogynist apparatus looks forward to us continuing the politics of deconstructing—theorizing about how different one group is from another—when there is collective power in understanding what makes us, our stories, and our experiences similar.

## Notes

1. Moya Bailey uses the term "misogynoir" to "describe the particular brand of hatred directed at Black women in American visual and popular culture" in a blog post, "They Aren't Talking About Me," for the Crunk Feminist Collective.

2. The term "gratuitous humiliation" is used by Lani Guinier and Gerald Torres in their book *The Miner's Canary*, page 279, to describe the way in which law enforcement subject people to specific acts of public humiliation as a means of social control.

## References

Bailey, M. (2010, March 14). *They aren't talking about me . . .* (blog post). Retrieved from www.crunkfeministcollective.com/2010/03/14/they-arent-talking-about-me

Bonilla-Silva, E. (2003). *Racism without racists: Color-blind racism and the persistence of racial inequality in the United States*. United Kingdom: Rowman and Littlefield.
Butterfield, S. (2004). Challenging American conceptions of race and ethnicity: Second-generation West Indian immigrants. *International Journal of Sociology and Social Policy, 24*(7/8), 75–102.
Caldwell, K. (2007). *Negras in Brazil: Re-envisioning Black women, citizenship and the politics of identity*. New Brunswick, NJ: Rutgers University Press.
Davis, A. (1974). *Angela Davis: An autobiography*. New York: Random House.
Davis, A. (1981). *Women, Race and Class*. New York: Vintage Books.
DeWitt, M. (Writer and Director), & Stepan, A. (Writer). (2002). *Brazil in Black and White*. [PBS documentary series episode]. In *Wide Angle*. United States: PBS Studios.
Guillard Limonta, N. (2016). To be a Black woman, a lesbian, and an Afro-feminist in Cuba today. *Black Diaspora Review, 5*(2), 81–97.
Guinier, L., & Torres, G. (2002). *The miner's canary: Enlisting race, resisting power, transforming democracy*. Cambridge and London: Routledge Press.
Hernández, T. (2013). *Racial subordination in Latin America: The role of the state, customary law, and the new civil rights response*. Cambridge: Cambridge University Press.
Hill Collins, P. (2000). *Black feminist thought: Knowledge, consciousness, and the politics of empowerment*. New York and London: Routledge Press.
Hintzen, P., & Rahier, J. (Eds). (2003). *Problematizing Blackness: Self-ethnographies by Black immigrants to the United States*. New York and London: Routledge.
hooks, b. (1992). *Black looks: Race and representation*. Boston: South End Press.
hooks, b. (2000). *Feminist theory: From margin to center*. Cambridge, MA: South End Press.
Lorde, A. (1984/2007). *Sister outsider: Essays and speeches by Audre Lorde*. Berkeley, CA: Crossing Press.
Morrison, T. (2008). How can values be taught in the university? In C. Denard (Ed). *What moves at the margin: Selected non-fiction* (pp. 191–198). Jackson: University Press of Mississippi.
Roberts, D. (1997). *Killing the Black body: Race, reproduction, and the meaning of liberty*. New York: Pantheon Books.
Waters, M. (1994). Ethnic and racial identities of second-generation Black immigrants in New York. *International Migration Review, 28*(4), 795–820.
Waters, M. (2001). *Black identities: West Indian immigrant dreams and American realities*. Cambridge, MA: Harvard University Press.
Williams, E. L. (2013). *Sex tourism in Brazil: Ambiguous entanglements*. Champaign-Urbana: University of Illinois Press.
Winddance-Twine, F. (1998). *Racism in a racial democracy: The maintenance of White supremacy in Brazil*. New Brunswick, NJ, and London: Rutgers University Press.

# Part II

## Evaluating Foundations and Generations

Chapter 7

# A Seat at the Table

## *Mary McLeod Bethune's Call for the Inclusion of Black Women During World War II*

Ashley Robertson Preston

> She [Mary McLeod Bethune] came out there and talked to us and told us that they [The War Department] did not want us in this service in the first place, so we had to set an example. And we did.
>
> —Brenda Lee Moore, 1996

On September 30, 2016, Solange Knowles released an album titled *A Seat at the Table*, which became one of the most talked about albums of 2016. *Huffington Post* called the work "a beautiful statement about what it means to be Black while acknowledging how the world makes it hard to celebrate life in a Black body" (Anthony, 2016). The younger sister of Beyoncé found a way to carve out her own unique space in the world of music. In her own words she states that the album is a "project on identity, empowerment, independence, grief and healing" (Johnston, 2016). Within the content of the lyrics she expresses social commentary on the state of Black America, a celebration of Black culture and self-assertion. The title *A Seat at the Table* sounds simple, but its interpretation is much deeper. Over the course of African American history, women have often had to create space where there was none. When no one offered a seat, they found their own. Studying the life of Mrs. Mary McLeod Bethune, one finds that just as Solange demanded a seat, Mrs. Bethune demanded the same not only for herself but also for Black women as a whole. Bethune once said:

> By the very force of circumstances, the part she has played in the progress has been of necessity to a certain extent subtle and indirect. She has not always been permitted a place in the front ranks where she could show her face and make her voice heard with effect. But she has been quick to seize every opportunity, which presented itself to come more and more into the open and strive directly for the uplift of the race and nation. In that direction, her achievements have been amazing. (Torricelli, 1999, 105–106)

It is in this statement that Bethune expressed how Black women were not always allowed in certain spaces but found ways to insert themselves despite resistance. Throughout her life, Bethune would often insert herself into situations in which most women were not allowed. Born in 1875 in rural South Carolina to formerly enslaved parents, Mary McLeod Bethune rose from very humble beginnings through hard work and persistence. She was the first in her family to be formally educated, and after being denied an opportunity to be a missionary in Africa she decided to become a teacher. In 1904, she traveled to Daytona Beach, Florida, with $1.50 in her pocket, and on October 3 of that same year she opened the Daytona Literary and Industrial School for the Training of Negro Girls (Hanson, 2003).

At the height of her career, Bethune served as the only woman in President Franklin D. Roosevelt's Black Cabinet, and in 1923 she became president of Bethune-Cookman College at a time when men led most institutions of higher learning. In 1936, Bethune became the first Black woman to head a federal agency when she accepted the position of Director of the Division of Negro Affairs for the National Youth Administration. She also created women's organizations such as the National Council of Negro Women to galvanize women to be involved in political and social issues in a male-dominated society. When the advent of World War II brought forth new opportunities for women in the workforce, Bethune seized this opportunity to fight for defense jobs, military positions, and recognition of the achievements of Black women.

## Victory Abroad, Victory at Home

In 1939, World War II began between European and Asian powers while the United States maintained its neutrality. It wasn't until the Japanese attacked Pearl Harbor on December 7, 1941, that the United States joined the allied forces and officially entered the war. Doris "Dorie" Miller fought during the attack on Pearl Harbor, manning a machine gun and saving the lives of some of his fellow troops by taking them to safety. Shortly after, he was awarded the Navy Cross for bravery, as he proved that Black soldiers were not only necessary but also dedicated to the protection of the United States. When the United States entered the war, Black troops served in France, Great Britain, and Tunisia, risking their lives far from home. As they fought to end the terrorist fascist reign of Adolf Hitler, they also decided it was time to end the reign of terror known as Jim Crow.

On January 31, 1942, cafeteria worker James G. Thompson wrote a letter to the editor of the *Pittsburgh Courier* on the subject of the War and asked, "Should I sacrifice my life to live half American?" (Thompson, 1942). Like many Black men, Thompson was concerned about both the possibilities of being drafted and how his sacrifice would affect his community. At a time when African Americans faced prejudice, segregation, and disenfranchisement at home, fighting abroad for the freedom of unknown constituents of fascist countries was illogical for many. In his letter, Thomas questioned whether democracy would come to the Black community as a result of the war. The allied forces of the war had taken on the slogan "V for Victory" to represent victory against the enemies. In keeping with the "V" symbol, Thompson called for a "double V" campaign in which "[t]he first V for victory over our enemies from without, the second V for victory over our enemies within" (Thompson, 1942). Thompson linked Black participation in the war as a war on two fronts, hoping that if they proved their loyalty to fighting the causes of America, then in turn America would honor the sacrifice of its soldiers by committing to equality and democracy.

As the war continued, the African American press, particularly *Chicago Defender* and *Pittsburgh Courier* promoted the ideals of the "Double V" campaign and criticized the United States for its hypocritical stance against fascism. The press was so influential in rallying African Americans that FBI head J. Edgar Hoover "believed that elements of the Double V campaign were seditious and therefore violated the Espionage and Smith acts" (Copeland, 2010, 7). In response, an agreement was made between African American newspapers and the government to lessen the combativeness of the articles, but the campaign continued. Throughout World War II, African Americans strategically linked the need to eliminate the evils of Jim Crow with the need to end fascism across the world, confirming their roles as international activists.

Although the bombing of Pearl Harbor marked a turning point in the involvement of America in the war, Bethune was well aware of the opportunities for advancement of women that had already become available. Many of those opportunities were not inclusive of Black women, nor did they consider them to be candidates. She wrote President Franklin D. Roosevelt in 1940, urging him to consider Black women for defense-related jobs: "I offer my own services without reservation, and urge you, in the planning and work which lies ahead, to make such use of the services of qualified Negro women" (McCluskey & Smith, 1999, 174) As president of the National Council of Negro Women, one of the largest women's organizations at the time, she represented member organizations including the National Association of Graduate Nurses, National Iota Phi Lambda Sorority, Inc., and Delta Sigma Theta Sorority, Inc. Her letter to the president was the voice of Black women from around the United States.

## The Women's Army Corps

After the December 7, 1941, attack on Pearl Harbor, the United States became fully immersed in the war. Due to the promotion of John Thompson's call for "Double Victory" throughout African American newspapers and the media, African Americans also became involved in the war, both on the front line as soldiers and in defense-related jobs. Although the campaign caught on, some remained skeptical about how the war would actually help African Americans. However, Bethune saw the war as an opportunity for the advancement of African Americans and promoted the war through NCNW and was a strong advocate for women's involvement.

At a time when men were going off to war by the thousands, Representative Edith Nourse Rogers of Massachusetts introduced a bill to Congress to create the Women's Army Auxiliary Corps Act (WAAC) in May 1941. The act would "create a voluntary enrollment program for women to join the U.S. Army in a noncombat capacity" (Wasniewski, 2006, 73) in positions such as clerical workers, cooks, phone operators, and medical-related jobs. Doing so would allow more men to be on the front line and free from noncombat positions. One year later, on May 14, 1942, the act became a bill, and the following day President Franklin D. Roosevelt signed it into law, making Oveta Culp Hobby the first director.

Behind the scenes it was Bethune who fought for the inclusion of African American women as WAAC members. In her 2011 memoir, *Justice Older Than the Law*, former WAAC officer Dovey Johnson Roundtree recalled watching Bethune meet with First Lady Roosevelt in attempts to get "her girls" involved in the war.[1] Roosevelt was leery about having African American women serve alongside white women, but Bethune did not back down. Roundtree wrote: "Watching Dr. Bethune fight so hard over so many months for a place for Black women in the military, I came to the conclusion that for all my reservations and fears, I couldn't turn away from her challenge" (McCabe & Roundtree, 2009, 52). It was due to Bethune's continued persistence that the first class of officers for the WAAC began their July 1942 training in

Des Moines, Iowa, with approximately 39 African American female officers in their number. Approximately 10.6% of the WAAC's members were to be African American women, and in its early phase Bethune saw to it that the number was fulfilled.

Bethune became a special assistant to Secretary of War Harry L. Stimson and was responsible for handpicking the first 40 members of WAAC. In choosing the members, she picked women who were college educated and whom she felt would best represent the race. She went throughout the United States recruiting on college campuses to find women to serve. On the first day of training, Bethune met the women in Des Moines and checked out the facilities to ensure that the women were in livable conditions (Hobby, 1942). Remembering the sobering effect of Bethune's visit, Roundtree wrote, "[s]he gathered her *girls* about her . . . and reminded us of our place in history" (McCabe & Johnson, 2009, 57). She also wrote that "Dr. Bethune transformed the atmosphere of those uneasy hours with a few carefully chosen words" (McCabe & Johnson, 2009, 57). Bethune didn't just throw the women into action; she paid a personal visit to ensure their safety and give them a boost of confidence. Over the years she would be a supporter of the women and a confidante in whom they could call on.

Bethune was also concerned about the general welfare of soldiers abroad and pushed for NCNW to be on the advisory council on soldiers' welfare. In a letter to Stimson published in the *Atlanta Daily World*, Bethune advised the general: "We still seek this end and urge upon you that Negro representation be included in this advisory council and in all future plans" (McCluskey & Smith, 1999, 174–175). In her protest, Bethune also reiterated the connections between inclusion of African Americans and democracy. She often told the government that African Americans receiving equal treatment and equal opportunities was a vital extension of American democracy. By 1943, NCNW was represented by Dorothy Porter as a member of the Advisory Council for the Women's Interests Section. The organization was formed to inform women about the welfare of soldiers and to distribute information about soldier's health, available recreational activities, and information on how women could contribute to the war. With Bethune and NCNW's involvement, the women asserted themselves into every aspect of the war. The first 39 African American women to go into the Corps were the first women to serve in the military other than nurses. Previous to their arrival, all military members had been men. For the women, it was a scary, yet historic time. In Roundtree's text she recalled explaining her desire to enlist in WAAC despite her grandmother and mother, who "regarded the military with fear" (McCabe & Johnson, 2009, 56). WAAC's members and their families did not know what to expect. As a recruiter and advisor, Bethune used her organization to calm the fears of African Americans. In the 1942 anniversary pre-conference issue of *Aframerican Women's Journal*, NCNW featured the WAAC. In the article "The W.A.A.C.—The Girl Who Wouldn't Be Left Behind," the journal emphasized the historical significance of the Corps, featured information about Director Oveta Culp Hobby, and provided an outline of the typical daily requirements of a WAAC member. The article also featured the names and contact information for the women who graduated from the officer's training school, encouraging NCNW to communicate with the women. Overall, the journal also updated the community on the conditions of the women of the Corps.

The women of the WAAC made a significant contribution to the winning of the war, and many of their roles gave more men the opportunity to serve in combat. In her book *When the Nation was in Need: Blacks in the Women's Army Corps During World War II*, former WAAC officer Margaret Settle Putney recalls the numerous jobs that women worked in during the war, including typists, clerks, telephone operators, librarians, nurses' aides, and laboratory technicians. Although many positions were available, the women found themselves having to fight to gain them, and Bethune had to persist in ensuring that the women were not selected to be WAACs in name only. Many thought that the Black women could not be useful in winning the war, including Major George F. Martin. According to Putney, "Martin said that his visit to the field installations revealed that some commanders 'are at a loss to determine how' Black personnel can be used" (1992, 74). Martin's leadership role as the control divisions director meant that his observations were not taken lightly; however, due to the suggestions of higher authorities, Black WAAC members were still given positions in the field.

Although she is often given little credit for her instrumental role behind the scenes of the WAAC, Bethune fought not only for their inclusion but for equal treatment; it is due to her persistence that the women were given active roles in the Corps. She visited WAAC sites, served as a listening ear to officers, and continued to push for a completely integrated military. After touring Fort Des Moines in Iowa and Camp Crowder in Missouri, she put forth nine suggestions, including full integration, opening occupations then closed to Black WAACs, and the abolishment of all-Black regiments (Moore, 1996, 54).

WAAC women served not only in the Corps in the United States, but also abroad. Under the leadership of Major Charity Adams Early, the 6888th Central Postal Directory Battalion was the only battalion of Black women to go overseas during World War II. Stationed in Birmingham, England, and Rouen, France, the battalion sorted and delivered mail to soldiers. This task was single-handedly one of the most important in the war because it was the only way that the soldiers were able to communicate with their families.

Soldiers waited for letters of good cheer to give them hope while fighting on the battle lines, while families awaited responses to assure their loved ones were still alive. The 6888th Battalion played a major role in keeping the morale of soldiers up during the war.

## NCNW's Support of the War

Bethune was in full support of America's position in World War II and encouraged African Americans to get involved in war efforts. In a speech "What Are We Fighting For?" she acknowledged the "hindrances" that kept African Americans from fully participating but urged them to continue to fight because "full democracy hinges upon the outcome of this war" (McCluskey & Smith, 1999, 247). She also reminded white America that they too had the duty of "removing obstacles" to ensure that African Americans could fully participate in the war. As the president of NCNW, Bethune fully involved the organization in war efforts. On June 3, 1945, the *S.S. Harriet Tubman* was launched and became the first Liberty Ship to be named after an African American woman. Previous Liberty Ships had been named after African American men, including Frederick Douglass and Booker T. Washington.

For Bethune and NCNW, the ship made a vital statement to the United States and to the world that African American women were willing to work to be included in the war, and also that they wanted to be recognized as equals. Funds to revamp the ship were raised solely by members of NCNW. By September 1944, the organization had passed a fundraising goal of selling $2,000,000 in war bonds and "[a] total of $3,452,361.75 bond purchases were credited to the drive" ("$3,452,000 Bonds for *S.S. Tubman*," 1944). Over the course of the year, the organization called on its member organizations, including sororities and professional organizations, to assist in selling United States War Bonds. By August 1944, the Los Angeles chapter of NCNW had surpassed their goal of $10,000 by $7,500 by selling bonds; all across the United States, other organizations were doing the same (*Chicago Defender*, 1944). The organization also used *Aframerican Journal* to advertise the sale of bonds as a way to communicate the significance of the ship with members.

During the launch of the ship, Tubman's family members, including her grandniece, attended the event. The women had accomplished an historic feat. The *S.S. Harriet Tubman* made history for African American women—not only as the first ship to be named after an African American woman, but as the only ship to be named after an African American woman during World War II. Out of 2,751 ships built during the war, only 17 were named after African Americans. Liberty Ships were used to take vital goods and cargo to soldiers fighting abroad. For NCNW, it was befitting to name the ship that would assist in liberation from fascism and racism after a woman who had brought hundreds of enslaved to freedom. The *S.S. Harriet Tubman* was one of the ways that the NCNW insured that the participation of Black women during World War II was recognized, and that the world understood their historic contributions.

## Women's Army for National Defense

On November 15, 1942, the Women's Army for National Defense (WAND) was founded by Lovonia Brown to serve as a volunteer organization in support of the efforts of World War II. Its motto, "We Too Serve America," was a declaration to serve against the odds. At the time, most predominantly white organizations, including the Red Cross and the Office of Civilian Defense, had not allowed Black women to serve in leadership or prominent roles. WAND was created by Black women to fulfill their patriotic duties on their own terms, and so that "Negro women would not always be relegated to the lowest positions where all of the hard work was done but with little glory" (Taylor, 1943). Lovonia Brown had previously been active in the clubwomen's movement in Chicago, and shortly after the founding of the organization she invited Bethune to serve as the First Officer in Command and General. Brown served as the Lieutenant General.

Bethune took the helm as General and diligently worked with WAND to create strategies to assist not only during but also after the war. WAND was well organized under her leadership and took the job of supporting the war seriously. In September of 1944, the organization hosted its first annual conference in Chicago, where its national office was located ("Mary McLeod Bethune selected chair," 1943). By this time there were 26 chapters of WAND in 14 states, including California, Mississippi, Virginia, Minnesota and New York. Each chapter was named after historic Black women, including Mary McLeod Bethune, Harriet Tubman, Sojourner Truth, and Hattie McDaniel. A "Miss Wand" was also selected after raising over $136 dollars for war bonds. Each member was given a uniform, which was quite similar to the WAAC's military uniform.

At the conference, reports presented on WAND activities, demonstrating that the organization had taken vigorous efforts to support the war. The women sent toys to the children of soldiers overseas, sent care packages to soldiers in their local areas, organized food/clothing drives to send to European allies, and raised money to purchase war bonds. Colonel Willa

Alston was awarded the Silver Award from the Department of Treasury for her individual fundraising efforts. To support women, WAND sponsored housing in Chicago (Irma Clayton Barracks) for women working in defense-related jobs and WAACs in need of housing (Litoff & Smith, 1997, 161). In 1945, when the war was coming to a close, the organization shifted its efforts toward postwar support and required every member to have a social service division with "an advisory council to aid soldiers, their families and dependents" (Taylor, 1945). WAND chapters also provided information about the GI Bill for returning veterans and gathered information on housing and employment to assist with the transition back into civilian life. By the end of 1946, many of WAND's activities started slowly coming to an end, but their work during the war had provided critical resources for military men and their families.

## Bethune in the Context of Social Justice Education

Scholar Ruth Lupton states that "[s]ocial justice in education demands, at the very minimum, that all students should have access to schools of the same quality" (2005, 589). Although the article highlights Bethune's work as an advocate for women during World War II, her demand for equality begun in her role as an educator. She consistently brought attention to the state of Florida for shortchanging its African American citizens in the area of funding for students. During a 1937 Bethune-Cookman College (B-CC) fundraising drive in New York, she alerted her audience of the unfair policies of the Sunshine State. According to Cleveland G. Allen's article in the *Chicago Defender*,

> [Bethune] stated that Florida spends $63.00 per capital on the education of a white child and less than $8.00 upon a race child. She told of the difficulty under which many of the children of Florida get an education, and said that one third of schools where Race children attend are without water and other modern conveniences. (*Chicago Defender*, 1937)

Bethune assured that the facts fell upon the ears of those who could help her, including Mrs. James Roosevelt (mother of President Franklin D. Roosevelt), former United States Senator Frederic C. Walcott, and New York State judge James Watson. It was in instances such as this that Bethune called wealthy whites to shift resources to her students so that they too could be educated. For her, it was access to resources that would be the vehicle to justice. She positioned herself among people who could do something about the issue and made a call to action. She was able to raise $207,482 during the fundraising drive, allowing her to provide invaluable opportunities for her students.

In 1936, President Franklin D. Roosevelt appointed Bethune to serve as the head of the Negro Affairs Division for the National Youth Administration (NYA). The NYA was part of Roosevelt's larger New Deal Program, which sought to stabilize the economic situation of Americans during the Great Depression. NYA was geared toward job creation and job training for youth aged 16 to 24. Again, Bethune used this position to bring attention to the needs of African Americans, pressing for more funds than the federal government had intended to give. After her first year, "an increase of $56,000 in NYA grants for race graduate students was approved and the number of Race students receiving NYA aid was increased from 26,000 to more than 35,000" (*Chicago Defender*, 1937). She also led the National Conference on the Problems of the Negro and Negro Youth to gain insight on where funds could be best used and delivered the reports of the conference to President Roosevelt.

As she worked tirelessly advocating for women during the War Bethune retired from her role as president of B-CC in 1942 (although she returned for the 1946–47 school year) but she continued to work to eliminate economic equalities, particularly amongst Historically Black Colleges and Universities (HBCUs). On April 25, 1944, Tuskegee Institute president Dr. Frederick D. Patterson and Bethune organized the United Negro College Fund (UNCF). Ultimately Bethune leveraged relationships with influential persons including President Franklin D. Roosevelt and John D. Rockefeller to garner support for UNCF. The organization sought to "appeal to the national conscience" and raise needed funds for its HBCU partners. Bethune relied on relationships formed during her work with the Roosevelt Administration and her position as president of the National Council of Negro Women to attract donors. The organization did well. In fact, "On its first drive, UNCF organization raised $760,000 (equating to over $8,000,000 in 2015). By November 1944, the fund raised $901,812, almost reaching its goal of $1,500,000." (Robertson, 2015, 37) Again, Bethune was able to shift resources to schools that were in dire need, thereby providing more access in hopes that it would equate to justice. In 2017 the UNCF is still a thriving organization that provides education for underserved students who might not otherwise have received it.

## The Liberatory Consciousness of Bethune

In her chapter "Developing a Liberatory Consciousness," Dr. Barbara J. Love examines the first step toward social justice as one that starts with individuals rising above internalized behaviors. She states:

> To be effective as a liberation worker—that is, one who is committed to changing systems and institutions characterized by oppression to create greater equity and social justice—a crucial step is the development of a liberatory consciousness. A liberatory consciousness enables humans to live their lives in oppressive systems and institutions with awareness and intentionality, rather than one the basis of socialization to which they have been subjected. A liberatory consciousness enables humans to maintain an awareness of the dynamics of oppression characterizing society without giving in to despair and hopelessness about that condition. (quoted in Adams, 2000, 470)

Mary McLeod Bethune was born in 1875 in the rural town of Mayesville, South Carolina. As a child she picked cotton and witnessed Black farmers being treated unjustly as they sought payment for their services. At an early age, something happened to her that she would never forget; one could argue the incident was a turning point and perhaps the moment that her liberatory consciousness was developed. In 1940 at the age of 65, Mrs. Bethune recounted a story of going to her mother's white employer's home and being discouraged from reading.

> I picked up one of the books . . . and one of the girls said to me "You can't read that—put that down. I will show you some pictures over here," and when she said to me "You can't read that—put that down" it just did something to my pride and to my heart that made me feel that some day I would read just as she was reading. I did put it down, and followed her lead and looked at the picture book that she had. But I went away from there determined to learn how to read and that some day I would master for myself just what they were getting and it was that aim that I followed. (Bethune, 1940)

For Bethune, this was the moment when she became aware of her possible limitations, and decided she would not allow them to defeat her. She became committed to changing her position in life; not long after, she became the first in her family to attend school. In the interview she recounted how on her first day of class she thought back to the moment of being told she could not read, stating "I felt that I was on my way to read and it was one of the incentives that fired me in my determination to read" (Bethune, 1940). She not only gained education for herself, but she later used her arithmetic skills in the community to assist farmers in getting fair pay. Growing up in a segregated environment, walking 5 miles to school, Bethune developed a liberatory consciousness that would allow her to rise beyond the oppressive systems set before her. She was intentional not only about gaining education but also using her education to assist others—this became her motivation as an educator and activist. Bethune fought for social justice not because it came easily to her but because she had decided she wasn't going to allow societal norms to dictate her future.

Recent books by historians have continued to keep Bethune's activism as a clubwoman and educator alive. *Mary McLeod Bethune in Washington: Activism and Education in Washington, DC* (2013) and *Mary McLeod Bethune in Florida: Bringing Social Justice to the Sunshine State* (2015) both address how Bethune effectively strategized to shift resources to African Americans to eliminate social inequality. *A Forgotten Sisterhood: Pioneering Black Women Educators and Activists in the Jim Crow South* (2014) identifies how Bethune and her contemporaries used education as a means of fighting discrimination and inequality. In all three texts, Bethune's role as a key factor in the social justice movement is highlighted.

One of the key goals of social justice education is to "enable people to develop the critical analytical tools necessary to understand oppression and their own socialization within oppressive systems and to develop a sense of agency and capacity to interrupt and change oppressive patterns and behaviors in themselves" (Mthethwa-Sommers, 2014, 10).

Essentially, social justice education will empower people to create change. An examination of social justice education would be remiss if it didn't include purveyors of liberatory consciousness, including Bethune. While this article focuses on her involvement in the military, Bethune was a dedicated educator for nearly 40 years. From the inception of her school, she was clear that she would not allow the environment that surrounded her students to stifle their education. Even when KKK members marched around her school, she did not allow herself to be defeated; in fact, her school's enrollment continued to grow thereafter. For one to act as an agent of social justice, historical connections must be made to those like Bethune to identify lessons and teachable strategies. Social justice relies on those who are willing to go beyond the socialization for which they're accustomed to in order to seek equality, be it for themselves or for others. In studying the actions of Bethune and her willingness to ignore the naysayers and the doors shut due to segregation, she can be seen as a clear example of what a liberatory consciousness can lead to.

## Conclusion

In May of 2016 President Barack Obama nominated Admiral Michelle Howard to serve as the head of U.S. Naval Forces in Europe and Africa. In 2014, Howard became the Navy's highest-ranking female officer and the first woman to become a four-star admiral. Her trailblazing path also includes becoming the first Black woman to command a Navy ship in 1999. Currently, Black women are joining the military in record numbers: "Black women now constitute nearly one-third of all women in the U.S. military. At around 30 percent, this number is twice their representation in the civilian population and higher than that of men or women of any other racial or ethnic group" (Melin, 2016, 1). Considering the high rates, one would think it would not have taken the navy over 230 years to promote a Black woman to its top position. Although the navy was founded in 1775, they did not recruit Black men until 1942.

The struggle for equality in the military has been continuous for Black women, and it all started with Bethune's demand for women's inclusion in World War II. She inserted Black women into a conversation in which they had previously been ignored; she rallied women to create their own spaces to carry out patriotic duties as American citizens. The pressure that Bethune put on the WAAC to accept Black women was a demand for social justice through opportunities that would lead to a permanent place for Black women in the military. Although only 39 women were initially allowed in the WAAC, their participation was groundbreaking—today, women such as Admiral Howard stand on the shoulders of Mary McLeod Bethune.

The efforts of NCNW to give credence to Harriet Tubman as a symbol of liberation inserted her name into war efforts by promoting her on a global level. The work of WAND provided resources in a segregated society for Black military men who may not have otherwise received anything. Overall, the organizations that Bethune worked with leveled the distribution of historic opportunities, created equality where there once was none, and raised women into leadership positions that transcended gender. When a seat at the table was not presented to her, Mary McLeod Bethune pulled up her own chair, leading to the inclusion of Black women even today.

## Note

1. This is the same Dovey Roundtree featured in this volume's Chapter 8.

## References

$3,452,000 bonds for *S.S. Tubman*. (1944, Sept. 9). *The Afro American* (p. 23).
Allen, C. G. (1937, July 3). Education of race in south neglected, says Dr. Mary M. Bethune. *The Chicago Defender* (national edition). Retrieved from search.proquest.com/docview/492469944?accountid=8596

Anthony, S. (2016, Oct. 4). Solange's "A Seat at the Table" Is a Bold Masterpiece. Retrieved from www.huffingtonpost.com/entry/solanges-a-seat-at-the-table-is-a-bold-pro-Black-masterpiece_us_57eea4dde4b082aad9bb16f7

Bethune, M. M. (1940). Interview with Mary McLeod Bethune. Florida Memory: State Library and Archives of Florida, Retrieved from www.floridamemory.com/onlineclassroom/marybethune/lessonplans/sets/interview

*Chicago Defender.* (1937, July 10). Special: Mrs. Bethune ends first year with NYA. Retrieved from search.proquest.com/docview/492592732?accountid=8596

*Chicago Defender.* (1944, Aug. 5). *S.S. Tubman* bond drive oversubscribed on coast (national edition, p. 9).

*Chicago Defender.* (1946, June 8). "No fight against fascism in world war II"—Du Bois. Retrieved from search.proquest.com/docview/492774788?accountid=8596

Copeland, D. (2010). *The media's role in defining the nation: The active voice.* New York: Peter Lang.

*Edith Nourse Rogers: Representative, 1925–1960, Republican from Massachusetts.* Retrieved from womenincongress.house.gov/member-profiles/profile.html?intID=209

Hanson, J. (2003). *Mary McLeod Bethune and Black women's political activism.* University of Missouri Press.

Hobby, C. O. C. (1942, Sept. 26). WAACs at work. *Chicago Defender* (national edition). Retrieved from search.proquest.com/docview/492631383?accountid=8596

Johnston, M. (2016, Oct. 3). Review: Solange's "A Seat at the Table" walks softly, speaks radically. Retrieved from www.rollingstone.com/music/albumreviews/review-solanges-a-seat-at-the-table-walks-softly-speaks-radically-w443183

Litoff, J., & Smith, D. (1997). *American women in a world at war.* Wilmington, DE: Scholarly Resources, Inc.

Love, B. (2000). Developing a liberatory consciousness. In M. Adams, W. Blumenfeld, R. Castañeda, H. W. Packman, M. L. Peters, & X. Zúñiga (Eds.), *Readings for diversity and social justice: An anthology on racism, anti-Semitism, sexism, heterosexism, ableism, and classism* (p. 470). New York: Routledge.

Lupton, R. (2005). Social justice and school improvement: Improving the quality of schooling in the poorest neighbourhoods. *British Educational Research Journal, 31*(5), 589–604.

Mary McLeod Bethune selected chair of Women's Army for National Defense advisory board, WAND chapters, and annual conference programs, 1943–1946 Folder 001390-0130234. (1943, Jan. 1). Proquest History Vault. Retrieved from congressional.proquest.com/histvault?q=001390-013-0234

McCabe, K., & Roundtree, D. (2009). *Justice older than the law.* Jackson: University Press of Mississippi.

McCluskey, A., & Smith, E. (1999). *Mary McLeod Bethune: Building a better world.* Bloomington: Indiana University Press.

Melin, J. (2016, Feb.). Desperate choices: Why Black women join the U.S. military at higher rates than men and all other racial and ethnic groups. *New England Journal of Public Policy, 28*(2). Retrieved from scholarworks.umb.edu/nejpp/vol28/iss2/8

Moore, B. L. (1996). *To serve my country, to serve my race: The story of the only African American WACs stationed overseas during World War*. New York: New York University Press.

Mthethwa-Sommers, S. (2014). *Narratives of social justice educators: Standing firm*. New York: Springer International Publishing.

Putney, M. (1992). *When the nation was in need*. Metuchen, NJ: Scarecrow Press.

Robertson, A. N. (2015). *Mary McLeod Bethune in Florida: Bringing social justice to the sunshine state* (p. 37). Charleston, SC: The History Press.

Taylor, R. S. (1943, Nov. 13). Federated clubs. *Chicago Defender* (national edition). Retrieved from search.proquest.com/docview/492706251?accountid=8596

Taylor, R. S. (1945, May 26). Federated clubs. *Chicago Defender* (national edition). Retrieved from search.proquest.com/docview/492697737?accountid=8596

Thompson, J. G. (1942, Jan.). Letter to editor. *Pittsburgh Courier* (p. 5).

Torricelli, R. G., & Carroll, A. (1999). *In our own words: Extraordinary speeches of the American century* (pp. 105–106). New York: Kodansha International.

Wasniewski, M. (2006). *Women in Congress, 1917–2006*. Washington, DC: U.S. G.P.O.

Chapter 8

# The Life of Dovey Johnson Roundtree (1914–2018)

## A Centenarian Lesson in Social Justice and Regenerative Power

KATIE MCCABE AND STEPHANIE Y. EVANS

This chapter offers lessons in social justice by presenting a case study of a groundbreaking activist's memoir. Legendary lawyer, Army veteran, and ordained minister Dovey Johnson Roundtree transformed the terrain of 20th-century America in all the public venues in which she worked over the course of her 50-year career. A member of the first class of Black military women, she fought segregation in a Jim Crow Army. In Washington, DC's white judicial system, she won high-profile criminal defense victories for the city's Black poor. In the male bastion of the African Methodist Episcopal Church, she led the vanguard of women ordained to the ministry. Her fight for justice also included more intimate forms of struggle, in her ministerial counseling role and as a grandmother mentoring a child. Dovey Roundtree's narrative, captured in collaboration with National Magazine Award winner Katie McCabe, exemplifies how justice must be understood in individual, social, and institutional terms. As will be seen in this chapter, she was a witness to major events in Black women's history; she certainly was an active part of making history as well.[1]

Much like the theoretical approaches of Pan-Africanism, feminism, or Marxism, social justice theory is invested in defining the roots of oppression and finding means to combat inequality. Social justice educators are committed to outcomes that improve quality of life for marginalized populations. In the opening chapter of this book, Tania Mitchell examines three mainstream approaches to social justice theory: distributive (equity of material resources), recognition (equity based on perceived difference), and procedural (the process of gaining equity). This delineation unpacks how injustice is defined, perceived, and experienced. McCabe's account of Dovey Roundtree's life illuminates contributions to justice on all levels: Dovey worked for legal justice in terms of equal access to resources (whether military service or transportation), equal access to justice (competent legal representation), and equal opportunity for growth (in her work as a woman minister and through acts of mentoring her grandchild to take advantage of all the world has to offer). The details of Dovey Roundtree's story lay bare the institutional, social, and political inconsistencies at the heart of the inquiry of justice work. Her story also centers on the complexity involved in understanding identity within discussions of lifespan in justice work and how the societal struggle for peace is deeply personal and rooted in the quest for inner tranquility.[2]

In this volume's preface, Barbara Love suggests guidelines for developing liberatory consciousness; for her, consciousness requires awareness and action based on historical understanding of oppression. Dovey Roundtree's narrative provides concrete examples of what conscious social justice work looks like, how it operates, and both tangible (legislative changes and judicial victories for underserved populations) and intangible (mentoring of grandson and ministerial services) measures of these efforts.

As cited in the introduction to this book, progressive approaches to education require interrogation of identities of facilitators, students, and curriculum. Also as noted in the introduction, Black women's memoirs are narratives of healing pain caused by violence in order to fashion a new vision of one's life. Consequently, Black women's memoirs constitute an act of not only personal, but social defiance, encouraging progressive action toward liberation. African American intellectual history is steeped in the spirituality and social consciousness that undergirds Black women's pursuit of rights and justice. Thus, Martha Jones and a collective of scholars who penned an introduction for the book *Toward an Intellectual History of Black Women* are correct to identify "race, gender, and justice" as the main thrusts of Black women's public intellectual history. Specifically, Black women authors write in ways that can teach educators how to broaden pathways to justice, wellness, and peace—individual as well as collective.

Black women have written life stories to teach critical lessons, particularly lessons pertaining to rights and justice. Through life narratives, Black women have encouraged readers to look back for wisdom, look inward for strength, and look forward for courage. Recognizing memoirs as a vital part of Black women's intellectual history allows readers to learn from historic intersectional experiences for several purposes outlined in Anna Julia Cooper's work on social regeneration: to recreate effective practices that lead to an inclusive society (retrospection); to define identity in ways that promote health and healing (introspection); and to engender a politics of resistance and activism to contribute to a more just society (prospection).

Autobiography and memoir sit at the crossroads of literature and history. There are rich traditions of authors who pen their stories and a growing number of critics and analysts who find meaning in those stories. Numerous Black women scholars have studied memoir as a form. Groundbreaking scholars in this field include Patricia Bell Scott and Juanita Johnson-Bailey, who co-edited *Flat Footed Truths: Telling Black Women's Lives* in 1998. Bell Scott also recently published *The Firebrand and the First Lady: Portrait of a Friendship: Pauli Murray, Eleanor Roosevelt, and the Struggle for Social Justice* (2016). The latter text explores letters between Pauli Murray and Eleanor Roosevelt and establishes Scott's expertise in the form of epistle and on the subject of social justice. Further, Johnson-Bailey is a pioneer scholar of the genre, having published a dissertation in 1994 on Black women's educational narratives. Tellingly, she identifies herself as a "narrativist."[3]

Other highly visible scholarship on memoir includes Joanne Braxton (1989), bell hooks (1998), Nellie McKay (1998), Margo Perkins (2000), Rosetta Haynes (2011), Layli Maparyan (2012), and Angela Ards (2015). Collectively, these works cover a broad scope of analysis but can be interpreted as clearly defining three ways in which memoirs speak to audiences: the past (bell hooks's memory), present (Braxton's self-creation; Maparyan's vitality), and future (McKay's resistance; Perkins and Ards's activism). This analysis engages the concept of Sankofa, a symbol in the Adinkra, West African system of meaning, represented by a bird whose feet point forward to move in positive directions while also looking backward to retain knowledge and wisdom of the past. This analysis also draws upon concepts of meditation (wellness) and improvisation (making a way out of no way). These ideas are grounded in Black women's narratives but are also influenced by arcs of critical scholarship.[4]

Though this chapter focuses primarily on memory and activism, relevant insight for healing is also present: "self-creation"—the look inside—is a temporal bridge between the past and future. Memoirs are mentors. In her essay "Womanhood: The Vital Element of Regeneration and Progress of the Race," Anna Julia Cooper wrote about women's central role in race progress and social regeneration:

> It is well enough to pause a moment for retrospection, introspection, and prospection. We look back . . . that we may learn wisdom from experience. We look within that we may gather together once more our forces, and . . . address ourselves to the tasks before us. We look forward with hope and trust. . . .[5]

Black women have long insisted, as the centenarian sister authors Sadie and Bessie Delany wrote, on "having our say." To date, the Africana Memoirs database houses more than 500 autobiographies by Black women from around the world. This online library includes widely diverse perspectives, ranging from Harriet Jacobs, Fannie Jackson Coppin, and Ida B. Wells to Maya Angelou, Anita Hill, and Ellen Johnson-Sirleaf. Dovey Roundtree's work is part of a growing library of Black women's narratives that has endured for several generations and continues to have volumes added regularly. While we focus on SJE as an educational activity, these narratives are filled with life lessons that reflect Black women's values and illuminate paths for future justice work in areas such as labor, medical fields, nonprofit, and business arenas.

Theorists like hooks, Braxton, and Perkins discussed narrative themes that outline a tri-part framework that defies linear representation of time. These concepts of writing through a dynamic concept of time (for the explicit purpose of addressing personal and social problems) can also advance our understanding of the relationship between authors and audience. Leading scholars of Black women's intellectual history, such as Martha Jones, identify a tradition of writing about "race, gender, and justice." So, how do Black women define social justice in their lives, work, and writing? A close look at narratives reveals a complex level of contributions best understood by carefully examining how Black women theorists situate race and gender within sociopolitical experience. To some extent, we are familiar with narratives that discuss human rights abuses of lynching, segregation, suffrage, and reproductive justice, but a more comprehensive study is necessary to fully examine the range of issues authors address in their reflections. Black women's centenarian narratives are irreplaceable primary sources for this endeavor.

Dovey Roundtree offers an expanded view and a deeper understanding of the journey to justice. Katie McCabe's account is a service to our understanding of the power of education and the necessity of universal participation in the fight for justice. Just as McCabe's award-winning story of cardiac pioneer Vivien Thomas led to a heightened public awareness of Black contributions to the medical field in print and in film, her dedication to assisting Roundtree with a full, published account of her life story heightens a national awareness of education, law, ministry, and the imperative to continue fighting for the rights of the next generation.

※

> It is exhausting, scary and difficult, in these troubled times, to incline students' heads toward social justice work. They need to know, always, that someone has come before, that they're not out

there alone, that it is possible to do this work and survive. *Justice Older than the Law* sustains me as a teacher and scholar and lifts my students to that higher ethical ground that Dovey Johnson Roundtree occupied. (Sharon P. Holland, Professor, Department of American Studies, University of North Carolina, Chapel Hill NC)

The African American women in my doctoral seminar in public administration saw the entire history of their people and their communities wrapped up in *Justice Older than the Law*. The book became a forum for them to challenge the ways in which American constitutional principles have failed to protect people of color. (Stephanie P. Newbold, Associate Professor, School of Public Affairs and Administration, Rutgers University, Newark NJ)

For Dovey Roundtree, the command to "be on your guard; stand firm in the faith; be courageous; be strong. Do everything in love" (1 Cor. 16:13–14) was the natural way that a social engineer conducted business as a lawyer and as a minister. For our current students, Dovey Roundtree's life clearly shows that a social engineer can promote and advocate for social justice in different capacities . . . to create a system and a profession that is all-inclusive and allows all to thrive. (Okianer Christian Dark, Professor and former Associate Dean, Howard University School of Law, Washington DC)

At the time of her death in 2018, one hundred and four years have passed since the birth of Dovey Johnson Roundtree in 1914 into a violent and segregated world, and 67 years since she first came before the bar of justice in Washington, DC, to battle for the rights of the poor and voiceless in a city where Black lawyers had to leave the courthouses to use the bathroom. She was driven, then, by what the Rev. Martin Luther King, Jr., called "the fierce urgency of now."

King's "now" has never been more urgent than it is today. At the time of this writing, Dovey Johnson Roundtree's beloved home town of Charlotte, North Carolina, is riven with anger, pain, and race hatred. On September 20, 2016, a Black man named Keith Lamont Scott was shot to death by a policeman, in the latest fatality in a wrenching series of Black deaths at the hands of law enforcement officers across America. Following Scott's death, the streets of downtown Charlotte, jammed with National Guardsmen and angry citizens demanding justice, plunged into in turmoil.

The work of social justice requires all the strength and courage we can summon, and in this fight, as Professors Sharon Holland, Stephanie Newbold, and Okianer Christian Dark have so eloquently pointed out, we need role models to sustain us. Katie McCabe recognized in Dovey Johnson Roundtree such a model when she first began to work with her 23 years ago on the book the two women co-authored, *Justice Older than the Law: The Life of Dovey Johnson Roundtree* (2009). "This, I knew almost immediately, was a woman of uncommon courage and moral fortitude, a woman whose fiercest desire was to speak to the next generation about the kind of justice she had sought all her life, a justice, she liked to say, that was 'older by far than the law,'" McCabe says. "I believed that if I could channel her voice, hundreds of thousands of others would be inspired by her example. I have seen both men and women moved to tears by her story, and more importantly, to action. May the fullness of her life, as set forth in *Justice Older than the Law*, continue to find its way into classrooms across America so that future warriors for justice may be raised up by her story and impelled to implement its lessons."

Following, in the words of Katie McCabe, is Dovey Roundtree's story.

Her life, she would say in later years, began with fear—the kind of terror known to very young children who are confronted either with terrible loss or extreme physical danger. The child Dovey Mary Magdalene Johnson knew both. There was, to begin with, the death of her father, felled in the autumn of 1919 by the second wave of the influenza epidemic brought home by the soldiers returning from World War I. She was 5 years old, and the emptiness inside her parents' house swallowed her up for days, until she and her mother and three sisters were taken in hand by Dovey's maternal grandmother, Rachel Bryant Graham, and whisked to the sanctuary of her home. In the tiny African Methodist Episcopal Zion parsonage where "Grandma Rachel" lived with her husband, the Reverend Clyde L. Graham, she set about healing the broken family.

Darkness of another sort shadowed Dovey's girlhood in Charlotte, North Carolina. From the time she could think, an unease about all things associated with white people insinuated itself into her consciousness. Huddled beneath the great wooden quilting frame where her grandmother and the neighbor ladies gathered to sew and gossip, Dovey heard whispers of the Klan and the horrors it perpetrated upon men in the neighborhood, men whose names she knew. On the terrible night when there came a thundering of hooves through the hot summer darkness and her grandmother shuttered up the house and doused the kerosene lamp and pushed the rest of the family under the kitchen table, Dovey's amorphous daytime fear of white people hardened into a knot of terror.

But the child who knew great sorrow and great fear also saw fierce and overpowering courage in the person of her grandmother, a five-foot-tall whirling dervish of a woman who beat back grief, poverty, danger, and the ugliness of racism with the entire force of her being. As a girl of 12 or 13, Grandma Rachel had survived an assault by a white overseer who had broken her feet when she rejected his sexual advances, and though she limped for the rest of her days, she moved determinedly through life. She had risen up, fighting, after the death of her young husband at the hands of the Klan, and with the AME Zion preacher who became Dovey's grandfather, she created a home that Dovey was forever to remember as a bastion against Jim Crow and a well of religious faith. A woman with only a third-grade education, Rachel Bryant Graham imbued her granddaughters with ambition and a deep sense of their own worth. The longest civil rights march she ever made, Dovey would later recall, was the mile she walked to downtown Charlotte when her grandmother yanked her off a segregated trolley car rather than permit her to endure the racial epithet the driver had flung at her. "Get that pickaninny out of here," he had nearly spat at Grandma when 6-year-old Dovey jumped on board and into the front seat. In one swift motion, Grandma Rachel had pulled the cord, taken Dovey by the hand, and marched with her in silence all the way to town and back, even as trolley after trolley passed them by and Grandma's limp grew worse and worse. What she told the family that night would stay with Dovey forever: "My chillun," she said, "are as good as anybody."

Grandma Rachel did more than preach self-reliance and self-worth. She offered her granddaughters a living example of Black achievement in the person of the internationally renowned woman who became her friend through the colored women's club movement: the great educator Mary McLeod Bethune. Bethune's rise from poverty to the status of presidential adviser and college president so inspired Dovey that she heeded the suggestion of her eighth-grade teacher that she apply to the elite Spelman College during the Great Depression. She worked three jobs to pay her tuition, and when she graduated, it was Bethune who placed her in the vortex of world events by selecting her in May 1942 for the first class of Black women in the newly formed Women's Army Auxiliary Corps.

In the crucible of a Jim Crow Army, the 28-year-old Dovey Johnson began forging her identity as an activist. Initially challenging the segregated mess halls as a lone protester, and then involving Bethune in the fight, she was quickly branded a "walking NAACP" and assigned to recruiting duty in the Deep South by white superiors who hoped to neutralize her influence over her Black comrades on the base. Instead, they unwittingly empowered her. Traveling alone and without Army protection across the South on buses and trains in 1942 and 1943, often at risk of her life, Dovey aggressively recruited African American women with the vision of postwar equality she had absorbed from Mary McLeod Bethune.

Scores of African American women rose to her challenge, enlisting in such numbers that the Army had difficulty placing them, given the reluctance of white male officers to train Black recruits. But the record stood, and in making it, Captain Dovey Johnson changed the racial face of the military before it was legally desegregated in 1948 by Presidential order.

She herself was transformed in the military, evolving into a public advocate for equality. When her Fort Des Moines commandant proposed a segregated platoon late in 1944 after having loosened the racial restrictions on the base, she took him on in a public meeting. Removing her Captain's bars to signal willingness to resign her commission if the Army persisted in its plan, she risked court martial and dishonorable discharge. But as a result of her speech about the Four Freedoms for which American troops were fighting, and the wrongness of segregation, the commandant rescinded the order for the all-Black platoon. In that moment, Dovey would later say, she discovered the lawyer in herself.

It required only the eloquence of Constitutional lawyer and activist Pauli Murray to set Dovey on the path toward law school. Her pursuit of civil rights through the law became a mandate so all-consuming that everything else gave way, including her marriage to her college sweetheart William Roundtree, whom she had wed after the war in the hope that he would join her at Howard Law School and take up the civil rights cause. But it was not to be; her cause was not his, and they quickly divorced. It was the law, she often said, that became her mistress.

When Dovey arrived at Howard Law School in the fall of 1947, the place pulsated with the brilliance of the legal minds leading the charge against "separate but equal" that would culminate in the groundbreaking 1954 Supreme Court ruling, *Brown v. Board of Education*. Thurgood Marshall, George E. C. Hayes, and James Madison Nabrit, Jr., shaped Dovey and her classmates in the mold of the great attorney who had recruited them for the fight, the legendary Charles Hamilton Houston. "A lawyer's either a social engineer or he's a parasite on society," Houston famously taught his protégés. Dovey took that to heart as she witnessed the assault on *Plessy v. Ferguson* from her seat in the law school's moot courtroom, where the NAACP Legal Defense Fund attorneys rehearsed their Supreme Court appearances for the law students and faculty.

Yet none of the great cases of her law school years hardened her resolve quite so sharply as her first case before the bar of the District of Columbia, filed on behalf of her grandmother and her mother, who had been wronged in a way she could not tolerate in their northward journey to one of the great celebrations of her life—her law school graduation.

They had held first-class tickets on the Southern Railroad for their trip from Charlotte to Washington—tickets Dovey herself had purchased at Union Station and mailed to them. When they had boarded in Charlotte, however, the conductor herded them out of the half-empty white car into the overcrowded Jim Crow coach, where they rode, standing, until at last her grandmother collapsed on the closed seat of the toilet a few miles outside Washington. The sight of her Grandma Rachel—then seventy-five years old—limping toward her on the platform at Union Station, and of her mother, flailing her arms and weeping, propelled Dovey head first into the DC courts even before she had taken the bar exam.

She prevailed upon her classmate and future law partner Julius Winfield Robertson to file the complaint in *Rachel Bryant Graham and Lela Bryant Johnson v. The Southern Railroad* in the U.S. District Court for the District of Columbia. Julius Robertson sued the Southern Railroad for breach of contract, and the moment Dovey was sworn in as a member of the bar, she entered her appearance in the case. Those two first-class tickets, she and Julius Robertson argued, constituted contracts—promises, in effect—of first-class passage.

She emerged from the fray shaken and enraged, not because she had lost, but because the pittance she won was so humiliating. She vowed that the next time she aimed at the face of Jim Crow in a court of law, she would not miss. From that moment in 1951, brand new to the bar and without a paying client to her name, Dovey Roundtree focused on the larger civil rights battlefield where, she believed, she might finally win justice for her people.

Washington, DC, in the early 1950s was no easy place to win justice for anyone if you were a Black attorney. A Black lawyer in those days had to leave the courthouse to use the bathroom or eat a meal. Mere survival was so difficult that Dovey pieced out her income with a full-time day job as an attorney-adviser in the Department of Labor, manning the desk at "Robertson and Roundtree" at night, while Julius Robertson, desperate to move his wife and growing family out of public housing, worked nights at the post office and took the day shift at the law firm.

And then, on a sweltering September afternoon in 1952, a client darkened their door with a case that changed civil rights history. The matter of *Sarah Keys v. Carolina Coach Company*, arising from the Jim Crow complaint of an Army private named Sarah Louise Keys, would over time reverberate across all 48 states and transform bus travel for Black passengers. That such a small case would wind its way into the 1961 Freedom Riders' struggle and empower Attorney General Robert Kennedy to mandate a permanent end to interstate bus segregation was an outcome neither Dovey Roundtree nor Julius Robertson could possibly have imagined.

The quiet, shy Sarah Keys, initially in the shadow of her father when she met with Dovey and Julius in 1952, was an improbable history maker. Her voice barely rose above a whisper as she described her midnight eviction from a bus in Roanoke Rapids, North Carolina, while she was traveling home on her first furlough. But her account of being forced to yield her seat to a white Marine spoke loudly to Dovey, who recalled her own experience as a WAC 8 years earlier, when she had been thrown off a Miami bus and commanded to do just what Sarah had done. She had felt compelled, then, to accede to the demand of the Miami driver in order to avoid being jailed or court martialed by the Army.

But this was 1952. In theory, she and Sarah Keys occupied different worlds. The Supreme Court had declared state Jim Crow laws inoperable on interstate buses in the 1946 case of *Morgan v. Virginia,* but the *Morgan* ruling had been rendered impotent by the crafty maneuvers of the Southern bus lines, who had put their own Jim Crow regulations in place within weeks of the decision's announcement. Dovey and Julius believed the time had come to challenge the carriers. When they filed suit in the U.S. District Court for the District of Columbia on November 19, 1952, on behalf of Sarah Keys, Thurgood Marshall and his NAACP Legal Defense Fund team were preparing to go before the Supreme Court of the United States to present oral arguments in the five cases subsumed under *Brown v. Board of Education.*

Pinning their hopes on a favorable ruling in *Brown,* Dovey and Julius pressed onward after the U.S. District Court dismissed the *Keys* complaint on jurisdictional grounds in February 1953, and they took the case before the notoriously segregationist Interstate Commerce Commission. What they asked, in their historic complaint, was that the ICC reevaluate its traditional interpretation of four key words in the Interstate Commerce Act, the words that forbade "undue and unreasonable prejudice" against bus and train travelers crossing state lines. Jim Crow seating, they argued, constituted such prejudice.

But in a September 30, 1954, decision, ICC Commissioner Isadore Freidson stated that *Brown's* ruling on public education, handed down 4 months earlier, had no bearing on the conduct of private business, such as that carried out by bus carriers. Dovey and Julius immediately filed exceptions to Freidson's ruling, in which they invoked both the commerce clause and the Supreme Court's reasoning in *Brown.* This time around, the full 11-man Commission reviewed the case, and as a group, they found *Brown* persuasive and highly relevant. One year after Dovey and Julius filed their exceptions, the ICC Commission saw fit, for the first time in its history, to condemn the doctrine of "separate but equal" in interstate bus transportation, and, in a companion case filed by the NAACP, to do the same for train travel. In a ruling made public 8 days before Rosa Parks took her historic stand in Montgomery, Alabama, the ICC explicitly repudiated the "separate but equal" doctrine in the field of interstate bus travel. The ruling had no bearing on travel *within* the segregated states; that would have to wait for Rosa Parks's defiance of the municipal laws of the city of Montgomery and the national protest movement her actions precipitated. But the *Keys* case, along with the NAACP's railway case decided the same day, affected every bus and train moving across state lines, and every station at which they stopped. Hailed by *New York Post* columnist Max Lerner as a "symbol of a movement that cannot be held back," the *Keys* ruling, and its companion train case, *NAACP v. St. Louis-San Francisco Railway Company*, made headlines across the country.

And yet, for all of that, 6 years would pass before the country felt the force of *Sarah Keys v. Carolina Coach Company*. From the time of the ruling in 1955 to the Freedom Riders' campaign in 1961, *Keys* remained dormant, its effect nullified by the lone dissenter in the case, who saw to it that the bus segregation banned by his 10 ICC brethren continued unabated. It was not until the Civil Rights Movement exploded across the South in the wake of Rosa Parks's historic action that the country was ready to listen to what the *Keys* ruling had said. In 1961, the world looked on in horror at the violence perpetrated upon the Freedom Riders in their campaign to implement the Supreme Court's 1960 *Boynton v. Virginia* ruling banning segregation in bus terminal restaurants—the one travel-related arena that hadn't been addressed in *Keys*. On May 29, 1961, Attorney General Robert Kennedy confronted the ICC in a petition citing *Keys*, and he pressed the Commission to deliver on it. Within 6 weeks, the ICC posted signs across the South mandating integrated seating in every vehicle crossing state lines, and in the stations, waiting rooms, and restaurants that serviced them. The stubborn fact of segregation in interstate travel had come to an end. The equality Dovey had sought so long ago for her mother and grandmother became, at last, the law of the land.

~

In the 6 years that separated *Keys* from the day in September 1961 when the ICC finally acted in accordance with its own 1955 order, Dovey Roundtree walked a path far removed from the protests across the South. She became a different sort of lawyer, one who labored not on the mountaintop of closely studied statutory victories, but down in the trenches where, she told people, "the stuff of life lay." The clients who found their way to her door were more often than not people in extraordinary pain—mothers fighting for their children, fathers fighting for their jobs, teenagers who had been preyed upon by the adults charged with their care, husbands and wives in bitter custody battles, victims of violent crimes, and perpetrators as well. Many came from her church community, and others were drawn to the firm because of Julius Robertson's influence as the publisher of a civil rights newsletter, *Stride*. The two of them took every matter that came their way, refusing to capitulate to the tradition among their Black comrades of referring clients to white lawyers. In 1956, they set a precedent by winning the maximum damage award allowed by the Federal Tort Claims Act at that time in a case involving a woman injured by an estranged spouse who had escaped from St. Elizabeth's Hospital. The win captured citywide attention, drawing Black lawyers to the offices of Robertson and Roundtree for advice on how to try personal injury and negligence cases. Clients, too, began seeking out Dovey and Julius in such numbers that they worked nearly around the clock to keep up, pressing themselves to the edge of endurance.

The pace of the practice broke Dovey's health. A lifelong diabetic, she suffered illness so grave in 1960 that she nearly died. Forced by the experience to a point of spiritual reckoning, she determined to pursue the ministry, a vocation to which she had been drawn from earliest childhood by the example of her grandfather. Though the African Methodist Episcopal Church barred women from the ministry, Dovey elected to embark on religious studies at the Howard University School of Divinity in order to prepare herself for ordination at such time that the AME bishops broke with their longstanding all-male tradition. As she regained her health, resumed her law practice, and moved forward with her evening courses, Julius Robertson pushed himself to the breaking point. On November 3, 1961, at the age of forty-five, he collapsed in the courtroom of a heart attack and died.

His death forced Dovey to yet another reckoning. Acutely aware during Julius Robertson's lifetime of the importance of having a male law partner, Dovey found the thought of practicing alone, as a Black woman, a daunting prospect. Her historic ordination in the vanguard of AME women ministers on November 30, 1961, just 3 and a half weeks after Julius Robertson's death, opened up the possibility of the ministry as a full-time career. But her passion for the law prevailed, and rather than abandon her practice, she chose to merge it with her ministry.

The challenges she faced in the wake of her partner's death were myriad—attracting clients, forging a dual role as minister and lawyer, purchasing a new office building, making a name for herself as a sole practitioner, and breaking down yet another racial barrier as the first Black member of the Women's Bar Association of the District of Columbia. Despite protests and threats of resignation by a number of WBADC's board members when she was nominated by her colleague and friend Joyce Hens Green (later a U.S. District Court Judge), she became the first African American member of that organization in 1962.

Through it all, she built a reputation as a one-woman legal aid society. It was a term no one used in those days, but in the minds of the city's Black poor, and in all of Washington's Black churches, Dovey Roundtree was known as the lawyer to seek in desperate times. And so it happened that when a Black day laborer named Ray Crump, Jr., was arrested and indicted without a preliminary hearing for the murder of Georgetown socialite Mary Pinchot Meyer in October 1964, his mother found her way to Dovey, pleading for help for the son she believed was innocent.

Dovey knew nothing of the background of the beautiful young divorcee who had been gunned down in broad daylight on the usually peaceful banks of the C & O Canal. It would be years before anyone learned of Mary Meyer's affair with President Kennedy, of her unprecedented Oval Office access, and of the diary she kept of the affair. The newspapers omitted all mention of her ex-husband's high position in the CIA, identifying him only as an author and lecturer. The CIA's longstanding paranoia about the outspoken Mary Meyer, their frantic search for her diary on the night of the murder, and their phone call to her brother-in-law Ben Bradlee hours before police had identified her body—these remained well-kept secrets for decades.

All Dovey knew in the autumn of 1964 was that she had no choice but to take the case of Ray Crump. The childlike, bewildered, incommunicative little man who sat before her in the DC jail struck her as entirely incapable of committing a murder as stealthy and meticulous as Mary Pinchot Meyer's. The gunman who had shot Meyer had no other goal but murder; there was no evidence of attempted robbery or rape. She had been shot at point blank range, once in the temple, once below the shoulder blade. And the person who had fired those shots had either fled with the murder weapon—a .38 caliber Smith and Wesson pistol, according to ballistics tests—or hidden it so well that the police had been unable to find it, despite weeks of searching the canal, the woods, and the Potomac River with divers and minesweepers.

Certain as Dovey was of Crump's innocence, she knew she faced an uphill battle. The government had woven a web of circumstantial evidence around him, based on the statements of two witnesses who had given similar descriptions of the clothing worn by the Black male at the crime scene, and the one who had been spotted trailing Mary Meyer. On the other hand, the prosecution had yet to produce a weapon, or any trace of evidence that Ray Crump had fired a gun that day. Nor was there any physical evidence linking Crump to the victim, or her to him.

Dovey pushed forward to trial, ignoring the warnings of her legal colleagues that she stood no chance. She pushed past the fear she felt at the anonymous late-night phone calls she began receiving after each of her daytime visits to the crime scene. Not even the death of her beloved Grandma Rachel, coming 5 days after she had entered her appearance for Crump, deterred her. For 8 months, from the moment she agreed to take the case for a fee of one dollar on October 28, 1964, until she entered the courtroom on July 20, 1965, she moved single-mindedly toward her goal: to win acquittal for a man she believed had been at the wrong place at the wrong time.

The white reporters, judges, and law students who packed the U.S. District Court for the District of Columbia in July 1965 to watch Dovey try the matter of the *United States v. Ray Crump* expected her to fail. But what those spectators remember today and still talk about when famous DC murders are revisited is not Dovey Roundtree's failure in the Crump case, but her breathtaking success. Her primary weapon was a police document, overlooked by the prosecution, that recorded the description of the suspect that the principal witness had given police. At 5 feet 3 inches and 130 pounds, Crump was 5 inches shorter and 50 pounds lighter than the man the witness had seen standing over the body. On this she built her case for the "little, little man" who became her lone exhibit, her small, eloquent answer to the tidal wave unleashed by the prosecution. During the 8 days of trial, she earned legendary status as the beautiful woman attorney who dared to try the most sensational murder case of the decade dressed in a pink and white suit, who made a mockery of the state's evidence, eviscerated their witnesses, and argued in soft Carolina accents and the ringing tones of a minister for the simplest of all principles: the sacredness of a man's good name. In so doing she shattered the circumstantial case erected against her client and cracked the iron wall of prejudice that had shut out Blacks from justice in the courtrooms of Washington since the Civil War.

When Dovey Roundtree won acquittal for Ray Crump in the murder of Mary Pinchot Meyer on July 30, 1965, she won more than a single victory, more even than freedom for her client. She became, in the wake of *U.S. v. Ray Crump*, one of the city's most sought-after criminal defense attorneys, appointed by judges to some of the toughest murder cases in the District of Columbia, including the notorious 1977 Hanafi Muslim case in which she won acquittal for John Griffin. She also opened doors to attorneys of color, both men and women, who followed her into the courtroom. From the time of her victory in the Crump case until her 1996 retirement, Dovey Roundtree fought battle after battle for "the little man." In 2000, she received the American Bar Association's Margaret Brent Women Lawyers of Achievement Award, and in 2011, the Women's Bar Association of the District of Columbia honored her with its Janet B. Reno Torchbearer Award.

In *Justice Older than the Law*, Dovey Roundtree speaks urgently of the final crusade in her lifelong war for justice:

> I have battled in my time for so many kinds of justice, fought for integration in the Army, pressed for racial fairness before the ICC, argued for the rights of hundreds upon hundreds of men and women in courts of law, but no battle of my half century at the bar has been so urgent as the one for the next generation. Age has taken my strength, and it has robbed me of my eyesight, but I have yet a voice, and I raise it this day, at this hour, for our children. If every matter before every court in American were foreclosed this moment as a litigable issue, there would yet remain the cause of our children. They are the case at bar. Theirs is the case I plead now.

To bring Dovey Roundtree's story into the classrooms of America is to take up her charge, to pass on to the next generation her consuming commitment to building a just and equitable society. The urgency of our racially troubled times demands no less.

༄

## Human Rights and Dovey Roundtree's Devotion to Freedom

> Whatever their strategies of self-construction, active resistance to oppression of all kinds has been at the center of the history of Black women's lives in this country from slavery to the present time. These narratives are as politically significant as more overt modes of protest. (Nellie Y. McKay, "The Narrative Self: Race, Politics, and Culture in Black American Women's Autobiography," 1998)

Both Dovey Roundtree's first-person narrative *Justice Older than the Law* and McCabe's insightful account show that Black women's life stories hold vital healing histories. When Frederick Douglass wrote about Harriet Tubman in an endorsement of her 1868 memoir, he lauded her "devotion to freedom" that was expressed largely "in a private way" under "a midnight sky and silent stars" (Tubman, 1868). Like Tubman, Roundtree and a host of other freedom fighters lived lives of fighting for their own freedom while advocating for human rights and social justice for others. Dovey Roundtree's struggle for social and political equality was intertwined with her own struggle for personal peace. Though she lived to be a centenarian—and therefore a model of sustainable struggle—she also recorded how challenging it was to find a healthy balance in her work. In sum, Roundtree's love for humanity included her humble quest for personal and spiritual peace, as well as political peace and legal justice.

Peace studies founder Johan Galtung notes three levels of violence: personal, social, and institutional. Dovey Roundtree's life narrative demonstrates her efforts on behalf of human rights and her pursuit of social justice, which, like the efforts of a multitude of other Black women, operates as an antidote to violence. Roundtree's activism, to use a word popularized by Angela Davis, was anti-violence. Roundtree's work for peace encompassed the pursuit of personal, social, and institutional justice. On a personal level, Roundtree's commitment to self-improvement can be seen in her struggle with health issues that included diabetes, cardiac disease, and exhaustion. Her contributions to social peace are reflected in her decision to pursue a life of ministry and bring a healing spirit to the communities in which she lived and worked. Clearly, her work for institutional peace in the form of courtroom battles for desegregation and her representation of underserved minorities in all-white judicial systems made an impact on the lives of individuals, but they also set a precedent for structural justice. Roundtree's devotion to freedom reflects the imperative quality of self-love necessary for Black women to recognize their own worth as human beings while also challenging social and political structures that dehumanize others. Building on the legacy of women like Pauli Murray, who also represented a blending of creative, legal, and spiritual identities, Roundtree's life is a primer in fundamental commitments to liberty and justice for all.

Memoirs and life stories like Roundtree's offer educators and scholar-activists instruction in what Dr. Cooper calls "regeneration": retrospection, introspection, and prospection. Several women's narratives offer context for Roundtree's reflective look at her journey. For example, Layli Maparyan looks inside to identify "vital health" in *The Womanist Idea*, Toi Derricotte creates her racial identity in *The Black Notebooks: An Interior Journey*, and Jan Willis looks inside to imagine her multifaceted spirituality in *Dreaming Me: Black, Baptist, and Buddhist*. Additionally, Lani Guinier uses her own struggle to shine the light on "zero sum" politics and advocate for a more equitable future in *Lift Every Voice: Turning a Civil Rights Setback into a New Vision of Social Justice*. Dovey Roundtree's work encompasses each of these areas, offering critical insight into how Black women operate within oppressive settings and transform themselves even as they transform society.

Toni Morrison seems to agree that one main purpose of human existence is to pass on knowledge—but she emphasizes that knowledge is not merely information, but wisdom that is information congealed through values. In her essay, "How Can Values Be Taught in the University?" Morrison challenges the myth of objectivity in higher education. She argues that, essentially, all education is values-based education. She outlines four steps in the process of education: to examine, evaluate, posit, and reinforce. As educators inside and outside of the university, we research Black women's intellectual history through memoirs in order to teach values of inner peace (health and wellness) and outer peace (human rights and empowerment).

The UN Universal Declaration of Human Rights (UN UDHR) indicates six levels of guarantees, ranging from Divine rights of each individual to rights concerned with participation in a civil and democratic society. Within this range of rights of self and other exist familial, social, and political safeguards. Essentially, rights are defined as relationships to God and nature, to one's self, community, nation, and to the world.

Given this framework, Black women's writing becomes more easily recognizable as a rich tapestry of epistles about basic guarantees needed for each human being to thrive and live a full life. The 30 articles that comprise the UN UDHR are prefaced by a set of resolutions that state the moral and political imperative to agree on basic needs of each human. When placed in this structure, it becomes clear that Black women writers like Dovey Roundtree have addressed human rights in all forms.

The UN UDHR puts forth 30 Articles that clarify dimensions of human rights; these rights—and how diverse populations define and pursue them—are essential for all who seek to more clearly study and advocate for social regeneration. Civil rights narratives have been explored by several scholars, particularly Vicki Crawford, V. P. Franklin, and Bettye Collier-Thomas. Human rights and social justice narratives have much to offer future generations who want to more clearly define what it means to have, as educator Dr. Cooper asserted, "this right to grow."[6]

Roundtree's life story, channeled and documented by McCabe, offers educational resources that can prove useful to contemporary teachers and professors. For example, *Justice Older than the Law* should be required reading in constitutional law classes as well as social work and pastoral professional courses. Yet, its instructive value is not confined to the classroom. Black women's wellness programs can benefit greatly by narratives like Roundtree's because they demonstrate the challenges and opportunities we have as Black women to pursue justice and to do so in a way that does not require our martyrdom. Freedom fighters are certainly, in the words of Fannie Lou Hamer, "sick and tired of being sick and tired." Narratives like Roundtree's (along with works by other nonagenarians and centenarians like Harriet Tubman, Anna Julia Cooper, the Delany Sisters, and chef Leah Chase) present inspiring examples of how Black women can fight for justice in a way that feeds our spirits. In the final analysis, Dovey Roundtree's life story reveals a paradigm that shows it is possible to have both social justice and inner peace. Regenerative power means tapping into an inner vitality that derives from and contributes to a collective vitality. Black women centenarian life stories offer lessons in sustainable struggle for social justice. This certainly is a lesson needed as the struggle continues. Dovey Johnson Roundtree transitioned on May 21, 2018, at the age of 104. Her life was profiled in a prominent *New York Times* obituary that attested to her contributions to breaking barriers—legal and otherwise.

## Notes

1. The material in this chapter is drawn from the book Katie McCabe co-authored with Dovey Johnson Roundtree, *Justice Older than the Law: The Life of Dovey Johnson Roundtree*, which was based primarily on personal interviews McCabe conducted with Dovey Roundtree from 1995 to 2004 in Washington, DC, Spotsylvania, VA, and Charlotte, NC, and on Roundtree's papers, housed in the National Archives for Black Women's History of the Mary McLeod Bethune Council House National Historic Site, located at the Museum Resource Center in Landover, Maryland. Context on the history of African American women in the Women's Army Corps is provided by Martha S. Putney's *When the Nation Was in Need: Blacks in the Women's Army Corps during World War II* (1992).

The case file on Dovey Roundtree's groundbreaking bus desegregation case, *Keys v. Carolina Coach Company* (64 MCC 769 [1955]) was destroyed by the National Archives and Records Administration, along with all other Interstate Commerce Commission motor carrier files. A portion of the file was preserved in the records of the Department of Justice Anti-Trust Division, DOJ Case Number 144-54-56. A copy of Attorney General Robert F. Kennedy's petition citing the *Keys* case (Before the Interstate Commerce Commission, Petition for Rule Making Filed by Attorney General on Behalf of the United States) is contained in ICC Docket No. MC-C 3358, May 29, 1961. For historical context on the legal history of Jim Crow in public transportation, Catherine A. Barnes's *Journey from Jim Crow: The Desegregation of Southern Transit* (1983) is invaluable.

The most comprehensive treatment of *Brown v. Board of Education* is Richard Kluger's two-volume work, *Simple Justice: The History of Brown v. Board of Education and Black America's Struggle for Equality* (1975). For background on the history of Black women in the ministry, see Teresa L. Fry Brown's *Weary Throats and New Songs: Black Women Proclaiming God's Word* (2003) and Jualynne E. Dodson's *Engendering Church: Women, Power and the AME Church* (2002). The trial transcript for *United States v. Ray Crump, Jr.* (Criminal Number 930-64, U.S. District Court for the District of Columbia) is available in the case files of the U.S. District Court for DC, housed in Landover, Maryland.

For background on the life and death of Mary Pinchot Meyer, which was updated for this chapter to reflect recent findings, see Peter Janney's *Mary's Mosaic* (2012) and Benjamin Bradlee's *A Good Life* (1995).

2. See Tania D. Mitchell, "Social Justice Theory" in *Black Women and Social Justice Education: Legacies and Lessons*, edited by Stephanie Y. Evans, Andrea D. Domingue, and Tania D. Mitchell.

3. Juanita Johnson-Bailey, "Making a Way Out of No Way: An Analysis of the Educational Narratives of Reentry Black Women with Emphasis on Issues of Race, Gender, Class, and Color" (1994); Patricia Bell-Scott and Juanita Johnson-Bailey, *Flat Footed Truths: Telling Black Women's Lives* (1998); Patricia Bell-Scott, *The Firebrand and the First Lady: Portrait of a Friendship: Pauli Murray, Eleanor Roosevelt, and the Struggle for Social Justice* (2016).

4. bell hooks and Nellie McKay in *Women, Autobiography, Theory: A Reader*, edited by Sidonie Smith and Julia Watson (1998); Joanne Braxton, *Black Women Writing Autobiography: A Tradition within a Tradition* (1989); Margo V. Perkins, *Autobiography as Activism: Three Black Women of the Sixties* (2000); Rosetta R. Haynes, *Radical Spiritual Motherhood: Autobiography and Empowerment in Nineteenth-Century African American Women* (2011); Angela A. Ards, *Words of Witness: Black Women's Autobiography in the Post-Brown Era* (2016); Layli Maparyan, *The Womanist Idea* (2012).

5. Anna Julia Cooper, "Womanhood: A Vital Element in the Regeneration and Progress of a Race." *A Voice from the South* (1892).

6. See Stephanie Y. Evans, *Black Women in the Ivory Tower, 1850–1954: An Intellectual History* (2007).

## References

Ards, A. A. (2016). *Words of witness: Black women's autobiography in the post-Brown era.* Madison: University of Wisconsin Press.

Barnes, C. (1983). *Journey from Jim Crow: The desegregation of southern transit.* New York: Columbia University Press.

Bell Scott, P. (2016). *The firebrand and the first lady: Portrait of a friendship: Pauli Murray, Eleanor Roosevelt, and the struggle for social justice.* New York: Knopf.

Bell Scott, P., & Johnson-Bailey, J. (1998). *Flat footed truths: Telling black women's lives.* New York: Henry Holt & Company, 1998.

Bradford, S., & Tubman, H. (1868). *Scenes in the life of Harriet Tubman.* New York: Heraklion Press.

Bradlee, B. (1995). *A good life.* New York: Simon & Schuster.

Brown, T. L. Fry. (2003). *Weary throats and new songs: Black women proclaiming God's word.* Nashville, TN: Abingdon Press.

Cooper, A. J. (1892/1998). A voice from the south, by a black woman of the south. Xenia, Ohio. In C. Lemert & E. Bhan (Eds). *The voice of Anna Julia Cooper: Including a voice from the south and other important essays, papers, and letters.* Lanham, MD: Roman & Littlefield.

Dodson, J. E. (2002). *Engendering church: Women, power and the AME church*. Lanham, MD: Rowman and Littlefield Publishers, Inc.

Evans, S. Y. (2007). *Black women in the ivory tower, 1850–1954: An intellectual history*. Gainesville: University Press of Florida.

Haynes, R. R. (2011). *Radical spiritual motherhood: Autobiography and empowerment in nineteenth-century African American women*. Baton Rouge: Louisiana State University Press.

Janney, P. J. (2012). *Mary's mosaic*. New York: Skyhorse Press.

Johnson-Bailey, J. (1994). Making a way out of no way: An analysis of the educational narratives of reentry black women with emphasis on issues of race, gender, class, and color. PhD dissertation, University of Georgia, Athens.

Kluger, R. (1975). *Simple justice: The history of Brown v. Board of Education and Black America's struggle for equality*. New York: Vintage Books.

Maparyan, L. (2012). *The womanist idea*. New York: Routledge.

McCabe, K., & Roundtree, D. J. (2009). *Justice older than the law: The life of Dovey Johnson Roundtree*. Jackson: University Press of Mississippi.

McKay, N. Y. (1998). The narrative self: Race, politics, and culture in Black American women's autobiography. In S. Smith & J. Watson (Eds.) *Women, autobiography, theory: A reader*. Madison: University of Wisconsin.

Perkins, M. V. (2000). *Autobiography as activism: Three black women of the sixties*. Jackson: University Press of Mississippi.

Putney, M. (1992). *When the nation was in need: Blacks in the women's army corps during World War II*. Metuchen, NJ: Scarecrow Press.

Chapter 9

# This Ain't Yo' Mama's Revolution— Or Maybe It Is

## *#TakeBackTheFlag and the New Student Activism*

SHENNETTE GARRETT-SCOTT AND
DOMINIQUE GARRETT-SCOTT

After the end of a well-attended protest to remove the Confederate-emblazoned state flag on the campus of University of Mississippi, a group of Ku Klux Klan (KKK) and League of the South (LOS) members "crashed" the protest. They marched into University Circle and approached the center of campus displaying Confederate "stars and bars" flags. Those news teams who had not shuttered their cameras, turned off their microphones, or put away their notebooks, rushed over to the scene of approaching white men and women with small children being pushed in strollers. Some of the protesters who were still milling about looked visibly shaken and moved as far away as they could from the procession. Most of the remaining protesters, however, gathered and openly confronted the Confederate supporters. They cursed at the Confederate supporters, taunting them with threats and calling them cowards.

I, Shennette Garrett-Scott, was one of the many faculty members who attended and participated in the protest. I stayed afterward, talking with a group of faculty members and staff who had hung back with the last protestors and attendees. We heard the Confederate supporters and saw the rush of media and students to meet them. The KKK and LOS members got as far as the lawn in front of the Lyceum, the oldest building on campus and the symbolic heart of the campus. Most of my colleagues who chose to share their opinion quietly criticized the students for engaging with the Confederate supporters. They criticized the actions of the angry protestors, most of them young college-aged Black men and women, shouting back and forth with the KKK and LOS. Then I heard, "This is not what Martin Luther King Jr. would have done," followed by a minor chorus of agreeing voices and nodding heads. I thought and then said, "Well, this ain't yo' mama's revolution."

For a few years now, headlines in *The Atlantic, New York Times*, and across the web highlight "the new" student activism on college and university campuses across the United States (Buckley, 2012; Wong, 2015; Wong & Green, 2016). The urgent and omnipresent issues of social justice call for advocacy, knowing that much work still remains to be done. However, what seems like a new or resurgent phenomenon is more accurately part of a wave or cycle of student activism. Students have always been important, foundational players in movements for social change; they have continued to remain at the forefront of social justice movements since the 1960s (Bradley, 2016; Carson, 1981; Cohen & Snyder, 2013; Franklin, 2014; Rogers, 2012; Wolters, 1975). What is new, however, is their willingness to use some tactics and strategies from the past, disregard others, and mobilize new technologies. One way to understand recent student activism is to explore one movement that gained national attention—the removal of the state flag from the University of Mississippi campus—through one of the student leaders of that movement. Dominique Scott, founder and president of USAS Local Students Against Social Injustice and former Regional Organizer for United Students Against Sweatshops, considers the advantages and challenges of the recent wave of student activism from the perspective and experience of an active student organizer.

In the spirit of this volume's focus on Black women and social justice education on college campuses, we decided to write about the #TakeDownTheFlag campaign from the perspective and in the voice of one of its organizers. Her voice and perspective are critical given Toni Morrison's still prescient query, "How can values be taught in the university?" (Morrison, 2001). Morrison's query takes on special resonance when students and even faculty reject many of the values communicated by their campuses—when they feel that the very architecture does violence to their sense of self-worth. Such is certainly the case on the campus of the University of Mississippi, where symbols of the state's Confederate, Lost Cause, and Jim Crow history and memory wage constant battle with the progressive sensibilities of a modern generation of faculty, staff, and students. Morrison (2001) makes clear that secular universities and colleges still embrace a moral imperative to communicate their values. Indeed, she asserts that the university "*produces* power-laden and value-ridden discourse" (Morrison, 2001, 277; emphasis added). Morrison's musings about values, combined with Patricia Hill Collins's (2000) insights about Black feminist epistemology, reveal that Black women play an important role in mediating bitter contests over the pursuit of arcane knowledge and abstracted "truths." They have a charge to make the university space one that promotes opportunity and advances democratic freedoms—particularly in spaces that embrace traditions and values rooted in pasts that systematically and willfully excluded women of color. They are no longer content to ask, "What values will be tolerated?" but instead insist "What happens when we interrogate the values themselves and find them wanting?" The "new" student activism interrogates values and traditions. Contemporary student activists imagine a different space of possibility. It makes sense then that universities, as sanctified places of investigation, must hallow testimony as well.

## The "New" Student Activism

We are quite familiar with the images of students sitting in at lunch counters and college administrative offices or linked arm in arm marching across bridges and along highways. Eerily similar images flash across our cell phone and tablet screens: students staging sit-ins and walk outs, tying up traffic for hours marching, even lying down in the streets. The recent wave of youthful protesters, however, has drawn as much criticism as praise from their contemporaries. Much of the criticism mirrors the same frustrations—and confusion—that some of my (Shennette) colleagues expressed toward students' reactions to the KKK and League members. Some of the UM student protesters "flipped the bird" and exchanged insults back and forth, images and actions that they gleefully posted on social media. Critics complain students have become too radical and divisive in their strategies and tactics. Such behavior and reactions, they believe, disrespect the sacrifices of past protesters. They also add that students today should emulate their forebears' respectable behavior in the face of the abominable behavior of their opponents (Jaschik, 2016; Miah, n.d.; Reynolds, 2015; Young, 2016).

Such complaints do disservice not only to today's young protesters but also to those of yesterday. The passive, turn-the-other-cheek style of protest promoted publicly by groups like the Southern Christian Leadership Conference was the exception, not the norm. Blacks routinely engaged in armed and physical self-defense; they even took on the role of aggressors against staunch segregationists. More important, much of the public disparaged even the most peaceful protesters as radicals and troublemakers. King himself, often held up as the paragon of respectable, morally grounded protest, was criticized as an extremist. A number of historians have worked to reorient historical memory, highlighting the interconnectedness of the Civil Rights and Black Power Movements and the radical roots of both (Gilmore, 2009; Jeffries, 2009; King & West, 2015; Ransby, 2000; Theoharis, 2013; Umoja, 2013).

Efforts calling attention to the eviscerated historical memory of the centuries-long Black movement for justice and democracy, in particular, undermine present-day student activists. Increased incidences of student activism spring from the same roots of disaffection that mobilize other disgruntled segments of society: namely, persistent inequities in opportunity. The high cost of education, stagnant wages, and feeble job growth, not to mention continued racially and sexually motivated legal and extralegal violence and discrimination have led to disaffection among many college students. They typically do not see voting as an effective strategy to bring about meaningful change, particularly for issues they see as unrelated to the electorate.

The "new" student activists use the campus space to raise their voices against various issues, including racism, bigotry, and homophobia; free-speech abuses; safe spaces for undocumented immigrant students and workers; mishandling of campus sexual-assault cases; and divestment from controversial industries. They also draw attention to provincial issues, such as on-campus hiring policies and tuition hikes. Beyond their campuses, youth call attention to real-world issues such as police brutality and state-sanctioned harassment and violence motivate. Students have used various methods of protest, including hunger strikes, silent protests, and tent cities. They have gone high tech, too, producing videos, electronic petitions, and hashtag campaigns that draw millions of views from around the world (Shoichet & Ansri, 2016; Wong, 2015; Wong & Green, 2016).

Their efforts have garnered mixed results. The President and Chancellor of the University of Missouri resigned in November 2015 after students and athletes protested. Princeton University, however, decided not to change the names of its Woodrow Wilson buildings.

Students' protests have drawn not only criticism but also repression. In February 2017, police placed the University of California at Berkeley campus on lockdown after students and other protestors set fires protesting a speech by a President Donald Trump supporter (UC Berkeley, 2017). The voice of one of these young activists, then, is essential in helping put into perspective the immense challenges and spaces of possibility for those who commit themselves to the struggle for social justice.

## From Whacktivist to Organizer: Dominique Scott

Beads of sweat dripped down my back as I rapped my knuckles on the apartment door. It was still early but already a brutally hot New Orleans summer afternoon in June 2015. As interns with Organizing Beyond Borders, UNITE HERE's summer organizing and training program, our intern team traveled around the city to discuss upcoming union contract negotiations at a local hotel in the French Quarter.[1] We were at the apartment complex to visit Maricel Rodriguez (the name has been changed), a strong voice at the hotel who had recently been placed on leave after she participated in a worker-led public demonstration. Maricel opened the door, smiled widely, and invited us in. We sat on her red couch, surrounded by pictures of smiling children, and talked for hours about her experiences as a housekeeper in the hotel. "They will fire us for any little thing we do, no matter how long we have worked there or that we have to feed our families. They don't care. They think just because I am not from this country they can treat me like less than them." Having worked 4 years in the fast-food industry myself, Maricel's message resonated deeply with me.

Growing up working class in a predominantly white, affluent neighborhood meant that I could never afford the things my friends could, like going to movies or shopping at the mall. I started working in the fast-food industry when I was 16; my dream job quickly turned into a nightmare. I continued working fast food in college to make ends meet. I endured racism, sexual harassment, wage theft, and disrespect at the counter and drive-thru window. I knew all too well the exhaustion of working long after my shift was supposed to be over. I understood the feelings of helplessness because of a manager's power over your livelihood. I knew the backbreaking and soul-killing work of continuously defending one's character and intelligence from the misconception of fast-food workers as aimless losers. My experiences as a worker influenced not only my activism but also my scholarly interest in understanding and combatting economic inequality.

I made a few transitions before I reached Maricel's door. My experiences at the University of Mississippi (UM) also gave me an education outside of the classroom. I confronted blatant bigotry, misogyny, elitism, and ableism. William Faulkner once wrote, "To understand the world, you must first understand a place like Mississippi." My experiences put places outside Mississippi, like Allen, Texas, the affluent white suburb I grew up in, and Oak Cliff, the Black and Brown working-class neighborhood my family "escaped" from, in perspective. In many ways, they were not so different. I joined the Afrikan Activist Student Alliance (AASA). We started my second semester at UM with a lofty goal: to eradicate white supremacy on campus. I thought we would be the Black Justice League. It turned out that we were actually a bunch of misfits who would not even make the cut as sidekicks. The best thing about the AASA was that our faculty advisor, African American Studies professor Bryan Cooper Owens, introduced me to works in the Black radical tradition: David Walker, Maria Miller Stewart, W. E. B. Du Bois, Assata Shakur, Frantz Fanon, James Cone, Bayard Rustin. My fellow AASA members and I were idealists who talked for months and months about how to fight "The Man" on campus, but we never made anything happen. In short, we were "whacktivists."

In my sophomore year, I enrolled in my first sociology course: Introduction to Sociology. The first day of class, my professor wrote on the board in large blue letters "sociological imagination." He explained that the term, coined by C. Wright Mills, meant that one could see and understand the connections between their personal life and the world (Mills, 1959, 6). Immediately I thought, "I think I have one of those: a sociological imagination." I never stopped believing I could still change things on campus; I just did not know how. I thought activism was all about protesting and marching. I had not yet connected myself to the people I read about. I officially changed my major from Pre-Medicine to Sociology; my organizing work and scholarship would become interdependent and complementary.

The summer before my sophomore year, I attended my first Solidarity Ignite (¡Si!) social justice organizing conference (Solidarity Ignite, n.d.; Wimberly, Katz, & Mason, 2015). At ¡Si!, I got my first real taste of organizing. I learned practical skills and strategies for activism around economic justice and labor issues. I also participated in the FightFor15, an international movement of fast-food workers resisting poverty wages and workplace exploitation (Fight for $15, The, n.d.). I felt empowered seeing people like me mobilizing and resisting these conditions. I went back to Mississippi and started my own group: Students Against Social Injustice or SASI (pronounced "sassy"). I changed my major to sociology. I no longer wanted to escape my own working-class struggles; I wanted to break down the barriers that kept all working-class people struggling.

One important lesson I learned at ¡Si! was to forge alliances. If I was going to change anything, I needed allies. While recruiting like-minded members for SASI, some friends and I felt it important to reactivate our then-defunct NAACP chapter. We spent the entire summer before my junior year rechartering the chapter. I also continued to learn how to effect change. I became an Organizing Beyond Borders (OBB) intern. I developed my social justice skills in workshops and through participating in demonstrations with local groups and workers around securing a livable wage. I worked with the UNITE HERE Local 2262 organizing and participating in labor protests. My more than four years of McDonald's experience came in handy; I was able to talk to hesitant English- and Spanish-speaking workers about how to advocate for their rights within the bounds of McDonald's bible, The Crew Member Handbook. I talked to them about how they could use written policies around issues like taking breaks, expressing grievances, and working overtime to assert some of their rights. I came to the attention of United Students Against Sweatshops, and USAS eventually hired me as its Mississippi Regional Organizer. As an organizer, I traveled around the country participating in demonstrations. I planned activities to raise awareness, trained other activists, and increased union membership. My experiences showed me that the University of Mississippi needed an organizer, not just an activist.

My sociological imagination connected theory with praxis; it blossomed through a combination of social justice training, classroom learning, hands-on research, and grassroots activism and organizing. During my junior year, I enrolled in two sociology classes that have proven invaluable to my work, Social Problems and Race and Ethnicity. In Social Problems, we worked on the university living wage campaign and learned how to use our scholarship to shape responses to inequality in our communities. In Race and Ethnicity, I learned how ideas like race and gender are constructed and reinforced to normalize and reproduce inequality. These lessons and others shaped every conversation I had with other students, every action planned, and every speech I made.

## This Ain't Yo' Mama's Revolution: #TakeDownTheFlag Is Born

I never gave up on my dream of a Black Justice League, but unlike previous years I now had training and a plan. SASI, NAACP, and other groups planned a variety of protest actions during the summer of 2015, but we galvanized around Confederate iconography after the mass shooting of the nine members of the Emanuel African Methodist Episcopal Church in Charleston, South Carolina, on June 17, 2015 (Williams, Williams, & Blain, 2016). Following the tragedy, there was a nationwide call for institutions to reconsider their use of Confederate iconography and memorabilia (Hunter, [2015]). We answered the call at the University of Mississippi (UM). Planning for the Take Down the Flag campaign (#TakeDownTheFlag) began by late June 2015. Our campaign called for the removal of the current Mississippi state flag, with its prominent display of the Confederate-battle-flag insignia.

Removal of the flag on campus, however, was only the first phase in our ambitious and long-term campaign to removal all symbols of white supremacy at the University. Our long-term campaign focused on not only the Confederate battle flag but also the Confederate memorial statue, Confederate burial ground, and street and building names on campus. We also targeted activities such as playing "Dixie" at football games and practices like using the nickname "Ole Miss" to describe the University (Brundage, 2000; Eagles, 2009; Hale, 1999; Neff et al., 2016; Upton, 2002).[2] The university's difficult struggle with racism in conjunction with exclusionary symbols fostered a space that was unwelcoming to students of color (Combs et al., 2016).

As part of SASI, I designed an escalation plan, which is sometimes called a strategic plan or strategic overview. In organizing for social change, an escalation plan creates a series of specific activities that build pressure and momentum on a target, growing steadily in strength and urgency. I modeled my plan on the USAS Escalation Model, which drew its organizing model from the Student Non-Violent Coordinating Committee. At its heart, it is a model for effective civil disobedience. The first step in SASI's plan was a letter-writing campaign. Working with a coalition of campus organizations, we created a list of demands. Some of our partners included UM Pride Network, our LBGTQIA umbrella organization; Latin American Student Organization (LASO); Vietnamese Student Association; and the College Democrats. We were also wise to tap into faculty groups. We counted the Critical Race Studies Group and the Slavery Research Group, which uncovers UM's historic relationship to enslaved people, among our allies.

Working with the campus NAACP, our coalition created a list of demands. These letter drops outlined a number of demands for the University, including the banning of the Confederate battle flag at campus events, an increase in minority spaces, and, of course, the removal of the Mississippi state flag from the center of campus. (See a copy of the first letter in the Appendix.) While awaiting a response from administration, we worked on the other steps. We continued to reach out to student groups and faculty on campus who we thought would be interested in joining our cause. As a result, we gained the support of a number of student organizations and got the backing of dozens of faculty and staff and their respective departments.

One way we solidified our alliances was through training and programs. I held solidarity meetings; we built a solid community base long before we held rallies, met with school administrators, and organized colloquia and workshops (Cohen, 1996). After about 3 weeks of rallying allies and planning a public forum, we finally got a meeting with administration. This meeting, though frustrating, allowed us to map our administrative allies and plan for the next step in the campaign. Following the meeting, we held a public forum co-sponsored by the University's Center for Inclusion and some academic departments titled "Confederate Symbols: A Conversation on Southern Heritage," and invited a panel consisting of historians, an anthropologist, a sociologist, and a representative from the Sons of Confederacy (Thornton, 2015). This forum educated the campus community about the history of the Confederate flag and its evolution, cultural symbolism, and long history and ties to the University. This forum marked our first public action on campus.

I then organized workshops in which I taught collective liberation principles, how to attract press coverage and manage interviews with the press, how to interact with hostile onlookers, and more. Following the forum, Allen Coon, a senator in the Associated Student Body (ASB), contacted us and offered his aid in bringing the issue before the student government. We authored a resolution to present to the ASB and began lobbying senators to vote yes for Resolution 15-3 (Resolution 15-3, n.d.).

To put further pressure on the ASB, we held a rally on campus that attracted a crowd of over 300. At the rally, members of the NAACP and other organizations led chants and roused the crowd. Black students spoke about their experiences with racism and exclusion and explained why the University must take down the flag. Following the rally, the Ku Klux Klan (KKK) and League of the South (LOS) arrived on campus to do their own counterprotest. Their protest erupted into a loud dispute between the white supremacists and the campaign supporters. Slurs were hurled at Black students, and the altercation began to disrupt classes, so the counterprotestors were escorted off campus. As they walked back to their cars, students followed, singing and chanting, arm-in-arm, "Na na na na, na na na na, hey hey hey, goodbye!"

Following the presence of the KKK and LOS on campus, the university came under new scrutiny. The rally attracted national and international media attention. Local and national television, radio, internet, cable news shows, and even international outlets such as the Korean Broadcasting System asked for interviews (*Democracy Now*, 2015a; *Democracy Now*, 2015b; Korean Broadcasting System, 2015; Swayze, 2015). Support also began pouring in. Faculty and staff released statements of support for the campaign. Students and faculty wrote articles in the campus and city newspapers, and students posted pictures with the hashtag #TakeItDownASB on social media websites. In mid-October, after weeks of waiting, the ASB Senate met to vote on Resolution 15-3, the resolution to remove the state flag from campus grounds. After a heated deliberation that went on for nearly 3 hours, the resolution passed with 33 in favor, 15 opposed, and 1 abstention. The following day, the Staff Council, Faculty Senate, and Graduate Council all passed resolutions of their own supporting Resolution 15-3. On October 26, 6 days after Resolution 15-3 passed, University Police removed the Mississippi state flag from the University campus. In recognition of my efforts, I was a co-winner of the 2015 NAACP Image Award Chairman's Award. In addition to my fellow UM colleagues Chukwuebuka Okoye and Tysianna Marino, I shared the award with other student activists from the University of Missouri Concerned Student 1950 Collective, Justice League NYC, and Brittany "Bree" Newsome. As one of my personal heroines, it was a great honor to share the award with Bree and other committed activists (Chairman's Award, n.d.; Smith, 2016).

My sociological imagination connected theory with praxis; it has blossomed through a combination of social-justice training, classroom learning, hands-on research, and grassroots activism and organizing. Collins (2000) stresses "experiential knowledge," or connecting experience and ideas, as an important aspect of Black feminist thought (25). Thus, through a sustained personal engagement with underrepresented communities inside and outside of the academy, I use activism and scholarship to shape my responses to inequality in our communities. In the classroom, on the campus, and in the streets, I developed programs to address the academic, psychological, and cultural needs of people of color, especially women, first-generation college, and at-risk students. I enact my commitment to collective liberation by building alliances and providing people with knowledge and tools that can help them change their lives and the world around them. My experiences in high school and college have taken me from a passive bystander to an idealistic activist to an assertive, analytical scholar-organizer committed to living and growing in solidarity.

## Or Maybe It Is Yo' Mama's Revolution: Reflections on Intersectional Activism

#TakeDownTheFlag received a lot of press, including international coverage, but the news magazines, programs, and papers vetted the voices, images, and pictures of the movement to construct a narrative of what they thought the movement was about. The media's images and focus drove a narrative that people came to accept, which gained legitimacy as people passed it along and retold it to each other. The media's narrative can be summed up in a picture that appeared in the Oxford (Miss.) *Eagle* newspaper in late October 2015 (Berryhill, 2015). The image shows four men. The second from the left is Justavian Tillman, president of the Black Student Union (BSU); then Allen Coon, a senator in UM's Associated Student Body (ASB) and president of the UM Democrats; and Chukwuebuka "Buka" Okoye, the president of the UM NAACP. The narrative that gained traction is that Coon got the idea to take down the flag, and he got the NAACP involved. The NAACP then got the BSU to host a rally. After the rally, the ASB voted to make a resolution to ask the university to remove the flag. Then, with a few ups and down, the school met our demands to take down the flag, and "we" won. Let me be clear: The fact that the media hijacks or misinterprets a movement's narrative is certainly not unique to our movement, but the consequences are still demoralizing.

Thus, one of my biggest regrets is that we did not have our own media team to take pictures and capture moments from the time we began planning the movement. We also should have documented our organizing—created our own archive. We should have kept lists of who was present and not present at meetings as well as copies of emails, texts, and social media messages; we should have taken videos and lots of pictures. I also wish we had been more public in the beginning. For some reason, we thought it was a good idea to move in silence. For example, we did letter drops and told no one about them. We should have invited more press coverage from the very beginning. The widespread narrative that survives means much of the heavy lifting has been effectively "*un*remembered" and, with it, the liberatory breadth and potential of the movement as well.

That October 2015 picture in the *Eagle* is a microcosm of this erasure. First, no women are in the picture. Consequently, few people even understand the critical roles that women played in making the movement happen. For example, early on and throughout the campaign Tysianna "Ty" Marino, Vice President of the NAACP, contributed a significant amount of invisible labor without which it would have been impossible for any movement work to get done. She booked rooms, sent emails, set up speakers, and created PowerPoint presentations and fliers. Hers was the kind of "woman's work" that, for a long time, largely went unacknowledged when people thought and talked about the Civil Rights and Black Power Movements (Intersectional Black Panther Party History Project, n.d.; Robnett, 1997).

The skewed gender dynamics in planning and organizing the movement killed some of my friendships, particularly my friendship with Buka Okoye. I will describe my own experience and not speak for anyone else's experience. I felt that a weird chicken-and-egg thing began to happen between Buka and me. I feel that he started to act as if he had a more important role than he did in reality. It could have been the media attention. The media constructed a narrative about the campaign focused largely on Buka, president of the NAACP. The media and then Buka, too, paid little attention to the other officers, executive board members, and members. The media sought out Buka for interviews and comments. Journalists sometimes settled for Ty (as vice president) or me (as secretary), but they made it clear that they were settling; they wanted to talk to Buka. Buka also did most of the public speaking. It did not take long for Buka to act as if he was more important than the rest of us. A few months into the campaign, he ignored our input and refused to listen to our ideas. The female officers and executive board members resorted to a facilitated interaction with Buka mediated by the NAACP faculty advisor, Dr. James "J. T." Thomas. It did little to change the situation.

I have heard others describe what happened between Buka and the women leaders as the "Martin Luther King Jr. complex." Buka acted self-important because people treated him like he was the most important person in the movement. On the other hand, perhaps he already felt he was more important, and the media and public attention only reinforced his self-assessment. At the rally, people remember Buka's speech, but they do not know that Ty is the one who got the stage and arranged the speakers. She contacted the Dean of Students office to make sure that we could make ambient noise at that time of day! If it had not been for Ty, Buka and the other speakers would not even have had a mic to talk into. Her work and the work of so many women have not just been minimized: Their work has been erased completely.

The picture in the *Eagle* and some images in other outlets reinforce the single or handful of charismatic leaders model of a social movement, much as people embody the Civil Rights Movement in King or a few other prominent folks or the way Black Power sometimes equals Malcolm X or Huey Newton in the minds of many. The messiah model obscures the work of multiple people and organizations behind the scenes. People do not see the work of labor unions like USAS. Gone, too, is any sense of the broader movement. Few people are even aware that removing the flag was only a small part of our strategic overview. We had a long list of demands, but we never made it public, which is another one of my regrets. The movement was always about space (Combs et al., 2016). We wanted the Confederate memorial moved to the Confederate cemetery on campus. We wanted the names of buildings named for slaveholders, prominent white supremacists, and prominent segregationists changed. We demanded institutional space. We wanted a larger voice and presence of students of color in the curriculum. For example, we advocated a diversity pedagogy and wanted diversity classes to be a required part of the core curriculum.

Instead of being able to articulate our larger vision, groups that played little or no role in the movement became center stage. The Black Student Union (BSU), for example, played no role in the campaign, but they somehow became a key player in the media's narrative and in people's memory. BSU members merely showed up for the rally. In fact, they actively worked against us during the bulk of the organizing. I am not saying they ignored the campaign or were just resigned, idle observers: They fought against us. In a way, I understand their resistance. The BSU has strong and extensive institutional ties to UM, far more than SASI or the recently re-chartered student chapter of the NAACP had at that time. The BSU received a lot of funding from the University. It had far more money than we did. It had an advisor who was the head of an important center on campus, on-campus office space, and institutional memory. The BSU has been on campus since 1969. I also interpreted the BSU as constrained by the politics of respectability (Cooper, 2015; ForHarriet.com, n.d.; Higginbotham, 1993; White, 2001; Wolcott, 2001). It had to keep up an image of Black-elite excellence, which is conceptualized in a particular way in the campus space and in the minds of certain people on campus. The BSU was not considered reactionary or militant, but we were. The BSU did not want to be lumped into the militant category. Whatever its radical roots, in some ways the BSU was complicit in upholding the status quo.

We were labeled radical. I laugh when I hear people say that. It is a comical characterization to me. I feel that the characterization has more to do with drawing distinctions between the new Black group on the block and the established BSU than seeking an accurate descriptor of our goals, tactics, and vision. When I think of our parent group, the Mississippi state NAACP, I chuckle a little more. The state organization was anything but radical, as far as we were concerned. We definitely confronted some generational divides. In 2015, after the flag had been removed from campus, members of the Executive Committee attended our first state conference in Jackson, Mississippi. Our chapter won a couple of awards, including the Juanita Jackson Mitchell Award for Legal Activism.

We were recognized repeatedly for #TakeDownTheFlag. The constant accolades made it difficult for us to fellowship with the other student chapters who attended the conference. Festering ideological tensions between historically Black colleges and universities (HBCUs), who were the overwhelming majority of the campus chapters represented, and predominately white institutions (PWIs) were only exacerbated by the failure of the state chapter to acknowledge fully the hard work of other chapters or even to allow us to share ways we all worked through the particular challenges that confronted us at our home institutions and in our local communities.

As I reflect on that experience at the conference, I have to admit that there may have been very little that the state organization could have done. It became clear to us almost immediately after arriving at the event that the HBCU chapters considered us less legitimate because we were "Ole Miss." Some students told us that because we chose to go to a PWI over an HBCU we should have known that we had to deal with racism. Someone actually said, "That's what you get." I cannot, however, homogenize the chapters. We did have some sympathetic people in different chapters who acknowledged that by choosing a PWI we did not choose to be treated unfairly. They did not essentially "blame the victim."

If I continue to be honest as I reflect on the movement, I must admit that I resented the state chapter. I did not appreciate what I saw as others taking credit for our work. We were a chapter under the state's umbrella and authority so it could say "we," but that mutual pronoun never sat right with me. The state chapter did not offer any assistance until the rally. It did call us and ask if we needed any help with the rally. By then, though, a lot of the heavy lifting had already been done. It did not give us any financial resources either, but I do not fault the state chapter. I did then, but now I understand that the campaign happened so fast—faster than any of us could have imagined or were prepared for. To be honest, our escalation plan anticipated strong and continued resistance. We expected the administration not to do anything, even actively to resist us. Our strategic plan had weekly activities through March 2016; we thought that we were in for a long fight.

Another reason I am still uncomfortable saying "we" when it comes to the state chapter and people who were not allied with our movement in the earliest stages is because of the personal harassment and violence that I experienced. In my mind, there was no "we" when *I* was followed home by a truckload of white men who threw trash and spit epithets and expletives at me. Trolls flooded my social media; they published personal information like my address and family members' names. Pundits wrote editorials personally attacking me. Some of the other officers and I received death threats through Yik Yak, an anonymous messaging smartphone application for college students. For some time after the rally, the Ku Klux Klan, the League of the South, and other white supremacist groups came to campus armed. The FBI offered me and some other organizers armed escorts, but we all declined even though we were fully aware those threats could turn into real violence at any moment. Though the experience probably took years off of the end of my life, the threat of violence played a role in the quick success of #TakeDownTheFlag. It prompted the University to act quickly. I believe that the administration did not want to appear to align itself with people and groups who appeared prepared to use racially motivated violence against students, faculty, and staff.

The results have been bittersweet. For example, in addition to removal of the flag from campus, the school no longer plays "Dixie" during football games (Dixie, 2016). The school administration erected a plaque contextualizing the Confederate statue in the Circle, the heart of the university (Vitter, 2016). Yet, a backlash has ensued. A rash of full-on Confederate stars and bars flags hung from students' dorm windows. The tailgaters in the Grove, a large, park-like area on campus, have always used that space to signify their whiteness to each other, but during and after #TakeDownTheFlag the numbers of Confederate tablescapes and other memorabilia multiplied exponentially. Even more people wore Colonel Reb costumes; I saw someone wearing a Confederate-flag jumpsuit. Once when Allen Coon and I were hanging out in the Grove during a football game, a group of people touched and harassed us. New protests, though, have been ignited. The contextualization plaque ignited a new round of protests from faculty, staff, and students who believed the wording avoided any acknowledgment of the obvious, particularly the Civil War and slavery.

What I remember most about the 2015–16 school year is that it was hostile. I felt as if anything could happen. That energy drained me and made it one of the most difficult and exhilarating semesters I have ever had. I feel proud of what we accomplished, but we paid a steep personal price in lost friendships, in feeling our lives were on the line, and in victories that often felt as if we really did not win much at all.

## The Future of Student Activism

In many ways, the new student activism departs from how we imagine the Civil Rights Movement of the 1950s and 1960s. The kinds of technology used is, of course, an obvious difference, though the Montgomery, Alabama, Women's Political Council's "Don't Ride the Bus" leaflets have much in common with Facebook, Instagram, and Twitter (Leaflet, 1955). The new technologies, however, do allow students to lobby, dialogue, and plan without ever having to join physically hand in hand. They also allow the movement to draft supporters from many quarters, even if some complain that clicking like or reposting pales in comparison to "real" activism.

In other ways, the Civil Rights Movement's legacy casts a long shadow. It still has many lessons to teach. The experiences of student activists and their supporters reminds us that the movement was not a moment when Blacks united to fight against their shared oppression. Nor did Blacks even share the same vision of what equal rights and equal access looked like. #TakeDownTheFlag, like the Civil Rights Movement, revealed that people possess differing levels of commitment, consciousness, and capacity for change. Student activists sometimes found themselves jockeying for position with constituencies that imagined they were natural allies. They also, however, found support in unexpected places as well. Most important, the new student and veteran activists share the life changing transformation that occurs in the context of fighting for social justice.

The #TakeDownTheFlag campaign was only the beginning, not the culmination, of demands for change and a more-inclusive campus at the University of Mississippi. SASI and other groups succeeded in ending the tradition of playing "Dixie" at college football games in the fall of 2016. Plaques contextualizing the Confederate iconography have begun to appear at various sites on campus. Moves are also being made to rename buildings and streets commemorating Confederate leaders and staunch segregationists. The

University hired a new Vice Chancellor of Diversity in 2016 and has initiated programs to identify, attract, and retain students of color. These accomplishments are laudable, but much more still needs to done. In addition, these changes have garnered criticism and backlash. In addition to demonstrations by alt-right groups, citizens groups have created Facebook and billboard campaigns demanding "Fly Our Flag." House Bill 280 proposes to force K–12 schools to fly the state flag. Students, too, continue to fly the Confederate stars and bars, and incidents of physical and verbal harassment directed against activists and students, largely unreported in the press, continue.

Thus, our story, Dominique's story especially, is not a finished one. Dominique represents a new generation of militant thinkers and doers who called out and then urged others to resist oppression. She and her fellow student activists are actively shaping the post-Obama discourse on race and social justice. This chapter records one young woman's personal struggle for social justice. It is in our power to build on her and others' examples to create a more just, inclusive, and empowering future for us all.

## Appendix

We have included a copy of one of the first letters SASI and the NAACP dropped as part of its escalation plan. Looking back, Dominique sees many changes she would have made to the letter, but we think it is an important part of the "archive" of #TakeDownTheFlag.

September 21, 2015
To whom it may concern,

We, the students, have formed a coalition of representatives from existing Registered Student Organizations committed to the complete eradication of social injustice at the University of Mississippi. Students Against Social Injustice or, SASI, has compiled a list of demands to make the University of Mississippi a more inclusive space for students of ALL identities. We want the campus to reflect ALL of the students and their unique heritages that contribute to the University and state of Mississippi.

1. We, *the students*, demand the University ban all use of Confederate memorabilia and iconography on every campus. This includes its use during sporting events and other events open to the public.

a. We believe that the use of the Confederate Flag on our campus impedes upon our ability to successfully navigate through our academic space and our workplace.

b. The Confederate Flag and other Confederate memorabilia serve as symbols of exclusion that detract from the campuswide effort for increased diversity and inclusion.

c. We understand that the banning of the flag is only the beginning step in a long process of shaping the University into a more open and inclusive space. However, the Confederate flag is a tangible symbol of hatred that the University must distance itself from.

d. This contention includes all visitors participating in any event sponsored by the University of Mississippi. It is the responsibility and duty of university officials to ensure all visitors are aware Confederate iconography is not to be displayed on any personal or real property secured in any given campus location. This means that the construction of tents or other personal property carried by visitors are to be free of all Confederate iconography and memorabilia.

2. We, *the students*, demand the Mississippi Flag be taken down from the circle.

   a. As the flagship school of the state of Mississippi, this university must move with all deliberate speed and urgency to set the precedent of the cruciality of inclusion. Like the Confederate flag, the Mississippi state flag hinders progress on this campus as it imposes upon the experiences of those who do not share in its supposed "heritage" and disenfranchises students as a whole to share a part in our campus community.

3. We, *the students*, demand greater representation in the decision for our new chancellor and that the IHL adopt new policy that provides students with an increased and diverse representative group to make decisions on our part in both the interview and search committees.

   a. We do not believe that the ASB President can adequately represent the experiences of all 16,667 students at the university. Our student body is comprised of individuals with many different identities and identity intersections. It is because of these identities that students experience the university in different ways and it is because of these identities that students are able to challenge the institution to progress and become more inclusive. The ASB president cannot possibly represent the lived experiences and issues that accompany this varied body, and therefore the students demand more fair and adequate representation in decisions regarding changes on campus.

b. We also do not believe that a singular graduate student can represent 2,754 graduate students, who again, are very diverse individuals with diverse experiences who will need representation as well on both committees to ensure that their needs and voices are taken into account. The student voice cannot be the "most important aspect of [the search and interview] committee[s]," a direct quote of the IHL president, if there is no true representation for students in selecting the next chancellor.

c. Therefore, we are calling upon both the university and the IHL to facilitate necessary accommodations to provide a more diverse student group to represent the entire student body as well as to change certain policies that prevent students from having proper representation as a whole on either committee.

4. We, *the students*, demand the strict enforcement of this ban on Confederate memorabilia. We demand the university adopt a zero tolerance for the use of the flag in any shape, form, or fashion on campus and that violators be removed from the campus immediately.

a. However, if removal will not be considered, policies must be constructed in a manner that reputes its display and demonstrates in a concise format consequences for any individual who continues displaying on campus any Confederate iconography.

5. We, *the students*, demand an increase in minority spaces across campus, specifically involving National Pan Hellenic Council organizations. To keep to task with the theme of inclusive-

ness and a campus that pursues a policy of attracting those of every racial, ethnic, and gender group, there needs to be further action on the part of this institution to provide them with more adequate spaces (e.g., Greek houses, minority office spaces) for participation and inclusion in the UM community.

We, *the students*, demand that the University of Mississippi initiate or encourage student and faculty led dialogues involving the theme of inclusion and acceptance across campus. We the students demand that this institution also sponsor social action (e.g., rallies, protests, die-ins) surrounding that particular theme to facilitate an even speedier development of reconciliation within our campus community.

Ten days ago, on Friday, September 11, SASI representatives came to your office with a detailed list of demands for the university. As we have yet to receive a response from you, we have taken the liberty to hand deliver another copy of our demands to your office personally. As Interim Chancellor, we understand that you too have a vision for the university and we believe that it is your duty to work hand in hand with students to make that vision possible. We look forward to hearing from you by Friday, September 25, to schedule a meeting for us to come together to generate solutions to these issues and form sustainable policy changes on campus. If we do not hear from you by then, we will follow up. If you have comments, questions, or concerns please contact us at sasilikesassy@gmail.com.

In solidarity,
Students Against Social Injustice (SASI)

## Notes

1. UNITE HERE is an international labor union, representing more than a quarter-million workers in Canada and the United States, formed from the combination of the former Union of Needletrades, Industrial, and Textile Employees (UNITE), and Hotel Employees and Restaurant Employees International Union (HERE). See the union's website at unitehere.org/who-we-are.

2. Despite claims that the term "Ole Miss" is merely a diminutive of the state's name, Ole Miss has racist overtones. It is a nickname for both a slave plantation and the mistress of the plantation. The popular use of the term dates from 1897. It reflects the school's efforts to evoke a nostalgic connection to the state's slave past as part of the Lost Cause narrative and to gesture to its racial (and class) exclusionary status quo.

## References

Berryhill, L. (2015, October 21). Ole Miss ASB says to remove flag. *Oxford Eagle* (MS). Retrieved from www.oxfordeagle.com/2015/10/21/ole-miss-asb-says-to-remove-flag

Bradley, S. M. (2016, Feb. 1). Black activism on campus. *New York Times*. Retrieved from www.nytimes.com/interactive/2016/02/07/education/edlife/Black-History-Activism-on-Campus-Timeline.html

Brundage, W. F. (2000). "White women and the politics of historical memory in the New South, 1880–1920." In J. Dailey, G. E. Gilmore, & B. Simon (Eds.), *Jumpin' Jim Crow: Southern politics from Civil War to Civil Rights* (pp. 115–39). Princeton, NJ: Princeton University Press.

Buckley, C. (2012, January 19). The new student activism. *New York Times*. Retrieved from www.nytimes.com/2012/01/22/education/edlife/the-new-student-activism.html

Carson, C. (1981). *In struggle: SNCC and the Black awakening of the 1960s*. Cambridge, MA: Harvard University Press.

The Chairman's Award (n.d.). NAACP.org. Retrieved from www.naacpimageawards.net/main_chairmans_award.html

Cohen, J. (1996). Procedure and substance in deliberative democracy. In S. Benhabib (Ed.), *Democracy and difference: Contesting the boundaries of the political* (pp. 95–119). Princeton, NJ: Princeton University Press.

Cohen, R., & Snyder, D. J. (Eds.). (2013). *Rebellion in Black and White: Southern student activism in the 1960s*. Baltimore: John Hopkins University Press.

Collins, P. H. (2000). Distinguishing features of Black feminist thought. *Black feminist thought: Knowledge, consciousness, and the politics of empowerment* (pp. 21–43). 2nd ed. New York: Routledge.

Combs, B. H., Dellinger, K., Jackson, J. T., Johnson, K. A., Johnson W. M., Skipper, J., Sonnett, J., & Thomas, J. M [University of Mississippi] Critical Race Studies Group (2016). The symbolic lynching of James Meredith: A visual analysis and collective counter narrative to racial domination. *Sociology of Race and Ethnicity*, 2(3), 338–353.

Cooper, B. (2015, March 10). *The end of respectability: Black feminism and ratchet politics*. The Havens Center for Social Justice Spring 2015 Visiting Scholars Program [Video File]. Retrieved from https://vimeo.com/121847236

Democracy Now. (2015a, Oct. 20). *"Heritage of hate": Univ. of Miss. students seek removal of Confederate battle flag from campus* [Video File]. Retrieved from www.democracynow.org/2015/10/20/heritage_of_hate_univ_of_miss

Democracy Now. (2015b, Oct. 27). *In student victory, U. of Mississippi removes state flag with Confederate emblem* [Video File]. Retrieved from www.democracynow.org/2015/10/27/in_student_victory_u_of_mississippi

Dixie will no longer be played at Ole Miss football games. (2016, Aug. 19). Retrieved from thedmonline.com/ole-miss-dixie

Eagles, C. (2009). *The price of defiance: James Meredith and the integration of Ole Miss*. Chapel Hill: University of North Carolina Press.

The Fight for $15. (n.d.). About us. Retrieved from fightfor15.org/about-us
ForHarriet.com (n.d.). Wrestling with respectability in the age of #BlackLivesMatter: A dialogue. Retrieved from www.forharriet.com/2015/10/wrestling-with-respectability-in-age-of.html#axzz4wYrlYf7a
Franklin, S. M. (2014). *After the rebellion: Black youth, social movement activism, and the post-civil rights generation*. New York: New York University Press.
Gilmore, G. E. (2009). *Defying Dixie: The radical roots of civil rights, 1919–1950*. New York: W. W. Norton and Company.
Hale, G. E. (1999). Stone Mountains: Lillian Smith, Margaret Mitchell, and whiteness divided. *Making whiteness: The culture of segregation in the South, 1890–1940* (pp. 241–280). New York: Vintage Books.
Higginbotham, E. B. (1993). The politics of respectability. *Righteous discontent: The women's movement in the Black Baptist church, 1880–1920*. Cambridge, MA: Harvard University.
Hunter, K. (2015). Remove the Confederate flag from all government places. MoveOn. org Petition. Retrieved from https://petitions.moveon.org/sign/remove-the-confederate-3
Intersectional Black Panther Party History Project (n.d.). Retrieved from https://iphp com.wordpress.com
Jaschik, S. (2016, October 24). Backlash to anthem protests. *Inside Higher Ed*. Retrieved from https://www.insidehighered.com/news/2016/10/24/alabama-and-greenville-backlash-anthem-protests-Black-students
Jeffries, H. K. (2009). *Bloody Lowndes: Civil rights and Black power in Alabama's Black Belt*. New York: New York University Press.
King Jr., M. L., & West, C. (Ed.) (2015). *The radical King*. New York: Beacon Press.
Korean Broadcasting System. (2015, Dec. 27). *Racism abolishment campaign resurrected* [Video File]. Retrieved from news.kbs.co.kr/news/view.do?ncd=3205481
Leaflet (1955, Dec. 2). " 'Don't Ride the Bus,' Come to a Mass Meeting on 5 December." Retrieved from kingencyclopedia.stanford.edu/encyclopedia/documentsentry/leaflet_dont_ride_the_bus_come_to_a_mass_meeting_on_5_december
Miah, M. (n.d.). BLM: A movement and its critics. *Solidarity*. Retrieved from www.solidarity-us.org/node/4518
Mills, C. W. (1959). *The sociological imagination*. New York: Oxford University Press.
Morrison, T. (2001, Spring). How can values be taught in the university? *Michigan Quarterly Review, 40*(2), 273–278.
Neff, J., J. Roll, & Twitty, A. with Grem, D. & McClure, J. (2016, May 16). A brief historical contextualization of the Confederate monument at the University of Mississippi. Retrieved from https://history.olemiss.edu/wp-content/uploads/sites/6/2017/08/A-Brief-Historical-Contextualization-of-the-Confederate-Monument-at-the-University-of-Mississippi.pdf
Ransby, B. (2000). *Ella Baker and the Black Freedom Movement, a radical democratic vision*. Chapel Hill: University of North Carolina Press.
"Resolution 15-3: A resolution of the Associated Student Body Senate requesting that the University of Mississippi cease flying the Mississippi state flag." Retrieved from www.olemiss.edu/faculty_senate/archives/Resolution-15-13.pdf

Reynolds, B. (2015, August 24). I was a civil rights activist in the 1960s. But it's hard for me to get behind Black Lives Matter. *Washington Post*. Retrieved from www.washingtonpost.com/posteverything/wp/2015/08/24/i-was-a-civil-rights-activist-in-the-1960s-but-its-hard-for-me-to-get-behind-Black-lives-matter/?utm_term=.7cdd3d322018

Robnett, B. (1997). *How long? How long?: African American women in the struggle for civil rights*. New York: Oxford University Press.

Rogers, I. H. (2012). *The Black campus movement: Black students and the racial reconstitution of higher education, 1965–1972*. New York: Palgrave Macmillan.

Shoichet, C. E., & Ansari, A. (2016, Nov. 16). Sanctuary campus' protests target Trump immigration policies. CNN.com. Retrieved from www.cnn.com/2016/11/16/politics/sanctuary-campus-protests

Smith, E. (2016, Jan. 20). Campus NAACP chapter wins 2016 Chairman's Award. *Daily Mississippian*. Retrieved from https://news.olemiss.edu/um-naacp-chapter-wins-2016-chairmans-award

Solidarity Ignite (n.d.). Retrieved from solidarityignite.org

Swayze, R. (2015, Oct. 20). Ole Miss student senate: Take state flag down. *USA Today*. Retrieved from www.usatoday.com/story/news/nation-now/2015/10/20/ole-miss-student-senate-take-mississippi-flag/74311954

Theoharis, J. (2013). *The rebellious life of Mrs. Rosa Parks*. New York: Beacon Press.

Thornton, L. (2015, Sept. 30). University's NAACP chapter holds panel on iconography. *Daily Mississippian*. Retrieved from thedmonline.com/universitys-naacp-chapter-holds-panel-on-iconography

UC Berkeley halts Milo Yiannopoulos talk amid violent protest. (2017, Feb. 2). BBC.com. Retrieved from www.bbc.com/news/world-us-canada-38837142

Umoja, A. O. (2013). *We will shoot back: Armed resistance in the Mississippi Freedom Movement*. New York: New York University Press.

Union of Needletrades, Industrial and Textile Employees (UNITE) and Hotel Employees and Restaurant Employees International Union (HERE). (n.d.). Who we are. Retrieved from unitehere.org/who-we-are

Upton, M. A. (2002). *Keeping the faith with the University Greys': Ole Miss as lieu de memoire*. (Master's Thesis). University of Mississippi.

Vitter, J. S. (2016, March 11). UM begins installing plaque offering context for Confederate statue. Retrieved from chancellor.olemiss.edu/um-begins-installing-plaque-offering-context-for-confederate-statue

White, E. F. (2001). *Dark continent of our bodies: Black feminism and politics of respectability*. Philadelphia: Temple University Press.

Williams, C., Williams, K. E., & Blain, K. N. (Eds.). (2016). *Charleston syllabus: Readings on race, racism, and racial violence*. Athens: University of Georgia Press.

Wimberley, D. W., Katz, M. A., & Mason, J. P. (2015). Mobilization, strategy, and global apparel production networks: Systemic advantages for student antisweatshop activism. *Societies Without Borders 10*(1). Retrieved from scholarlycommons.law.case.edu/swb/vol10/iss1/3

Wolcott, V. (2001). *Remaking respectability: African American women in interwar Detroit*. Chapel Hill: University of North Carolina Press.

Wolters, R. (1975). *The new Negro on campus: Black college rebellions of the 1920s*. Princeton: Princeton University Press.

Wong, A. (2015, May 21). The renaissance of student activism. *The Atlantic*. Retrieved from www.theatlantic.com/education/archive/2015/05/the-renaissance-of-student-activism/393749

Wong, A., & Green, A. (2016, Apr. 4). Campus politics: A cheat sheet. *The Atlantic*. Retrieved from www.theatlantic.com/education/archive/2016/04/campus-protest-roundup/417570/

Young, D. (2016, Nov. 21). Those "I'm not my grandparents; you can catch these hands" shirts are disrespectful as fuck (and wrong). VerySmartBrothas.com. Retrieved from verysmartbrothas.com/those-im-not-my-grandparents-you-can-catch-these-hands-shirts-are-disrespectful-as-fuck-and-wrong/comment-page-3

Chapter 10

# We Got a Lot to Be Mad About

## A Seat at Solange's Table

BETTINA L. LOVE AND SARAH ABDELAZIZ

Education is often conceived within the bounds of the classroom. It emanates from textbooks, and through those entitled "Ms.," "Mrs.," "Professor." The academy, or the institution of education, requires certain patterns of speech and methods of relation. Some professors and students may attempt to break these restraints, but the institution is an overall homogenizing force, rewarding certain bodies, while disciplining others (Berry & Mizelle, 2006; Evans, 2008; Fleming, 1983; Kim, 2003). Blackness, queerness, and womanness are unprivileged in the academy. Even in spaces that seemingly appreciate it, such as Black Studies or Women, Gender, and Sexuality studies, aggressions erupt within and from outside. Meanwhile, Black women in the academy find their lives, vigor, and intellectualism budding not only within the binds of textbooks and the PDFs of peer-reviewed journals, but at dinner tables, in bars, at rallies, and on the radio (Evans, Taylor, Dunlap, & Miller, 2009; Gutiérrez y Muhs, Niemann, Gonzalez, & Harris, 2012). Social Justice Education recognizes that much of what influences us and creates us is beyond the confines of a book or a classroom (Freire, 1985; hooks, 1994). We want to privilege here the arts, and how music has been a forum for Black women to practice social justice and education. Specifically, we want to privilege the most recent album by Solange: *A Seat at the Table*.

Solange's *A Seat at the Table* is, for us, an exemplar of Black woman–led, social justice education. Solange Knowles, of the famous Knowles clan, was immersed in various forms of sonic art from childhood and has been a recording artist for close to 2 decades. However, *A Seat at the Table*, released in September of 2016, is arguably her magnum opus. The 21-track album is a bookend and the continuance of a conversation on Blackness in America, and a nod, specifically, to the joyful arduousness of womanhood within that space. *A Seat at the Table* occupies a space of love, celebration, anger, sorrow, and playfulness. The 21 tracks weave in and out of masterful songs that are delicately named, songs such as "Weary," "Mad," "F.U.B.U," "Cranes in the Sky," "Don't Touch My Hair," "Rise," and "Where Do We Go." We believe that Solange created a beautiful conversation among Black women in a moment that has been increasingly opening the conversation of the violability of being Black into the larger, visible, public sphere. The dual importance of Solange as Black and as a woman is of increasing importance, as social justice movements tend to exclude the feminized, even when they are the originators of movements.[1]

*A Seat at the Table* makes a profound and lasting intervention. The space that Solange occupies as the public figure of a highly recognizable family makes the conversation provoked by her album public, yet by simultaneously centering the album on Black women, Solange creates more intimate spaces within the larger audience, allowing conversations amongst one another to emerge. Our analysis of Solange's lyrics and album cover engages with the long tradition of Black popular music serving as a "primary vehicle for communally derived critiques of the African-American experience" (Neal, 1998, xi). For this reason, so much of Black popular music narrates America's anti-Blackness, the sensibilities of Blackness that emerge from racial trauma, and joys of being Black despite America's insistence on oppression. We enter the work as cultural critics with a deep understanding and appreciation for how Black cultural creativity provides "modes of cultural excellence in an ethos of white disbelief in Black humanity" (Dyson, 1993, xiv).

Upon first glance, *A Seat at the Table* is already complex and intriguing. The title of the album invites a certain type of understanding: Arguably, "a seat at the table" implies a question. Having a seat at the table invites ideas of inclusivity and democracy and all of the problematic ways with which these ideologies propose, but do not instate, equality. The phrase "a seat at the table" does not question the notion of a table, but perhaps even validates it, as though getting a seat at the table will dismantle hundreds of years of oppression or as though it will dismantle the table itself, or structures that bind, constrain, kill. "A seat at the table" might be a necessary step toward invalidating structures of oppression at its best, but at its worst, it enlivens the structure, allowing a legitimacy to persist in that which has always been broken. And yet . . . our first sight of the album is Solange, hair clips in hair, unwaveringly looking at us, face unadorned. A Black woman in a space so naked and politicized: hair being done.

Intimate, but not vulnerable, Solange appears to us powerful, in control. Somehow, due to the way she has positioned her head, she looks down at us ever so slightly. She is making it very clear that she has us fastened within her gaze. Already the album occupies a space of dissonance. The idea of a seat at the table conjures social justice as reform, similarly to how the notion of "speaking truth to power" does. This is the album's first foray into a space that allows for seeming impossibilities to co-exist; a theme that can be observed throughout the volume of songs. Simultaneously, the sight of Solange's face occupies politicized spaces of rejection, acceptance, and defiance. The simple act of appearing in such a way is politicized in its refusal of certain norms. We could perhaps imagine this image in twinness with young, Black, feminine Panthers emerging with their afros, loudly declaring Black as beautiful. The album picture flies in the face of binding norms such as Eurocentrism, and the often violent way with which the image of "woman" is manicured and maintained. It is from the first glance then that Solange begins her process of social justice education. She allows us to gaze at her in a space that has been much contested—a Black woman's hair—and from within that space, she emanates love for family and defiance toward her enemies.

The first song on the album, "Rise," includes the repeated refrain,

*Fall in your ways so you can crumble*
*Fall in your ways so you can sleep at night*
*Fall in your ways so you can wake up and rise*

The title of the song, "Rise," is seemingly in opposition to the motif of falling. Once again, Solange challenges us. Paired with the cover of the album which effortlessly blends dualities, falling and rising can be seen as part of the same process, that of the self-love and resolve required to be an affirming Black woman in a place which disregards life so easily. "Falling into your ways" tends to imply negativity: we fall into our ways as we go back to old lovers, pick smoking back up, or miss deadlines. Solange suggests that we also fall into our ways as we come to love ourselves and understand ourselves to be good and eclipsing ideologies of "worth" (Few & Bell-Scott, 2002; Few, Stephens, & Rouse-Arnett, 2003; hooks, 2000). Defying narratives of linear self-growth, Solange's acknowledgment of the dialectic nature of love for self radiates a wisdom that guides individuals and movements through the many pitfalls and triumphs that will inevitably come.

Opposition and contradiction are forces that find home within and on the bodies of the marginalized. Though fabled as absurd, impossibility and contradiction exist without immediate resolution. The impossibility of contradiction is realized within the experience of Black women, for instance. Occupying the space of absolute sexualization and societal rejection, ascribed life and boundless death, cultural icon and absolute other, contradiction is not impossibility, but rather, the endless dance of contention. Solange litters her album with contradiction and impossibility from the very image of her album cover to the many songs within it. This first song on the album sets forth the liminal zone from which the album emanates, pulling us into and out of what is possible.

## Assembling Black Art while White Rage is Raging

In an interview with *The Fader*, Solange revealed that the album, a loosely packaged personal memoir, was recorded over the course of 4 years. During this period of Solange's creative musings, people of color, indigenous people, queer folks, and non-Christians in the United States, or folks who are a combination of these identities, were witnessing, mourning, and experiencing first-hand, white rage. White rage is what the United States of America is founded on; it is a byproduct of whiteness. Drawing from the work of Critical White Studies (CWS), Matias and colleagues (2014) argue that whiteness functions as a normative script of white supremacy that maintains racist systems and does not acknowledge how whiteness is "historically, economically, and legally produced" (3). Increasingly, the world watches as unarmed, poor, trans, mentally ill, people of color, children—the most vulnerable in our society—are murdered by the resolute power of whiteness. According to Carol Anderson, author of *White Rage: The Unspoken Truth of Our Radical Divide* (2016), "The trigger of white rage, inevitably is Black advancement. It is not the mere presence of Black people that is the problem; rather it is Blackness with ambition, with drive, with purpose, with aspirations, and with demands for full and equal citizenship" (2). During Solange's album production, the carnage of Black life was witnessed in an endless cycle of 15-second loops via social media.

On February 26, 2012, white rage murdered 17-year-old Trayvon Martin. Trayvon's killer would be acquitted of second-degree murder and manslaughter due to a judicial system that is a functioning artifact of whiteness. Trayvon's death and his murderer's acquittal were the impetus of the Black Lives Matter Movement; the movement grew, and continues to grow, in strength, numbers, and visibility.[2] The Malcolm X Grassroots Movement (2013) reported on the state-sanctioned violence endured by Black people: Every 28 hours a Black person is killed by the police or a vigilante. *A Seat at the Table* is a dialectic ode to the movement as it wrestles with the daily struggles of "Blackness with ambition" in a world of white rage.

In the same *Fader* interview, Solange stated that her life and work have been deeply impacted by the writings of Claudia Rankine. During the making of the album, a close friend of Solange's suggested she read Rankine's book, *Citizen: An American Lyric*. When discussing how Rankine's work influenced her intense feelings about the power of language to express her interior thoughts, Solange says,

> Claudia was someone who directly inspired my writing because her poetry cuts through in a really unique way. She leaves certain things up for your interpretation, while also being very direct. I identified with that so much. That has always been something, in terms of my songwriting, that I've strived for. I want people to have a personalized experience, but I want my role to be clear within that. *Citizen* just so powerfully expressed many things I'd been feeling that I just thought, *Oh wow, okay. I can actually name these incidents in a very personal way.* And I think that, in the past, I might have been a bit more reluctant in my songwriting to be so clear in the narrative—I use a lot of analogies, and I try to have a certain sense of poetry in my writing—but I feel like she really helped inspire me to be more direct in my feelings.

Although in some ways, indeed, direct, Claudia Rankine's *Citizen: An American Lyric* makes attempts at an analytical deciphering of it purposefully evasive. The book is all poetry, part anecdote, artwork, and narrative. It artistically explores the experiences of being a racialized other in America, viewing and being viewed as object. *Citizen* does not employ one methodology, seemingly because it evades such stringent calculation. Solange similarly intersperses her album not only with the melodic but with the spoken recordings of those around her. Both Solange and Rankine allow for multiple subjectivities— Solange through featuring speakers such as her mother, father, and Master P, and Rankine through role playing the subjectivities of those other than herself. Rankine's writing is a dive into the privileging of affect theory as a method of expression. The objectification and annihilation of being Black is the impulse to use the methodology of affect theory, as Rankine acknowledges the incoherency of fluidly telling this story. Similarly, Solange's album speaks not just through straightforward lyrics, which we could spend multitudinous pages ruminating on. It is the feelings that Solange is sometimes able to name, and at other times only able to make space for, which are the album's true catharsis and invocation.

*Citizen* is comprised of seven chapters filled with the life experiences of society's invisible and most vulnerable. Rankine meticulously illuminates the microaggressions that people of color endure daily which accumulate into a slow death when living against a "sharp white background" (53). As Rankine writes, existence for people of color consists of "anger built up through experience and the quotidian struggles against dehumanization every brown or Black person lives simply because of skin color" (24). While focusing on the ways in which racial injustice "murders people of colors' spirits" (Love, 2013, 2016) like a recurring nightmare, *Citizen* cogitates the state sanctioned violence toward Black people. Rankine's intersectional meditation on race stretches from an examination of Serena Williams and how her Black excellence is constantly under siege by white rage, to the way white rage explodes into fits of murder upon bodies such as Trayvon Martin's (36). Rankine's words at times capture the anger and emotions of Black suffering, as people of color witness, mourn, and internalize Black death. When she is unable to capture the absolute contradiction—the absolute illogic of anti-Blackness—Rankine leaves blank space on her pages, art in the margins, and a wealth of dashes, leaving space for the unspeakable. As Rankine so hauntingly summarizes, "because white men can't police their imagination Black men are dying" (135).

Rankine's book and Solange's album are assemblages. The book and album recognize themselves as the incoherency that is experienced by being Black in a world that relies on the simultaneous invisibility and hypervisibility of Blackness. Such an impossible situatedness—of Blackness as made into object by whiteness and therefore acted upon violently, and Blackness as subjectivated even in the presence of humiliation and disappearance into its own autonomous presence—can seemingly only give rise to an assemblage of response. This form of knowledge production is an education specific to the marginalized. It is education that moves in a nonlinear fashion, rejecting straightforward narratives that could never capture difference and multiplicity.

This form of knowledge production is a form of Black women social justice education not just because of the identities of those speaking, but because of the very method that is employed. Rankine's method of exposure is one that is in fact very teleological in that it recognizes the Black body is necessarily without teleology: there can be no sense made of such intensive disregard and brutality. In fact, the words used to describe the treatment of Black people in this world ("brutality," "disregard") are words that cannot encompass the scope of terror, such that an articulation of the objectification of being Black and female, to Solange or Rankine, is simply an articulation of the events that unfold as being named Black and female. What denotes the terror is not the anecdote itself, but the haze around its utterance. So that when Rankine tells this tale in the span of one page,

> In line at the drugstore it's finally your turn, and then it's not as he walks in front of you and puts his things on the counter.

> The cashier says, Sir, she was next. When he turns to you he is truly surprised.
>
> Oh my god, I didn't see you.
>
> You must be in a hurry, you offer.
>
> No, no, no, I really didn't see you. (77)

Or when Solange's father states,

> I was the first, one of the first. My first day, a state trooper caught me, put me in the backseat of the car, and meeting the other Black kids, was six of us. And seeing all of those parents, and also KKK members having signs and throwing cans at us, spitting at us. We lived in the threat of death every day. Every day. So I was just lost in this vacuum between integration and segregation and, and racism. That was my childhood. I was angry for years . . . angry, very angry.

The words aren't the full brunt of the blow, but the space between them. The inarticulable creation of each breath, space, and pause. Rankine and Solange utilize not the straightforwardness of emotion that tries to name, but the vaporality of affectation, which appears in the utterances and between them, and refuses naming as a necessity to its incomprehensibility. Black women–led social justice education does not mistake pauses for gaps in knowledge, rather it understands this to be a part of the process of knowledge production (Gay, 2014; Adichie, 2015). Black women–led social justice education recognizes that language will fail to name the inarticulable.

### Poking a Bear: Master P, Black Ambition, and "For Us By Us"

New Orleans is Solange's muse: the site of her radical imagination. In a *Vogue* interview, the Houston, Texas, native called the Crescent City "magical." She spoke of how interesting New Orleans is to her because of the city's unique Black history that is comprised of performance, pleasure, and resistance. New Orleans is also significant because Solange's roots can be traced back to Iberia Parish, Louisiana, about 120 miles from New Orleans. New Orleans allows Solange to masterfully position her music on the axes of art, Black folks' lives, and the joy of being Black. Scholar Mark Anthony Neal (1999) writes in his book, *What the Music Said: Black Popular Music and Black Public Culture*, that Black popular music can be described as "power, politics, and pleasures" because it is "largely about communities, communities under siege and in crisis, but also communities engaged in various modes of resistance, critique, institution building, or simply taking time to get their 'swerve on'" (1999, x). *A Seat at the Table* is a lyrical avalanche of Blackness behind the snare beat of New Orleans' ethos. In the album, Solange weaves the lives of two of the most influential New Orleanian rappers of all time: Master P and Lil Wayne. The song "Mad," which features 16 bars from Lil Wayne, is a sonic rendering of James Baldwin's thesis of Black rage.

Baldwin (1984) writes: "To be a Negro in this country and to be relatively conscious is to be in a rage almost all the time" (205). Moving Baldwin's acumen to rhyme, Lil Wayne's verse highlights the perpetual arduousness of being Black; he raps: "Yeah, but I, got a lot to be mad about. . . . When I wear this fucking burden on my back like a motherfucking cap and gown . . . Man, you gotta let it go before it get up in the way. Let it go, let it go." In this verse, Lil Wayne is grappling with the reality that white supremacy lives on the literal backs of people of color. The unbearable weight of this very personal burden, stifling as it is, can easily crush whoever stands beneath it. Wayne warns of "let(ting) it go" before it does. Although much more easily said than done, the importance of Wayne's verse recognizes the tension between the personal and the structural, importantly not erasing the significance of either.

Following Lil Wayne, the southern, New Orleansian, gritty, sonic aesthetic of the album is solidified with the voice of New Orleans rap god, Master P. Master P punctuates the album with testimonial interludes of Black ambition and struggle against the ever-present veil of white mediocrity. Throughout the album, Master P's interludes bring sonic testimony to Black ambition. Before the song "For Us By Us," in which Solange sings, "All my niggas in the whole wide world/All my niggas in the whole wide world/Made this song to make it all y'all's turn/For us, this shit is for us." Master P unequivocally articulates Black ambition coupled with keen entrepreneurship skills in the face of the record industry's' legacy of colonizing Black music for profit. Master P states:

> They offered me a million dollar deal, and had the check ready. Said I wouldn't be able to use my name. I was fighting my brother, because "Man, you shoulda took the million dollars!" I said "No, what you think I'm worth? If this white man offer me a million dollars I gotta be worth forty, or fifty . . . Or ten or something." To being able to make "Forbes" and come from the Projects. You know, "Top 40 Under 40." Which they said couldn't be done. Had twenty records on the top "Billboard" at one time. For an

independent company. Black-owned company. You know, going to the white lady's house where my Grandmother lived at, and say, "Look, you don't have to work here no more Big Mama! We got more money than the people on St. Charles Street." And I, I took that anger and said, "I'mma put it into my music." I tell people all the time, "If you don't understand my record, you don't understand me, so this is not for you."

Here, Master P acknowledges the words of Kwame Ture: "Black visibility is not Black Power." By refusing a deal that would have propelled him to more notoriety than he had ever experienced, Master P demonstrated the recognition that visibility, when "handed down" by an other that controls unequivocally, does not constitute power, but rather the empty shell of symbolic power. Master P's refusal, brazen as it was, helped carve out his space of power in the game for years to come.

Six years before Master P released his 4x platinum album, *MP Da Last Don,* Daymond John, J. Alexander Martin, Keith Perrin, and Carlton Brown, four Black entrepreneurs from New York City, launched the clothing company F.U.B.U. The acronym stood for, "For Us By Us." The name and company was one of the first Black-owned companies to monetize the exclusion of White folks within Hip Hop culture. In 1998, F.U.B.U sales grossed over $350 million worldwide. The title of the track, "For Us By Us," signals to people of color, especially those who came of age in the late 1990s at the height of hip hop's global takeover, that Black art must move beyond just visibility to self-sufficiency, wherein artists of color can have the ability to control their art and voice independent of the music industry's plantation model. The stories of these men are of capitalist ideas of empowerment: a For Us By Us model that signals to white folks that we can beat them at their own game of selling Black culture. But, when all is said and done, is that liberation? Despite Master P's achievements, we understand that liberation for people of color must be collective—meaning, until "the most marginalized Black people, including but not limited to those who are women, queer, trans, femmes, gender nonconforming, Muslim, formerly and currently incarcerated, cash poor and working class, disabled, undocumented, and immigrant" (Black Lives Matter, 2016, para. 3) are not limited by opportunity or duress, the idea of liberation is hollow at best. An empowerment based off of the maintenance and validation of capitalism can only ever be empowerment for a few, at the cost of the majority. We have to question whether the idea of For Us By Us really means anything if we are merely switching roles with our oppressors.

Robin D. G. Kelley (2002) reminds us that "virtually every radical movement failed because the basic power relations they sought to change remain pretty much intact. And yet it is precisely alternative visions and dreams that inspire new generations to continue struggle for change" (78). The emancipatory nature of the song and its title is seductive, but it is not a blueprint for dismantling power. Perhaps instead, it's a fight song for the struggle. Solange's music falls within the long legacy of Black women entertainers using their music as pedagogical spaces to spread the ideas of and advance civil rights. From Bessie Brown, Ella Fitzgerald, Lena Horne, Nina Simone, Abbey Lincoln, and Mahalia Jackson to Solange, Black women's music has done the seminal work of building collective identity formations for movement building. For example, on the track, "For Us By Us," Solange sings, "When you driving in your tinted car/And you're a criminal just who are you . . . When a nigga tryna board the plane/And they ask you, "What's your name again." She adds "For us, this shit is from us/Get so much from us/Then forget us." "For Us By Us" is a mixture of emotions. Solange so vividly captures the pain, frustrations, and anger with living inside of white folks' trivializing and violent imagination. The song is a powerful narrative of resistance to whiteness. Solange captures the collective experience of white supremacy as it pummels the Black body, and in response, she evokes white rage, telling it, "Don't feel bad if you can't sing along/Just be glad you got the whole wide world? This us / This shit is from us / Some shit you can't touch" (Solange, 2016). Solange makes it clear that "some shit" white people cannot take from us. Her stance is pro-Black, affirming, and something that needs to be said. The song "For Us By Us" is about more than money or power, it's about Black humanity and dignity.

## Intimacy, Vulnerability, and the Logic of Love

Although littered with songs that articulate the complexity of being a Black woman in America, the most "forward" of songs on *A Seat at the Table* are arguably "F.U.B.U." and the clap-worthy titled song, "Don't Touch My Hair." These two songs capture a tension in the album: that of being unflinchingly for the perpetuation of Black-only experience, space, and reflection, and that of accepting the dominant narrative of the United States as possibility and opportunity for all. This tension, as previously noted, was apparent in the pairing of the album title and the album photo. It is these songs that most clearly express the rage felt toward whiteness that appropriates and preys upon Black people. In "Don't Touch My Hair," Solange explores many of the themes surrounding Black women's hair. Not only pillage to the exoticism of the refrain, "Can I touch your hair?," Black women's hair is arguably subject to more scrutiny than any other bodily feature in modern history. Black women experience the exoticism of non-Blacks touching their hair as though hair doesn't grow from Black women's' heads as it does from everyone else's'. Black women experience scrutiny for the ways they decide to wear their hair: When worn naturally, it is read as unkempt and disheveled, when worn pressed, or preferred as weave, Black women are thought to be sell-outs, self-hating, or promoting ideals of Eurocentrism.

Black women's hair is always a political space, hence the importance of Solange's album cover. "Don't Touch My Hair" beautifully weaves the clear boundary that Solange is drawing around herself and all other Black women, and the vulnerability that hair, specifically Black women's hair, occupies. This tension between vulnerability and defiance is a literal line by line dance that Solange plays. The first line of the songs begins with the refrain, "don't touch my hair." Throughout the song, hair begins to be substituted with other nouns, "don't touch my soul," "my crown," "my pride." Hair is not just the protein that accumulates from follicles in the scalp—hair is intimacy, strength, and vulnerability. Hair is not left alone, be it by the grower of the hair or by its observer. Hair is disciplined and subject to scrutiny, but hair can also be celebrated. It is a "crown." This song demonstrates the complexity of keeping the intruders at bay, while also wrestling with seemingly contradictory forces such as love and hate, territorialism and openness, pride and humiliation, inwardly.

Though songs such as, "F.U.B.U," "Don't Touch My Hair," "Mad," and others are all more complex than their titles might suggest, it is "Cranes in the Sky" that has left us (Bettina and Sarah) lingering in wonderment and disorientation. To both of us, this song one day represented love life, the next day, mass affect, the next day, self-love. This song, out of all the others, proved the most difficult to pin down. It was in this realization—that the song refused simple naming—that assuredness began to set in. There are names that educators, activists, and laymen speak to point to the terrors that structure modern life: racism, homophobia, capitalism, classism (Adams & Bell, 2016; Anzaldua, 1999; hooks, 1994). However, it is the conglomerate of daily experience that gives these categories any meaning at all. Racism can be taught as a set of institutions, practices, and interrelations that consistently inscribe race as inherent and everlasting and within a spectrumed hierarchy. These categories are helpful in that they steer the personal toward the political—they allow an understanding of aggressions and misfortunes out of the neoliberal realm of personal responsibility to the historical comprehension of genocidal chains of command. However, it is the latently formed consciousness of difference in treatment from our peers, the strenuous labor of our mothers, the violence between or absence of our parents, that gives us an inkling that "something ain't right." Solange captures the inner dialogue that we battle with due to outside and inward force. Part love song to self and other, part depressed admittance, and all unresolved tension, "Cranes in the Sky" is poetry and truth, as are many of our existences.

The vulnerability of this song cannot be mistaken. Solange wrote the song 8 years ago in one night. The honesty and intensity of the process is revealed through the song, if not it's background story. Shot in nine different cities, "Cranes in the Sky" is a literal journey through the self. There is universality and specificity in "Cranes." Who has not tried to drink "it" away? To sleep "it" away—to sex "it" away? It is the "it" that provides the anchor and the detail: the "it" of Black women everywhere being lower than most lows, but for that, higher than most highs. Solange's journey is a journey of knowledge of the self, and a raw recognition that many of us find ourselves frightened of. It is her honesty and her vulnerability that truly makes this album educational in the most social justice of ways—it is the honesty to be true to what we do and who we become when we are under mountains of pressure that creates self-worth, that beautiful avenue of freedom fighting.

## What Black Women Teach Us

One aim of this book is to document and acknowledge Black women's social justice practices that take place outside the academy. A constant site of Black women's legacies as social justice educators is Black motherhood. *A Seat at the Table* is a generational sonic ode to how Black mothers teach their children to love being Black. Solange is the daughter of Tina Lawson and the sister to megastar Beyoncé; Solange, herself, is a mother. Throughout the album, Solange reveals the way she teaches her 12-year-old son, Daniel Julez Smith, to understand his Black boy magic and her simultaneous fear of having him taken from her. However, Solange's mother does the heavy social justice mamma lifting on the album in the interlude "What Tina Taught Me." She says:

> I think part of it is accepting that it's so much beauty in being Black and that's the thing that, I guess, I get emotional about because I've always known that. I've always been proud to be Black. Never wanted to be nothing else. Loved everything about it.
>
> It's such beauty in Black people, and it really saddens me when we're not allowed to express that pride in being Black, and that if you do, then it's considered anti-white. No! You just pro-Black. And that's okay. The two don't go together.
>
> Because you celebrate Black culture does not mean that you don't like white culture or that you putting it down. It's just taking pride in it, but what's irritating is when somebody says, you

know, "They're racist!," "That's reverse racism!" or, "They have a Black History Month, but we don't have a White History Month!" Well, all we've ever been taught is white history.

So, why are you mad at that? Why does that make you angry? That is to suppress me and to make me not be proud.

This lesson of Black love is evidently instilled in the way that Tina's daughters go about their art. In April of 2016, Beyoncé released the visual album *Lemonade*. *Lemonade* was laced with African symbolism across the diaspora: References to the Middle Passage and African spirituality were seamlessly and intentionally placed throughout. Solange's creative approach differs from her sister's, but still commands these historical and contemporary narratives of Black life. Regardless of their different styles, these women are Tina's children. Her words in the interlude reflect the righteous rage and indignation for how loving being Black provokes white rage. And for all of the truth and beauty behind Tina's message, we must ask: Is she right? With all due respect of our elders, Tina's statement, "Because you celebrate Black culture does not mean that you don't like white culture or that you putting it down" is problematic. Her statement highlights the ambivalent state that this album occupies. Tina's statement on white culture reads as an apology for the strength in her words proceeding; to say it plainly, we must *not* celebrate white culture because white culture upholds and perpetuates white supremacy. Whiteness is an enemy to be defeated, not a compatriot to be heralded.

Political sociologist Eduardo Bonilla-Silva (2006) argues that the two-sided or "balanced" approach to racial harmony is structurally unreachable through this mindset. We have to reject white culture in its totality because it is fundamentally anti-Black, violent, and oppressive. Being pro-Black means understanding that there is no counterpart to the stance. White folks who are truly about the work of justice must be pro-Black with the understanding that they are rejecting whiteness, and thus, a colonizer's mindset. There is often an apology or a hedging interspersed in the words of pro-Black messages; we can't help but read Tina's words in this way. Tina's ambivalence is historically structured; whiteness, when it has not violently crushed what is pro-Black, tends to violently curate it, causing this state of ambivalence between recognizing whiteness as inherently anti-Black and espousing a multicultural fantasy.

## Speaking with Solange: A Conversation Among Friends

Solange's album gives us what texts such as the one we are producing here, are sometimes unable to offer us: the lyrical and sonic measure for that which escapes the bounds of formally structured sentences and linear rationale. For that reason, we love her, and we take her album as a method of education that reflects the historical creativity of Black women who have found ways to engage in social justice through every conceivable measure possible. For as sure as the legacy of oppression toward Black women and non-cis males is true, is as true as the magical ways that Black women have adapted to abhorrence, to create life in the void.

We look to Solange's album not just as a manifestation of her doubtless talent as an artist, but as a snapshot of a moment in history that has the world listening to the ever-increasing veracity of the phrase, "Black Lives Matter." Just as we look to Solange as an educator of sorts, so must Solange—and by way, us—look to the historical moment of mass mobilization as her educator. Social justice educators have taken note of the ways in which mass movement sparks a budding intellectualism and new forms of relation. And in the continuance of that legacy and this dialectic conversation that occurs in Tweets, in the annexes of Spotify, on the streets, at our dinner tables, and in our bedrooms, we understand the way in which Black women–led social justice education is a hopeful offering of a new way to learn and grow: a way that gives space for historical weight, a way that recognizes linearity as simplistic. As Black women continue to teach us, and as we speak to one another over the deafening alienation which seeks to partition our existences, we learn that nothing short of the pursuit for total liberation is our greatest teacher.

## Notes

1. For an extensive understanding of Black Lives Matter see https://policy.m4bl.org/platform

2. It is important to note that BLM is a movement created by three queer Black women: Patrisse Cullors, Opal Tometi, and Alicia Garza.

## References

Adams, M., & Bell, L. A. (Eds.). (2016). *Teaching for diversity and social justice.* New York: Routledge.

Adichie, C. N. (2014). *We should all be feminists.* New York: Vintage.

Anderson, C. (2016). *White rage: The unspoken truth of our racial divide.* New York: Bloomsbury Publishing.

Anzaldua, G. (1999). *Borderlands/La frontera: The New mestiza* (2nd ed.). San Francisco: Aunt Lute Books.

Baldwin, J. (1984). *Notes of a native son* (Vol. 39). New York: Beacon Press.
Berry, T. R., & Mizelle, N. D. (Eds.) (2006). *From oppression to grace: Women of color and their dilemmas in the academy.* Sterling, VA: Stylus.
Bonilla-Silva, E. (2006). *Racism without racists: Color-blind racism and the persistence of racial inequality in the United States.* New York: Rowman & Littlefield Publishers.
Dyson, M. E. (1993). *Reflecting Black: African-American cultural criticism* (Vol. 9). Minneapolis: University of Minnesota Press.
Evans, S. Y. (2007). *Black women in the ivory tower, 1850–1954.* Gainesville: University Press of Florida.
Evans, S. C., Taylor, M. Dunlap, & D. Miller (2009). *African Americans and community engagement in higher education: Perspectives of race in community service, service-learning, and community-based research.* Albany, NY: SUNY Press.
Few, A. L., & Bell-Scott, P. (2002). Grounding our feet and hearts: Black women's coping strategies and the decision to leave. *Women and Therapy, 25,* 59–77.
Few, A. L., Stephens, D. P., & Rouse-Arnett, M. (2003). Sister-to-sister talk: Transcending boundaries and challenges in qualitative research with Black women. *Family Relations, 52*(3), 205–215.
Fleming, J. (1983). Black women in Black and White college environments: The making of a matriarch. *Journal of Social Issues, 39*(3), 41–54.
Freire, P. (1985). *The politics of education: Culture, power, and liberation.* Translated by Donaldo Macedo. South Hadley, MA: Bergin, 1985.
Gay, R. (2014). *Bad feminist: Essays.* New York: Harper Collins.
Gutiérrez y Muys, G., Niemann, Y. F., Gonzalez, C. G., & Harris, A. P. (2012). *Presumed incompetent: The intersections of race and class for women in academia.* Boulder: University Press of Colorado.
Hamilton, C., & Ture, K. (2011). *Black power: Politics of liberation in America.* New York: Vintage.
hooks, b. (1994). *Teaching to transgress: Education as a practice of freedom.* New York: Routledge.
hooks, b. (2000). *All about love: New visions.* New York: William Morrow & Company.
Kelley, R. D. (2002). *Freedom dreams: The Black radical imagination.* New York: Beacon Press.
Kim, M. M. (2002). Historically black vs. white institutions: Academic development among black students. *Review of Higher Education, 25,* 385–407.
Love, B. L. (2013). "I see Trayvon Martin": What teachers can learn from the tragic death of a young Black male. *The Urban Review, 45*(3), 1–15.
Love B. L. (2016). Anti-black state violence, classroom edition: The spirit murdering of black children. *Journal of Curriculum and Pedagogy, 13*(1), 22–25.
Malcolm, X Grassroots Movement (2013). Operation ghetto storm: 2012 annual report on the extrajudicial killings of 313 Black people by police, security guards, and vigilantes. Atlanta: Malcolm X Grassroots Movement. Retrieved at mxgm.org/operation-ghetto-storm-2012-annual-report-on-the-extrajudicial-killing-of-313-Black-people

Matias, C. E., Viesca, K. M., Garrison-Wade, D. F., Tandon, M., & Galindo, R. (2014). "What is critical whiteness doing in our nice field like critical race theory?" Applying CRT and CWS to understand the white imaginations of white teacher candidates. *Equity & Excellence in Education, 47*(3), 289–304.

Neal, M. A. (1999). *What the music said: Black popular music and black public culture.* New York: Routledge.

Rankine, C. (2015). *Citizen: An American lyric.* UK: Penguin UK.

# Part III

## POSITING PEDAGOGY

Chapter 11

# Black, Female, and Teaching Social Justice

*Transformative Pedagogy for Challenging Times*

ROBIN BROOKS

Matters of social justice are increasingly pervading U.S. society and the greater global community. From news headlines to social media memes, people are confronted with the reality of inequalities and various forms of discrimination. Ignoring the fights against civil and human rights violations that are often reminiscent of the U.S. Civil Rights Movement of the 1950s and '60s is virtually impossible for people living in the United States. Famous quotes from revered ancestors such as Martin Luther King, Jr., are boldly displayed on signs and T-shirts at marches, protests, and community meetings throughout the nation. Unsurprisingly, college professors like me witness the ills of society spill onto our campuses and into our classrooms. In addition to participating in community protests against injustices, students are organizing protests on college campuses to demand an end to racially insensitive and discriminatory atmospheres at their universities. As in the larger society, many of the issues being combatted have long been a part of campus culture, but current events highlight their existence. As college professors, we aim to help students understand and become better informed about their surroundings so they learn the importance of contributing meaningfully to society. Diversifying our pedagogical practices and embracing a social justice education (SJE) approach, especially during challenging times, is critical to underscoring the reality of inequalities and equipping students with the necessary analytical thinking skills to resist them.

Situated within an SJE framework, this chapter represents some of my experiences teaching undergraduate students at predominantly white institutions (PWIs) during recent times of intensified racial tension in the United

States; the chapter focuses on the variety of pedagogical resources I use in my courses to teach social justice issues. Though my academic area is within the humanities, specifically literary studies, the material presented can act as a guide for other academic disciplines. The role of self-awareness and professors' personal teaching philosophies are significant matters that need attention in any discussion of SJE. Consequently, I submit details of my teaching persona as well as my overall style of teaching. Specific supporting resources to facilitate my SJE approach, however, make up the crux of the chapter. The skill of flexibility in lesson planning and execution is key in achieving goals of SJE, as being open to different perspectives unlocks different avenues of connecting and learning. Moreover, the courses we teach vary based on numerous factors, such as class size, time of day, and student dynamics, so I admit the presence of imperfection in the material presented throughout the chapter. The information can be amended, tweaked, and substituted as needed.

## Pedagogical Choices and Influences

For proponents of SJE, self-awareness is crucial, as it influences instructional choices. In fact, this chapter is based on the premise that "our social group memberships and positionality, along with our social identity, affect various aspects of our teaching, such as our pedagogical approaches and curriculum design" (Bell, Goodman, & Varghese, 2016, 397).[1] Numerous studies, including the collection of essays *Presumed Incompetent: The Intersections of Race and Class for Women in Academia* by Gabriella Gutierrez y Muhs and colleagues, discuss not only how our various intersections impact our teaching but also how we are perceived by students, colleagues, staff, and administrators. I am a Black female with a PhD, an authority figure many of the students I come across are not accustomed to seeing. I stand a couple of inches above 5 feet and appear younger than my age. I also have a southern accent and wear natural curly hair.

Whether we like it or not, physical appearance impacts our perceived competence and influences people's perceptions. While business casual attire is what I wear when I teach because I adore the stylishness and flair it offers, I am cognizant that matters as superficial as style of dress can sway people's opinions of me. Historian Tanisha C. Ford's *Liberated Threads* (2015), moreover, examines how Black women throughout history have used dress as intentional and political tools for their activism. Scattered across the nation, the small amount of Black female tenure-track professors as well as how our teaching evaluations can receive lower markings because of students' biased perceptions are factors that keep me attentive to my positionality in the classroom.[2]

The role of stereotype-based judgments, including how Black professors are expected to entertain, also are not lost on me.[3]

Ultimately, knowledge of these realities causes me to be strategic in my course and classroom preparation and to take critical steps in creating an inclusive environment. From day one of the semester, I present an organized classroom structure, reflected in the syllabus and course introductions, to prepare students to view my course as a safe space to have tough and, sometimes uncomfortable, discussions. Several scholars note that climate and classroom dynamics are integral or "central to social justice education" (Bell, Goodman, & Ouellett, 2016, 66). These measures allow me to establish my credibility and lay the foundation for students to trust me. As a result, I have their attention when it is time to engage matters of social justice.

Further, my teaching philosophy facilitates communicating core concepts of SJE, such as the importance of recognizing and, subsequently, acting against injustices. My constructivist paradigm suggests learning is an active process and the belief that a student-centered approach best aids that process.[4] With this premise, my teaching philosophy incorporates three main facets: critical reflection, writing as a mode of inquiry, and critical consciousness. I have discovered that transformative learning, which ultimately leads students to be independent thinkers, requires critical reflection and the challenging of presuppositions among students. Understanding that students come to class with a variety of learning styles, skill sets, and personalities, I begin my courses modeling active learning and demonstrating how to analyze texts critically. This approach can take on a variety of forms, including open-class activities. Such exercises serve multiple purposes: They make the critical analysis or thinking process visible; they allow students to compare their problem-solving or meaning-making processes; they demonstrate benefits of participation in collaborative learning; and they further help me create a supportive learning environment in which students express their ideas without fear of negative judgment.

Additionally, I encourage students to think of writing as a mode of inquiry or a process that helps them discover and uncover their ideas about the course material and related information.[5] Whether teaching an introductory or upper-level course, I allow students to choose their relevant writing topics, as I recognize that students have different interests, backgrounds, and reasons for taking the course. This practice generates original, imaginative projects from them. Still, I never want students in my courses to write simply for writing's sake; instead, I encourage students to develop critical consciousness, a practice advocated by Paulo Freire, enabling them to consider the social, economic, and political contexts pertaining to the course material.[6] Barbara J. Love (2013), preferring the phrase "liberatory consciousness," expresses my sentiments when she writes, "[a] liberatory consciousness enables humans to live their lives in oppressive systems and institutions with awareness and intentionality, rather than on the basis of the socialization to which they have subjected" (601). In the end, I prompt students to connect the literature to contemporary situations and issues to advance their understanding of their role in American society and the larger global community.

## Resources to Facilitate Class Activities

Using different types of class activities and assignments throughout the semester has helped to ensure that most students comprehend the course material, thereby becoming critically aware of various systems of oppression and ways to challenge them. In this section, I delineate a variety of effective resources I incorporate in class sessions that also easily lend themselves to adaptability within lesson plans in regard to current events. In other words, these resources allow me to be flexible and equipped to slightly augment lesson plans to include recent events or unexpected incidents, including tragedies, associated with a key theme or issue in the course material. Further, they allow me to smoothly and strategically insert the current events into the lesson in a way that students will not complain that I am off topic. This section outlines examples of how I use the resources, and I include anecdotes of various dynamics that I have observed play out in my classroom that brought me to these specific pedagogical tools and choices. I begin with video media, expanding on educational videos and news clip videos, before concluding with a few other types of videos. Then, I describe how I employ social media posts, audio, the internet (especially government websites), pictures, and additional resources in my SJE practice.

I have included the resources mentioned here in several literature courses, including those that focus on African American, Latino/a American, Asian American, Native American, and/or Caribbean literatures. In these courses, the students and I explore a number of SJE topics, such as the historical and contemporary elements of race, racism, privilege, unequal educational systems, sexism, gender rules, social identity, socialization, prejudices, discrimination, oppression, social action, stereotypes, intersectionality, human rights, and legal systems.[7] I use the resources as a part of my teaching methods, which include student-led discussions, pair/group work, individual and panel presentations, debates, and interactive lectures, in order to engage every student. Diverse teaching strategies prepare students to achieve learning outcomes of expressing not only their knowledge and comprehension of the course materials but also their ability to interpret and assess them. No matter the method, I elicit students' critical analysis and reflective practice to help them become better writers, researchers, and communicators on social justice matters, which are lifelong skills that stretch beyond their academic careers.

*Video Media*

I find visual literacy to be significant for today's students because contemporary culture is hypervisual, so being able to evaluate images and visual media can enhance students' skill sets. As a result, I use a variety of video, TV, and film clips in my courses. Still, I am mindful always about "using technology in ways that help rather than harm goals of social justice" (Domingue, 2016, 370). By far, these particular resources are among the most popular in my courses. Several types of video clips are valuable, including ones from educational videos, music videos, local/national/international news segments, TED talks, and other lectures. YouTube has been an invaluable tool for accessing such videos. Scenes from TV shows and films as well as documentaries are also quite effective in my courses.

Before I incorporated videos to demonstrate controversial ideas in my courses, some students would be hesitant to believe either me or the subject at hand. Angela P. Harris and Carmen G. Gonzalez (2012) explain such reactions, emphasizing that "the culture of academia is distinctly white, heterosexual, and middle- and upper-middle-class. Those who differ from this norm find themselves, to a greater or lesser degree, 'presumed incompetent' by students, colleagues, and administrators" (3). After viewing the videos, some students would have an "a-ha!" moment or add to the discussion by mentioning a situation or experience that related to the video, and thus, the controversial subject. Instead of being annoyed that some students needed further "evidence" to believe the course material or me, I chose to embrace the reality that video media could act as a tool to elaborate on difficult topics and further aid in establishing my intellectual authority. Exercises utilizing these resources tend to really capture students' attention and help them better understand and remember course readings and concepts.

Educational Videos

By educational videos, I mean straightforward videos usually created by an organization meant to inform about a particular topic. Some literary readings feature protagonists who face various hardships and struggle to live a productive life, such as Junot Diaz's *Drown*, in which Dominican characters in a working-class area confront many adversities. To illuminate the underlying issues portrayed in such readings, the African American Policy Forum's

"Structural Discrimination: The Unequal Opportunity Race" video is effective as it offers a visualization of structural racism.[8] It is an animation that illustrates runners of different racial backgrounds on a running track; the racial minority individuals are hindered by obstacles such as rainstorms, ditches, and a pond of sharks. The animation presents a simplified, "user-friendly" approach for students to grasp real impediments many minorities face, including wealth disparities, discrimination, poor schooling, underemployment, and a shortened lifespan. The video concludes with a message that national legislation helps level the playing field. Such a video is a useful tool to generate various views on a controversial issue and help clarify course materials.

A number of readings in my courses, no matter which literature course, examine the subject of privilege and its role in characters' lives. Much information about different forms of privilege appears in SJE literature and, without a doubt, this can be a very touchy or sensitive area for students at PWIs.[9] Many times, I witnessed physical changes when the subject surfaced, including changes in students' facial expressions, body language, and demeanor. Some students assumed that I was about to launch a brutal lecture on "imperialist white supremacist capitalist patriarchy" (182), to borrow a popular phrase by bell hooks (2003).[10] While these perspectives are certainly at the heart of the matter, I have found that videos allow me to introduce them in a more palatable manner.

A helpful tool, the BuzzFeed video "What is Privilege?" addresses the uneven playing fields and advantages that some people have by specifying different types of privileges.[11] In the video, participants begin in standing positions at the same line in the middle of the room. They move forward or backward depending on the number of privileges they have. The exercise attempts to make privilege visual, and the participants discuss their thoughts about their final positions—how far up or behind they ended. Students become informed about additional privileges such as religious privilege, gender privilege, and heterosexual privilege beyond the more familiar ones, like class privilege. Unfortunately, the privilege not to have your racial background paraded around as a mascot is one that Native Americans do not possess. Offensive to many people, the Washington Redskins, Atlanta Braves, Florida State University Seminoles, University of North Dakota Fighting Sioux, Miami Carol City Senior High School Chiefs, and McMinn County High School Cherokees are examples of mascots or nicknames based on Native Americans held by professional sports teams, universities, and high schools.[12]

As a result of students' association with and sometimes fanaticism of sports culture, I find the national campaign Change the Mascot's video "Proud to Be" an effective tool to open discussions of stereotypes, prejudice, human rights, and genocide. Referring to what it calls a racial slur, the campaign created the video to convey their desire for the NFL's Washington Redskins to change its mascot. The short video shows various pictures of Native Americans as the backdrop to the narration that simply calls out descriptions of Native Americans, such as "proud," "forgotten," "Blackfoot," "Navajo," and "indomitable." It ends with a picture of a Washington Redskins' helmet on a field next to a football before the final words of the video: "Native Americans call themselves many things. The one thing they don't . . ."[13] The viewer is meant to finish the sentence with the word "Redskins." Students begin to think more deeply about why the humanity of Native Americans has been ignored and continues to be ignored on many fronts given the controversy over the Dakota Access Pipeline protest that began in 2016 in which their rights to impede the construction of an oil pipeline that threatens their water supply and cultural resources have been being questioned.

News Video Clips

I have used local, national, and international news clips while discussing readings that reference aspects of criminal justice systems, such as the police and law enforcement. In this #Black Lives Matter era, some of my students clam up when I, their Black professor, broach the role of this subject in the readings. The disproportionate rates of people of color in regard to negative interactions with the law make it unsurprising that writers of color entertain the subject. Indeed, legal scholar Michelle Alexander (2012) expresses that several law enforcement methods "have been employed almost exclusively in poor communities of color, resulting in jaw-dropping numbers of African Americans and Latinos filling our nation's prisons and jails every year" (98).

June Jordan's "Poem about Police Violence" and Audre Lorde's "Power" are examples of such readings that depict the reality of Alexander's statements, and these readings always lead to discussions of events involving African Americans and police violence. To analyze such readings and to discuss people's attitudes about dealing with police encounters, I have shown an ABC news clip, "One Black Parent's Strict Dress Code Rules for His Kids: 'No Dark Clothes, No Hoodies,'" that featured an upper-class African American attorney, Lawrence Otis Graham, detailing guidelines for his sons that he thinks will lessen their chances of being targeted by police.[14] He stated that his sons, especially after Trayvon Martin's death, are not allowed to wear hoodies unless it is a rain coat or winter coat, and their attire consists of khakis, polos, sweater vests, and loafers. They also are not allowed to bring bags into stores or carry anything in their hands that could be mistaken as a weapon.

The video impressed upon students the real fear caused by racial profiling and police brutality that many Black parents have about not truly being able to protect their children, no matter their class status. Some students thought Graham's rules were extreme, which led to further discussion about what can be done to change these circumstances. Likewise, the call for protests when tackling this topic is common. Since local protests are happening in many places, I have been able to show additional news clips of people protesting across the nation for a variety of reasons as well as students at different universities protesting on campuses.

When covering a reading that addresses self-rejection or self-hate and the negative effects of racial inequality, I have shown video clips of updated studies based on psychologists Kenneth and Mamie Clark's 1940's doll tests in which young children of different races are presented with the task of choosing between Black and White dolls.[15] Alongside the Clark study, I discuss how Anderson Cooper and CNN created a variation of the test in 2010, what they call a "scientific pilot study," in which children had to answer questions and point to different pictures of dolls that ranged in shade from light to dark.[16] Their results (like many other studies on the topic) show that, even today, preference for the White dolls is still prevalent among young children of various racial backgrounds. Many of the children see the darker-skinned (Black) images as least intelligent, least attractive, and least liked by others. Self-rejection, unfortunately, is an issue many college students face, and I have learned that their sudden bashful behavior with this topic is sometimes associated with their self-perceptions. The video offers them a safe way to explore the subject.

## TED Talks, Music Videos, TV Shows, Movies

Additional video media aid my social justice focus. Lectures or TED talks, such as Peggy McIntosh's "How Studying Privilege Systems Can Strengthen Compassion" (along with her article "White Privilege: Unpacking the Invisible Knapsack" that lists examples of white privilege), tend to enlighten students about the reality of race privilege in everyday circumstances.[17] In like manner, a decades-old lecture by Jane Elliott, creator of the "Blue Eyes/Brown Eyes Exercise," in which she asks White audience members to stand if they would not mind being treated the way our society treats Black citizens is rather intriguing. When no one stands, she states, "That says very plainly that you know what's happening. You know you don't want it for you. I want to know why you're so willing to accept it or to allow it to happen for others."[18] Students in my courses recognize how relevant Elliott's question remains today. Interestingly, a 2016 music video, "Warzone" by rapper T. I., ends with these words from Elliott. His video re-enacts several high-profile police brutality cases that have led to #BlackLivesMatter protests; however, his video depicts a role reversal by having White actors play the victims and Black actors play the policemen. Like many music videos, this one offers provocative sociopolitical commentary. In the past, I have shown scenes from television series and movies as well so that students could compare course readings with the portrayals. Additionally, documentaries by Marlon Riggs and Michael Moore help examine systems of oppression on individual and societal levels.[19]

Social Media Posts

Social media is a very popular mode of communication, and students are familiar with and active on different social media sites, such as Facebook, Twitter, and Instagram. Acting as a facilitator, I incorporate entertaining instructional tools, such as social media technology, to introduce a topic or help guide class discussions. I have found that I can use social media, like other resources, to bear witness to the validity of contentious subject matters. Students have admitted that the various posts from social media platforms helped shake them from their preconceived notions and doubts about what they were examining. While I am still bewildered sometimes by the lack of belief, I am grateful that my method was successful in aiding their comprehension. For example, illegal immigration remains a hot-button, politicized topic, and I have used tweets from elected officials to ask probing questions about undocumented immigrants. When analyzing Jimmy Santiago Baca's "So Mexicans are Taking Jobs from Americans," Iowa's Congressman Steven King's tweet highlights current realities and sparks deeper discussion. King, during President Obama's 2015 State of the Union Address, tweeted, "#Obama perverts 'prosecutorial discretion' by inviting a deportable to sit in place of honor at #SOTU w/1st Lady."[20] He uses the term "deportable" to describe an undocumented college senior whose parents brought her to the United States from Mexico illegally when she was a year old. Under the Trump administration, students now are able to identify a plethora of troubling posts, especially tweets, that they use to analyze the content of readings on this topic and to further understand the wider debates in the nation about building border walls and Deferred Action for Childhood Arrivals (DACA). The reality that some college students, who could be their peers, are undocumented tends to really personalize the subject.[21]

Moreover, popular memes shared hundreds of times across social media are also useful in underscoring certain themes, such as stereotypes, subordination, and domination. In debates about what constitutes a riot versus a protest and how race figures into the separation between the two, memes comparing White fans committing all sorts of vandalism after a sporting event with people of color marching in the streets with signs have been eye-opening for students. They become aware of bias in media coverage as well as the role of media headlines in shaping people's perceptions. In *When Whites Riot: Writing Race and Violence in American and South African Culture*, Sheila Smith-McCoy explains that the term "riot" is so much associated with Blacks that "[it] remains difficult even to conceive of the idea of a white racial riot" (5). One particular meme that I show in my courses draws attention to racial double standards by placing pictures of Black protesters covered with the words "destroying the community," "animals," and "thugs" next to pictures of White rioters covered with the words "booze-filled revelers," "mischief," and "rowdy."[22] The juxtaposition of the pictures forces viewers to contemplate the reasons for the different titles and the insinuations of similar titles.

## Audio

Mindful that some students are auditory learners, I use audio throughout my courses as well. Music lyrics, poetry lines, and speeches accompanied by the song, spoken word, and speech performances can provide emphasis for students. Despite being released in the early 1970s, Marvin Gaye's song "What's Going On" continues to offer relevant commentary on social issues of today. Students find the song uncanny because many of them are literally trying to figure out what is going on in their society. In the past, I have had students volunteer to sing the Black national anthem "Lift Every Voice and Sing." Students unfamiliar with the song became aware of the sound and beat that accompany the lyrics, which correspond to the struggles of African Americans, and note how the overall tone presents an emotional appeal. Caribbean poet Jean "Binta" Breeze's poem "Third World Girl" comes to life when listening to her read it, and the references to imperialism and sexism that it underscores are better impressed upon students. Similarly, Amiri Baraka's performance of his poem "Dope" incorporates sounds that facilitate comprehension of the poem. Additionally, the audience interaction in the recording of Malcolm X's sermon "The Ballot or the Bullet" offers a participatory feel for listeners. Democracy and voting are central matters in the sermon, matters at the fore of many social justice dialogues.

## Internet: Government and Organization Documents

Classroom access to the internet is a valuable resource in many respects. I have been able to show students how to locate documents from the government and organizations for research purposes as well as discussion starters. I began incorporating these documents in various ways when I became aware of just how much some students blindly followed what they heard in the media.

Some students would insist that their misguided perspectives were accurate. An SJE approach is committed to interrupting the socialization processes that reproduce oppression. Misinformation, lack of information, and ignorance are reasons some people pass on assumptions (versus facts). Indeed, Maurianne Adams and Ximena Zúñiga (2016) explain that "[s]tereotypes are reinforced by selective attention to behaviors that match stereotypes and ignore or rationalize behaviors that contradict them" (99). One stereotype-based assumption, as an illustration, is that Blacks are the majority of those receiving government assistance or "free handouts" in the United States. To dispel the myth, I show data about the Supplemental Nutrition Assistance Program (SNAP), formerly known as the Food Stamp Program, which is available on the United States Department of Agriculture's website. Many students are surprised to learn that the majority of those receiving SNAP are White Americans.[23]

Further, the website for the anti-sexual violence "It's On Us" Initiative is helpful when addressing sexual assault, sexism, and gender roles or expectations in creative literary works. Cuban-American playwright Nilo Cruz's *Anna in the Tropics* and Jamaican writer Erna Brodber's short story "Suzzette" in *The World is a High Hill* are examples of readings possessing these themes and exploration of the website in my courses have helped students feel more comfortable addressing these topics. The Obama administration launched the initiative in 2014 to eliminate sexual assault on college campuses. However, Betsy DeVos, Donald Trump's choice for U.S. Secretary of Education, has made changes to how universities handle sexual assault cases by eliminating a part of the Obama-era government policy on September 22, 2017.[24] Still, the itsonus.org website is useful in providing easy-to-remember tips and resources about sexual violence, and it has a pledge and list of campus partners (a plus if students see their university's name) so that students can take part in the movement. Students recognize that they can enact what they are learning immediately.[25]

PICTURES

Social justice educators and academics in various other fields also cover topics of xenophobia, war, law, and peace.[26] I have found that pictures, particularly of tragic events from the past, can "speak" to students and immediately nullify doubts about the seriousness of certain topics. The similarity between images documenting the World War II history of U.S. Japanese internment camps with those of the Jewish Holocaust serve as viable illustrations for the reading and analysis of Dwight Okita's "In Response to Executive Order 9066." President Franklin D. Roosevelt's signing of the order resulted in the relocation of thousands of Japanese Americans after Japan bombed the U.S.

naval base at Pearl Harbor. Students note the irony that they have learned more about Germany's concentration camps than the United States' variation of the camps. The role of racism and other systems of oppression in the decision are a part of the discussion as well.

Readings that highlight other racist and discriminatory legal decisions, such as the 1896 U.S. Supreme Court case *Plessy v. Ferguson*, pair well with pictures of racial segregation signs, such as water fountains denoting "For Colored Only" and "For Whites Only." Plus, pictures are beneficial when examining texts such as Oonya Kempadoo's *Tide Running* and Diana McCaulay's *Dog-heart* to help identify the interrelated connections of imperialism, tourism, xenophobia, and human rights violations. Pictures of glamorous Caribbean tourist hotels and attractions juxtaposed with pictures of poverty-stricken local Caribbean residents' neighborhoods are striking and bring to life the narrative descriptions.[27]

## Additional Resources

Editorial or political cartoons can be effective in conveying key points associated with social justice course material as well. When evaluating readings that mention the destruction of Native American people, such as Leslie Marmon Silko's "[Long Time Ago]," two particular thought-provoking cartoons alluding to social group memberships, social identities, and stereotypes are worthwhile. One cartoon depicts an obese White male character dressed in gear for the fictional team "Warrior Savages."[28] He is holding a flag with the team's name and wearing tribal paint on his face along with a makeshift headdress. Clearly, his attire is meant to mimic that of Native Americans and connotes stereotypical behavior. The cartoon also indicates ignorance, which is a key factor in how oppression is reproduced, as the words "Go Savages Kill 'Em" are written across his bare chest, and he is saying to the Native American in front of him, "But I'm honoring you, dude!" The thin Native American character stands with a troubled look on his face, seemingly baffled at the obliviousness of the other character's insulting appearance. The extremes of the two characters' appearances accentuate the absurdity. In the same way, the second cartoon, "You Don't Look Like an Indian," depicts a young White boy saying these words to his Native American friend while a cloud with images of the Cleveland Indians' logo, Redskins' helmet, and Pocahontas float above his head.[29] Both cartoons allow for exploration of the myths about Native Americans and their traditions that are passed down from generation to generation among those in the wider U.S. population.

In addition to political cartoons, university newsletters and administrators' emails have become strategic tools in my classroom recently. Due to the intensified attention to injustices in the media, an increased number of university administrators are sending out campus-wide emails referencing the issues, and articles in university newsletters feature the issues as well. I find that these documents offer me a savvy way to speak to a critical current event in our society (even if not directly related to a topic we are addressing in the course at the time). Interestingly, many students do not read the emails or newsletters. After reiterating the importance of reading them, I pull them up on the screen and pinpoint the key points. I ask students what the lines mean and why the university would see the matters as so pressing to facilitate students recognizing the urgency of being aware of what is happening in their surroundings.

## Proven Strategies

While using various resources has been effective in my classroom, I am always mindful of my and the students' interactions as well. To de-center myself and encourage active participation and dialogue, I sometimes join students in a circular desk arrangement/seminar-position. I always try to speak to multiple sides of a controversial issue, as critical thinkers should consider various perspectives. In her discussion of pedagogical principles for SJE, Maurianne Adams (2016) helps explain my rationale:

> Participants need to feel from the very beginning that the learning community will be inclusive, personalized, and experiential. They need to know that they will be challenged, but they will be safe as they engage with difficult issues on which many of them will have different perspectives. (38–39)

Like Adams, I agree that it is important for students to know that they are safe even as they are being asked to come up to a higher level of thinking. Furthermore, I sometimes welcome storytelling in my courses to help with this and to create a more personalized tone. I ask students for examples from their lives or whether they have heard of something. To display openness, I also bring in my experiences to illustrate some points.

Demeanor while teaching, especially about these issues, is important to me as well. No matter how personal an issue is with me, I remain calm and not combative. This has not been easy always, however. Sylvia R. Lazos (2012) informs that "male and female instructors find maintaining authority in the classroom and at the same time keeping the atmosphere warm . . . to be challenging" (180). Aware of my authority, I do not want students to think they must agree with me; instead, I encourage them to share their individual point of views. Still, an ultimate goal in my courses, admittedly, is to recruit allies who will advance social justice.

Ultimately, my experiences teaching about social justice in my courses have buoyed my hope in our youth—our future. At times, I have been despondent about the state of affairs in the United States and the world. Witnessing civil and human rights abuses on a regular basis concerning the treatment of people of color has affected me on a personal level. In fact, it is traumatic to be inundated with tragedies. Having a self-care regimen that includes physical and breathing exercises, counseling, and fun or fulfilling activities keeps me healthy. Still, watching students expand their worldviews and exhibit a desire to challenge systems of oppression and domination is heartening. It encourages me to continue to stay updated on national and global happenings, attend relevant conferences, seek networking possibilities with social justice–minded scholars and activists, and check my biases so that I can continue to advance my teaching and share the information with them. In the last few years, many scholars have demonstrated their commitment to equity, fairness, and justice by creating and widely circulating syllabi such as the Black Lives Matter Syllabus, Ferguson Syllabus, #StandingRockSyllabus on #NoDAPL, #SayHerName Syllabus, Lemonade Syllabus, and #blkwomensyllabus. I, too, aim to remain committed to taking action that will bring about a transformed status quo.

## Notes

1. For more on this topic, see Bell, Goodman, and Varghese (2016).

2. For information on Black female professors' statistics, see Harris and Gonzalez (2012, pp. 2–3). Also, there are several studies on bias in student evaluations. For instance, see Lazos (2012).

3. See McGee and Kazembe (2015) for more on expectations to entertain.

4. See special issue on Forty Years of Radical Constructivism in Educational Research for more on constructivist approaches. In particular, see Dykstra (2014).

5. For more on writing as a mode of inquiry and composition, see Susan Miller (2009), especially Juan C. Guerra's chapter "Putting literacy in Its Place: Nomadic Consciousness and the Practice of Transcultural Repositioning," Victor Villanueva, Jr.'s chapter "Maybe a Colony: and Still Another Critique of the Comp Community," and Jacqueline Jones Royster's "When the First Voice You Hear is Not Your Own."

6. For more on critical consciousness, see Freire (1993) and Adams (2016).

7. Bell, Funk, Joshi, and Valdivia (2016) discuss a number of these topics.

8. See the video "Unequal Opportunity Race" at www.youtube.com/watch?v=eBb5TgOXgNY.

9. See Bell, Funk, Joshi, and Valdivia (2016).

10. hooks uses this phrase throughout her scholarship, including in her book *Teaching Community*.

11. See BuzzFeed's video at www.youtube.com/watch?v=hD5f8GuNuGQ.

12. After much controversy, the University of North Dakota retired the name Fighting Sioux in 2012 and replaced it with the Fighting Hawks. In contrast, the Seminole Tribe of Florida gave Florida State University "a written resolution from the Tribal Council affirming its enthusiastic support for the university's use of the Seminole name, logos and images." For more information, see unicomm.fsu.edu/messages/relationship-seminole-tribe-florida.

13. See the video at www.changethemascot.org/proud-to-be-video.

14. See abcnews.go.com/Nightline/video/Black-parents-strict-dress-code-rules-kids-27544055

15. For more on the Clark's doll study, see Clark (1963).

16. Kenneth and Mamie Clark's doll studies found that Black children associated the White doll with positive traits and the Black doll with negative traits; in other words, they were being negatively impacted by racial inequality. Their research played a significant role in the 1954 U.S. Supreme Court case *Brown v. Board of Education of Topeka*. CNN and Anderson Cooper's version is the AC360 Doll Study. A clip is available at www.youtube.com/watch?v=DYCz1ppTjiM. An additional clip of CNN's version, "Study shows how children view race bias" is available at www.youtube.com/watch?v=EQACkg5i4AY.

17. For more, see McIntosh (1990, 2012).

18. Various clips of Elliott's lecture are available on YouTube. The transcript for the video, *Essential Blue Eyed*, is available at www.newsreel.org/transcripts/essenblue.htm.

19. For more on Blacks and documentaries, see Klotman and Cutler (2000).

20. For the tweet and an article on it, see www.cnn.com/2015/01/21/politics/king-tweet-deportables.

21. For more on immigration, see Menjivar (2015).

22. See the meme at www.theroot.com/blog/the-grapevine. Black_people_riot_over_injustice_white_people_riot_over_pumpkins_and_football

23. See www.snaptohealth.org/snap/snap-frequently-asked-questions.

24. Some governors such as Tom Wolf of Pennsylvania have been emboldened to introduce state legislation that is associated with the "It's On Us" Initiative to protect victims of sexual assault.

25. For more on sexual violence on college campuses in particular, see Harris and Linder (2017).

26. See Harrison (2005) for essays on such topics.

27. Nixon (2015) discusses the divide between tourists and local residents and related topics in her scholarship.

28. The cartoon is by Lalo Alcaraz and is available at www.pocho.com/prophet-time-travel-cartoonist-native-team-mascot.

29. The cartoon is by John Branch and is available at publications.newberry.org/indiansofthemidwest/indian-imagery/stereotypes.

## References

Adams, M. (2016). Pedagogical foundations for social justice education. In M. Adams, L. Bell, D. J. Goodman, & K. Y. Joshi (Eds.), *Teaching for diversity and social justice* (3rd ed., pp. 27–53). New York: Routledge.

Adams, M., & Zúñiga, X. (2016). Getting started: Core concepts for social justice education. In M. Adams, L. Bell, D. J. Goodman, & K. Y. Joshi (Eds.), *Teaching for diversity and social justice* (3rd ed., pp. 95–130). New York: Routledge.

Alexander, M. (2012). *The new Jim Crow: Mass incarceration in the age of colorblindness.* New York: The New Press.

Bell, L., Funk, M. S., Joshi, K.Y., & Valdivia, M. (2016). Racism and white privilege. In M. Adams, L. Bell, D. J. Goodman, & K. Y. Joshi (Eds.), *Teaching for diversity and social justice* (3rd ed., pp. 133–181). New York: Routledge.

Bell, L., Goodman, D. J., & Ouellett, M. L. (2016). Design and facilitation. In M. Adams, L. Bell, D. J. Goodman, & K. Y. Joshi (Eds.), *Teaching for diversity and social justice* (3rd ed., pp. 55–93). New York: Routledge.

Bell, L., Goodman, D. J., & Varghese, R. (2016). Critical self-knowledge for social justice educators. In M. Adams, L. Bell, D. J. Goodman, & K. Y. Joshi (Eds.), *Teaching for diversity and social justice* (3rd ed., pp. 397–418). New York: Routledge.

Clark, K. B. (1988). *Prejudice and your child.* Middletown, CT: Wesleyan University Press.

Domingue, A. D. (2016). Online and blended pedagogy in social justice education. In M. Adams, L. Bell, D. J. Goodman, & K. Y. Joshi (Eds.), *Teaching for diversity and social justice* (3rd ed., pp. 369–396). New York: Routledge.

Dykstra, D. I., Jr. (2014). Radical constructivism and social justice: Educational implications. *Constructivist foundations, 9*(3), 318–321.

Ford, T. C. (2015). *Liberated threads: Black women, style, and the global politics of soul.* Chapel Hill: University of North Carolina Press.

Freire, P. (1993). *Pedagogy of the oppressed* (Rev. 20th anniversary ed.). New York: Continuum.

Gutierrez y Muhs, G., Niemann, Y. F., Gonzalez, C. G., & Harris, A. P. (Eds.). (2012). *Presumed incompetent: The intersections of race and class for women in academia.* Logan: Utah State University Press.

Harris, A. P., & Gonzalez, C. G. (2012). Introduction. In G. Gutierrez y Muhs, Y. F. Nieman, C. G. Gonzalez, & A. P. Harris (Eds.), *Presumed incompetent: The intersections of race and class for women in academia* (pp. 1–14). Logan: Utah State University Press.

Harris, J. C., & Linder, C. (2017). *Intersections of identity and sexual violence on campus: Centering minoritized students' experiences.* Sterling, VA: Stylus Publishing.

Harrison, F. V. (Ed.). (2005). *Resisting racism and xenophobia global perspectives on race, gender, and human rights.* Lanham, MD: AltaMira Press.

hooks, b. (2003). *Teaching community: A pedagogy of hope.* New York: Routledge.

Klotman, P. R., & Cutler, J. K. (Eds.). (2000). *Struggles for representation: African American documentary film and video.* Bloomington: Indiana University Press.

Lazos, S. R. (2012). Are student teaching evaluations holding back women and minorities?: The perils of "doing" gender and race in the classroom. In G. Gutierrez y Muhs, Y. F. Nieman, C. G. Gonzalez, & A. P. Harris (Eds.), *Presumed incompetent: The intersections of race and class for women in academia* (pp. 164–185). Logan: Utah State University Press.

Love, B. J. (2013). Developing a liberatory consciousness. In M. Adams, W. Blumenfeld, C. Castaneda, H. W. Hackman, M. L. Peters, & X. Zúñiga (Eds.), *Readings for diversity and social justice* (3rd ed., pp. 601–605). New York: Routledge.

McGee, E. O., & Kazembe, L. (2015). Entertainers or education researchers? The challenges associated with presenting while Black. *Race Ethnicity and Education, 19*(1), 96–120.

McIntosh, P. (2012, Nov. 5). How studying privilege systems can strengthen compassion: Peggy McIntosh at TEDxTimberlaneSchools. Retrieved from www.youtube.com/watch?v=e-BY9UEewHw

McIntosh, P. (1990). White privilege: Unpacking the invisible knapsack. *Independent School, 49*(2), 31–36.

Menjívar, C., & Kanstroom, D. (2013). *Constructing immigrant "Illegality": Critiques, experiences, and responses.* New York: Cambridge University Press.

Miller, S. (Ed.). (2009). *The Norton book of composition studies.* New York: W.W. Norton & Co.

Nixon, A. V. (2015). *Resisting paradise: Tourism, diaspora, and sexuality in Caribbean culture.* Jackson: University of Mississippi.

Smith-McCoy, S. (2001). *When whites riot: Writing race and violence in American and South African culture.* Madison: University of Wisconsin Press.

Chapter 12

# Moments in the Danger Zone

*Encountering "Non-Racist," "Non-Racial," "Non-Color-Seeing," Do-Gooders*

MICHELLE R. DUNLAP, CHRISTINA D. BURRELL, AND PENNEY JADE BEAUBRUN

> Give a person a fish, and you feed them for a day, but teach a person to fish, and you feed them forever.
>
> —Anne Isabella Thackeray Ritchie

There's that moment when a well-liked or even maybe even well-loved, well-intentioned, wonderfully "non-racist" supposedly social-justice-seeking person tells you that they see no color, or their parents saw no color in their entire lives, or every problem on earth is all about socioeconomics and not at all about race, and blah, blah, blah. We can't emotionally tolerate it anymore, mostly because both history and contemporary research after research study is not tolerating it anymore as it reveals that we do *all* see color, and as early as 6 months of age (Bronson & Merryman, 2009). Further, by denying it, more harm is exacted on minorities in either micro-aggressive or macro-aggressive forms, whether it is consciously perceived or not (Schofield, 1986; Sue, 2010). Not to mention that denying it warps social justice efforts by allowing people to ignore racial history, with them having bought into the idea that social justice is giving people something that they don't have enough of rather than fixing the structures that historically have caused the inequities. The contemporary scientific fact is that humans do see color throughout our lives, and if we think we don't or that we shouldn't, we become dangerous to those who already are the most disenfranchised, misunderstood, shunned, or otherwise excluded in our society (Dunlap, Burrell, & Beaubrun, 2017; Evans, Taylor, Dunlap, & Miller, 2009; Schofield, 1986). Thus, the colorblind are more likely to put the blame for disenfranchised others' plights mostly on the victims themselves instead of on the discriminatory structures that have played a key role in hindering whole groups of people. This is because the colorblind can't *see* those structures—they are colorblind to them (Dunlap et al., 2017; Schofield, 1986). As two former students and a professor of color educated and working in predominantly White, often liberal, higher education and social service environments, we have faced our share of micro- and macro-aggressions. Having come from African American, Haitian, and biracial African/Euro American backgrounds, we are all too familiar with the pain that colorblind do-gooding can do, and its deleterious impact on social justice efforts and individual and community understanding. If partners can't get past this first, initial phase of just hearing one another, with open eyes, willing to look, see, and learn from one another, then they most likely won't get far enough into their engagement to actually get something productive and social-justice enhancing done.

This chapter discusses the role of our mindset for listening to the unheard, seeing beyond the lone minority representative, and understanding White privilege, colorblindness, and early racial identity development stages. We also share the resources and strategies we use to try to best traverse these interpersonal challenges while attempting to conserve our energies for the students, colleagues, and communities with whom we engage who have interest in learning and growing with us as we work collaboratively within social justice efforts.

## Identifying Key Interpersonal Challenges

We've been *learning* while *engaging* in higher education environments and grassroots communities for 60 combined years of our adult lives. These environments include educational settings, faith-based organizations, social-service settings, nonprofit organizations, community youth-oriented engagements, and community family support endeavors. We learn while also teaching, service-providing, volunteering, or otherwise facilitating in these environments. Thus, we often find the lines blurred between learner and teacher/facilitator, as we go about our engagements within a variety of communities. We find that the three of us share commonalities in our personal philosophies for engaging about difference, diversity, race, racism, racial-identity development, and colorblindness as we traverse the aforementioned environments. Like many Black women professionals engaged across venues, we negotiate these environments frequently in the course of our responsibilities, but also with the hope of inspiring some degree of shaking up of others' sometimes rigid and stereotypical notions about communities of color—which historstatistically (our invented word) are disproportionately poor. By shaking up stereotypic notions and pushing for a more informed advocacy, we hope that social justice interests also will be shaken up and motivated. At the same time, we don't want our heads cut off in the process—in other words, we'd rather not lose our support systems, our jobs, our friends, our health, and so on, but the reality is that we all know a fair share of women who have paid far too great a price for trying to be heard, resisting oppression, and/or fighting for what is right. Being brave in spaces can be much riskier for us, and certainly can cost us more (Hamblin, 2017).

Topics surrounding race and other identity categories such as sexuality, politics, and religion can be particularly touchy topics in general. When these conversations occur in settings where participants' identities conflict across single or multiple categorical lines, they can be significantly more difficult (e.g., a conversation about sexuality between an opinionated conservative heterosexual person and an outspoken gay, lesbian, or bisexual person, who may or may not be of the same race or gender). Having difficult, brave, even contentious conversations is not the problem—it's being able to hear the unheard partners, and move forward having seriously taken into account what has been said. We have selected what we see as four of the main obstacles that hinder not only conversations about race, other diversities, and social justice, but also social justice action. Our list is not exhaustive by any means, but we see it as a starting point for delineating some of the challenges that we (and no doubt many others) have experienced in our years of educational and community engagement even with well-intentioned, liberal do-gooders who still don't get that they have not cornered the market on understanding minorities, racism, poverty, and the diversity of community perspectives that exist with respect to our society's inequities and injustices.

*Challenge 1: Not Being Heard and Not Listening*

It's been our experience as women of color that sometimes unaware but well-intentioned do-gooders approach us and those with whom we partner in the community in ways that are perceived as maternalistic, condescending, and suggestive that the speaker has not heard one word that we have tried to communicate. It would be helpful if everyone could just stop and listen—not for the purpose of responding right away—but just to listen and digest, in order to process and at least grapple with what the other person is trying to say. Far too often, we are experiencing a do-gooder who attempts to "chastise" us in one way or another for our own feelings and impressions of the world around us or, worse, tries to tell us how we should feel. Two or three or four times of that from someone, and we've already emotionally checked out and moved on to the next thing on our very busy list of responsibilities. The opposite can also happen. For example, in many courses and community environments, when the time comes for liberals, and especially White liberals, to speak about race or other sensitive topics, it is not uncommon to observe them to shut down right away when challenged (Ladson-Billings, 1996). This leaves an unfair burden on minorities to do all of the grappling, risk taking, and speaking on these issues. Every time we speak, we put our neck on the line—and why should that burden fall only on us. Our observation is that the liberal colorblind would like the privilege to speak, but not the burden of possibly getting their heads chopped off, so to speak, if others don't like what they are saying. This is a burden, however, that minorities live with every second of their entire lives. Another challenge involves do-gooders distancing themselves from conversations by speaking about others' experiences without grappling with their own issues, socialization process, and experiences. These individuals may initially provide input as if from an outsider's perspective, rather than by making "I" statements that indicate first-hand experiences or ownership of feelings and experiences that they themselves hold. From the perspective of others observing this, such depersonalization of the issue(s) may serve the purpose of removing oneself from any emotional attachment that may come with whatever they are sharing. Diversity work can be stressful emotionally, especially for students in early stages of racial identity development (Dunlap, 2011, 2013). As a protective measure, some may create a buffer against whatever response or rebuttal another person may have to their statement, story, or experience that they may share with them. This tendency to avoid the conversation or keep it at a very basic level takes away the ability to create any new, more authentic, understanding of one another, as any hopes for advancing the conversation on race, other differences, and/or social justice to any significant extent are diminished.

While we are promoting the idea of increasing our comfort with difficult dialogues so that there is greater ease in sharing, we are not promoting the idea that healthy conflict is always negative. We believe that completely shutting down or holding back during difficult discussions may be detrimental to the advancement of the conversation, while healthy conflict can lead to more authenticity in discussion and ideally provide those dialoguing with viewpoints that foster better understanding and social justice efforts in the future. Some collaborators have engaged dialogues proactively and consistently rather than waiting for future incidents. As minority former students, we have observed that when race topics were being discussed in academic settings, many students from a variety of backgrounds who shared their dilemmas and opinions with the groups did not appear as attentive to others' issues. They seemed mostly eager to share their side of the story but did not seem as eager to listen to their peers who may have different experiences and opinions. As a result, no one seemed to have left the room with solutions to the problems or any general deeper understanding about how others experience race or other diversities. Thus, some left with the same point of views that they had before attending the classes or meetings, which made us feel that our and perhaps others' valuable time and mental and emotional energy had been wasted. From the perspective of a minority faculty who has served on many diversity-related committees both inside and outside of academia, the experience has been similar to that of students. It is similar in that faculty, staff, and administration also struggle with issues of race, power, difference, silence, and so on. Whatever age group, diverse collaborations, even with colorblind do-gooders who may think they have already "arrived," will be more successful when there is space and respect for authentic sharing and earnest listening and processing. Without it, any endeavor may likely mirror the social inequities against which we often have already unsuccessfully fought.

*Challenge 2: Expecting the Minority Spokesperson*

In situations where minorities are in the minority, both in terms of power relations and *numerically* speaking, conversations surrounding race can be especially difficult in meetings, classrooms, and other such settings. Many community members, professors, and fellow students expect minorities to know or relate to certain topics due to their apparent racial, ethnic, gender, sexual orientation, or class categories. Occasionally, these facilitators of meetings or even professors may target a minority as a "spokesperson" unconsciously based on this assumption. Such action can create varying levels of discomfort in the student or person being targeted. In the classroom, if the student is the only minority in class or is the "token" minority student chosen as a spokesperson for the entire group, this discomfort may be escalated (Dunlap, Beaubrun, & Burrell, 2009). When members of a minority are targeted in this way, they may not have a readily available answer or opinion, which can be embarrassing, even humiliating—especially when the facilitator, teacher, or other students appear to expect the targeted individual to have a canned, well-formulated response. If an individual is targeted multiple times during a conversation or is repeatedly targeted throughout the span of the meetings or course, the person may come to dislike the class, the teacher, committee work, and/or fellow participants. They might also isolate themselves from the situation, emotionally checking out, or skipping meetings altogether to avoid being put in an uncomfortable situation. Diversity-related work is hard enough, but when colorblind do-gooders get the notion that it should be primarily the work of the few minorities in a situation, it overburdens the already burdened few, and allows the do-gooders to skate by without having to get into the trenches of this hard work.

*Challenge 3: Colorblindness—Ignoring Diversity and White Privilege*

From time to time we are called on to serve as diversity consultants to organizations or agencies. The biggest challenges that we observe in those situations are: (1) people who think they see no color, therefore they have no need for diversity training; (2) people who have a friend of color, spouse of color, child of color, neighbor of color, or office-mate of color who think that ensures their non-racism and makes them a diversity expert. They thus believe they have no need for further learning, teaching, or sharing about diversity issues; and (3) people (and these are the most difficult) who take pride in helping the poor, the illiterate, the sick, the less fortunate, and so on while remaining convinced they see no color. This latter group is often convinced that they have not a biased thought anywhere in their imagination for reasons such as their parents never in their entire lives saw color, or they never heard of the N-word until they were 52 years old, or perhaps they took a 2-hour (usually 90 minutes or less) diversity course in 1991 that taught them everything they needed to know about diversity to cover them until the end of time. This can present quite a challenge for consultants like ourselves who believe that 50% of the most effective diversity work is internal and long term—that is, it's on the facilitators' and participants' internal selves, and over the course of entire lifespans. Therefore, we are very upfront with whomever we are engaging that our work will be a partnership, and most likely will barely scratch the surface of possible learning that can happen. Nonetheless, learning to posture ourselves for listening, and in terms of how to observe and ask questions and engage dialogue may be the skills that, when continually developed, are just as important as learning specific histories and "facts" about cultures/races/ethnicities that themselves are variable from individual to individual and day to day. So, what we've learned from the participants with whom we've consulted is that knowing how to ask questions, listen, and observe is just as important as knowing histories, well-researched cultural tendencies, and so on. In other words, learning *how* to position ourselves for engagement and *learning* is just as important as the passing on of specific knowledge because what we think we know about a group can change from person to person, group to group, and moment to moment. Both history and process, together, are important.

Recent research that we've conducted suggests that those who work hands-on with disenfranchised communities still also can hold colorblind ideologies, and further, these colorblind ideologies are associated with negative impressions of youth. To be specific, in a recent data analysis of 200 social workers and teachers, it was revealed that the more that these social service providers ascribed to colorblind ideology, the more significantly aggressive and out of control they saw a group of minority children they were asked to evaluate, even when controlling for race, gender, and social desirability (Dunlap et al., 2017). Therefore, naïve, colorblind ideologies, as in past studies, continues to be a challenge for community members who are engaging with well-intentioned, colorblind do-gooders.

Whenever race is discussed, the concept of White privilege (McIntosh, 1990) is often unwittingly overlooked or perhaps defensively ignored among some of our classmates and colleagues. An example of a White privilege is being able to walk into a store at the mall and not have the staff assume you are there to steal, or being able to use checks and credit cards without it being assumed that you may not be financially responsible (Dunlap, forthcoming; McIntosh, 1990). Throughout our experience of being minorities on majority White campuses and communities, we have participated in numerous race conversations with White students and faculty. We have observed that some are unaware of their unearned daily privileges, while others are, and yet others may choose to ignore their privilege perhaps as a defense mechanism (Dunlap, 2011, 2013; Dunlap, Scoggin, Green, and Davi, 2007; McIntosh, 1990). Many White students are unaware of their privilege because they have never been confronted with a situation that actualizes it for them. So, once they enter conversations, experience media, or engage in community settings that help bring their Whiteness and the unearned day-to-day privileges that often accompanies that Whiteness, they can begin grappling with what it means to be a White person in a broad range of U.S. society environments. Those grappling with this may need extra support and resources that will enable them to acknowledge and recognize where they are situated with respect to race, class, privilege, and oppression (Dunlap, 2011, 2013; Tatum, 1992). This will enable them to better understand how the cycle of privilege, racism, and discrimination is perpetuated in our society, and what role it has played in their social justice endeavor(s).

*Challenge 4: Ignoring Racial Identity Development*

The concept of Racial Identity Development (RID) was defined by Janet E. Helms in her White Racial Identity Development Model and by William Cross in his Black Racial Identity Development Model (Helms, 1995; both reviewed in Dunlap, 2011 & Tatum, 1992). Individuals can be situated anywhere between being seemingly oblivious to the existence of racism altogether to being significantly aware of racism. Whites, specifically, can fall along the range of believing that they and our society are totally free of racism to being fully aware of their own racial identity and the privileges or disadvantages that accompany them, and can use their awareness as a home base from which to branch off and explore other groups with a more open mind, better informed, and with appropriate intentions. People of color may fall on one end where they place Whiteness on a pedestal and attempt to assimilate and be accepted, while others may actively seek to immerse themselves to one degree or another in their own culture so as to have a stronger cultural identity with their own group. Many people do not fit neatly into one or the other of these two models, as they may not consider themselves to be exclusively White or Black racially, therefore other models have been developed in order to assist anyone in thinking about and grappling with how the socially constructed concept of race and its history across the world has shaped us individually (Atkinson, Morten, & Sue, 1989; Dunlap, 2011, 2013).

In spite of the growth in racial identity models since the early '90s, we still find—both in academic and nonacademic settings—that most people have not yet done the work of grappling with their own racial identity stages. Therefore, they may not yet be able to examine their own developmental progress with respect to race and other diversities, much less anyone else's. In classrooms and other working environments where racial identity development has not been addressed, individuals may find it more difficult to understand the origins of the experiences and points of views of their peers. They may have difficulty engaging authentically with others because they have not yet confronted the ways in which racial identity development stages have shaped and are affecting their own and others' viewpoints. Some may be unwilling or unable to see the validity in what their peers are sharing with them because of the stage of racial identity development in which they find themselves (Dunlap et al., 2007; Dunlap 2011, 2013; Tatum, 1992). This hinders growth of individuals who are unaware of their racial identity progression, and often is frustrating for individuals who have explored such matters and are versed in their developmental progress.

Our stage of racial identity development, especially if it is an early stage or level, may not allow people to quickly connect that socioeconomic issues go hand in hand with race, and have an even more devastating and long-term impact on Blacks and other minorities than anyone (Dunlap 2011, 2013; Tatum, 1992). As the old saying goes, when White America catches a cold, Black America already has pneumonia, figuratively speaking, and research has truly confirmed this (Adelman, Smith, & Cheng, 2003). We've also noticed a tendency for well-intentioned grassroots do-gooders to want to help poor and/or minority communities exclusively by giving them things such as food, clothes, and school supplies, which is helpful indeed, and we would never suggest that this not be done. But we find ourselves feeling some frustration when we don't see more efforts devoted to also incorporating a progressive component so that providing assistance is combined with teaching strategies and methods for demanding social justice and equity while also working to become more independent or self-sufficient. In other words, besides volunteers bringing clothes and food to those in need, can't we also work on efforts to educate and empower those with whom we assist, which is a deeper level of engagement requiring the development of mutual trust? Otherwise, what we see happening is that our community-based volunteering help and efforts go out to the same families for years, decades, and even generations without families and their loved ones having the opportunity to engage a learning base that will help to both question the system while also working to move themselves out of their circumstances, if at all possible, and into a more empowered situation.

It's been our experience that when suggesting this to well-intentioned do-gooders, while they are highly motivated to keep *giving* fish, they may not be as motivated to put resources into teaching the poor and disenfranchised *how* to fish. It's been our experience that the more adept at critical thinking a person is, and the higher they are in their racial identity development, the more willing they may be to offer resources and supports for longer-term, more sustainable solutions, in addition to short-term immediate remedies. So, referring back to our "give a fish" notion, from our perspectives, first comes giving, then accompanied with that comes teaching or empowerment, and then accompanied with that comes social justice in which we can work toward structural change. We should always be striving to move toward greater sustainability and structural change, if we can, in our community engagements. Those still in denial about whether structural racial inequities still exist may be stuck at the exclusively "giving a fish" stage. We can no longer exclusively bring people food and clothes. Thus, understanding the role of racial identity development is helpful to us as we try to engage with diverse groups and work collaboratively toward self-empowerment and community social justice goals.

The four areas outlined above involve the interpersonal, and from our experience are preconditions to our ability to really see people for who they are, rather than for the stereotypes that we might imagine them to be, and thus to move forward to empowerment and social justice. In other words, if we don't have our minds right, how are we going to collaboratively build something, fix something, rectify a wrong, and truly engage in social justice? We'll be too busy exclusively collecting and handing out tons and tons of fish to figure out what needs to be changed in the system so that individuals won't have to rely their whole lives and for generations to come on that same handing out of fish. The negative effects of all four of the key interpersonal challenges we have discussed can be diminished when students and faculty are educated on topics such as White privilege and racial identity development, and when there are various resources and supports made available to help facilitate conversations and collaborative efforts so that partners can more effectively move forward with their social justice collaborations.

## Interpersonal Strategies and Resources

One's mindset can affect how one opens or closes themselves to really seeing the bigger picture beyond assumptions. Sometimes, being angry with or dismissive of the bearer of new information is easier, and often less effective. Over the years, a variety of methods, strategies, and resources have been engaged to assist with the interpersonal beginnings of community engagement and social justice work (Dunlap et al., 2017; Dunlap, 2000b, 2011, 2013; Dunlap et al., 2009; Dunlap et al., 2007; Evans et al., 2009). We will discuss some of the interpersonal strategies we have found to be helpful in community engagement and social justice endeavors in the sections that follow.

*Strategy 1: Reframing*

Decades ago, co-author Dunlap found that some students had difficulty seeing her as teaching about "children" whenever she incorporated children and families of color into her Children in a Multicultural Society course lectures. She did this in an effort to counter the exclusively White text discussions that were common in those days. She would get questions, complaints, and course evaluations questioning whether she should be talking about culture and race in a child development class. In other words, child development was seen as a White middle-class phenomenon, and to have to hear about the similarities and differences in developmental concepts and assumptions regarding other groups of children made some students feel they were being cheated out of their education. Some of these same students also saw her as having ulterior motives if and when she mentioned anything about the historical contexts of poverty, privilege, access, and disparities that their children and families faced. This made her life and teaching difficult for a short time. She brought this to her department chair, and together they tried to determine how Professor Dunlap could better support both herself and her students. Since there were no other African American women professors on campus at that time with whom she could consult, they turned to professors in similar situations at other institutions, the two men of color at our institution at that time, White allies doing multicultural work, and the reading resources available at the time (two of which she still uses: McIntosh, 1990; Tatum, 1992).

Professor Dunlap also found herself inspired to give her students a hypothetical analogy from the field of medicine. She asked them that if she were a heart surgeon who also happened to be good at brain surgery, would that make her any less of a surgeon in either area? They all agreed, no. She explained, then, that if she brings not only the conventional curriculum to them, and is expert at that as her education, training, and experience demanded, but also brings multicultural expertise to give them a fuller and deeper educational experience that will better prepare them for the real world, then she is doubly expert, and not less expert at either one. The resistant students seemed to get that, and were less resistant (Williams, Dunlap, & McCandies, 1999). Sometimes people need assistance in understanding how diverse research and perspectives strengthens their work rather than dilutes it.

*Strategy 2: Readings*

We have found particular materials to be extremely useful over the years. One crucial resource has been Beverly Tatum's article, "Talking about Race: The Application of Racial Identity Development in the Classroom" (1992), and the other Peggy McIntosh's article "Unpacking the Invisible Knapsack" (1990). Students and community partners tend to love these two resources even to this day and have relied on them for two decades. Because these two articles tend to focus on Whiteness and Blackness exclusively, sometimes Asian, Latina, Indigenous, and biracial students would complain or find themselves confused as to where they fit within the models. So, over the years, Professor Dunlap developed alternatives models and resources that anyone, no matter their background, could use to examine their current stage, level, or depth of racial identity development (Dunlap, 2011, 2013) or what kind of diversity they may be experiencing in their community engagement (Dunlap, 1999, 2000b; Dunlap et al., 2007). So, to sum up, concerning her students, what she has learned is that when helping to prepare them for community engagement, they find it very useful to explore their own social location and understanding of themselves, their assumptions, and stereotypical ideas and expectations (Dunlap, 2000b, 2011, 2013). Exploration of racial identity development (Dunlap, 2011, 2013; Tatum, 1992) and, if applicable, White privilege (Dunlap et al., 2007; McIntosh, 1990) assists students and community partners in examining themselves and their own developmental stages with respect to reflecting on and grappling with race and racial issues, which also helps them to understand others who are at different stages than they are. This then can assist partners in their social justice endeavors, as interpersonal relations is the first step in any engagement. Collaborative partners can begin to see one another as potentially *in process*, and can use their own experiences and sharing to help engage and teach others, and learn from others, with Racial Identity Developmental theory, White privilege, resistance to colorblindness, and so on as backdrops for processing their engagements with others. As Black women in academia, we do not think we would ever want to teach or take a course without using Racial Identity Development as the preliminary self-work for ourselves and those with whom we engage (Dunlap, 1999; Dunlap et al., 2009).

*Strategy 3: Multimedia Documentaries*

Based on our experiences, we would agree that when well-trained professors and facilitators include constructive methods in their engagement strategies such as multimedia resources, participants likely feel more comfortable about expressing themselves regarding race and other diversity issues (Dunlap, 2000a, 2011; Williams et al., 1999). When minorities, alone, are not being targeted and the environment is not only inclusive but also welcoming, discussions surrounding diversity and social justice can be more gainfully facilitated. But in many situations such diversity unfortunately does not exist. While the following is not a substitute for appropriately diversifying an environment, it is one strategy we have used while also challenging organizations to improve the diversity of their staff, governing boards, and other areas needing attention. In our experience, media resources in combination with other communication dialogue strategies can help shift focus from the few minorities in a training and onto a media stimulus in which characters tell a story that can be critically analyzed by all participants (Dunlap, 1999, 2000a, forthcoming). All participants have the opportunity to project their thoughts, feelings, emotions, stories, and connections onto the characters and circumstances in the media, and then move from that to more personal engagement and eventually social justice discussions with each other.

Multimedia resources cannot substitute for the human diversity for which we should earnestly strive, but they can have some impact on our interpersonal development, as illustrated by the way that television and other media have shaped individual lives and society in general. Within a multicultural educational setting, media that offer realistic portrayals of the struggles, injustices, and added layers of stress that African Americans and other minorities encounter daily (Hamlin, 2017) are helpful for provoking conversation surrounding multicultural issues that may lead to greater diversity and social justice efforts (Omi, 2006). Through our studies and work at the college we have encountered numerous materials that have served as educational tools and stimulated authentic dialogue across groups in our classrooms (Dunlap, 2000, forthcoming; Dunlap et al., 2009). These tools are particularly useful because they appear not to provoke the same degree of defensiveness and resistance among students and community partners that discussions or readings alone often provoke (Dunlap, forthcoming; Williams et al., 1999). When culturally relevant multimedia are combined with readings and/or course discussions, we have noticed that the four hindrances discussed earlier are reduced.

Documentaries in particular can be very useful. For example, one of the tools professor Dunlap uses in both her Adolescent Development and her Children and Families in a Multicultural Society courses is the documentary *A Girl Like Me*, created for a high school literature project by then-student Kiri Davis (2005). This documentary explores the stereotypes and distorted viewpoints of what it means to be beautiful in mainstream America and how these views affect Black children, especially females. *A Girl Like Me* was modeled after the Kenneth Clark doll studies conducted first in the late 1940s. Essays and studies can be paired with such films, such as the essay "See Baby Discriminate" (Bronson & Merryman, 2009), which Dunlap uses in conjunction with *A Girl Like Me*. In this essay we are shown how racial attitudes are perpetuated in children even younger than 3 years old. We see how minority parents are more likely to explicitly talk about racism with their children than their White counterparts, and we see how this lack of openness in race discussions leads to children forming their own uninformed opinions and meanings about other racial and ethnic groups (Bronson & Merryman, 2009). This article is an eye-opener for many individuals who believe that colorblind practices in early childhood are most appropriate. These two resources together suggest that ideas about race begin in early childhood and should be addressed earlier than we have done in the past. Also discussed in conjunction with *A Girl Like Me* was a study conducted by the Black Women for Black Girls Giving Circle (BWBGGC, 2009), which explored not only the struggles that accompany being a Black girl but also the resilience we may hold seemingly from birth, according to the researchers. This is yet another essay to pair with documentaries to use as learning tools for students when difficult race discussions arise.

A fourth resource is *Race the Power of Illusion* (Adelman, 2003), a three-part documentary focused on understanding what race is and how the concept of race disproportionately advantages people who are White. The third and final segment of the documentary focuses on how institutions and policies advantage some groups at the expense of others. It also conveys how housing became a racialized matter, including the emergence of suburbs and ghettos. In her freshman seminar Black Children and Families, professor Dunlap used this film as a tool in discussing both current issues such as housing discrimination and its impact on children and families today, as well as the origins of these issues over the centuries. The use of these kinds of resources provided many students and community partners with a wider perspective of the racial situation in America (Dunlap, 1999). Another exceptionally useful resource is Ava DuVernay's (2016) *13th*, which offers an in-depth and shocking examination of the preschool-to-prison pipeline in historical context. We have all noticed that the use of film invokes a variety of reactions from students and community partners that otherwise might not be shared, such as surprise that racism and self-image remain issues with which minorities must grapple in our society. If employed strategically, these documentaries can be used in classrooms and community environments to foster more engaged and less silent or volatile educational discussions of multicultural, policy, and social justice issues for children and adults of all ages. With the aid of these tools, we can more actively engage students and community partners in conversations that are more productive than if we attempted to do so without the use of projective resources.

*Strategy 4: Multimedia Feature Films*

Feature films (e.g., *Crooklyn*) used in classrooms and community engagement settings can also reduce some of the hindrances previously discussed. In our experience, the silences that can occur out of fear of speaking and sharing can dissipate, and the tendency to single out minorities as spokespersons for their racial group can be minimized. This may be because, as mentioned previously, students and community partners are able to project their emotions, opinions, and frame their reactions around the individuals depicted in the film as opposed to using solely their own experiences as a basis for discussion (Dunlap, 1999; Dunlap et al., 2017). Such resources may make it easier for students or community partners to engage in discussion that allows them to branch off into more contemporary discussions related to social justice issues and endeavors at hand.

*Strategy 5: Additional Resources*

Based on our experiences, other recommendations for creating more multiculturally friendly classrooms and community engagement venues conducive to open and progressive conversations include providing an inclusive environment with a diverse staff and ample diverse resources for those who will engage in that environment. These resources should come in many forms—books, films, documentaries, posters depicting multicultural individuals as opposed to only White individuals—and be readily accessible to everyone. We also recommend that if multimedia resources are used they be paired with appropriate readings, discussion, or experiential activities (e.g., service learning), and that students or community partners should be provided with ample time to process the media. Because students and community partners all have unique experiences and understandings of race due to individual differences, processing time is necessary so they can hear and share their reactions and questions with peers, teachers, and/or facilitators.

While we have suggested several particular resources, others are also readily accessible, such as the website www.teachingtolerance.org. Websites of this nature provide free teaching kits and classroom or community activities to help teach a diverse array of students and groups.

In this chapter we have shared both written and multimedia resources that many instructors and other friends have found extremely helpful (even our do-gooder friends who just don't get why we aren't always impressed by what they are saying or doing) . . . and then there are those who, no matter what resources you suggest, will not consider any view other than their own. This is when we must make the decision to conserve our energies for those who truly want to engage in a two-way, not a one-way, conversation.

In summary, race is one of America's taboo topics. Discussions surrounding race-related issues can trigger varying degrees of emotional responses and create a silent and tense atmosphere among individuals involved in the attempted discussion; this can be counterproductive to the interpersonal relations required for truly collaborative social justice work. Such a situation tends to perpetuate the cycle of racism, discrimination, stereotyping, and victim-blaming already so deeply rooted in American society. When these negatively stereotypical ideas are passed directly and indirectly along to our students and/or community partners, any hope of improving race relations and social justice in America diminishes. We believe the use of approaches and resources discussed in this chapter can help overcome obstacles and set an atmosphere of equity in collaboration toward social justice. We hope the information presented here can be used to improve the interpersonal experiences of both minority and mainstream individuals in settings where there are means to do so, such as in schools, community collaborations, and other social and social justice environments. Such practice tends to better engage students and community partners, helping us move beyond "do-gooding" toward social justice endeavors that promote the equitable changes we all want to see in our society.

## References

Adelman, L., Smith, L., & Cheng, J. (2003). Producers, PBS Series, Part 3—The House We Live In. *Race: The power of an illusion*, Vol. 3. California Newsreel.

Atkinson, D. R., Morten, G., & Sue, D. W. (1989). A minority identity development model. In D. R. Atkinson, G. Morten, & D. W. Sue (Eds.), *Counseling American minorities* (pp. 35–52). Dubuque, IA: William C. Brown.

Black Women for Black Girls Giving Circle of the Twenty-First Century Foundation (BWBGGC) (2009). *Black girls in New York City: Untold strength and resilience*. Washington DC: Institute for Women's Policy Research, pp. 1–63.

Bronson, P. & Merryman, A. (Sept. 5, 2009). See baby discriminate. *Newsweek*.

Clark, K. (1955). *Prejudice and your child*. Boston: Beacon Press.

Dunlap, M. (1999). Tolerance and intolerance for African American children and families: Lessons from the movie *Crooklyn*. In J. Robertson's (Ed.), *Teaching for a tolerant world*, Urbana, IL: The National Council of Teachers of English, Committee on Teaching about Genocide and Intolerance, 121–146.

Dunlap, M. (2000a). Teaching about children and families in a multicultural society. *Transformations: The New Jersey Project Journal for Curriculum Transformation and Scholarship*, *11*(1), 28–34.

Dunlap, M. (2000b). *Reaching out to children and families: Students model effective community service*. Lanham, MD: Rowman & Littlefield Publishers.

Dunlap, M. (2011). Thriving in a multicultural classroom. In C. P. Harvey & M. J. Allard (Eds.), *Understanding and managing diversity*. Upper Saddle River, NJ: Pearson/Prentice Hall.

Dunlap, M. (2013). "Cross-cultural community engagement, Elizabeth Kubler-Ross's model of death and dying, and racial identity development." In H. Fitzgerald, J. Primavera, and C. Burack (Eds.) *Going public: Civic engagement, the scholarship of practice*. East Lansing: Michigan State University Press.

Dunlap, M. (forthcoming). *Shopping while Black: Minority experiences in retail marketplaces & other consumer environments*.

Dunlap, M., Beaubrun P. J. & Burrell, C. (2009). Minority perspectives on enhancing engagement and belonging in a liberal arts environment. *Metropolitan Universities: An International Forum*, Vol. 20/1.

Dunlap, M., Scoggin, J., Green, P., & Davi A. (2007, Spring). White students' experiences of privilege and socioeconomic disparities: Toward a theoretical model. *Michigan Journal of Community Service-Learning*, 19–30.

Dunlap, M., Shueh, T. F., Beaubrun, P. J. & Burrell, C. (2018). Belief in colorblindness and perceptions of minority children during a fictionalized parent-child discipline scene. *Journal of Ethnic & Cultural Diversity in Social Work*, *27*(2), 193–213. doi: 10.1080/15313204.2017.1344946. Retrieved at www.tandfonline.com/eprint/AzpBSS4VBcGtF9iEfS2s/full

DuVernay, Ava (2016). *13th* (documentary film). Netflix.

Evans, S. Y., Taylor, C. M., Dunlap, M. R., & Miller, D. S. (Eds.). (2009). *African Americans and community engagement in higher education*. Albany, NY: SUNY Press.

Fox, J. [Prod./Dir.]. *An American love story.* (1999). NY: Zohe film Productions, www.pbs.org/lovestories

Hamblin, J. (2017). Why succeeding against the odds can make you sick. *New York Times*, January 27, 2017. www.nytimes.com/2017/01/27/opinion/sunday/why-succeeding-against-the-odds-can-make-you-sick.html?

Helms, J. (1995). An update of Helms's White and People of Color racial identity models. In J. G. Ponterotto, J. M. Casas, L. A. Suzuki, & C. M. Alexander (Eds.), *Handbook of multicultural counseling* (pp. 181–198). Thousand Oaks, CA: Sage.

Ladson-Billings, G. (1996). Silences as weapons: Challenges of a Black professor teaching White students. *Theory into Practice*, 35(2), 79–85.

Lee, S. [Prod./Dir.]. Lee, J. [Writer]. *Crooklyn.* (1994). Universal City, CA: MCA Universal Home Video.

MCC [Prod.]. Free indeed: A video drama about racism [1995, videocassette], Akron, PA: Mennonite Central Committee and MCC U.S.

McIntosh, P. (1990). White privilege: Unpacking the invisible knapsack. *Peace and Freedom*, July/August.

Omi, M. (2006). In living color: Race and American culture. In S. Massik & J. Solomon (Eds.), *Signs of life in the USA: Readings on popular culture for writers.* Boston: Bedford/St. Martins.

Reed, T. [Prod./Dir.]. *Once upon a time when we were colored.* (1996). Los Angeles: Republic Entertainment/BET Pictures.

Reel Works Teen Filmmaking (Producer), & Davis, K. (Director) (2005). *A girl like me* [documentary]. United States.

Schofield, J. W. (1986). Causes & consequences of the colorblind perspective. In J. Dovidio & S. Gaertner (Eds.), *Prejudice, discrimination, & racism* (231–253): San Diego: Academic.

Smith, L. [Prod.] & The Corporation for Public Broadcasting. (2003). *Race: The power of an illusion.* San Francisco: California Newsreel.

St. Pierre, S. [Prod.] Too good to be true? (The story of Marva Collins). *60 Minutes.* New York: Columbia Broadcasting System.

Sue, D. (2010). *Microaggressions in everyday life: Race, gender, and sexual orientation.* Hoboken, NJ: Wiley.

Tatum, B. (1992). Talking about race: The application of racial identity development theory in the classroom. *Harvard Educational Review*, 62(1), 1–24.

Warnock-Graham, O. [Prod./Dir.]. *Silences.* (2006). Octave Films.

Williams, M., Dunlap, M., & McCandies, T. (Fall, 1999). Keepin' it real: Three Black women educators discuss how we deal with student resistance to multicultural inclusion in the curriculum. *Transformations*, 10(2), 11–22.

Chapter 13

# And the Tree is NOT ALWAYS Happy!

## A Black Woman Authentically Leading and Teaching Social Justice in Higher Education

COLETTE M. TAYLOR

> *On November 11, 2016, I began re-reading Shel Silverstein's,* The Giving Tree, *an appreciation gift signed by a group of my former students in 2006. I was inspired to pick the book off the shelf due to the flood of distressed messages I had been receiving from former students. As I read their inscriptions, I began to cry. The crying itself was not normal for me, but what started out as misty tears became a cataclysmic waterfall. One would have thought I had lost a friend or family member. Instead, it was the culmination of incredible sadness and disbelief. Perhaps, in some ways, these feelings were based on the fact that I might have let these students down . . . taught them idealistic concepts of social justice without preparing them for the reality . . . arising from the clashes between class and economic privilege, race/ethnicity and White privilege, gender and male privilege, and the intersections of each of these privileges.*

As I gazed at the familiar sketch on the cover of *The Giving Tree*—a tall tree, tree top spilling off the page, and a little boy looking up at it, I began to reflect on how often I have utilized this well-worn book. Throughout my career as a higher education professional, I have frequently used this well-known text to remind undergraduate students—most privileged students—about generosity and social justice. But should there have been more to it than that? If you recall, *The Giving Tree* tells the story of a relationship between a young boy and a tree. As the boy grows older, he wants more, and the tree sacrifices its apples, branches, and trunk for him. Only when he is an old man does the boy rejoin the tree, and the tree is happy.

Upon reflection, I am unsure if I fully understood the story as a younger Black woman; I was certain that the tree had done the right thing. Beautifully, the tree gave everything for the boy, and I tried to emulate this as a higher education leader. Giving everything I had, I taught my students about leadership and social justice. However, having grown older and encountered more and different challenges as a social justice educator, I am less inclined to see the tree's reactions as healthy. While the sacrifices of the tree are commendable, the decision to keep giving to the boy pays no attention to the tree's own needs or identity.

As a leader, teacher, and advocate for social justice, current events have me, a self-professed transformative social educator, struggling to answer: What does it mean to be an authentic social justice educator in higher education? This chapter summarizes the difficult task of searching for the meaning of authenticity as a Black woman social justice educator.

Baudrillard (1994) articulated that the real world is no longer understood as real because reality no longer exists. Determining authenticity in the simulacrum (from Latin, meaning likeness or similarity) is challenging if not impossible because the notion of authenticity requires a comparison to reality. Facing this reality—and in reference to the metaphor used in *The Giving Tree*—means accepting that the tree is NOT always happy when practicing social justice leadership.

## Defining Social Justice Leadership as a Black Woman

Social justice is defined in multiple ways in the literature (Blackmore, 2002; Furman & Gruenewald, 2004; Gewirtz, 1998; Goldfarb & Grinberg, 2002) depending on the context. Gewirtz (1998) offers an operational definition of social justice centered on the ideas of disrupting and undermining arrangements that promote marginalization and exclusionary processes in organizations. For others, social justice includes practices driven by respect, care, recognition, and empathy. It is "the exercise of altering these [institutional and organizational] arrangements by actively engaging in reclaiming, appropriating, sustaining, and advancing inherent human rights of equity, equality, and fairness in social, economic, educational, and personal dimensions" (Goldfarb & Grinberg, 2002, 162). Simply defined, social justice leadership means that education leaders make issues of difference such as race, class, gender, and other historically and currently marginalizing conditions in the United States central to their leadership and advocacy practice.

Existing literature on diversity, equity, and social justice in education illustrates how the intersection of race and gender as experienced by the Black woman leader often forces one to act as a bridge for others and between others in complicated contexts.

> As a group, Black women are in an unusual position in this society, for not only are we collectively at the bottom of the occupational ladder, but our overall social status is lower than that of any other racial group. (hooks, 1984, 16)

Students often learn about the lives of Black women by reading the works of such Black women as Sojourner Truth, bell hooks, Angela Davis, Toni Morrison, Alice Walker, and Maya Angelou as assignments in literature or history classes. These works, including essays, speeches, poetry, and scholarly research, illuminate the struggles of negotiating the identity of both being Black and a woman encountering the effects of racism and sexism in society, but can often be seen as just detailed illustrations of racism and sexism in society.

The theoretical framework grounding this chapter focuses on the marginalization of Black women as an oppressed group and the works necessary by Black female scholars to resist such oppression (Collins, 2000; Hill Collins, 1989). As Howard-Hamilton (2003) notes, the dominant society members (through theoretical models, assumptions, and research) have articulated the experiences of Black women according to their experiential understanding. "Black feminist thought, then, specializes in formulating and rearticulating the distinctive, self-defined standpoint of African American women by African American women" (Hill Collins, 1989, 750).

With this understanding, Black female researchers can correct and challenge inaccurate narratives by clearly expressing the experiences of African American women based on the realities of their own lived experiences. "Since Black feminist thought both arises within and aims to articulate a Black women's group standpoint regarding experiences associated with intersecting oppressions, stressing this group standpoint's heterogeneous composition is significant" (Collins, 2000, 32). Due to personal experiences, Black women educators can shed light on the realities of social justice leadership to students by sharing their own diverse backgrounds such as socialization encounters, cultural adaptations, and assimilations as well as the negotiating of practices to authentically act as bridges in the quest to educate our students about social justice leadership.

## Higher Education, Identity, and Intersectionality in the Simulacrum

The 21st-century democratic higher education system was designed to reconcile the individual as a part of and apart from society. Kincheloe (2001) articulated that democracy requires a critical consciousness, or understanding of the world, to deconstruct the national(ist) meta-narrative. This narrative can be problematic because the central story of both individuals and society in the United States is that of White, European, Christian males. Specifically, higher education in the United States grew from Eurocentric roots tied to a hierarchal system within the colonial foundation of higher education (Altbach, 2001).

As a strategic part of a university's organizational structure, higher education professionals often are placed to support students within the constructs of the centuries-old higher education systems of practice (Chang, 2002). In this environment, higher education leaders experience diverse and complex challenges associated with both formal and informal interactions among students, faculty, and other educational professionals related to stereotyping, discrimination, inequality, and social justice.

As a Black woman administrator in higher education, it is easy to lose focus on one's own identity while addressing the needs of students, as well as the incessant political and social pressures that take a toll both professionally and personally. The concepts of various privileges—class and economic privilege, race/ethnicity privilege, White privilege, gender privilege, male privilege—and the intersections of these impact one's work every day. In *Teaching to Transgress*, bell hooks (1994) eloquently describes the "mind/body split," through which she points out that it is a social privilege to call yourself "unbiased," to not include your social identity in your work.

Anyone who calls themselves "unbiased" is inauthentic. All people interact with this world based on a specific perspective, and that perspective affects everything anyone does. It is a privilege not to see oneself as having a bias or particular agenda (because, really, everyone, including White, straight, middle-to-upper class, cisgender, able-bodied men, carry their biases and agendas). Thus our work as social justice educators actively, authentically, and consciously must become infused with our own perspectives and identities.

To better grasp these perspectives in our work, intersectional analysis of race, class, gender, and other social divisions is needed to understand the lived realities of the individuals with whom we work. Intersectionality, coined by Crenshaw (1989, 1991), expresses the concerns about Black female marginality in mainstream theorizing that were voiced by Black feminists such as Angela Davis, Patricia Hill Collins, and Audre Lorde (Cho, Crenshaw, & McCall, 2013).

By providing a complex ontology, intersectionality demonstrates "really useful knowledge," that systemically reveals the everyday lives of Black women who are simultaneously positioned in multiple structures of dominance and power as gendered, raced, and classed "others." Balancing various responsibilities in their lives, Black women come from diverse cultures, religions, and nation-states and live in the dominant modalities of race, class, and gender (Brah & Phoenix, 2004), which adds complexity to the patchwork of their lives. As social justice educators in higher education, Black women must balance these multiple roles while navigating the politics of the academy. To tackle social justice issues within higher education, one must acknowledge and understand the nature of power relations and how race, class, and gender interact with the lived experiences of Black female educators in their places of leading and teaching.

## Black Women in Higher Education

The Digest of Education Statistics reports that Blacks make up 7% of American college and university faculty and staff (National Council of Education Statistics, 2012). Statistics show that Black women earned 68% of all associate degrees, 66% of bachelor's degrees, 71% of master's degrees, and 65% of all doctorates awarded to Black students in 2009 and 2010 (NCES). By both race and gender, Black women make up a higher percentage (9.7%) of underrepresented students enrolled in college than any other group, topping Asian women (8.7%) and White women (7.1%). Although women hold almost 52% of all professional-level jobs, Black women lag substantially behind representation in leadership positions with less than 2% of leadership roles in the United States. These statistics highlight the fact that despite recent participant gains, Black women are subjected to both racism and sexism no matter where they work, but those working in higher education, because they have achieved a privileged status, are also the targets of classism. Frazier (1957), in addressing issues of the Black bourgeoisie, said "the frustration of the majority of the women . . . is probably due to the idle or ineffectual lives which they lead" (222). A different story could be heard when listening to the voices of Black women educators authentically working for social change.

To accurately hear these voices, one must understand that cultural identity and intersectionality are important issues when considering the concept of authenticity. Gee (2000) defines identity as "being recognized as a certain kind of person in a given context," and writes that "all people have multiple identities connected not to their internal states but to their performances in society" (99). Identities are expressions of who we are; the way we speak and act fluctuates depending on the various situations leaders find themselves in and the identity that one wishes to construct or reveal at the time. Taylor (1992) argues that one's identity is partly shaped by its recognition and misrecognition by others. He asserts that nonrecognition or misrecognition "can inflict harm, can be a form of oppression, imprisoning someone in a false distorted and reduced mode of being" (25).

Gee's (2000) theoretical framework of the concept of identity expresses the need to study how people construct their identities through their interactions with others. Black female social justice educators, like myself, need to acknowledge the masks that people of color hide behind or the faces that they choose to reveal while working in predominately White higher education environments. It is important to examine how individuals define who they are in certain circumstances, and how these identities encourage Black women to make certain choices depending on the impressions needed to be made. Charles Taylor (1992) argues that modern identity stresses the importance of one's inner voice and capacity for authenticity—in other words, the ability to find a way of being true to oneself. Equality doctrines emphasize the concept that each person is capable of marshaling his or her practical reason or moral sense to live an authentic life. According to Taylor (1992), the politics of difference has appropriated the language of authenticity to describe ways of living that are true to the identities of marginalized social groups.

The difference between Black culture and White educational systems has been the focus of pedagogical research for the last century (Tuitt, 2010). As Zamani stated, "given the complex intersection of race and gender, more attention should be paid to the educational, social, and political positions of African American women in post-secondary education" (2003, 6). Howard-Hamilton (2003) articulated the concept of the outsider within, whereby African American women have been, in ever-increasing numbers, invited into the higher education setting yet are still considered and often treated as outsiders with the little voice within these walls. As Black women enter the academic community, their identities interact with the dynamic community influences, causing a transformation of that personal identity into the "perceived" identity.

Because of this interaction and transformation, individuals often see themselves as changed people, people with two identities. Successfully obtaining a position, whether as an administrator or a faculty member can be challenging in itself. What can be even more challenging is successful progression in an academic environment where you are an authentic leader for social justice.

## The Journey of a Black Female Social Justice Educator in Higher Education

A Black woman's journey as a social justice educator in higher education takes her into the "Heart of Whiteness." The destination is often described as a place where the homogenous identity of the Black woman, is created by "a white gaze which perceives her as a mute visible object" (Casey, 1993, 111). An intersectional conception of oppression is often distinguished, particularly in higher education, from an account of systems of oppression that theorizes them as "interlocking" (Collins, 2000). Interlocking systems of oppression help to secure one another, and tracing the complex ways that both race and gender interlock in higher education is vital. Black female social justice educators know from experience how women are promoted into positions that exist symbiotically but hierarchically. They understand, for example, how domestic workers and professional women are produced so that neither exists without the other. Social policies in the United States, upheld by race, gender, and class politics, enables the pursuit of middle-class respectability in highly oppressive ways.

Various forms of oppression are "interlocking," as described by McWhorter, because they cannot be separated in the lived experience: "race, sex, and class are 'simultaneous factors'" in the lived experience of oppression (McWhorter, 2004, 55). As Black female social justice educators, many of us feel that we should let our intersectionality influence our work. This intersectional model describes the articulation of oppressions in authentic lived experience—in other words, using one's experience with structural intersectionality to educate students about the reality of social justice. Crenshaw (1989) introduced the concept of structural intersectionality, which speaks to a model of identity that labels the unique situation of hyperoppressed, paradigmatically Black women. This analytical model of structural intersectionality illumes the complexity and irreducibility of race and gender oppression experienced by Black women in higher education.

Black female social justice educators experience life as a member of a group of people who experience themselves as members of an oppressed community by their recognition by others as people of common descent (Appiah, 1990). Functioning within an oppressed society in the power structure of higher education day in and day out takes a toll on Black women's perspectives of who they are and their value in the society in which they live and work. We have unique experiences in higher education that many of our students do not have. As educators, we need to share these experiences with our students. Some middle-class students attending predominately White institutions are not unaware of the disparities between their own communities and surrounding affluent communities. Students notice these differences, but without knowledge and consciousness of the institutionalized systems of oppression, they lack an understanding of why the disparities exist.

As seasoned social justice educators, we should not view social justice education as an option but as an obligation. James Baldwin's (1984/1955) words come to mind as I consider the questions of critical consciousness, obviousness, and authenticity:

> One writes out of one thing only—one's own experience. Everything depends on how relentlessly one forces from this experience the last drop, sweet or bitter, it can possibly give. This is the only real concern of the artist, to recreate out of the disorder of life that order which is art. (7)

The effectiveness of social justice educators depends on their personal search for authenticity or critical consciousness. Self-reflection and the transformation of attitudes and beliefs about their experiences help leaders understand their authentic selves in several ways. There's institutional culture, there's societal culture, and there's one's own cultural background. Trying to balance the positive and negative experiences created by these cultures as an African American woman working in predominately White communities can lead to the devaluation of personal and professional identities. Many social justice educators tend to have the first-hand experience that people tell them that they do not look or act Black. We *are* Black. When I meet people who tell me I do not act Black enough, I say, "I might be different, but Black is who I am, not what I think I am."

I believe that social justice education has two aspects: truth and empowerment. One should always strive to teach the truth, no matter how brutal or controversial it may be, and to empower students. Therefore, sharing one's own experience as Black women in higher education is essential. All the many injustices can make students and educators alike feel hopeless, particularly those who come from historically marginalized backgrounds. The world is not without hope, however. Wherever injustice exists, there are always those fighting for change.

## A Search for Authentic Social Justice Leadership

A strong social justice leadership program increases student self-awareness and helps students embody intentional practices that reflect the values of a more just society. By taking up the challenge to transform society, educators have a responsibility to prepare students to take on enormous challenges and face significant resistance. It is irresponsible not to educate them on ways to weather the storms that will result. This was evident in the response of my former students to their "perceived" failure during the recent elections. The sadness experienced was not due to a failure in their social justice education, but a lack of understanding that the work of leading for social justice is never easy. My former students, based on their reactions, clearly demonstrated that the experiences that I provided were less than authentic. The lack of personal connection to oppression allowed them to have an unrealistic sense of social justice. Clearly, like the boy in *The Giving Tree*, my students had not faced, truly faced, the struggle of true social justice until this moment. Moreover, I, like the tree, never challenged them to discover that I could not provide them what they most need—an authentic social justice struggle.

Glenn (2000) suggests that a search for authenticity in a hyperreal world may be a waste of time, that there is nothing we can know as authentic. Upon reflecting on my personal experience while re-reading *The Giving Tree*, Black women social justice educators should recognize that it is important to build a collective understanding of the importance of using our authentic selves to educate our students. In actuality, all institutional members should be a part of a social justice collective, but in reality, it is a role of those who live the oppressed experience daily to speak truth to power.

On reflection, this means practicing what we teach and becoming resilient in our quest for authenticity. Taking a clue from *The Giving Tree*, the best way to become more resilient is to develop the capacity to be a compassionate and adaptable *mindful* leader. Black female social justice educators need to meet adaptive challenges as leaders who are consciously able to step out of habitual reactions and engage with a shifting reality in new and more sophisticated ways (Kegan & Lahey, 2010). In other words, we must learn to cultivate and transform ourselves into authentic, mindful practitioners of social justice. To do this, a critical skill we should develop is the capacity to be mindful. Practicing mindfulness, in this context, requires us to be present and aware of our multiple identities as well as the identities of others around us; to recognize our own perceptions (and potential biases) in the moment; and to harness the emotional reactions and actions needed in order to meet today's social justice education more authentically (Boyatzis & McKee, 2005; Kabat-Zinn, 1990).

Mindfulness refers to one's awareness and attention to immediate experience, whereas the authenticity construct refers to awareness of aspects of one's self (i.e., values, beliefs, emotions, etc.) (Lakey, Kernis, Heppner, & Lance, 2008). To become mindful practitioners, Black women must learn not to become distracted from the chaos that surrounds the struggle for social justice. I therefore suggest we study and practice mindfulness. When challenged to the breaking point, do not act or speak right away. Take a few moments and just breathe. Allow for the space to evaluate the situation from multiple perspectives, regarding it from a place of freedom and peace, not anger or frustration. In a critical moment of social justice advocacy, this space allows clarity for decision making rooted in a principle of non-harm and authenticity.

Teaching social justice can be hard and emotionally exhausting work, especially in an environment where an institution's rhetoric often does not match its members' actions. Therefore, Black women educators also need to create a supportive community and space for reflection, regrouping, and mobilization. As Howard-Hamilton (2003) states: "[S]urvival for Black women is contingent on their ability to find a place to describe their experiences among persons like themselves" (25). Often, we find ourselves alone on our campuses bearing the burden of exemplifying the core values of diversity and social justice for our students. This community should be a place for Black women to openly describe their experiences—the good and the bad, to inform and incite empowerment for Black women educators working on college campuses (Reason & Broido, 2005). Networking and communing with colleagues who share one's experiences, interests, concerns, and even frustrations will help individuals negotiate and navigate the potholes and battles embedded in social justice and activist work.

## Conclusion

Teaching social justice is a calling for individuals determined to transform lives and changing the world. While the work can often generate frustration, disappointment, and sometimes disillusionment, it is imperative to reflect on the message of *The Giving Tree*. As a Black woman educator, I cannot give up and "be unhappy" during these turbulent times. For me, I have learned to be mindful and focus on the greater prize—finding social justice for every person and a better world for us all. When practicing mindfulness, I feel renewed and nourished by remembering that our "lineage is ancient and that my roots like those of the mesquite" (Anzaldúa, 1987, 234). This idea reminds me of my identities and the strength I can draw from them as I approach the complex, contested work of social justice education. In the end, teaching social justice and social change is not easy. Having students experiencing failure along the way is not bad. It inspires me to remain steadfast and committed to reconstructing a world that is more humane, equitable, and just, and to "become happy" like the giving tree.

## References

Altbach, P. G. (2001). The American academic in comparative perspective. In P. G. Altbach, P. J. Gumport, & D. B. Johnstone (Eds.), *In defense of American higher education* (pp. 11–37). Baltimore, MD: John Hopkins University Press.

Appiah, A. (1990). But would that still be me? Notes on gender, "race," ethnicity, as sources of identity. *Journal of Philosophy, 87*, 493, 497.

Anzaldúa, G. (1987). *Borderlands/La frontera: The new Mestiza*: San Francisco: Spinsters.

Baldwin, J. (1984/1955). *Notes of a native son* (Vol. 39). Boston: Beacon Press.

Baudrillard, J. (1994). *Simulacra and simulation*. (S. Glaser, Trans.). Ann Arbor: University of Michigan Press.

Blackmore, J. (2002). Leadership for socially just schooling: More substance and less style in high risk, low trust times? *Journal of School Leadership, 12*, 198–222.

Boyatzis, R., & McKee, A. (2005). *Resonant leadership*. Harvard Business School Press: Boston.

Brah, A., & Phoenix, A. (2004). Ain't I a woman? Revisiting intersectionality. *Journal of International Women's Studies, 5*(3): 75–86.

Casey, K. (1993). *I answer with my life: Life histories of women teachers working for social change*. New York: Routledge.

Chang, M. J. (2002). Preservation or transformation: Where's the real educational discourse on diversity? *The Review of Higher Education, 25*(2), 125–140.

Cho, S., Crenshaw, K. W., & McCall, L. (2013). Toward a field of intersectionality studies: Theory, applications, and praxis. Intersectionality: Theorizing power, empowering theory, special issue. *Signs, 38*(4): 785–810.

Collins, P. (2000). *Black feminist thought*. New York: Routledge.

Crenshaw, K. (1989). Demarginalizing the intersection of race and sex: A Black feminist critique of antidiscrimination doctrine, feminist theory and antiracist politics. *University of Chicago Legal Forum*, 139–167.

Crenshaw, K. W. (1991). Mapping the margins: Intersectionality, identity politics, and violence against women of color." *Stanford Law Review, 43*(6), 1241–1299.

Frazier, F. (1957). *Black bourgeoisie*. Simon and Schuster.

Furman, G. C., & Gruenewald, D. A. (2004). Expanding the landscape of social justice: A critical ecological analysis. *Educational Administration Quarterly, 40*, 49–78.

Gee J. P. (2000–2001). Identity as an analytic lens for research in education. *Review of Research in Education, 25*, 99–125.

Gewirtz, S. (1998). Conceptualizing social justice in education: Mapping the territory. *Journal of Education Policy, 13*, 469–484.

Glenn, J. (2000). Fake authenticity: An introduction. *Hermenaut, 15*.

Goldfarb, K. P., & Grinberg, J. (2002). Leadership for social justice: Authentic participation in the case of a community center in Caracas, Venezuela. *Journal of School Leadership, 12*, 157–173.

Hills Collins, P. (1989). The social construction of Black feminist thought. *Signs, 14*, 745–773.

hooks, b. (1994). *Teaching to transgress: Education as the practice of freedom*. New York: Routledge.

Howard-Hamilton, M. (2003). *Meeting the needs of African American women*. San Francisco: Jossey-Bass.

Kabat-Zinn, J. (1990). *Full catastrophe living: Using the wisdom of your body and mind to face stress, pain and illness*. New York: Delacourt.

Kegan, R. & Lahey, L. (2010). *Immunity to change: How to overcome it and unlock the potential in yourself and your organization*. Cambridge, MA: Harvard Business Press.

Kincheloe, J. (2001). *Getting beyond the facts: Teaching social studies/social sciences in the twenty-first century*. New York: Peter Lang.

Lakey, C. E., Kernis, M. H., Heppner, W. L., & Lance, C. E. (2008). Individual differences in authenticity and mindfulness as predictors of verbal defensiveness. *Journal of Research in Personality, 42*(1), 230–238.

McWhorter, L. (2004). Sex, race, and biopower: A Foucauldian genealogy. *Hypatia, 19*(3), 38–62.

National Center for Education Statistics, Institute of Education Sciences (2012). *Digest of education statistics 2011*. Washington, DC: U.S. Department of Education.

Reason. R. D., & Broido, E. M. (2005). Issues and strategies for social justice allies (and the student affairs professionals who hope to encourage them). In R. D. Reason, E. M. Broido, T. L. Davis, & N. J. Evans (Eds.), *Developing social justice and allies* (New Directions for Student Services, no. 110) (pp. 81–89). San Francisco: Jossey-Bass.

Silverstein, S. (1964). *The giving tree*. New York: Harper & Row.

Taylor, C. (1992). The politics of recognition. In A. Gutmann (Ed.), *Multiculturalism and the politics of recognition* (pp. 25–74). Princeton, NJ: Princeton University Press.

Tuitt, F. (2010). Enhancing visibility in graduate education: Black women's perceptions of inclusive pedagogical practices. *International Journal of Teaching & Learning in Higher Education, 22*(3), 246–257.

Yosso, T. (2005). Whose culture has capital? A critical race theory discussion of community cultural wealth. *Race Ethnicity and Education, 8*(1): 69–91.

Zamani, E. (2003). African American women in higher education. In M. Howard-Hamilton, *Meeting the needs of African American women* (pp. 5–18). San Francisco: Jossey-Bass.

Chapter 14

# Effectively Teaching the One Course on Race and Culture

*Critical Explorations from a Black Woman Social Justice Teacher Educator*

KEFFRELYN D. BROWN

Concerns with equity and social justice plague K–12 education, and this is perhaps most evident in the field of preservice teacher education. Individuals charged to prepare the next generation of K–12 teachers struggle to provide teacher candidates with the knowledge, skills, and experiences needed to work effectively with all students (Darling-Hammond & Bransford, 2005). Unfortunately, in teacher education, this work is often attempted through the context of one course on multicultural education. As a female Black American scholar, researcher, and teacher educator whose work focuses on the relationships among race, culture, teaching, and curriculum, I am particularly keen to this charge because I teach such a course.

Among scholars committed to preparing teacher candidates to teach for social justice and equity, there is ongoing discussion about infusing critical multicultural curriculum in all aspects of the teacher preparation program. There is concern around the impact any one course might play in preservice teachers' acquisition of critical sociocultural knowledge (Brown & Kraehe, 2010; Sleeter, 2008). The content for the one course is wide and broad, and often related to the idiosyncratic decision making of individual instructors (Gorski, 2009). What students learn or fail to learn, then, depends on the curricular and pedagogical choices of the instructor.

In this chapter I critically explore my process as a Black female scholar and teacher to effectively teach the single course offered to teacher candidates on the sociocultural knowledge of schooling and teaching. By sociocultural knowledge, I refer to the social, cultural, economic, political, and historical knowledge that informs how societies and schools operate (Brown, 2012). I draw from my experiences creating, teaching, and revising an undergraduate course from fall 2006 to fall 2008 and most recently in fall 2016 that explores how sociocultural factors play a role in the schooling and teaching process. I privilege the role of critical sociocultural knowledge, along with theoretically/empirically informed pedagogical and curricular choices that play in preparing teachers to teach for cultural relevance and social justice.

My development of the course directly related to studies I conducted on my teaching (see Brown & Kraehe, 2010a, 2010b; Kraehe & Brown, 2011). I wanted students to develop a critical sociocultural knowledge base that was theoretically complex and that challenged deficit-oriented perspectives of students, families, cultures, and communities, while simultaneously helping teachers recognize the vital role and responsibility they play in their students' learning processes. This stance aligned with commitments of teaching that is culturally relevant and socially just. I advocated teaching that affirms students' cultural- and community-based knowledges and resisted practices that reinforce diminished opportunities for students to learn.

The extant literature on teacher education discusses the characteristics of and experiences related to teaching multicultural education courses (Hollins & Guzman, 2005). It is less common for teacher educators to critically reflect on their pedagogic and curricula choices over time, that is, the impact these choices have on student learning and how the instructor decides to teach the course in the future. I argue that *what* teachers do and *why* they do it in the classroom *matters*. These actions always occur in the context of a teacher's positionality. Thus, I take seriously the issue of teacher reflexivity on curricula and pedagogic choices made in the context of teaching in a university-based teacher education program. In doing this, I respond to recent calls made by scholars to seriously consider how teacher educators can more effectively help teacher candidates acquire critical sociocultural knowledge about teaching (Gorski, 2009; Milner, 2010) when asked to do so in only one course.

## Preparing Teachers to Teach for Equity and Social Justice

The struggle to prepare teacher candidates to become teachers for equity and social justice is well documented in the teacher education literature. These difficulties may result from several sources, including preservice teachers' lack of prior experiences with diversity (Grant & Sleeter, 2006) and their resistance to issues related to diversity, social justice, and equity (Sleeter,

2001). Others cite problems with insufficient teacher training and preparation related to limited knowledge possessed by program faculty (Gay, 2000; Nieto, 2000), program incoherence (Sleeter, 2008), and/or ineffective field experiences (Zeichner, 1996). What is common across all of these explanations is that many teacher candidates leave their programs lacking the knowledge to work effectively with students of color and those from other historically marginalized student populations.

In spite of the many explanations given for why teacher education programs struggle to prepare teachers to work effectively with all students, many of these struggles are situated in self-study research. Here, teacher educators/researchers examine the practice-based challenges encountered when teaching for equity and social justice (Hollins & Guzman, 2005). This is vital work because teacher educators have the responsibility to teach all of their students, including those that exhibit resistance. Yet it is also a tenuous, emotionally fraught space for teacher educators of color because they negotiate a hidden, yet real, emotional toll in their work (Brown, 2016).

First, teacher educators of color generally shoulder the burden of teaching these courses to an overwhelmingly White preservice teacher population (Moule, 2005) that often has little formal or experiential knowledge about race, culture, and schooling (Sleeter, 2008). Second, when teaching these courses, students and others often leverage microaggressions toward teacher educators of color that undermine their authority and question their intellect and ability to teach in nonbiased, objective ways (Dixson & Dingus, 2007). Third, the micro-level experiences of teacher educators of color embody the content they teach about race and culture, either by way of their own schooling experiences or those of their own children and other close acquaintances. What, then, are the pedagogical implications on a female teacher of color, committed to preparing teachers to teach in culturally relevant and socially just ways?

## Tackling the Challenges: Accounting for Praxis

In fall 2006 I began a tenure-track faculty position at a large research university in the southwest. During this semester, I taught my first instantiation of the Sociocultural Influences on Learning Course. I held two instructional goals. First, I wanted to illustrate how sociocultural factors played a role in the schooling process and that schooling and teaching practices either reinscribed or pushed against these conditions. Second, I wanted students to critically reflect on the sociocultural knowledge of schooling and teaching they entered the course possessing.

After having taught both undergraduate and graduate level courses focused on sociocultural content knowledge, I observed that students gained understanding of course content when they engaged with various types of materials. I worried about how my own positionality as a Black woman teaching a course that directly addressed race might impact my primarily White students. I recognized that we needed a common start place to begin our work. For these reasons, I included a set of historical readings that put into the context the longevity and depth of inequitable schooling conditions associated with marginalized groups of color. In addition to selected course readings, I included multimedia film clips from documentaries on race, gender, social class, and the history of schooling in the United States, as well as situation comedies related to race.

Students also participated in learning activities to engage with the ideas presented in the course. Students engaged in large- and small-group discussions around course readings. Small-group discussions were structured, with students discussing a specific topic or set of questions I developed. I used a jigsaw configuration (Aronson, 2002) in which students in a home group were assigned a different reading to complete. Students who read the same reading met in a small group to discuss the main points of their assigned reading. All students were responsible for sharing what they learned from their assigned readings with members in their home group. This allowed students to easily tackle large amounts of reading and encouraged them to learn in a sociocultural, collaborative way. Large-class discussions were both structured (i.e., fishbowl discussion in which a group of students sits in a circle and discusses with each other while another group of students sits outside of the inner circle, listening to the inside circle talk—e.g., see McKeachie & Svinicki, 2010) and unstructured in nature. Students also participated in small-group activities. They created visual representations and collages of key course terms and constructs, and completed several formal class assignments. They submitted a weekly summary sheet for session readings; wrote an educational autobiography; read and presented a group project around a book related to sociocultural factors in school and/or society, and crafted a final reflection paper.

After completing the course in fall 2006, I began a longitudinal research study that examined how teacher education candidates acquire sociocultural knowledge about schooling and teaching across their teacher education program. The students recruited for the study took my Sociocultural Influences on Learning course in fall 2006 and were planning to begin the professional development sequence of teacher preparation in spring 2007. While students cited gaining more awareness of the role sociocultural factors played in schools, many also felt overwhelmed and incapable of successfully teaching all of their students in the midst of sociocultural factors. Only one student exhibited some resistance, primarily around supporting a deficit view of Black students regarding achievement. However, many participants viewed sociocultural factors as connected only to the identities of students, the students' families, and the communities where students lived. Sociocultural factors were positioned as obstacles, often deficiencies that needed remediation. They were not recognized as playing out in all aspects of the schooling and teaching process, including how students are organized in schools; decision making around teaching, curriculum, and student learning; and teacher beliefs/perspectives about students, parents, and families. Participants did not recognize how their own future teacher lives were implicated in the sociocultural context of schooling, nor how their practices might challenge or reinscribe inequitable practices found in schools.

I realized that in spite of my initial planning and focus on exposing students to how sociocultural factors create inequitable opportunities for students to learn, I did not consider how best to scaffold the presentation of materials and activities in the course. I selected what I considered enlightening and engaging course materials and activities. I realized this was not enough. I wanted more than merely student engagement in the course. I wanted students to acquire a deeper, more complex knowledge base around sociocultural factors and schooling. For this to happen, I needed to accomplish three goals. The first was to identify the "big theme" or story that I wanted to tell in the course. The second was to select materials and engaging activities that powerfully illustrated the theoretical frames, ideas, and key concepts I wanted the students to learn. The third was to recognize how each element of the course (e.g., course readings, pedagogic activities) complemented, and/or possibly contradicted, each other and impacted the overall knowledge base I wanted students to acquire by course end.

I also realized that in my quest to get students to talk about what I assumed were, for some, challenging and new topics and ideas in class (e.g., inequity, racism, gender inequality, sexuality), I focused too much on students' verbal engagement in class session, rather than on providing them specific learning opportunities in class to make connections between key ideas explored in the course. My privileging of discussion, in all of its different iterations, took precedent in how I organized small- and large-group discussions and activities.

Existing literature in teacher education discusses the important role that discussion can play in student learning (Levin, 1995), particularly when discussing simulated, real-life case scenarios. I assumed that I was doing a good job as a teacher if I could get the students to talk—both to each other and to me—about course content. What undergirded my belief was the assumption that students would acquire sociocultural knowledge if they actively read the assigned readings prior to class, listened to my mini-lecture on the day's topic, interacted with the related session's supplementary course materials (e.g., film clips), and participated in activities—primarily, discussions—with each other. Yet, rather than focus on what actual knowledge connections students were making when socially engaged with their peers and the content knowledge in the activity, I gauged their learning on whether they were verbally engaged with the material, the activity, and each other.

*Second Instantiation of the Course*

By spring 2007, I recognized some of the limitations of my initial approach to teaching the course. I wanted students to acquire more complex understandings of the role of sociocultural factors in schooling and teaching that challenged deficit-oriented perspectives. I also wanted them to view teachers as efficacious change agents for social justice and equity. My first task was to outline key concepts and frameworks for the course. I also created a set of key terms related to these frameworks (see Appendix 1 for a truncated list of the key terms and concepts I identified as important to the course). Additionally, I noted where these ideas might contradict one another (i.e., cultural/social capital explanations for inequitable schooling and holding deficit-oriented perspectives of students', their cultural groups, and/or their families). I also made sure that course readings addressed one or more of the key theoretical frames, concepts, or terms. I had to adopt new readings to meet these criteria. I also dropped and created new course assignments.

Previously, the students did not take a midterm, but I thought I would create a take-home midterm in which students could select from several different assessment options. These options allowed students to choose whether to answer a traditional essay question, complete an analysis of two self-selected films focused on sociocultural factors, or create a school-based case study, short story, or script that addressed issues of race, social class, or gender. Regardless of the option selected, students had to draw from key terms that I provided and cite readings from the course syllabus. This activity served multiple purposes. I was able to gauge how well students were understanding and integrating course content. I was also able to hold students accountable for reading the course materials weekly since they knew they would have to use the readings in their midterms. In addition to the midterm, students completed a summary sheet for each class session reading and wrote an educational autobiography and a final reflection paper. I dropped the collaborative book project because I did not think it moved students closer to the learning goals I set for the course.

When I taught this iteration of the course, I was struck by some of the changes I noticed in the students and in my work as a teacher. I found that class discussions seemed more focused, along with the work products that students presented. I saw more evidence that students were understanding key ideas from the course. What I continued to struggle with was how to engage students in a variety of pedagogic activities, primarily viewing films, within the 90-minute time frame we had for each class session. I felt that showing more video and engaging students in a more diverse set of in-class activities would open additional avenues for them to immerse in the content and their own learning.

As had been the case with the first instantiation of the course, during the second instantiation of the course I did not encounter much resistance from students to the class content. I had one overtly resistant student who initially questioned the role of race in creating inequitable schooling conditions. He also frequently challenged my ideas. Over time, his stance, perhaps more than his perspectives, shifted as he became less defensive toward me and his peers in the course. I felt that he found a place to sit and grow in the course, specifically when I allowed him the opportunity to illustrate his growing understandings using a medium that he found personally engaging—zine writing.

*Third Instantiation of the Course*

By spring 2008, I felt confident that I could develop a course in which students left understanding the main things I wanted to them to learn about the sociocultural knowledge of schooling and teaching. However, I felt constricted by the time frame of the course to engage the various pedagogical activities I wanted to use. I decided to change the course meeting time to a weekly 3-hour class session.

This meant further cuts to the course reading list. I did not change the course assignments. I decided to approach the course from a case-based pedagogical perspective. I made this decision because the course already drew from multiple kinds of "cases." These came in the form of course readings and in-class activities I used to illuminate key terms, concepts, and/or frames (Darling-Hammond & Hammerness, 2002; Sykes & Bird, 1992).

At the end of our fall 2007 semester discussion about the course, students noted the course readings and multimedia presentations were impactful to their learning. What stood out about these materials was how they provided a clear example of how the key course terms and concepts operated in real-life situations. While getting my masters, I collaborated with a group of faculty members at the Harvard Medical School to produce case-based curricula to use in high school biology classes that served students of color. This experience introduced me to the idea of case-based pedagogy. I sought out literature on how this approach was used in multicultural teacher education courses. Though case-based pedagogy was becoming increasingly more popular in the literature, with notable exceptions (Kleinfield, 1990, 1998; Mesa-Baines & Shulman, 1994; Nieto 2008/1992, 1999; and most recently with Gorski & Pothini, 2013), this literature did not address multicultural (teacher) education courses (Moje & Wade, 1997).

Situating the course in a case-based framework would make it easier for students to understand my rationale for asking them to engage with various kinds of course materials and participate in various kinds of learning activities. I called this an *eclectic case-based pedagogy*, and it incorporated the use of four distinct kinds of cases. *Ethnographic cases* offered students clear, empirical examples of how key concepts covered in the course by showing how race, gender, and class play out in schooling and in the classroom. These cases were located in primarily research articles, book manuscripts, book chapters, and newspaper articles. *Autobiographical cases* provided students an opportunity for critical personal reflection that related to the content covered in the course. Drawing from course readings and key terms from the course, students addressed how sociocultural factors operated in their schooling. *Multimedia cases* gave students realistic examples and demonstrations of how race, class, and gender are produced and presented through multimedia cases. These were reflected in PowerPoint presentations, film and television clips, songs, and music videos. The *collaboratively produced video case* was created by students. They worked in groups of two or three to produce a project that examined how race, class, or gender played out in a schooling context. The case included a written narrative of the case itself, a reflection sheet that explained the key themes in the case, three to five reflective questions aligned with the case, and a presentation of the co-created and edited video performance of the case to the class.

For the first time, I also realized that I had never theoretically reflected on my *approach* to teaching. What I had done previously was select teaching methods that I thought were effective based on my own experiences as a learner (in my undergraduate and graduate studies) and/or that I had heard or read about from my teacher educator colleagues. In much the same way that teacher candidates experience an apprenticeship of observation, I had learned how to become a teacher educator through my own learning experiences.

Yet several theoretical orientations framed my instructional decision making. These were *sociocultural learning theory* (i.e., help students acquire knowledge by drawing from social interaction and familiar cultural tools); *visual studies* (i.e., use art, including popular culture, to engage students in critical reflection about the world); *critical pedagogy* (i.e., attend to micro and macro social reality to illuminate both how societal practices sustain oppressive conditions and how groups and individuals resist and disrupt such conditions); and *culturally relevant pedagogy* (i.e., focus on relationship, cultural awareness, community-building, and consciousness raising).

On the first day of the course, I shared my approach to teaching and rationale for organizing the course, including why I thought it was a useful strategy. I continued to refer back to this discussion across the semester to reinforce what we were doing and why we were doing it in the course.

After making these changes to the course, I (with the help of a grad student TA) initiated a study to examine students' learning experiences in the class (Brown & Kraehe, 2010a, 2010b). Students cited three learning opportunities afforded to them in the class. The first was *guided participation*, in which students interacted with various cases in the course in order to learn new theoretical concepts and terms. The second related to *dismantling and building connection*, in which students engaged with different kinds of cases, specifically the autobiographical case. Students made connections between the theoretical concepts of the course and occurrences in their own and others' real-life contexts. Third, they engaged in a *close in(tro)spection of schooling and society*. Here, they reflected on their hidden assumptions and acknowledged how their own teaching was embedded in power relations that they could challenge or help to reinscribe (Brown & Kraehe, 2010b).

Teaching the class in this way proved fruitful. Students showed evidence of and cited gaining new and more complex sociocultural knowledge. I also encountered a few overtly resistant students. Interactions with these students were challenging, as they often made comments that were intellectually uninformed but also emotionally painful to hear as a Black woman committed to social justice and helping all of my students learn. I had four students across three offerings of the course who questioned if race played a role in creating inequitable societal and school relations. In one semester, I had two White males who were initially antagonistic to the course. While one eventually softened, engaging in both small- and large-group discussions in ways that were productive to his own learning, the other continued to challenge me during every class session. In another semester, I had a White woman who felt comfortable using the n-word in class—she argued it was simply a word with no real value. As a result of my pushback, she eventually dropped the course. In another semester, I also encountered a White female who was uncomfortable having me as her teacher. While I was eventually able to get her to actively participate in small- and large-group discussions, she continued to hold on to deficit-based perspectives of people of color.

The successes I may have had in helping to push my students to learn did not negate the emotional labor I negotiated every class session as I navigated my multiple identities as a Black woman teacher committed to teaching for social justice. These hidden costs were not visible to my students, but I carried their weight in the moments of planning, teaching, and reflection.

## Discussion and Implications

In this chapter I explored my intentional work as a teacher educator of color committed to preparing teachers to teach for equity and social justice. My identity, like all teachers, is part of this work. It is tied to how students view me and the knowledge that I ask them to engage with and learn. Because of this, I am convinced that it is only through serious consideration and critical reflexive praxis that one's teaching can improve. My experiences as a Black female teacher educator have inevitably informed my understanding of sociocultural knowledge. This knowledge, while gathered over a lifetime, is experientially linked to my over 20 years as a researcher and teacher, both in K-12 and university settings. This knowledge has not come easy, nor has it been cheap. Yet it would be inaccurate to assume that just because I am a person of color and/or because I possess this knowledge base, I can effectively teach others this knowledge. Effective teaching is intentional and can occur only when one has time to plan, reflect, and refine.

Faculty members committed to preparing teachers to teach for social justice and equity know how good teaching looks. It is relevant to students' backgrounds and lives and takes into account their prior knowledge, so they can co-construct and develop more complex understandings. It also requires substantial content and pedagogic knowledge, sustained, critical reflection, and a willingness to continue growing as a pedagogue.

My critical reflections suggest it is possible to offer a course that asks students to consider the powerful role that sociocultural factors and teacher decision making has in schooling, while also recognizing the importance of challenging deficit-oriented perspectives. This teaching work requires deep, often difficult, ongoing personal critical reflection of pedagogy and curricula materials by the instructor. Since I implemented the last instantiation of this course, students in my courses have demonstrated a change in depth and complexity of understanding of sociocultural knowledge, schooling, and teaching (Brown & Kraehe, 2010b). Yet for all my reflective and intentional teaching, I sometimes still encounter varying degrees of resistance or other emotionally challenging responses from students.

In the face of calls in teacher education to infuse multicultural content across all course and fieldwork experiences (Sleeter, 2008), faculty members who teach the one multicultural teacher education course must have the opportunity to critically reflect on effective ways to approach their instruction (Cochran-Smith, 2003). Teacher education programs that hold a commitment to preparing teachers to teach for social justice and equity should provide faculty members the opportunity and reward structure needed to reflect on and develop just such good instruction. These institutions must also account for the unique challenges that junior, untenured faculty of color endure when teaching these courses (Williams & Evans-Winters, 2003).

One of the ongoing challenges I face is helping students understand how to successfully navigate through the complex sociocultural factors that operate and create inequitable learning opportunities in the daily work and decision making of teachers (Brown & Kraehe, 2010b). As a Black woman, this is deeply emotional and challenging work. It means managing our own deeply emotional responses to our teaching while helping students progress in their own learning—processes often laden with resistance, guilt, fear, and confusion. Helping students feel more capable to work through the tensions that frame the local context of teaching is challenging yet worthwhile work. For it is only through facing our own struggles as teacher educators that we can appreciate and help our students appreciate the awesome task that defines effective and socially just teaching.

## Appendix 1. Truncated List of Key Terms and Concepts Identified for the Course

1. Sociocultural influences in learning
2. Othering
3. Normalcy
4. Deviance
5. Equity
6. Equality
7. Meritocracy
8. Deficit thinking
9. Student resistance
10. Institutional inequality
11. Privilege
12. (School) tracking
13. Social construction of race
14. Colorblind ideology
15. Essentializing
16. Institutional racism

17. Capital
    a. Cultural capital
    b. Economic capital
    c. Social capital
    d. Symbolic capital
18. Discourse
19. Social class
20. Gender performativity
21. Individual habitus
22. Organizational habitus
23. Sexism
24. Social construction of gender
25. Symbolic violence
26. Pedagogy
27. Curriculum
    a. formal curriculum
    b. societal curriculum
    c. hidden curriculum
    d. null curriculum
28. Multicultural education
29. Critical Pedagogy
30. Culturally relevant teaching/culturally responsive teaching
31. Funds of knowledge

## References

Aronson, E. (2002). Building empathy, compassion and achievement in the jigsaw classroom. In J. Aronson (Ed.), *Improving academic achievement: Impact of psychological factors on education* (pp. 213–225). San Diego, CA: Elsevier

Brown, K. D. (2016). Race and emotions in the researching of teachers and teaching. In M. Zembylas & P. Schutz (Eds.), *Methodological advances in research on emotion and education* (pp. 179–189). New York: Springer.

Brown, K. D. (2012). Trouble on my mind: Toward a framework of humanizing critical sociocultural knowledge for teaching and teacher education. *Race Ethnicity and Education*, *16*(3), 316–338.

Brown, K. D., & Kraehe, A. (2010a). When you only have one class, one chance: Acquiring sociocultural knowledge using eclectic case pedagogy. *Teaching Education*, *21*(3), 313–328.

Brown, K. D., & Kraehe, A. (2010b). The complexities of teaching the complex: Examining how future educators construct understandings of sociocultural knowledge and schooling. *Educational Studies*, *46*(1), 91–115.

Cochran-Smith, M. (2003). Learning and unlearning: The education of teacher educators. *Teaching and teacher education, 19*(1), 5–28.
Darling-Hammond, L., & Bransford, J. (Ed.) (2005). *Preparing teachers for a changing world: What teachers should learn and be able to do* (pp. 232–274). San Francisco: Jossey-Bass.
Darling-Hammond, L., & Hammerness, K. (2002). Toward a pedagogy of cases in teacher education. *Teaching Education, 13*(2), 125–135.
Dixson, A. D., & Dingus, J. E. (2007). Tyranny of the majority: Re-enfranchisement of African-American teacher educators teaching for democracy. *International Journal of Qualitative Studies in Education, 20*(6), 639–654.
Gay, G. (2000). *Culturally responsive teaching: Theory, research, & practice*. New York: Teachers College Press.
Gorski, P. C. (2009). What we're teaching the teachers: An analysis of multicultural teacher education coursework syllabi. *Teaching and Teacher Education, 25*, 309–318.
Gorski, P. C., & Pothini, S. G. (2013). *Case studies on diversity and social justice education*. New York: Routledge.
Hollins, E., & Guzman, M. T. (2005). Research on preparing teachers for diverse populations. In M. Cochran-Smith & K. Zeichner (Eds.), *Studying teacher education* (pp. 477–548). Mahwah, NJ: Lawrence Erlbaum.
Kleinfeld, J. (1990). The special virtues of the case method in preparing teachers for minority schools. *Teacher Education Quarterly, 17*(1), 43–51.
Kleinfeld, J. S. (1998). The use of case studies in preparing teachers for cultural diversity. *Theory into Practice, 37*(2), 140–147.
Kraehe, A., & Brown, K. D. (2011). Awakening teachers' capacities for social justice with/in arts-based inquires. *Equity and Excellence in Education, 44*(4), 1–24.
Levin, B. B. (1995). Using the case method in teacher education: The role of discussion and experience in teachers' thinking about cases. *Teaching and Teacher Education, 11*(1), 63–79.
McKeachie, W., & Svinicki, M. (2009). *McKeachie's teaching tips: Strategies, research, and theory for college and university teachers* (13th ed.). Belmont, CA: Wadsworth Publishing.
Mesa-Bains, A., & Shulman, J. H. (1994). *Diversity in the classroom: A casebook for teachers and teacher educators*. Hillsdale, NJ: Lawrence Erlbaum Associates.
Milner, H. R. (2010). What does teaching education have to do with teaching? Implications for diversity studies. *Journal of Teacher Education, 61*(1–2), 118–131.
Moje, E. B., & Wade, S. E. (1997). What case discussions reveal about teacher thinking. *Teaching and Teacher Education, 13*(7), 691–712.
Moule, J. (2005). Implementing a social justice perspective in teacher education: Invisible burden for faculty of color. *Teacher Education Quarterly, 32*(4), 23–42.
Nieto, S. (1999). Culturally relevant teaching with cases: A personal reflection and implications for pedagogy. In M. A. Lundeberg, B. B. Levin, & H. L. Harrington (Eds.), *Who learns what from cases and how? The research base for teaching and learning with cases* (pp. 179–196). Mahwah, NJ: Lawrence Erlbaum Associates.

Nieto, S. (2000). Placing equity front and center: Some thoughts on transforming teacher education for a new century. *Journal of Teacher Education, 51*(3), 180-187.

Nieto, S. & Bode, P. (2008[1992]). *Affirming diversity: The sociopolitical context of multicultural education.* Boston: Pearson.

Sleeter, C. (2001). Preparing teachers for culturally diverse schools: Research and the overwhelming presence of Whiteness. *Journal of Teacher Education, 52*(2), 94-106.

Sleeter, C. E., & Grant, C. A. (2006/1986). *Making choices for multicultural education: Five approaches to race, class and gender* (5th edition). New York: John Wiley & Sons.

Sykes, G., & Bird, T. (1992). Teacher education and the case idea. *Review of Research in Education, 18*, 457-521.

Williams, D. G., & Evans-Winters, V. (2005). The burden of teaching teachers: Memoirs of race discourse in teacher education. *The Urban Review, 37*(3), 201-219.

Zeichner, K., & Melnick, S. (1996). In K. Zeichner, S. Melnick, & M. L. Gomez (Eds.), *Currents of reform in preservice teacher education* (pp. 176-198). New York: Teachers College.

Chapter 15

# Social Conceptions and the Angst of Mentoring Women of Diverse Backgrounds in Higher Education

Brenda L. H. Marina

It has been evidenced how little attention has been paid to the relationship of mentoring and the sociocultural dis/advantages for women's career paths in academia. There are consequences for women who lack mentorship throughout their educational career, and the lack of educational scholarship on mentoring women coupled with the sociocultural dynamics and conditions of academia is a concern. Findings from my qualitative research and literature analyses on women of diverse backgrounds in general and women of African ascent in particular in higher education provide evidence (or the lack of evidence) regarding the determinants for breaking the glass ceiling that has received little attention and gives rise to this conversation (Marina, 2015). Considering the past 36 years, a range of social ideologies has been identified as intervention strategies for breaking the glass ceiling in academia.

From my womanist (Maparyan, 2012) standpoint, the glass ceiling is referred to as the highest level a professional woman can attain in a given professional field without running into an impasse in terms of achieving higher goals (Marina & Fonteneau, 2012). There was a time when the term "glass ceiling" was used mostly to refer to mainstream, upwardly mobile white women entering male-dominated professions; however, the term is more broadly used here to include all women from various professional points of view. From a social justice perspective, similar to Adams, Bell, and Griffin (2010) and Adams and Griffin (2016), this work values the discerning patterns that are often invisible yet reflect systemic aspects of oppression functioning in various contexts. The amalgamation of the glass ceiling effect and mentoring women of diverse backgrounds in academia adds a dimension to our social justice discussion as new and different voices are added to the traditional notions of academic discourse, where glass shattering transformation can occur (Marina & Fonteneau, 2012).

Narratives by and about the experiences of women of diverse backgrounds in the United States and beyond the borders of this nation shed needed light on the ways in which mentoring influences identity formation and internal coping mechanisms in environments often characterized by marginalization (Stanley, 2006a; Vargas, 2002). Through these narratives, women of diverse backgrounds serve as "quasi-mentors" and create spaces for other women to develop and enhance their sociocultural identities to survive and thrive in academia.

To unpack the identity analyses, I briefly depict "mentor influenced" discussions. These were discussions about the experiences of African American women in graduate school as compared to their White peers. Two other African American women explained how women who navigated through the STEM environment had to find their own way. They discussed how women who were less satisfied in the academic workplace are less likely to stay in STEM careers if they *felt* they were less likely to advance within their career. Then there were two older-than-average women (one Native American/German, the other Norwegian/French) as students who became friends and peer-mentors focused on social support. They noted that research consistently indicates that men are better positioned than women to secure organizational mentoring relationships (Ely, Ibarra, & Kolb, 2011; Sandberg, 2013) and that women are often disadvantaged in traditional formalized mentoring structures (Searby, 2010; Zachary, 2009). These discussions I classified as "on the road to academe."

Considering another group of conversations, one White woman discussed power dynamics and how women are often cut off from more senior mentors, which perpetuates a system that exists on a "sink or swim" mentality. My African Jamaican colleague discussed formal mentoring and workplace socialization; "while formal mentoring for faculty in higher education is a prominent feature or becoming more common in countries such as England, the United States and Australia, in small island states such as Jamaica, formal mentoring for new academics is not yet ingrained in the institutional practices at one of the chief institutions of higher education."

Further, from a Pan-Asian perspective, another colleague discussed the negative consequences of ambiguous philosophical issues around gender and ethnicity. My colleagues from the United Kingdom (UK) followed with a similar theme, noting that the Higher Education Institutional (HEI) environment is characterized by a distinct absence of sponsorship and developmental mentoring, resulting in very few female professors. These discussions I classified as "Tapping on the Glass Ceiling in Academe."

Continuing my analyses, Tammy and two of her colleagues, all African American, described collaborative efforts that enhanced their professional development. Their discussions posited the deeply rooted institutional, organizational, departmental, and individual values, beliefs, and perceptions that perpetuate issues surrounding race and gender that inhibit the success of minoritized female faculty, emphasizing Black female faculty (Hull, Bell Scott, & Smith, 1993; Morrison, 2001). More specifically, they described an institute that played a role in the development of social capital by facilitating peer mentoring, which is necessary for success in the academy (Collins, 1986; Gregory, 1999). Three other colleagues (one from Turkey, the other two of African ascent with one being a male) chimed in about a grassroots support program with activities provided by a university for its faculty, with an emphasis on female faculty. This program functions on the premise that the socialization process of junior female academics does not have to adapt to the male patterns of academic socialization. Further, it was made clear that a feminist construct for promoting women in academia is certainly not inferior to that introduced by senior males in years past. Finally, the topic of professional associations created for women who select disciplines that are historically underrepresented by women in general and persons of color in particular further conjectured the need for critical social justice conversations supported by White feminists, Black feminists, and feminists of color (Guy-Sheftall & Cole, 2010). These discussions are classified as "Steps Toward Successful Mentoring in Academe."

Moreover, Patricia Hill Collins (1990) writes that African American women often invoke their own concrete experiences and those of other women and communities of color in the selection of topics for investigation. As such, the scholar and researcher within me challenges the status quo and espouses to ideals of social justice and equality by bringing insights to expose the extent to which social conceptions in mentoring have supported or failed these women. Within this chapter, women differently situated but engaged in academic workspaces have taken part to bridge some of the knowledge gaps where culture implies a set of beliefs, assumptions, norms, and traditions are incorporated into the lives of those in a group. Women (and one supportive male) describe mentoring experiences that influenced their sociocultural identity development and internal coping mechanisms in educational environments often characterized by marginalization.

To further the notion of "differently situated," bear in mind that culture exists in countries, racial and ethnic groups, and organizations and institutions, and within each of these there may be subcultures that have their own set of beliefs and values (Kochan & Pascarelli, 2003; Morrison, 2001). Similarly, context, is a framework, situation, circumstance, or environment. As such, this chapter proffers sociocultured and gendered perspectives on mentoring from varied racial and ethnic backgrounds: African American, African American with a German parent, Asian (United Kingdom), Black, White, White with Scandinavian and Native American (Chippewa) parents, White with one German parent and one Norwegian/French parent, English (United Kingdom), Jamaican, Korean, South African, and Turkish. Moreover, these perspectives on mentoring are from varied education levels, disciplines, and workspaces: business, education, mathematics, social work, STEM, undergraduate, graduate, early career, tenure-track faculty, tenured faculty, and administrators.

I examined the stories of women of diverse backgrounds through the lens of the theory of intersectionality offering a discussion on cultural patterns, variations, and similarities in mentoring utilizing Yosso's (2005) theory of cultural capital. The theory of intersectionality (Crenshaw, 1991) suggests that various culturally and socially constructed categories, such as race, gender, and class, interact on multiple and often simultaneous levels, contributing to systematic social inequality. Through this intersectional lens, I attempt to illuminate how our mentoring experiences as women across cultures and around the globe are interconnected.

Following the work of Kochan (2002) and Kochan and Pascarelli (2003), I considered each narrative as a case from which to extrapolate data. I conducted a content analysis to situate this discussion about mentoring within the context of the sociocultural aspects of a glass ceiling in academia. The emergent themes from the intersecting realities of each woman present theoretical contributions, personal advice, and insights for mentoring to improve the current context of higher education for women, and thus promote the shattering of the glass ceiling in academia. I have intentionally studied the concrete experiences of women of African ascent (Collins, 1990), while at the same time striving to extrapolate wisdom and meaning from other women of diverse backgrounds. Our concrete experiences, uniquely individual, are at the same time collectively connected.

All of the women communicated a unique narrative and journey of continued persistence; consequently, several African American women used autoethnography (Muncey, 2010; Siddique, 2011) to analyze and reflect on their experiences to celebrate rather than demonize their individual story (Chang, 2008). I uncovered salient themes that emerged from the narratives that were eloquently shared about the positives and negatives of mentoring experiences in academia. Consistent with the precepts of intersectionality, these themes reference various culturally and socially constructed categories, such as race, gender, class, and ageism, which interact on multiple and often simultaneous levels, contributing to systematic social inequality, or in other words, a glass ceiling in academia (Marina, 2015). Glass walls and ceilings have been systematically constructed as a consequence of sociocultural attitudes, behaviors, and practices (Marina, 2011). Further, considering a sociocultured critique, Yosso's (2005) Theory of Cultural Capital scaffolded the discovery of cultural patterns, variations, and similarities for mentoring. Yosso names six forms of cultural capital that marginalized groups (in this case, women are the marginalized group) bring into the conversation: aspirational, navigational, social, resistant, familial, and linguistic capital. Yosso's theory complemented the notion of intersectionality and illuminated the complexities of issues faced by women of diverse backgrounds in general and African American women in particular.

Drawing from Yosso (2005), I briefly describe three of the forms of capital that were applicable for mentoring and academia in this particular case. *Aspirational capital* refers to the ability to sustain high aspirations even when one's circumstances make them seem impossible to achieve, such as living in poverty or, in this particular case, remaining diligent in carving out a space for women in historically male-dominated structures. *Navigational capital* refers to the skills to navigate through social institutions, particularly institutions that systemically disadvantage marginalized persons. *Social capital* refers to the networks of people to whom women can turn to obtain information, emotional support, and access to key institutional personnel, such as those who may help them through the tenure and promotion process. These three forms of cultural capital can be used as identity markers for both mentors and mentees to consider as areas to identify barriers and address concerns.

Two African American women particularly described their graduate school experiences and discussed the role mentoring played in their identity development. They wanted . . . *role models who embodied confidence, poise, and who embodied success . . .* so there would be *footprints for them to follow.*[1] The two African American women navigating the STEM discipline shared . . . *we needed emotional support, guidance, and direction for coping with the social issues and politics surrounding degree attainment.* One of the women poignantly noted . . . *I lost valuable time finding my own way and encountered many detours, roadblocks, and brick walls. Navigating as a Black female in an environment that was traditionally for White males was clearly a challenge.* Our Scandinavian/Native American and Norwegian/French colleagues said . . . *during our graduate school experiences, formalized mentoring structures were very limited. Informal mentoring and/or peer mentoring proved to be the mechanism to help lessen the feelings of isolation and face obstacles as we navigated through academe.* Embarking on graduate education, the African American women appeared to have encountered glass ceiling structures and obstacles to a greater degree. Systemic disadvantages were the major concern thwarting the *navigational capital* during the critical years of graduate education.

One White woman described academic socialization as . . . *neither consistent nor an institutionalized process, and dependent upon the discipline, institution, or individual . . . socialization occurred mainly on-the-job, through trial and error, and with little formal training or formal mentoring.* Similarly, my African Jamaican colleague noted that *formal mentoring as an aspect of workplace socialization is not embedded in the organizational culture for several higher education institutions in my country.* The two women from the United Kingdom furthered the notion that both informal and formal mentoring relationships are beneficial. These women firmly believed that *informal mentoring relationships have been the basis for our academic socialization,* however, . . . *there remains the need for the adoption of formal processes and structures to support the professional well-being of faculty and staff.* While social capital was the dominant theme with this group of women, there was one Korean woman whose early life reflections hint to the development of aspirational capital. The early lessons (mentoring) she gained as a protégé caused her to remain diligent in male-dominant spaces.

The theme of social capital continued as other African American women discussed that *mentors were needed to build the social capital necessary for success and survival in academia.* Peer mentoring and informal mentoring experiences were reiterated as extremely effective tools to build social capital. While four other African American women added their voices to the social capital issue (a social justice issue), their contention about the differential gender-based socialization process in academia applied to aspirational capital as they found structures not necessarily conducive to thriving in academia; however, they persevered and continue to tap on glass ceilings. Adams and colleagues (2013) portend that we need to affirm and value social and cultural differences and challenge the social norms and policies in institutions where difference is profoundly unequal.

## The Angst of Mentoring Away the Glass Ceiling

While each woman spoke about mentoring experiences, relationships, and programs, several also suggested that women in large part are responsible for mentoring away the glass ceiling. For example, two respondents noted that they were intentional in selecting graduate programs with African American faculty members who shared their research interests and perspectives in higher education. Similarly, Virginia and Krystal said that African American women should not be afraid to seek support from individuals. Alison pointed out that it is women who carry the responsibility to move inside the margins and to help other women create their identities. As social justice educators, mentors, and role models, to tap on the glass ceiling, it is our responsibility to engage, inform, and provoke, as eloquently noted by Morrison and Denard (2008) in "What Moves at the Margin."

**Reflections and building confidence.** I also suggest that women are in large part responsible for mentoring away the glass ceiling. The women in this study support this notion, as they collectively suggest that critical reflection and building one's confidence can construct and maintain empowering definitions of self (Marina, 2015). Jennifer and Jeanette felt that *scholarly reflection on one's own experiences helped us to understand the experiences, issues, and obstacles we faced along the journey.* Vanna, Abe, and Andy suggested that being mindful and reflective on one's own experience in academia is an important ingredient of meaningful mentoring. Through reflection and critical dialogue, Julie's mentor helped her to reach her own conclusions, which spurred the development of her confidence and self-esteem. Charlotte, regularly reflected on her mentoring process, which broadened her scope for change and new ideas. Wilma's mentoring alliance improved her sense of worth as a scholar, and Joni noted that her mentoring relationship with her peer was the beginning of rebuilding her confidence as a faculty member. These self-initiated, self-reflective experiences suggest that, with diligence in identifying aspirational, navigational, and social capital issues (a reflective process), individual confidences created by women will be bolstered. As we make these connections with our own identities, we are better equipped to call attention to discrepancies between the rhetoric and practice of social justice in our academic spaces (Ross, 2016).

**Peer mentoring and informal and formal mentoring.** Several women (and one male) described peer mentoring as key for them, and every woman mentioned informal or formal mentoring networks, relationships, or programs. It was suggested that such relationships with other caring and nurturing women increase positive self-identity and self-efficacy (Packer-Williams & Evans, 2011). Peer mentoring was described as an opportunity that brought peers together as sisters, which met a need for faculty of color. Because faculty of color receive less social support than their White counterparts (Jackson, 2004; Ponjuan, Martin Conley, & Trower, 2011), peer relationships provide greater access to mentoring (Thomas, Hu, Gewin, Bingham, & Yanchus, 2005). A colleague from South Africa described her first mentoring experiences in her new leadership role as "corridor" mentoring. While she looked for a clear process of mentoring from her dean, she found herself asking questions of her peers as she passed them by in the corridors of the institution.

Informal mentoring relationships were the supports necessary for PhD journeys, helped in the development of identities as mentors, and were the fundamental part of students' socialization processes in the academy. It was an evident and common theme that due to missing or inadequate formal mentoring, women in the academy relied on themselves and others for support and guidance (Fries-Britt & Kelly, 2005; Myers, 2002). It was suggested that formalized mentoring programs at the university level must be created and supported for women by women for the professional well-being of new members to the academy. If institutions moved from informal mentoring to more formal mentoring programs, the diverse needs of early career professionals aspiring to leadership roles may be met; the benefits of formal policies and programs that provide formal, structured mentoring experiences should not be overlooked.

## Words of Wisdom for Mentoring Away the Glass Ceiling in Academia

Some of the women in this study now serve as mentors because of the supportive networks and environments they experienced. For others, the opposite is true: they now serve as mentors because of the lack of mentorship throughout their academic and or professional journey. Considering the intersecting realities (Crenshaw, 1991; Davis, 2008) of these African American women and the other women of diverse backgrounds, insights are offered for mentors, mentees, and educational intuitions and organizations. Whether it is the uneven terrain and journey that occurs from the onset of graduate education for women of diverse backgrounds (disciplines, cultures, age variance, etc.), or career issues and concerns that call attention to the positive and negative aspects of mentoring for women (Adams et al., 2013; Marina & Ross, 2016), or institutions responding to the sociocultural dynamics from within and without (Morrison, 2008), there is glass to be broken.

**A Word to tap on the glass for mentees.** Mentorship, in various forms, is critical for cultivating the self-definition necessary to resist the oppressiveness of university environments. The mentoring experience can facilitate emotional and sociocultural adjustments that come with the journey within institutions, disciplines, or departments. Further, a team of mentors can help reduce those feelings of isolation, low confidence, cultural alienation, and disillusionment that women often feel in male-dominated spaces (Herzig, 2004; Ponjuan, Martin Conley, & Trower, 2011). It is wise to build a team of mentors and have at least one mentor who can relate to the personal (e.g., gender-wise, social, cultural, racial, geographical) issues faced by women. Some of the women in this chapter preferred mentors who "looked like them"; however, their overall advice was that women should be open to mentorship from other well-intentioned and qualified individuals (e.g., mentors from other ethnic groups and/or genders or institutions). Being open to mentorship that was previously unconsidered is an opportunity to capitalize on being at the right place at the right time for career development, advancement, and potential success (Marina, 2015). Ming Fang He (2016) encourages *clashing with the traditional . . . thriving in-between landscapes of education . . .* to confront issues of social justice to bring positive social and educational change.

**A word to tap on the glass for mentors.** Mentors of women must be intentional about mentoring by identifying the aspirational, navigational, and social capital challenges and assist with gaining access to critical knowledge, networks, and other professional development opportunities. Insights into the sociocultural dynamics of an institution will help mentees understand how to engage and build relationships with key people in the academy. As such, mentors must continue developing strategies to increase the number of women working in leadership roles in academia and decrease feelings of isolation and alienation within courses, departments, colleges, or disciplines (Adams et al., 2013; Stanley, 2006b). Moreover, it is necessary for women mentors to share their stories (Bell, 2010) to empower and facilitate a better understanding of other women's experiences.

**A word to tap on the glass for institutions.** The remnants of deeply rooted institutional, organizational, departmental, individual values, beliefs, and perceptions (Morrison, 2001) that perpetuate sociocultural issues that impede the success of women in academia must be obliterated. Institutions can benefit by diminishing exclusionary practices that impede mentoring, from ageism (DeJong & Love, 2010; Ostrom-Blonigen & Larson-Casselton, 2016) to racism (Bell, Love, & Roberts, 2007). While mentoring support is needed to increase the number of women of diverse backgrounds working in leadership roles in academia, the goal should be to change and sustain institutional culture shifts that go beyond merely adding women. Institutions should take note that effectively mentored women are more likely to stay at the university, receive more grant income, obtain a higher level of promotions, and have more positive perceptions of themselves as academics compared with nonmentored female academics (Marina, 2016). As such, incentivizing mentoring programs is a win-win proposition.

A consistent institutionalized process for academic socialization with some common starting points would likely pave the way for women to begin and advance in their careers. However, the consideration for the differing paths taken and the modification of "one-size fits all" models for mentoring relationships could better meet the needs of women seeking mentors (Peña & Wilder, 2011). There is strong evidence of the benefits of informal mentoring relationships for academic socialization; as such, higher education institutions should take decisive and proactive steps to develop and maintain structures and processes to support both informal and formal mentoring relationships and programs.

## A Final Word on Mentoring

My South African colleague seemed to capture the essence of every articulated voice in these conversations. Collectively, these voices tell a story, a story about social justice; Bell (2010) calls it *storytelling for social justice*. Because social justice for the individual and for the collective is very important from the South African view, I will let her heart *speak* to our minds. Fatima was excited about the new opportunity for a leadership role, however, when she found that she was not being mentored as she expected, she reached out to peers and those who had done what she was trying to do. She also tapped into the untapped resources in the organization—the janitorial staff, who were very helpful in many ways. Fatima would say, "you must reach out." There were times when Fatima simply had to learn it her own way—self-learning. She tapped into her own assets; she had to read and use her computer to gain her own social capital. Fatima would say, "you must reach in." I support this social justice action, as I described such similar conundrums in *Mentor Myself? The Juxtaposition of Identity Development for Women of Color in Higher Education* (Marina, 2016). As Fatima reflected on her experiences, she found mentoring policies and agendas that were not fully executed. She also found that the women at the upper levels were not accessible; it seemed that they enjoyed saying that they broke that glass ceiling and wore it like a badge—they didn't want that trophy taken away from them. Fatima would say, "you must reach down."

It is my hope that both men and women may come to embrace the need to work within the context of knowing that what he or she does in any education discipline is a contribution to something higher than him- or herself (Bell, 2002). As a woman of African ascent, I must remind myself that I have assumed a role as leader, advocate, and collaborator in a male-dominated system to address ethical and equity concerns in the socioenvironmental and political contexts (Marina, 2016; Sefa Dei, 2002) of academia. If we as African-ascendant educators, scholars, researchers and mentor/teachers immerse ourselves in the spaces that are congruent with what we know in body, mind, and spirit, we can construct more authentic paradigms for women and deconstruct the boundaries and norms of Western ways. Where mentors of color are absent or scant on university campuses, we must constantly reassess our academic impact and continually create intellectual spaces in academe that affirm and support mentoring women of color. Mentors can enhance the aspirational, navigational, and social capital of women in higher education by extending their reach. In our reaching, we are teaching; we can transform social conceptions and break glass ceilings. *Reach out, reach in, reach down!*

## Note

1. Italicized text represents quotes from interviews.

## References

Adams, M., Bell, L., & Griffin, P. (2010). *Teaching for diversity and social justice.* New York: Routledge.

Adams, M., Blumenfeld, W., Castaneda, C., Hackman, H., Peters, M., & Zúñiga, X. (2013). *Readings for diversity and social justice.* New York: Routledge.

Adams, M., & Griffin, P. (2016). *Teaching for diversity and social justice.* New York: Routledge.

Bell, D. *Ethical ambitions: Living a life of meaning and worth.* New York: Bloomsbury.

Bell, L. (2010). *Storytelling for social justice: Connecting narrative and the arts in anti-racist teaching.* New York: Routledge.

Bell, L. Love, B., & Roberts, R. (2007). Racism, and white privilege curriculum design. In M. Adams, L. Bell, & P. Griffin (Eds.), *Teaching for diversity and social justice: A source book for teachers* (pp. 123–144). New York: Routledge.

Chang, H. (2008). *Autoethnography as method.* Walnut Creek, CA: Left Coast Press.

Collins, P. H. (1986). Learning from the outsider within: The sociological significance of Black feminist thought. *Social Problems, 33*(6), 514–532.

Collins, P. H. (1990). Black *feminist thought: Knowledge, consciousness, and the politics of empowerment.* New York: Routledge.

Crenshaw, K. (1991). Mapping the margins: Intersectionality, identity politics, and violence against women of color, *Stanford Law Review, 43*(6), 1241–1299.

Davis, K. (2008). Intersectionality as buzzword: A sociology of science perspective on what makes a feminist theory successful. *Feminist Theory, 9*(1), 67–87.

DeJong, K., & Love, B. (2010). Ageism and adultism. In M. Adams, W. Blumenfeld, C. Casteneda, H. Hackman, M. Peters, & X. Zúñiga (Eds.), *Readings for diversity and social justice* (pp. 533–540). New York: Routledge.

Ely, R. J., Ibarra, H., & Kolb, D. M. (2011). Taking gender into account: Theory and design for women's leadership development programs. *Academy of Management, Learning & Education, 10*(3), 474–493.

Fries-Britt, S., & Kelly, B. T. (2005). Retaining each other: Narratives of two African American women in the academy. *Urban Review, 37*(3), 221–242. doi: 10.1007/s11256-005-0006-2

Guy-Sheftall, B., & Cole, J. (2010). *Who should be first: Feminists speak out on the 2008 presidential campaign.* Albany: State University of New York Press.

He, M. (2016). Thriving in-between landscapes of education. *The Sophist Bane, 8*(1), 47–56.

Hill, C., Corbett, C., & St. Rose, A. (2010). *Why so few? Women in science, technology, engineering, and mathematics.* Washington, DC: American Association of University Women.

Holmes, S. L., Land, L. D., & Hinton-Huston, V. D. (2007). Race still matters: Considerations for mentoring Black women in academe. *The Negro Educational Review*, 58(1/2), 105–129.

Hull, G., Bell Scott, P., & Smith, B. (1993). *But some of us are brave: All the women are white, all the blacks are men: Black women's studies*. New York: The Feminist Press at CUNY.

Jackson, J. (2004). The story is not in the numbers: Academic socialization and diversifying the faculty. *NWSA Journal*, 172–185.

Gregory, S. T. (1999). *Black women in the academy: The secrets to success and achievement*. Lanham, MD: University Press of America.

Herzig, A. (2004). Slaughtering this beautiful math: Graduate women choosing and leaving mathematics. *Gender and Education*, 16(3), 379.

Kochan, F. (2002). Examining the organizational and human dimensions of mentoring: A textual data analysis. In F. K. Kochan (Ed.), *The organizational and human dimensions of successful mentoring programs and relationships* (pp. 269–286). Greenwich, CT: Information Age Publishing.

Kochan, F., Kent, A., & Green, A. (Eds.) (2014). *Uncovering the hidden cultural dynamics in mentoring programs and relationships: Enhancing practice and research*. Vol. 4: Perspectives in Mentoring Series. Charlotte, NC: Information Age Publishing.

Kochan, F., & Pascarelli, J. (2003). *Global perspectives on mentoring: Transforming contexts, communities, and cultures*. Greenwich, CT: Information Age Publishing.

Maparyan, L. (2012). *The womanist idea*. New York: Routledge.

Marina, B. L. H. (2016). Mentor myself? The juxtaposition of identity development for women of color in higher education. *The Sophist Bane*, 8(1), 29–33.

Marina, B. L. H. (Ed.) (2015). *Mentoring away the glass ceiling in academia: A cultured critique*. Lanham, MD: Lexington Books.

Marina, B. L. H. (2014). A cultural connection to identity development for graduate female students of color. In F. Kochan, A. Kent, & A Green (Eds.), *Uncovering the hidden cultural dynamics in mentoring programs and relationships: Enhancing practice and research* (Vol. 4: Perspectives in Mentoring Series; pp. 63–77). Charlotte, NC: Information Age Publishing.

Marina, B. L. H., & Fonteneau, D. Y. (2012). Servant leaders who picked up the broken glass. *Journal of Pan African Studies*, 5(2), 67–83.

Marina, B. L. H. (2011). Breaking ground and breaking barriers in a globalized world. In S. Fullerton & D. Moore (Ed.), *Global business trends contemporary readings 2011 edition* (pp. 117–122). Ypsilanti, MI: Academy Business Administration. ISBN 1-887676-03-1

Marina, B. L. H, & Ross, S. (2016). *Beyond retention: Cultivating spaces of equity, justice, and fairness for women of color in U.S. higher education*. Research for Social Justice: Personal~ Passionate~ Participatory Inquiry Book Series. Charlotte, NC: Information Age Publishing (IAP).

Morrison, T. (2001). How can values be taught in the university? *Michigan Quarterly Review*, 40(2), 273–278.

Morrison, T., & Denard, C. (2008). *What moves at the margin: Selected nonfiction*. Jackson: University Press of Mississippi.

Myers, L. (2002). *A broken silence: Voices of African American women in the academy*. Westport, CT: Greenwood Publishing Group.

Muncey, J. (2010). *Creating autoethnographies*. London: Sage.

Ostrom-Blonigen, J., & Larson-Casselton, C. (2015). Navigating the turbulent boundaries of a Ph.d. program: A supportive peer-mentoring relationship. In B. Marina, *Mentoring away the glass ceiling in academia: A cultured critique* (pp. 41–58), Lanham, MD: Lexington Books.

Packer-Williams, C. L., & Evans, K. M. (2011). Retaining and reclaiming ourselves: Reflections on a peer mentoring group experience for new African American women professors. *Perspectives in Peer Programs, 23*(1), 9–23.

Peña, M., & Wilder, J. (2011). Mentoring transformed: When students of color see diversity in leadership. *Diversity in Higher Education, 10*, 345–363.

Ponjuan, L., Conley, V. M., & Trower, C. (2011). Career stage differences in pre-tenure track faculty perceptions of professional and personal relationships with colleagues. *The Journal of Higher Education, 82*(3), 319–346.

Ross, S. (2016). Dangerous terrain: Reflections of a Black woman teacher educator working within predominantly white universities. *The Sophist Bane, 8*(1), 5–10.

Sandberg, S. (2013). *Lean in: Women, work, and the will to lead*. New York: Knopf.

Searby, L., & Collins, L. (2010). Mentor and mother hen: Just what I needed as a first-year professor. *Advancing Women in Leadership Journal, 30*(20), 1–16.

Sefa Dei, G. (2002). Spiritual knowing and transformative learning. Working paper #59. Retrieved from nall.oise.utoronto.ca/res/59GeorgeDei.pdf

Siddique, S. (2011). Being in-between: The relevance of ethnography and auto-ethnography for psychotherapy research. *Counseling and Psychotherapy Research, 11*(4), 310–316.

Stanley, C. A. (2006a). An overview of the literature. In C. A. Stanley (Ed.), *Faculty of color: Teaching in predominantly White colleges and universities* (pp. 1–29). Bolton: Anker.

Stanley, C. A. (2006b). Summary and key recommendations for the recruitment and retention of faculty of color. In C. A. Stanley (Ed.), *Faculty of color: Teaching in predominantly White colleges and universities* (pp. 361–373). Bolton: Anker.

# Part IV

# REINFORCING ACTIVISM AND COMMUNITY BUILDING

Chapter 16

# Navigating the Complexities of Race-Based Activism

CHERJANÉT D. LENZY

> I think, us as Black people have so far to go in understanding who we are. I feel we get activism, we understand that we should and deserve to be living a better life than we are, but we truly don't understand who were are as people . . . I feel . . . in my experience of any organization that I have been to, they always fall short. Maybe I have all these different complexities within that, but . . . I'm not part of really any organization, because of these reasons, I don't feel a whole complexity when I'm in them. And I feel some parts of me have to be silent because of that.
>
> —*Nilta X*

Honoring our full selves within activist spaces is uncharted territory. Often, we are required to center one component of our identity to participate in all-encompassing social movements. In turn, situating the complexity of identity within a social justice or activist framework seems to be a minimal occurrence. Founders of the #BlackLivesMatter movement and the corresponding #SayHerName campaign sought to explore these issues (Crenshaw, Ritchie, Anspach, Gilmer, & Harris, 2015; Rickford, 2016). However, media attention has focused the #BlackLivesMatter movement on Black men. In turn, the experience of those with multiple identities engaged in this or similar race-based activism is not entirely understood.

For this chapter, I selected one woman's story extracted from a larger study that explored the experiences of college-aged Black women engaged in race-based activism. What emerged from the original study were four separate unique experiences of Black women that centered on the overarching theme of the complexity of Black womanhood. Though each participant shared how they felt, activist spaces did not always allow space for their full selves. It became clear that insight on how each participant understood their intersectionality was the most salient discussion in our conversations. Thus, to tell their stories collectively seemed to suggest that their experiences were the same. Though similarities were present, significant experiences seemed important to be highlighted. Therefore, Nilta's story will be shared here. The dynamic of having more formal education than the other participants may have had an impact on Nilta. Her reflection on her lived experiences seemed to provide strong understanding of her identities, social issues, and interpersonal relationships that clearly emerged from our conversation. This saliency allowed for abstraction from the group to highlight key themes found across participants while providing a seamless narrative.

## Literature Review

Black women's leadership and lived experience are impacted by the intersecting identities of race and gender (King, 1998; Simien, 2003). Together, the interlocking systems of racism and sexism create a compounding oppressive experience (Crenshaw, 1991). Black women navigate the complexity of intersecting identity that in turn impacts their participation and engagement in identity-based activist movements. For instance, past engagement in activism such as the Civil Rights Movement highlights how Black women managed their lived experiences in activist spaces (Simien, 2003).

As demonstrated in the Civil Rights Movement and early feminist movements, Black women have found themselves on the margins of discussions on both racial issues and women's issues (Evans, 2015; hooks, 2000). Discussion about gender issues within racial justice movements was limited by concerns they would distract from the larger movement's success (Simien, 2003). In kind, Black women were rendered invisible in the women's liberation movement as White middle-class women's concerns were centralized (Evans, 2015). The erasure of Black women's experiences with oppression is commonplace. Societal perceptions that all who identify as Black have similar experiences, or all women deal with similar issues, have created an assumption that oppression across an identity group looks the same (Purdie-Vaughns & Eibach, 2008; Schug, Alt, & Klauer, 2015).

Interestingly, though, Black women have been integral in racial justice movements (Edwards, 2000; Horsford, 2012; Simien, 2003). During the Civil Rights Movement, many Black women acted as bridge-building leaders by connecting the community to the larger social movement, acting as critical organizers and mobilizers (Alston & McClellan, 2013; Horsford, 2012; Robnett, 1996, 1997). For instance, some members of the Black community were not instantly on board with the racial justice activism during the time. Black women often worked in the community and focused on individuals' social location to help convince them of the importance of the movement and gain their support (Robnett, 1997).

However, the work Black women did during this time was not applauded in the same ways as Black male leadership. Gender roles of the time put Black men in mainly positional leadership roles. These men held positions such as director, while women mostly filled administrative roles (Robnett, 1996). In essence, Black men were the face of the movement while Black women did the behind-the-scenes work (Barnett, 1993).

It appears the behavior of Black women in race-based activism has taken on a similar role in movements today. For instance, current activism around the #BlackLivesMatter movement has seemed to minimally recognize or completely erase the contributions of Black women, Queer people, and Trans* people in the movement (Lindsey, 2015; Taylor, 2016). Though this was not the original intent of the movement, it seems the media attention and community focus has defaulted to lifting the experiences of Black men over Black women (Garza, 2016; Rickford, 2016).

As of this writing, no studies explore why Black women's issues that connect to their intersectional identities are not situated in either race-based or gender-based activist platforms. Though there is literature exploring Black women or women of color and activism (Harvell, 2010; Linder & Rodriguez, 2012; Rainey & Johnson, 2009) and discussion of how Black women were involved in activism during the Civil Rights Movement (Barnett, 1993; Edwards, 2000; Horsford, 2012; Millner, 1996; Simien, 2003), no studies look specifically at why activist platforms minimize how Black women are impacted by racism and sexism and how that impact is not centered in activist work. While new literature has begun to address Black women's marginalization in race-based activism (Lindsey, 2015; Rickford, 2016; Taylor, 2016), accompanying research has yet to appear.

In contemporary activism, a difference in Black women's and Black men's experience with police violence highlighted in media can be seen through the activism of the #BlackLivesMatter movement. Though three Black women, two of whom are Queer, started the #BlackLivesMatter movement, there has been little focus on the experience of Black women with police brutality and other violence. Though the #SayHerName (Crenshaw et al., 2015) campaign did ignite a redirection of conversation to acknowledge the ways Black women have suffered police brutality and called attention to the numerous women that died from this violence, focus quickly shifted back toward Black men. This renders the experience of Black women virtually invisible and perhaps creates the assumption that Black women deal with this violence, discrimination, and racism less frequently than their male counterparts.

Despite their many contributions, Black women and their interests remain at the margins of race-based activist movements. Due to the intersecting identities of race and gender, Black women combat both racism and sexism. The multiple oppressive experiences endured by Black women are often left out of activist platforms and general understanding. Additionally, the discussion of sexism centers on the experience of White women, while racism is centered on the Black male experience (Purdie-Vaughn & Eibach, 2008; Schug et al., 2015; Sesko & Biernat, 2010; Thomas, Dovidio & West, 2014).

## Methodology

Four college-aged Black women were selected for this study via purposeful sampling (Jones, Torres, & Arminio, 2014). Participants spanned the locations of the Rocky Mountain Region and a Northeastern state; three were college graduates, and one was a current graduate student at a 4-year public university. Each shared their experiences with intersectionality in race-based activist spaces through semi-structured interviews. Before the interviews, participants were asked to consider their intersecting identities (Carbado, Crenshaw, Mays & Tomlinson, 2013; Crenshaw, 1991) as Black women, and bring with them a list of the most pressing issues they felt Black women faced and that they would be engaged in activism around if possible. The prompt framed our conversations, guiding participants to hone in on specific experiences that illuminated challenges with intersectionality and single-issue activist spaces. Nilta's story clearly presents the dynamic of wrestling with these issues and communicates themes found throughout other participants' stories. Focusing on her narrative provides synchronized travel through one person's journey. Her story is chronicled in the pages that follow.

## Intersectionality

The interplay of race and gender together impacts the lived experiences of women of color in significant ways (Crenshaw, 1991). The impact of the systems of racism and sexism together bring along with it power dynamics that influence how women of color must navigate the world (Jordan-Zachery, 2007). Specifically, the link among oppressive structures, such as racism, classism, sexism, and heterosexism offer a compounding effect experienced by women of color only. However, activist spaces seem to center one identity in activist platforms, which does not account for the multiplicity of identity that is innate among all persons. Moreover, neither feminist nor anti-racist spaces account for the collective impact of racism and sexism; rather, one or the other is addressed, while women of color are oppressed by both systems (Crenshaw, 1991).

## Nilta X

Nilta X's story highlights how she came to understand her identity through various college experiences. Along her journey, she wrestles with the cultural implications of her multiple identities and how these impact how she shows up as an activist. Her story is followed by implications and suggested future research.

### Developing Identity and Blackness

Nilta began the journey to understanding her identity in community college. After realizing her plan to become a nightclub owner was more involved than she anticipated, she decided to attend college to put off "real life" a little bit longer. However, she was thrust into the reality that racism is constant and protruding when she was greeted by hateful signage posted on the property of a townsperson across from her college. Though Nilta did not describe the sign, images of lynchings, beatings, and other racist violence came to mind.

> This is a very small, confederate, tiny, little town . . . didn't know that, didn't know it existed . . . being first generation to this country my mother doesn't know too much about like the actual American history . . . I never really knew about things . . . I knew who the KKK was . . . but when I got to [college] a former KKK member lived across the street from the school and he loved his history so much that he had a display . . . [that was] the first thing I drove up to.

Surprised by her new surroundings, Nilta found herself in an environment that was not like previous spaces she had been. Her identity was something she had been very sure of, but now she was forced to process what her identity meant to her in this new place. She began by educating herself about her cultural history, and through this discovery new understanding about her identity materialized.

> I had a whole lot of free time to read . . . Tumblr was like my go to . . . I loved Tumblr . . . I was like so fascinated . . . I started reading, and reading . . . Brazilian history . . . because it tells you who you are, where you came [from] . . . I was like "What do you mean? What's Afro-Brazilian? Like you mean there's more Africans in South America?" I was . . . fascinated . . . then I started listening to a lot of YouTube videos . . . everything there just sang about what White supremacy was and things just started clicking . . .

Through her discovery of information, Nilta began to have a self-awareness that opened her up to new ways of understanding her own experience. She became president of the Black student organization on campus, started a step team, and also worked in admissions. Through each of these experiences she was being shaped as a Black student, but there was still more ahead of her that would require her to delve deeper into her identity.

Nilta's self-discovery opened up once she completed community college and started attending a 4-year university. She joined her college's Black women's organization on campus and expressed this is where she felt she had a voice.

> It was like a different type of voice like *actually* being a Black woman, and I say *actually* because it was like that identity was super hard to own for the longest time because I didn't even know what that meant . . . going to [college] it was like a whole different type of Black woman, so it was like really great . . . you can be surrounded by beautiful Black women who do or do not share similar identities or similar stories with you but that's how you build that sisterhood, by understanding how complex our Black sisterhood is.

Connecting with this student organization was significant for Nilta because it began to shape her identity as a Black woman. Nilta's identity as Brazilian impacted her sense of self and gave her great pride. Still, her understanding of her Blackness was continuously developing.

> I feel my mom knew that this country is a little different in how we could walk around but she never was like, "This is what it is," she would always just say "You are who you are," . . . So I never knew what a Black woman was because my mom didn't identify, she still doesn't identify because that to her, that to us, is like being American.

Nilta's relationship with her mother and her mother's own identity influenced her understanding of herself. Though her mother did not connect with being a Black woman, per se, Nilta's college life was shifting her understanding and connecting her to a community that embraced her.

> I would say college is what made me realize I was a Black woman . . . being treated like a Black woman in the aspect of being disrespected by other people telling me that . . . I'm not as pretty as someone because [of] my skin . . . and that's when it came to me like, "Oh my gosh I'm really a Black woman, people see me that way!" And do I? I didn't know what that really meant, and then further on in college I was like "YES, I'm a Black woman!" like own that identity . . . like I've been through so much that has shown me what it is to be a Black woman . . . my culture is Black . . . I think it's just a beautiful thing to be a Black woman . . . I had to figure out what a Black woman meant to me, not what society says it was supposed to be.

Nilta's involvement both on campus and in her student organization helped her define her Black identity. Being perceived as Black was significant and solidified her Blackness. This realization shifted her processing and allowed her to begin internalizing her identity and finding ways to express and own this in a personal way.

*Black versus Brown Identity*

As Nilta's identity as a Black woman became more concrete, her two worlds of being Black and Brazilian sometimes seemed as though they were colliding. As Nilta embarked in activism she was faced with the expectation to compartmentalize her identity and pick which aspects of her identities to bring to the forefront.

> Race is something that gets juggled around here, everywhere you go in the U.S., I have to talk about it . . . when I'm in more [of] the U.S. setting and trying to talk about activism [and when I am] also including my Brown brothers and sisters, people [start] looking at me side-eyed . . . like I'm both, what do you want me to do . . . just forget about them?

Nilta's desire to be engaged in activism was strong and continued to be nourished throughout her college experience. However, finding a space that incorporated all of herself in these activist spaces was not happening. From social and leadership organizations to personal affiliations, Nilta felt that her intersecting identities were not being fully embraced. After Nilta became a member of a Latina sorority, others who expected her to join a historically Black sorority questioned her, again not embracing both her racial and ethnic identities. Though Nilta was proud of her choice, she still felt challenged by the confrontation.

> The first question was like, "Oh I thought you were Black," and I was like, "But I am Black and you don't know your history . . . because if you knew your history you would know that the bare minimum are in the U.S. and like Brazil is a very large compass of African people." So like to me I was very shocked . . . I knew it was coming, I just didn't know how it was going to come towards me . . . I constantly have to battle that.

Nilta tried to balance her identities of being Black, Brown, and Brazilian but it seemed the assumption was that since she claimed a Black identity all her connections would also be Black. Her intersectionality was not necessarily honored by Black-specific organizations. Not only were her multiple identities not acknowledged, in some cases it was not recognized at all because she was solely viewed as being a Black woman.

> I'll choose to . . . be in my [Greek] letters and then when I do, some people question it, like . . . "You didn't choose to go to Divine Nine [National Pan-Hellenic Council] . . . ?" It's that constant struggle that I have to fight with . . . Can we as people understand and honor the complexity that people have within their ethnic and racial identities? I bounce back and forth, with the question . . . is it better to be mixed and have it be noticed or better to be mixed and not have it noticed? For myself, it's not noticeable. . . . So it's like which one? Cause for me . . . it took a long, long, long, long, time to identify the way I do, because of that constant back and forth, back and forth.

*Intersection of Spirituality*

Though Nilta had been reflective and intentional in wrestling with her multiple identities she struggled with others not being as intentional in trying to understand. As she continued on her college journey, she soon discovered that the limiting of her identity was not reserved only for her racial and ethnic identities but others as well.

> Another intersectional identity is my spirituality . . . and how do I see myself as a being of this world. Being Black, you're supposed to be Christian . . . I have to walk into places that are singing gospel music, blasting it out loud . . . I'm just thinking, how many other Black people are not Christian and don't come into this space because we play this kind of music?

Though Nilta's Blackness was becoming salient for her, she still felt like somewhat of an outsider. Her spiritual identity intersected with her Black identity and meant something different from how others were expressing their Blackness. The monolithic idea of Blackness did not allow space for multiple ways of being. In thinking about her activism and the activist organizations she participated in—campus student organizations, local chapters of the #BlackLivesMatter movement, and Freedom Riders—Nilta always felt that her whole self was not necessarily recognized in these spaces, which made it difficult to fully embrace these groups.

*Identity Shaping Activism*

If activist platforms did not have a single-issue focus perhaps space would be created for intersectional connections to issues. For Nilta her gender, ethnicity, race, and spirituality collectively influenced how she defined herself. In addition, the activist work she was committed to was also influenced by her identity and made her show up in the work differently.

> How has my identity shaped the path that I choose for my activism? Or how has it prevented it? Because one of the things I think about a lot is, I find myself having to always explain, how I know so much about Latina culture and how much I know about Black culture.

Nilta was hoping to find ways that her Latina and Black cultures could coexist. Still, it seemed that other intersectional identities also could not fully be central in her activist work. She recalled how her gender was often minimized, if not erased, both in activist spaces and in the Black community in general. In particular, Nilta discussed how patriarchy shows up in these spaces. She suggests that Black men are so overwhelmed by the racism they experience that they forget they can also oppress Black women. In Nilta's experience Black women do much of the work in activism and the Black community, but that work often goes uncelebrated or even squelched.

> We can be the mothers of society, be the mothers of our community, but behind closed doors. Then our sons, our fathers, our uncles, are the ones who get the shine . . . But it's like what did I do for you to get you here? Because of the trauma that our Black men also go through . . . it seems like there's a big ole wall or something that they can still not get past, that they still have privilege for being a male period . . . When can we actually have these conversations?

Nilta also felt pressure to allow the cycle of patriarchy that she was experiencing to continue due to cultural standards in the Black community. Though she wanted to discuss the way Black men were participating in oppression, it felt challenging for her to do anything about it. She expressed feelings that were specific to navigating relationships that proved difficult and sometimes overwhelming.

> If I could call it an emotion, it's an emotion that I feel like my Black men, when I speak out that I feel like I'm betraying them in some way . . . When can we actually have a raw conversation that [Black men] have privilege? It's not a bad thing, cause [Black men] can use that privilege to help uplift us, but we are not there yet, well some folks are not there yet.

Nilta believed the psychological effects of racism clouded Black men from seeing the intersections of identity that is present for Black women. In some spaces, Black men wanted Black women to support them in their fight against racism; if they did not, this would mean they were against them. However, fighting for racism in some cases may have required Black women to forego fighting against their gender oppression. Further complicating relationship dynamics was the idea that Black women are expected to support Black men in seeking racial equality, but Black men do not seem to have the same sense of responsibility toward Black women in their fight for gender equality. Interestingly, Nilta had experiences in her activism where some organizations were intentional in centering the voices of Black women through leadership tactics and group policy. Still, this was not a perfect place.

> Even within that [organization] though we still had issues of what it is to be a Black man [and] how you could still be using

> patriarchy and not understand that. There were definitely those times, but I feel like those are constant conversations that are always going to be had. But it also tells me that if this Brotha is sitting next to me . . . we still have that one goal or that common goal . . . is still there. If you are sitting next to me that means you are still willing to learn. If two people [have a] common goal and . . . are working hard, there can be change.

Though Nilta felt that understanding patriarchy was challenging for Black men, she was hopeful that there could be growth and change. Still, she wrestled with what the intersections of being Black and a woman looked like in everyday life. Racism and sexism have a unique impact on Black women, and Nilta thought that understanding this complexity was important.

> I think . . . Black folks don't understand that, that's where the mishaps of misunderstanding is . . . We get it; all [our] genders are Black . . . but what separates [Black women] from all the other genders is . . . this outstanding fear that we have had created for us . . . we stay [in] fear of walking, daylight, nighttime, it doesn't matter, because [in] daylight, we could just look suspicious and [like] we just robbed a bank . . . [In the] nighttime . . . you can turn into a sex object.

Nilta's explanation of the complexity of the multiple identities of being a Black woman showcased how the interplay of racism and sexism is significant. She also believed that in activist spaces little discussion is had about this dynamic, and when she attempted to bring it up, it was often brushed off and the conversation shifted back to Black men.

> When can we actually have these conversations? Why is it that I have to sit here and be uncomfortable in this room and vocalize that I am, and I only get ten seconds and then we go right back [to the original conversation]? [The] ten seconds of being talked about I think [is] one of the things that frustrates me. Because it's like can we have those conversations? Most of the time [it's] no . . . [it's] the same situation [in] talking I fear turns . . . loud becomes defensive, aggressive . . . [and] whether or not men are taught how to express their emotions that way . . . that's exactly what happens . . . I think that's one of the things I'm trying to balance. How can I break that [cycle] of not wanting to talk about those moments? We cannot just talk about women for ten seconds; give her, her little shout out . . . that's the problem. That's

been the problem . . . and it's not like we want the attention, it's the fact that this is a real matter; we are dying at the same exact rate. We are getting locked up at the same exact rate. We are not getting paid . . . the list goes on but all we see is the men taking on that role.

Nilta details her feelings of sometimes being worried and somewhat in fear of Black men when trying to raise issues that specifically affect Black women. If the examples of racism and sexism that impact Black women—incarceration, low pay, and death—are brought up, she is concerned that emotions would heighten to possible uncontrollable levels. This fear itself that her body as a Black woman would be at risk may result in her silence instead of engagement in discussion.

Ultimately, Nilta's experience with activism coupled with her intersecting identities is one that is tangled, involved, and complicated. However, her experience does begin to showcase why identity is not monolithic and how oppression impacts identity.

## Recommendations

Understanding how interlocking systems of oppression impact Black women provides an overarching view of how persons with multiple identities experience oppression differently (Bell, 2016; Crenshaw, 1991). Thus, social justice educators should engage with these concepts to support Black women participating in activist work. Considering the following recommendations can push us to center our commitment to activism while also teaching our values (Morrison & Denard, 2008).

*Social justice educators should begin to include ways of supporting those with multiple identities in navigating single-issue activist spaces to advocate for issues that impact them on numerous levels.* Black women often have to siphon out pieces of their identity when engaging in activist work. Empowering Black women to situate issues that impact their multiple identities in single-issues spaces acknowledges their lived experiences while encouraging disruption of traditional ideas of race-only activism.

*Facilitate conversations on sexism that center Black women's stories and emphasize the complexity of how racism and sexism are linked.* There is often an unspoken expectation to prioritize race over other identities. This may encourage Black women to shelve experiences with sexism for the sake of seeking racial justice. Providing spaces that allow Black women to process their own identities and accompanying oppression will allow them to find ways to incorporate gender issues into their activist work.

*Create intentional dialogue and curriculum that teaches activism.* Though social justice educators encourage and support activist work, we may rely on "on-the-job-training" to teach the inner-workings of activism. However, creating intentional spaces to dialogue about techniques, provide processing time, and develop action plans could empower more women to be engaged in the process. Creating these spaces allows different ideas of activism to naturally materialize instead of defaulting to an adoption of a cookie-cutter approach.

Focusing on these three ideas will begin to nourish and develop Black women wishing to connect their intersecting identities with justice-seeking. Further, embracing these ideas provides space for collective community thinking and consciousness-raising that aligns with the heart of social justice education (Adams, 2016).

## References

Adams, M. (2016). The theoretical and activist foundations that inform SJE pedagogy. In M. Adams & L. Bell (Eds.), *Teaching for diversity and social justice* (pp. 30–37). New York: Routledge.

Alston, J. A., & McClellan, P. A. (2011). *Herstories: Leading with the lessons of the lives of Black women activists.* New York: Peter Lang.

Barnett, B. M. (1993). Invisible Southern Black Women leaders in the Civil Rights Movement: The triple constraints of gender, race, and class. *Gender and Society, 7*(2), 162–182.

Bell, L. (2016). Theoretical foundations for social justice education. In M. Adams & L. Bell (Eds.), *Teaching for diversity and social justice* (pp. 3–26). New York: Routledge.

Carbado, D. W., Crenshaw, K. W., Mays, V. M., & Tomlinson, B. (2013). Intersectionality: Mapping the movements of a theory. *Du Bois Review: Social science research on race, 10*(2), 303–312. doi: 10.1017/S1742058X13000349

Crenshaw, K. W. (1991). Mapping the margins: Intersectionality, identity politics and violence against women of color. *Stanford Law Review, 43*(6), 1224–1299.

Crenshaw, K., Ritchie, A. J., Anspach, R., Gilmer, R., & Harris, L. (2015). *Say her name: Resisting police brutality against Black women.*

Edwards, A. E. (2000). Community mothering: The relationship between mothering and the community work of Black Women. *Journal of the Motherhood Initiative for Research and Community Involvement, 2*(2), 87–100.

Evans, S. M. (2015). Women's liberation: Seeing the revolution clearly. *Feminist Studies, 41*(1), 138–149.

Garza, A. (2016). A herstory of the #BlackLivesMatter movement. In J. Hobson (Ed.), *Are all the women still white?* (pp. 23–28). New York: State University of New York Press.

Harvell, V. G. (2010). Afrocentric humanism and African American women's humanizing activism. *Journal of Black Studies, 40*(6), 1052–1074.

hooks, b. (2000). *Feminist theory: From margin to center*. London: Pluto Press.
Horsford, S. D. (2012). This bridge called my leadership: An essay on Black Women as bridge leaders in education. *International Journal of Qualitative Studies in Education, 25*(1), 11–22.
Jones, S. R., Torres, V., & Arminio, J. L. (2014). *Negotiating the complexities of qualitative research in higher education: Fundamental elements and issues* (2nd Ed.). New York: Routledge.
Jordan-Zachery, J. (2007). Am I a Black woman or a woman who is Black? A few thoughts on the meaning of intersectionality. *Politics & Gender, 3*(2), 254–263.
King, D. K. (1988). Multiple jeopardy, multiple consciousness: The context of a Black feminist ideology. *Signs, 14*(1), 42–72. doi: 10.1086/494491
Linder, C., & Rodriguez, K. L. (2012). Learning from the experiences of self-identified women of color activists. *Journal of College Student Development, 53*(3), 383–398.
Lindsey, T. B. (2015). Post-Ferguson: A "herstorical" approach to Black violability. *Feminist Studies, 41*(1), 232–237.
Millner, S. Y. (1996). Recasting civil rights leadership: Gloria Richardson and the Cambridge Movement. *Journal of Black Studies, 26*(6), 668–687.
Morrison, T., & Denard, C. C. (2008). *What moves at the margin: Selected nonfiction*. Jackson: University Press of Mississippi.
Rainey, S. A., & Johnson, G. S. (2009). Grassroots activism: An exploration of women of color's role in the environmental justice movement. *Race, Gender & Class, 16*(3–4), 144–173.
Rickford, R. (2016). Black Lives Matter: Toward a modern practice of mass struggle. *New Labor Forum, 25*(1), 34–42.
Robnett, B. (1996). African-American women in the Civil Rights Movement, 1954–1965: Gender, leadership, and micromobilization. *American Journal of Sociology, 101*(6), 1661–1693. doi: 10.1086/230870
Purdie-Vaughns, V., & Eibach, R. P. (2008). Intersectional invisibility: The distinctive advantages and disadvantages of multiple subordinate-group identities. *Sex Roles, 59*(5–6), 377–391.
Robnett, B. (1997). *How long? How long?: African-American women in the struggle for civil rights*. New York: Oxford University Press.
Schug, J., Alt, N. P., & Klauer, K. C. (2015). Gendered race prototypes: Evidence for the non-prototypicality of Asian men and Black women. *Journal of Experimental Social Psychology, 56*, 121–125.
Sesko, A. K., & Biernat, M. (2010). Prototypes of race and gender: The invisibility of Black Women. *Journal of Experimental Social Psychology, 46*(2), 356–360.
Simien, E. M. (2003). Black leadership and civil rights: Transforming the curriculum, inspiring student activism. *Political Science and Politics, 36*(4), 747–750.
Taylor, K. Y. (2016). *From #BlackLivesMatter to Black liberation*. Chicago, IL: Haymarket Books.
Thomas, E. L., Dovidio, J. F., & West, T. V. (2014). Lost in the categorical shuffle: Evidence for the social non-prototypicality of Black women. *Cultural Diversity & Ethnic Minority Psychology, 20*(3), 370–376.

Chapter 17

# Storytelling

*Advising Black Women Student Leaders in White Spaces*

Lydia Washington

The purpose of using storytelling as an advisor model is to empower, motivate, and make an impact. This chapter traces my personal experiences as a Student Affairs professional and connects experience to theory to center storytelling in the role of advising. I was once at a Black History Month dinner, and a Black woman student leader made a statement that stuck with me for a very long time, "*When it comes to leadership for me, one day I lack the motivation, but have the empowerment to press through. Then the next day, it switches where I have the empowerment but not the motivation to carry on leading as a Black woman student leader in this lily-white space.*" I believe it is our job as advisors to listen, have empathy for, and be vulnerable with our Black women student leaders because it has a major impact when it comes to making sure they lead with both empowerment and motivation (Collins, 2000).

My graduate assistant, who identifies as Black Cape Verdean, appreciates the way that I conduct our one-on-one meetings. For example, I share my insight and use the method of storytelling when I know she is having a bad day because of her experiences of being silenced in her graduate program. At times, I have supported her by telling her to time off so she can focus on working through tough moments, often brought about by feeling invalidated in the classroom or on campus. For my undergraduate Black women student leaders, I set times once a week on my calendar to just have lunch with them and do a "temperature check" by using storytelling. This creates supportive space for them to demonstrate vulnerability when they talk about their leadership challenges. When I have created these spaces during advising time, Black women student leaders found strength in storytelling just like I did when I was in my undergraduate experience with my professor.

We cannot let students lead in fear or suffer in silence in these white spaces. Black women advisors need to be supportive of each other and hold each other accountable when we notice our students are suffering in silence in their involvement experiences. As advisors, we should remember that we are part of the magical journey of these student's identity development and experiences. Our students are our next generation of artists, teachers, doctors, mothers, engineers, partners, and more. Although disproportionate service responsibilities are a reality for Black women advisors, we must not take for granted the opportunity to teach and demonstrate how to listen, to have empathy and show vulnerability when it comes to telling our stories to our students. If we are going to do the work as social justice educators for our students, we can create space through storytelling in advising as an important example of true engagement. You never know, years later those moments might be pivotal in a person's first steps toward healing.

Recently, one of my former students tagged me in a Facebook post that demonstrated the potential impact one can have. She expressed gratitude for how I supported her during a pivotal moment in her life as student leader in the Student Government Association. As I read her message, I was going through a period of doubt, disconnection, and loss of self in my own professionally journey as an advisor. This message was sent after 8 years of being Facebook friends with her. At that time, I had been advising student leaders at my institution for about 10 years and had hit a professional brick wall. Once I decided to enter in the field of Student Affairs, one of my main goals was to always support and uplift Black women student leaders at predominantly white institutions (PWIs). My experience at a PWI changed my life forever, and I wanted to make sure I was present and available for Black women student leaders through my field of Student Affairs. My professional wall started to build brick by brick, year after year, day after day; the wall was built from the many adversities I faced in the field. Like most Black Women do when this wall starts to build up, I started to question my self-worth and skill sets. I began searching for ways to reconnect. It was not until I received this special tag of gratitude that I was reminded that my story will always have value and serve as an important resource in my work with students. The message that my former Student Government Association (SGA) president sent re-centered me and strengthened my resolve to continue,

> ... words cannot express the gratitude I have. People may not realize but that was probably the hardest time in my life and you were there for me like a rock. When neutrality was an important

role for administration to play you never forgot that I was a young, Black woman who too needed to feel like I could cry . . . get angry and react. You gave me a book of daily readings which I still have till this day. The small acts of kindness in you sharing with me your book meant and still means the world because for a long time that book gave me courage and settled by mind.

This message reached so many levels of emotions for me. After many years of not talking to this student, this message was a reminder that sharing my story with her had a major impact on her resistance to oppressive environments and persistence as a Black woman student leader. Sharing my story with her was important because, as a past leader in SGA, hers was not an easy journey to travel. I too took a governance role, and it almost cost me my life. I was blessed to have Black women mentors at my undergraduate institution to tell me their stories, and that helped me push through to survive toward graduation. I just never thought I would be in a role where I directly advised a student in this capacity to share my own story as student leader. I used the art of storytelling as my method to create supportive spaces for Black women student leaders in predominantly white collegiate environments.

In my everyday practice as a social justice educator, I have found it important to hone the art of storytelling, especially in the capacity of advising student leaders. Storytelling is a universal human practice; we learn, maintain culture and community, and bridge collective realities with individual experiences (Bell, 2010). Using storytelling as an advising model for Black student women leaders is important; as many of us come from marginalized populations as well, they need to see and hear from us. Haddix (2013) writes, *"I will believe it when I see it . . ."* which is often the attitude held by Black women students who feel they are not represented in their curriculum, classroom, or on campus. I resonate with this statement as an adviser because leadership requires listening, patience, and love when we are sharing stories. We must affirm, acknowledge, validate, and legitimate student existence as leaders (Haddix, 2013). The art of storytelling has several vital elements, including listening, having empathy, and embracing vulnerability. Black women advisors can authentically learn from each other's differences and foster inclusive learning environments by engaging these three elements, particularly when advising Black women student leaders. The purpose of this chapter is to provide a social justice model of storytelling by using my experiences as a case study to support future practice. This chapter is also written for Black women advisors who struggle to find ways to connect with efforts to advise, empower, and mentor.

## Storytelling: Words and Power

"Aggressive," "harsh," "direct," "attitude," "petty Betty," and "insensitive" are all words that have come across my desk from others when advising or working with Black women students in my 10-plus years of advising within higher education. I have heard these words used to describe Black women when in conflict with others. As an advisor, these same words have been used against me by staff members when I am advising students who hold different identities than me in my office. I never had an opportunity nor cared to challenge those individuals in my work space regarding why they felt this way toward Black women. In retrospect, there are some questions I would ask to create a more fruitful dialogue. The first question that came to mind was, "How have I impacted your work in this space? Define, within your life experiences, what aggressive, direct, harsh, insensitive etc. mean to you?" Creating clarity and having dialogue about why such words are so often attributed to Black women are imperative to help people understand why this is unacceptable and to be an agent of social change.

Early in my career, I did not recognize why stereotypes would be happening to Black student women leaders and me because I never took the time to process and give myself space in my day-to-day work life to figure this out. The moments where students complained about how Black women were combative. These moments triggered me emotionally because most of these women in leadership roles shared similar experiences that I personally experienced in respect to my leadership experiences. As I have taken the time to process why this occurs, I decided to refocus my energy in a positive manner. For the past 2 years, I have sought ways to support Black women student leaders and advisors by employing storytelling.

In my experience, storytelling has been one of the best ways to help people understand each other's differences with compassion. The first time I taught a class on racism, for example, my co-facilitator and I based our course design on creating opportunities for our students to share their experiences of racism. Students were brave to share with us that storytelling within the class helped create stronger spaces and helped them feel comfortable sharing with one another. In *Understanding Education for Social Justice*, Hytten and Bettez (2011) lament that, despite the great efforts in social justice education work, genuine dialogue is a missing aspect of our practice. I believe genuine dialogue is established through storytelling. Hytten and Bettez (2011) identify seven skills, practices, and dispositions of activists in social justice education. Of these seven skills, three skills can be demonstrated through storytelling: engaging in explicit discussions of power, privilege, and oppression; conducting artful facilitation that promotes critical thinking; and building critical communities. These skills, in my opinion, can only happen if you know how to listen, have empathy, and experience and demonstrate vulnerability.

One also may ask, "How can listening and voicing contribute to personal and collective transformation when it comes to advising?" Black female student leaders need storytelling in white spaces because it can strengthen leadership development and prepare them for their career postgraduation. Storytelling is transformative because each narrative provides examples of hope and resiliency. It can also play a role in intervention for our Black women student leaders when they are facing crisis or conflict. Transformative experiences are helpful for Black women student leaders and can allow them to lead fearlessly in white spaces, even when facing intimidation. These students need to know it is ok to vent, to feel, to cry, to be angry, and to process what they might be going through in their leadership experiences.

## Three Elements of Storytelling in Advising

When advising student leaders, I engage three principles: listening, empathy, and vulnerability. The first major element in learning the art of storytelling is having effective dialogue when listening. In *Dialogue Groups: A Practical Guide to Facilitate Diversity Conversation*, Huang-Nissen (1999) explains that you are to listen by using your ears, mind, eyes, and heart. When advisors are using storytelling with their students, these four listening tools are essential to ensuring a transformative experience when creating spaces of effective dialogue through storytelling for Black women student leaders. When Black women student leaders go through conflict with other student leaders, it's important as advisors to adapt Huang-Nissen's (1999) notion of being fully engaged in listening in order to understand why conflict happens. Information in this chapter highlights the need for an engaged advisor because of the many micro-aggressions and the oppression experienced by marginalized populations of student leaders.

Fleming (1984) offers research about how PWIs are not always accepting institutions for Black students. The most important aspect of this author's research is that all departments need to be aware of the "inadequate support" for Black students at PWIs. Fleming stated that because of "inadequate support," Black students develop identity problems that sap their intellectual energies (xiii). Black female student leaders who have internalized their negative experiences and have not received counseling can damage their college experience by not having a strong academic and psychological well-being (Allen, 1999). Faculty and staff have the biggest influence on students' self-worth (Rodolfa, 1987). Knowing the major impact and influences that advisors have, storytelling can be an empowering method toward creating the positive environments in these white spaces for Black student leaders.

Showing resonance when listening is a clear sign of *empathy*, which is the second major element in storytelling when advising. McCormick (1999) defined empathy as the ability to experience the same feeling as someone else. This author also stated how people confuse empathy with sympathy when trying to listen to others telling their story. I do agree with this author that better listening requires empathy and perspective, but I would have to disagree that understanding is required to have empathy during storytelling. My interpretation of what it means to have empathy is that understanding someone's story has its limitations based on the different identities we all hold. It is imperative to show empathy during advising Black women student leaders. My experience has shown me that many have not been socialized to show empathy toward others, and this shows up in their student involvement.

As a Black woman advisor, I have connected with many Black women student leaders who lead with urgency and effectiveness. When in conflict, some write off Black women leadership as bossy, dictatorial, and ineffective. It is important to show empathy and to acknowledge their emotions and the impact of their feelings so that it creates a space of vulnerability to talk about it with their advisor. The Facebook post from my former student body president highlighted the need for a space to feel, react, and be angry. I offered that space for her in our advising appointments.

The last element in storytelling would be vulnerability. Vulnerability is only successful in storytelling when there are spaces that people feel they can open up in. Witherell (2010) stated that good dialogue is a ". . . commitment of energy, space, anticipation, intense listening, attentive response, and a belief that we can learn profoundly from others." The author also compared good dialogue to making a musical composition. I love this example as a visual learner; in my own thoughts, I can *see* some that have special meaning to me. These songs have the perfect voice, great harmony, and words that touch my soul. Leaders join student organizations that relate to their sense of identity during their college experiences. I firmly believe Black female student leaders join organizations as an act of survival against the multidimensional aspects of trauma they experience before and during college. Social isolation for Black women student leaders is important to recognize because it can cause mental stress and depression (Kitzrow, 2003). By using storytelling, we create spaces for the student and advisor to listen to each other, have empathy, and show vulnerability to see past some of the ugliness that we encounter when engaging in student leadership in white spaces.

## Reflections of Developing Leadership

Black female student leaders are able to create a sense of belonging on college campuses by joining in formal or informal peer groups (Chickering & Reisser, 1993). When these students decide to join these white spaces, as advisors, we have to think about the intersectionalities that display for Black women student leaders would immediately be engaging in when trying to create comfort in white spaces. Chickering and Reisser (1993) stated that joining student organizations creates the most impact for students during their undergraduate experiences. Knowing this, it is important to have a very impactful advising model, which includes storytelling, when Black women student leaders are joining student organizations. As Black women advisors, it is our responsibility to use storytelling as a guide for advising and creating a space using the elements of listening, empathy, and vulnerability. We should also be sharing to our students *the good, the bad, and the ugly* when strengthening their engagement in white spaces. When Black women advisors help their student leaders to create a supportive space to develop their self-identity, many factors come to light of how fearlessly they experience shifts positively in their involvement.

As social justice educators, this should be our goal in creating supportive spaces for Black women student leaders' to be vulnerable. This actually is the hardest to show and receive in settings of storytelling as Black women advisors. As little Black girls, most of us are taught to protect ourselves and not to display any aspects of vulnerability during our development as youth. Vulnerability is a major element for having storytelling take place when it comes to advising Black female student leaders. Not having space to exhibit vulnerability could be a missed opportunity to experience what a supportive space feels like. I remember, from my own experience of being vulnerable, sharing my undergraduate story with one of my students who was going through depression. I saw signs that she started isolating herself from all group members, the lack of sleep and showing up at group meetings ready to fight against every issue in the group. I took her to lunch one day just to check in with her. This lunch was not easy because the whole time she was guarded and kept telling me she was OK and that I did not have anything to worry about. I looked her in her eyes and just listened to her and showed compassion. Slowly, some of the things she mentioned I knew were items that she felt should be very small but were very big to her and contributing to her unhappiness at the institution. I resonated with her statements about pushing through because she did not have a choice but to graduate from college for her family. I then opened up and told her my story of suffering in silence with depression during my undergraduate involvement in student government. I began to let her know the feelings and emotions and how suffering in silence is not the best way to deal or survive.

When I made the choice to share my story with her, it was *deja vu* all over again. I started to think about when my college professor and mentor in my studies shared her personal stories with me of perseverance and resistance through her experience with depression. I remember being in her office thinking . . . *not* my professor, she is the Beyoncé of professors; she holds us down on campus, her groundbreaking research book about the ivory tower is changing my life about higher education, and her leadership shows us how to protest in solidary as student leaders to pressure our school newspaper that allowed a derogatory term to be printed.

That experience when my professor shared her story never left my mind; I remember listening to her and thinking, this is very brave of her to disclose this to me. I resonated with a lot of her story of resiliency while being a professor on tenure track, and it gave me hope and the understanding that there was more to life than just existing outside of the trials I was experiencing in my student involvement. This experience with my professor shaped me to always be my authentic self when mentoring and advising Black women student leaders. It is exhausting at times, but the reward is greater when you see these leaders push through their adversity after sharing your moment of vulnerability. As Black women advisors in white spaces, we have to lead by example to teach our Black women leaders how to be vulnerable. We are not invisible, and it is not mentally healthy to create a false perception of invulnerability in higher education or in the world.

## Conclusion: Reflective Practice

In closing, the major elements in storytelling are to listen, have empathy, and demonstrate vulnerability. I have found these practices to be very successful in creating meaningful and lasting experience within the work of advising Black women student leaders. For many, speaking of our different backgrounds, life-changing experiences, and our trials and tribulations creates conflict and perpetuates signs of weakness. On today's college campuses, Black women students are experiencing major psychological issues and are in need of more support in addition to on-campus counseling centers. I share these reflections with all advisors, but especially for the benefit of Black women advisors; our main goal should be to create a positive and supportive space in predominantly white higher educational settings to help Black female students to think critically (Gellin, 2003). Black women student leaders face unique challenges in achieving academically and integrating socially at PWIs because their values might differ from those of the majority of the student body (Tinto, 1998). We can empower Black women student leaders to use their differences and values as an asset to the student body. Cultural biases and low socioeconomic status are often the biggest impediments Black women face when it comes to their student involvement. In white spaces we, as advisors, can use storytelling to ease these impediments. When marginalized students face oppressive forces, we should not be afraid to tell our story to help find them find ways to survive.

By listening, having empathy, and embracing vulnerability, I am positive we can authentically learn from each other's differences I have had some hard conversation about work/life balance, burnout, imposter syndrome, love and relationships, depression, anxiety, and perfection. Storytelling has helped me become a powerful and engaging advisor because showing empathy while I am being vulnerable and listening shows students that I am human.

In this chapter, I have presented examples of the ways in which storytelling can be a strong form of authentic dialogue. It is important to create spaces with other advisors to hold each other accountable for self-love and work/life balance. Storytelling is not a model for solving issues Black women advisors and advisees face day to day. The goal of centering storytelling as an advising model is to have dialogue about challenges and experiences and, by doing so, create more opportunities for transformative leadership.

## References

Bell, L. A. (2010). *Storytelling for social justice: Connecting narrative and the arts in antiracist teaching.* New York: Routledge.

Chickering, A. W., & Reisser, L. (1993). *Education and identity* (2nd ed.) San Francisco: Jossey-Bass.

Collins, P. H. (2000). *Black feminist thought: Knowledge, consciousness, and the politics of empowerment* (2nd ed.). New York: Routledge.

Fleming, J. (1984). *Blacks in college.* San Francisco: Jossey-Bass.

Gellin, A. (2003, Nov./Dec.). Effects of undergraduate student involvement on critical thinking: A meta-analysis of the literature, 1991–2000. *Journal of College Student Development, 44*(6), 746–762.

Haddix, M. (2013). Visionary response: Listening "face-to-face" and "eye-to-eye": Seeing and believing black girls and women in educational practice and research. *Counterpoints, 454,* 191–199.

Huang-Nissen, S. (1999). *Dialogue groups: A practical guide to facilitate diversity conversation.* Blue Hill, ME: Medicine Bear Publishing.

Hytten, K., & Bettez, S. C. (2011). Understanding education for social justice. *Journal of Educational Foundations, 25*(1/2), 7.

Kitzrow, M. A. (2003). The mental health needs of today's college students: Challenges and recommendations. *NASPA Journal, 41*(1), 167–181.

McCormick, D. W. (1999). Listening with empathy: Taking the other person's perspective. In A. L. Cooke, M. Brazzel, A. S. Craig, B. Greig (Eds.), *Reading book for human relations training* (8th ed.). Arlington, VA: NTL Institute.

Rodolfa, E. R. (1987). Training university faculty to assist emotionally troubled students. *Journal of College Student Personnel, 28,* 183–184.

Tinto, V. (1998). Colleges as communities: Taking research on student persistence seriously. *The Review of Higher Education, 21*(2), 167–177.

Witherell, C. S. (2010). Composing narratives and opening spaces-exploring intercultural and gender themes through dialogue. *New Directions for Adult and Continuing Education* (126), 63–75.

Chapter 18

# Reflections on Moving Theory to Praxis

*Dialectical Engagements of Black Women Faculty in an Urban High School Space*

CHRYSTAL A. GEORGE MWANGI AND KEISHA L. GREEN

This chapter provides reflections on our experiences as two Black women faculty members developing a youth participatory action research (YPAR) project at Hillside Tech High School (pseudonym). Specifically, we consider the ways in which our positionalities, worldviews, and approaches to social justice education framed our preparation and expectations of the project as well as impacted our experience and engagement with it. Our chapter emphasizes the integration of theory and praxis, a primary goal of social justice education work (Adams, 2016; Freire, 1970). We share the lessons we learned in order to demonstrate moving educational theory to praxis as well as the joys, challenges, and complexities inherent in engaging YPAR work within schools that can be dehumanizing spaces for youth of color (Irizarry & Brown, 2014). To provide greater context, we begin the chapter with a description of Hillside Tech and the data we collected. Next, we present our conceptual framework, which incorporates endarkened feminist epistemology (Dillard, 2006) and double-dutch methodology (Green, 2014). In alignment with this framework, we describe our positionalities as Black women faculty that inform our reflections and lessons learned in engaging theory and praxis in the development of social justice education work.

## Hillside Tech

We engaged in this project at Hillside Tech (pseudonym), a predominantly Puerto Rican career and technical (CTE) high school in New England. Eighty-five percent of students in this district come from low-income backgrounds, 80% identify as Hispanic/Latinx, and 48% report that English is not their first language. This project was embedded in an 11th-grade English language arts course called "Our Literate Lives Matter: Education Narratives of 'Hillside' Youth," facilitated by a research team led by two Black women education scholars. The course, comprised of 15 students, centered on improving academic readiness and literacy through (1) using culturally sustaining pedagogies and curriculum that centers the multiple identities, cultural backgrounds, histories, experiences, and language practices of students to promote academic achievement (Ladson-Billings, 2014; Paris, 2012; Paris & Alim, 2017); (2) development of critical consciousness and a social justices lens related to the educational system, pathways, and options after high school; and (3) development of research skills using youth participatory action research.

We used a critical ethnographic approach to collect and analyze data from and with students in the course taught every other day for 90 minutes over one academic year. Critical ethnography centered our inquiry on how the educational environment was constructed, shared, and navigated by the students and school staff, as well as by us as instructors. This approach aligned with our emphasis on youth engagement for social change and justice (Carspecken, 1996; Madison, 2005). Data were drawn from individual interviews, focus groups, participant observation, students' photographs and written narratives, and our instructor reflections captured through memos.

## Conceptual Framework

This chapter is informed by two concepts: endarkened feminist epistemology and double-dutch methodology. Both of these approaches are culturally sustaining, meaning they provide space for plurality of identity, language, and culture to exist and thrive. As Black women educators, our framework rejects assimilation or confirmation of dominant, hegemonic practices and outcomes and instead centers on an intersectional and reflexive process for engagement in educational research and practice.

We use endarkened feminist epistemology (EFE) as a framework for centering our positionalities as Black women scholars. Dillard defines this concept as

> [h]ow reality is known when based in the historical roots of Black feminist thought, embodying a distinguishable difference in cultural standpoint, located in the intersection/overlap of the culturally constructed socializations of race, gender, and other identities,

and the historical and contemporary contexts of oppressions and resistance for African American women. (2006, 3)

The term "endarkened" shifts away from majoritarian white feminist or "enlightened" thought and instead centers on the multiple and overlapping identities of Black women, including race, gender, nationality, class, and sexuality (Dillard, 2000, 2003). Informed by the work of Hill Collins (1990), hooks (1989), and other Black women scholars, EFE intersects Black feminist theory with education research and practice. The characteristics of EFE align with our desire to merge education theory and praxis as well as to acknowledge the dynamic nature of social justice education. EFE extends Black feminist thought by situating it within a diasporic context (Okpalaoka & Dillard, 2012). As Black women, this diasporic worldview guides our positionality as one of solidarity, but also of tension with the predominantly Puerto Rican students and predominantly white staff that we engaged with through our project.

Endarkened feminist epistemology acknowledges and elevates the unique lived experiences of Black women and the expertise built through those experiences. Yet, Dillard (2000) also expresses that individual experiences must be part of building and elevating community. Thus, the focus is not solely on the individual, but on the interplay between people, shared experiences, and sustained relationships developed through social engagement and the responsibility that communities of color have to one another. In short, "research as responsibility, answerable and obligated to the very persons and communities being engaged in the inquiry" (Dillard, 2006, 5). In describing our experiences, we draw from three assumptions of EFE: (1) how you define yourself shapes your participation and responsibility to the community in which you conduct research; (2) research is not ahistorical—it reaches backward into the past and is also outward facing into the future; and (3) power relations structure identity relations within research (Dillard, 2000). These assumptions inform how we see ourselves in our work and the ways in which we engaged in our work at Hillside Tech.

Whereas an EFE captures our perspective about research, a double-dutch methodology offers an approach to engaging in research that considers how, where, and when to enter research contexts (as outsider/insiders or researchers/teachers/scholars/mentors). Drawing from a reference to the inner-city game of double-dutch, Robin D. G. Kelley (1998) describes the kind of richness and nuance in skill and technique necessary when jumping the two ropes, much like navigating qualitative educational research involving urban youth from historically marginalized communities. Though seemingly unrelated, the qualitative research method of participant observation is like playing double-dutch. It is inherently complicated and dynamic as the participant observer seeks to at once participate as a "member" of a group and critically observe the ways in which the participants perceive, make meaning of, and reproduce the interactions that define the group over time. The good jumpers (read "researchers") will be skillful and agile enough to improvise and acquire an awareness of rhythm, knowing when and how to enter (Green, 2011; Kelley, 1997; Winn, 2011).

Double-dutch methodology (DDM) provides an alternative way of thinking about qualitative research inclusive of particular strategies. The first part of DDM involves "learning the ropes" (Gaunt, 2006, 37), or critically exploring researcher positionality. For example, what are the intersecting identities that researchers bring to the research context? And, what are the multiple roles and shifting orientation that a researcher may experience during the research process? The second component of DDM includes "plant[ing] both feet" (Gaunt, 2006, 174), or considering the main theoretical standpoints on which DDM or a humanizing qualitative research approach is based. Specifically, what theoretical lens(es), conceptual framework(s), or set of principles informs DDM as a new way of thinking about and doing research. Finally, the third component of DDM entails "keeping time and rhythm," or engaging in participant observation that is complicated, contextually stylized, and improvisational. In particular, during fieldwork, how and when do qualitative researchers, utilizing the method of participant observation, engage as "a participant observer at times, an observer at other times, and a participant at still other times" (Paris, 2011, 8)? Moreover, DDM is concerned with privileging the everyday interactions, voices, and experiences of the participants. This approach to research invites reflexivity, relevance, and reciprocity, which is transferable to researchers in other disciplines, particularly scholars of color who are struggling with the notion of needing to be "distant" and "neutral" observers in spaces or research contexts that include participants from oppressed or marginalized communities. This set of strategies informed our research design, data collection, and analysis of the Hillside Tech project.

## Our Positionalities

We are two Black woman tenure-track assistant professors at a public land grant state university. I (Keisha Green) came to the project with a background in educational studies, specializing in literacy, language, and culture. Previous work in and with communities of color, particularly youth of color, influenced my desire to continue engaging in schools serving marginalized students. I (Chrystal George Mwangi) came into the project with a background in higher education, specializing in college access and post–high school planning for marginalized communities. Although I had worked with youth of color through college outreach programs, I was interested in working with students in their high school to more fully understand and support their educational experiences. Both of us share a belief in the importance of youth of color developing a critical consciousness, and we both use critical and culturally sustaining frameworks to inform our research and community engagement.

We were two assistant professors coming to teach one high school class at Hillside Tech for an academic year. Our approach to curriculum and instruction was not bound or linked to district- or school-level constraints or policies. Thus we exercised and enjoyed a certain degree of autonomy in lesson planning, grading, and classroom management. Both of us were nonfluent Spanish speakers working with students who were predominantly bilingual. Neither of us was from the local area and had lived in the state for only 1 or 2 years at the beginning of the project. Given our positionalities relative to the context of Hillside, we believed that who we were, how we identified, and how we were perceived could provide both benefits and challenges in working with the students, teachers, and administrators.

## Reflections on Moving Theory to Praxis

Our reflections are organized around two important aspects of our learning and engagement at Hillside Tech, the first being our expectations of the project and how we entered it (theory-informed) and the second being what we actually experienced and enacted (praxis). While educators hope for congruency between the two, educational spaces and social justice work are not static, sterile contexts. Thus, we share our experiences to demonstrate how we as social justice educators used our expertise, frameworks, and positionalities to prepare for the project as well as how these factors influenced how we navigated the realities of the work. Our reflections emphasize how we developed the project, specifically (1) meeting and working with Hillside Tech teachers and administrators and (2) developing and enacting the curriculum that guided the "Our Literate Lives Matter" course.

### Meeting and Working with Teachers and Administrators

***How we entered.*** For both of us, engaging in community-based research often comes as a result of established relationships and trust built over time. Yet, this project was different in that a colleague approached us to work with the high school as part of a larger partnership in the school district to incorporate culturally sustaining pedagogies. Although we were excited at the opportunity and wanted to be a part of our colleague's efforts in the district, there were also challenges to beginning a project in this way. For example, we were not involved in initial conversations about how the program would be structured or what the expectations from the district would be. Both of us believe strongly in spending time in a community space prior to formally engaging in a partnership or project, but neither of us had ever visited the high school. Given these factors, we spent a large part of our summer in conversation about whether this project aligned with our worldviews and if it was even feasible. Ultimately, we trusted our colleague and believed that in working together the project could be successful. However, given our stance on the importance of social engagement and community building through research (Dillard, 2006) and the need to logistically plan the project, we knew it was important that we build a relationship with the teachers and staff at the high school as soon as possible.

Our first meeting with the school administration left us feeling very positive in their support for our work, but also apprehensive about their expectations. On one hand, they had the tangible resources we would need. For example, the school offered more than we expected regarding technology resources and were willing to give us autonomy in how we taught the class. Therefore, "on paper" we felt set up for success. On the other hand, given our understanding of the complex and political nature of school environments (Freire, 1985; Irizarry & Brown, 2014), we knew it was important to consider what was beneath the surface as well. In doing so, we learned that the administrators had hand-picked the students for our course, calling them the "best of the best" and "quality students." Scholarship tells us that these terms are often codes reflecting a deficit-based discourse and dominant cultural beliefs about who is a "good student" and who is a "bad student" (Ladson-Billings, 2007; Lei, 2003). We did not want our work to reify any stratification that might have already been present at the school or create an exclusive environment. And yet, given the climate of the school district we were aware that the school leadership likely had their own agenda that we were unaware of as newcomers. Green (2014) illustrates our position through DDM in explaining, "the work is located in a context, therefore my feet land within a 'game' already in motion" (156). Although we were grounded in our own frameworks as scholars and educators, we recognized that enacting these frames within a new space would be complex and require both learning and negotiation.

To foster our knowledge of the school environment and to continue building relationships with community members, we attended the school's first professional development program of the year for new and returning teachers. When the principal introduced us, he explained to everyone that the teachers and students would be subjects in our research project. This immediately made us cringe given that our goal was to work with teachers and staff, not conduct research on them from a distance (Dillard, 2000). This early incident made us reflect on how we perceived ourselves and our role in the school alongside the perceptions of the school community and how they were positioning us. While the principal situated us within a position of power as researchers, we were also keenly aware of being two of very few Black people, and even fewer Black women in the space. Most of the teachers in attendance were white. This observation became more pronounced during a fishbowl activity during which the principal selected seven teachers to come to a table and discuss the school's goals and vision. All of the teachers except one was male, and all appeared to be white. The rest of the teachers were supposed to listen to the discussion and take notes on what was said. The principal later acknowledged how homogenous his selection was, but the incident provided a clear illustration of how easily exclusion happens and the relationship between identities and power (Dillard, 2000). It also made us think, "If there are voices being silenced in gendered and racialized ways among school staff, how is similar exclusion also showing up with students?"

One Latina administrator expressed to us that at their convocation ceremony, many of the teachers who stood up to say that they had been teaching for 10 years or 20 years in the district where white as well. This administrator explained that many of these teachers had not changed their teaching practices even as the school district's student demographics had shifted over the years from majority white students to majority Puerto Rican students. She used an example, saying she felt that the habitat (school's student population) had changed, but the teachers felt that they, themselves, did not have to change. Instead, their philosophy was that the students should assimilate. Yet, she countered that, in fact, when your habitat changes, you do have to change in order to survive and thrive, and thus the teachers should evolve as well. Her frustrations reinforced our desire to engage in culturally sustaining pedagogies through our class, but also made us consider how our approaches might be perceived/supported (or not) by the rest of the school. Her insights and these early interactions with school administrators and teachers gave us much to think about as we continued to plan for the approaching academic year.

*How we engaged.* Although we spent the majority of our time engaging with the students in our class, it was always our intent to work with the administrators and teachers as well. Yet, we quickly realized it would be challenging to foster those relationships. Like many schools short on resources and staff, the administration simply did not have time to fully engage with us, given other priorities. For example, we had hoped to meet a few times a year with the school leadership to discuss the class and to eventually present our work to teachers at the end of the year. We were not able to achieve these goals, because of scheduling challenges, and instead predominantly communicated with school leadership through email or in passing at the high school As a result, much of our communication was through requests to administration rather than working directly with them. Thus, the relationship felt more transactional than collaborative, which runs counter to how we envisioned our presence in the space. In reflection, we also realize that this limited our ability to advocate for students and reinforced our outsider status.

We felt this limitation most when one of our students got into an altercation at the high school and was facing out-of-school suspension. After learning of the altercation, we wrote an email to the principal advocating that the student not be suspended:

> We see in him an immense capacity that can continue to grow with continued support, encouragement, and opportunities to stimulate his intellect and creativity. As educators, we believe the school environment is one of the primary contexts in which this can happen and thus we ask that he not be removed from this environment. Research confirms that suspension may carry a greater risk . . . we are willing to work with school administrators, guidance counselors, and teachers to consider an alternative conflict resolution, as well as a plan for completing the school year successfully.

The principal responded via email thanking us for the letter and reiterating the strong possibility that the student would still be suspended (and indeed he was suspended). We understand that the principal's decision was based on many factors, some of which we were likely not privy to, and do not suggest that his decision was wrong. However, this and other incidents made us question our role at the high school. Were we simply there to work with the students in our classroom space? Were we student advocates? Should we predominantly be observers when it came to the school environment outside of the classroom space? Similar to DDM (Green, 2014), we struggled with when and how we could "jump in" to the game and when we should wait to catch our rhythm. Overall, we were able to develop community inside our classroom and connected with some teachers and administrators, but primarily we maintained an outsider identity as we walked the halls of the high school.

Yet, the challenges that we experienced in building relationships with teachers and administrators were not one sided. Given our positionality as pre-tenure faculty members at a Research I institution, we also had a number of limitations in how we could focus our time. We did not have a grant or teaching release time from our university to work at the high school. While we received informal praise from many of our colleagues in pursuing our project, we were also told that it was not going to be formally rewarded in our tenure process unless we developed associated publications or grants. This issue aligns with the concept of cultural taxation (Padilla, 1994), or the notion that faculty of color are often expected by their institutions to show commitment to minoritized populations through research and service, but during the tenure process that work is often marginalized. For many faculty of color, including ourselves, the additional "tax" comes in having to identify other areas or ways in which to demonstrate our scholarship, which increases our workload (Padilla, 1994). Therefore, we struggled in our ability to commit our time to the needs of teachers and administrators at the high school even when they did approach us wanting to collaborate, given the demands of the project itself and expectations from our university. For example, when a teacher asked if we could help him plan a cultural event for the high school, although we provided him with resources and contacts, we declined being involved in the actual planning because we knew that we would not have the time or capacity to help coordinate the event. This was a missed opportunity to engage the school community beyond our classroom space, and at the same time was necessary in terms of what we could feasibly commit to doing while managing our own research, teaching, and service commitments. Through EFE, Dillard (2000) suggests that how you define yourself shapes your participation and responsibility to the community you are in, and we found that this was impacted not only by our social identities as Black women but also in our professional identities as pre-tenure faculty.

## Developing and Enacting the Curriculum

***How we entered.*** We approached developing and enacting the curriculum through our complementary disciplinary lenses, both rooted in equity and social justice. I (Keisha) am interested in critical English education and youth literacy practices in and out of school. And I (Chrystal) am concerned with the educational experiences of students of color and structures of opportunity and educational attainment for underrepresented populations. Together, our research agendas document and emphasize the needs of students of color from preschool through college, career, or post–high school. In particular, we know from our research that Black and Brown students benefit from having access to curricular content, teachers, and support systems—in and out of schools—that are culturally responsive. Therefore, knowing our students would be predominantly Puerto Rican, and mainly Spanish speakers, we prioritized designing a curriculum that foregrounded Puerto Rican literature, history, identity, and culture. Like most public schools in the nation, the standardized English language arts curriculum at the high school was not particularly reflective of the Puerto Rican student body or local Puerto Rican community. Instead, according to the high school website, the 11th-grade standards and reading lists featured a list of classically canonical British and American literature texts, certainly inclusive of Shakespeare's plays, as well as novels by the usual dead white men: Hawthorne, Hemingway, Twain, and so on. Beyond *The Color Purple* and *Native Son*, there were scarce texts representative of a diverse student body, and definitely no texts listed that would indicate a nearly exclusive Puerto Rican student population. And after touring the school, including our classroom for the year, we glimpsed the familiar thick literature anthologies for high schoolers stacked in a corner of the room. Notably there were no sets of novels or decorative displays of multicultural texts, young adult literature, or Puerto Rican (or Latinx) authored poems, essays, or biographies.

These observations influenced our decisions to consider engaging literature on the diversity of the Latinx experience, specifically that of the Puerto Rican, Afro Latinx diaspora. We selected poems and essays related to Puerto Rican "hybrid" identities and experiences (Puerto Rican in the context of "urban" United States). And we endeavored to create opportunities to think critically about whether these "hybrid" identities and experiences were/are valued, salient, or central to the culture of current school contexts, curriculum, and instruction, as well as the imagined or real higher education context. Through this curriculum we wanted students to engage in "story-ing" their lives or co-writing narratives of their educational experiences and college or career aspirations (Kinloch & San Pedro, 2014). Among the Latinx writers we proposed for the curriculum were poets Martin Espada, Willie Perdomo, and Mayda del Valle—each having pieces about identity, culture, and language.

To contextualize Puerto Rican poets and poetry in the United States, we considered including the text *Aloud: Voices of the Nuyorican Poets Cafe,* a history of the legendary Nuyorican (New York Puerto Rican) poets cafe and its poets. Importantly, we considered young adult texts and memoirs by Judith Ortiz Cofer (*An Island Like You: Stories of the Barrio)*, Piri Thomas (*Down These Mean Streets*), Julia Alvarez (*How the Garcia Girls Lost Their Accents*), and Esmeralda Santiago (*When I Was Puerto Rican: A Memoir*). Readings such as *Who Is Black?* by Puerto Rican public intellectual Rosa Clemente and *Ballin' and Becoming Boricua: From Roxbury to Rio Piedras and Back Again* by Shabazz Napier (Puerto Rican basketball player for the Portland Trailblazers, formerly a college player for the University of Connecticut) with Jason

Irizarry, were included in the lesson plans as a way to explore Puerto Rican diasporic identity and grapple with terms such as "Boricua" and "Afro Latinx."

Essentially, each of our curricular decisions, particularly our text selections, were rooted in culturally sustaining pedagogies (Paris & Alim, 2017). In other words, the curricular module and lesson plans were divided into three parts: cultivating a classroom community; exploring personal narratives and understanding systems of inequality and inequity at a microlevel; and eventually examining systems of oppression at a macrolevel, centering their school context and their own particular surrounding community. This curriculum was designed "to perpetuate and foster—to sustain—linguistic, literate, and *cultural* pluralism as part of the democratic project of schooling" (Paris, 2012, 93). Of course, we were ambitious about the scope and depth of the year-long curriculum. And we could not start without getting to know the students. Building on critical English language arts teacher and teacher educator Linda Christensen's (2000) notion of cultivating community from chaos, we decided to prioritize building community before "teaching" any particular curricular content.

Additionally, because we were aiming to design a course that would reflect the sociocultural realities of the students, we also created opportunities for critical reflection and consciousness raising, adopting a critical pedagogy and engaging students in critical literacy during which students would be encouraged to question their school policies and position themselves as experts in their own lived experiences. For example, we drafted lesson plans that included activities to help students examine notions of race, power, and oppression. One activity, the oppression tree, was included to assist students in understanding the complex and cyclical nature of oppression and systemic inequity. The tree roots are a metaphor for the systems of oppression (e.g., racism, sexism, homophobia), the trunk represents the culture, practices, and beliefs that are a conduit for systemic oppression, and the branches or leaves represent the visible outcomes such as underemployment, housing discrimination, or underresourced schools.

To reinforce class content, we planned for guest speakers—many of whom were local artists, activists, and critical education scholars—to facilitate class sessions on the class themes. In particular, we scheduled guest speakers, including a Latina guest speaker who was a representative of the local #BlackLivesMatter chapter, to facilitate a workshop on colonization, race, and identity. We also made efforts to meet our goal of assisting students with exploring college and career pathways. For example, we planned for a course session on the implications of "whitening" a resume using study results related to how employers perceive applicant names.

The final element of the curriculum, and perhaps the goal of the project, was youth participatory action research (YPAR), a methodology for engaging youth that encourages them to question and critique the social norms and dominant narratives that contribute to injustice and oppression. In his writing about the Latinization of U.S. public schools, Irizarry (2011) observes that "conditions under which students are educated are rarely addressed as part of the curriculum" and warns that "continuing to construct educational experiences that fail to address the sociocultural and sociopolitical realities of youth and their communities is a futile endeavor . . ." (22). With that in mind, we planned to use the YPAR components of the curriculum to provide opportunities for students to investigate issues relevant to their school context. In sum, we considered the context in which the high school was situated, and accounted for the historical, political, social, and cultural context of the city, all of which influenced our development of a social justice curriculum for high school students.

*How we engaged.* Although we were committed to enacting a culturally sustaining pedagogy, and strove to develop a curriculum that would be responsive to and reflective of the student demographics, histories, and subjectivities, we soon realized that crucial information was missing during our planning process–namely, an understanding of individual student learning preferences, students' previous academic achievement and interests, and the feasibility of our plan within the parameters of a 90-minute class block. Having developed the curriculum for the school year over the previous summer, we were prepared to engage students with a critical Puerto Rican literature course punctuated with participatory action research. As we commenced to implement the lesson plans, it was not long before we were confronted with two assumptions. The first assumption was our belief that our decision to center Puerto Rican history, culture, and language would be embraced and celebrated by Puerto Rican students, whom we soon discovered did not necessarily have much prior knowledge of or feel strong connections to Puerto Rican diasporic history, literature, or political contexts. This kind of heritage knowledge was not inherently viewed as an asset to their current circumstances. Our second assumption was that students would know how to think, write, and speak critically. For example, students were often asking for more direction or authoritative stances from us and were reluctant to share their own opinions. Some of students' inexperience with thinking critically could be attributed to the current "skill and drill" nature of the test-driven schoolwide curriculum. At other times, silence from students during small-group or whole-class discussions was linked to interesting gender dynamics. Over time we noticed boys classically "taking up space" in the classroom with their bodies and voices, while the girls in the classroom tended to be more vocal in smaller group dynamics or in their writing assignments. As a research team, we decided to experiment with meeting with the students in affinity groups, so class time was occasionally spent in self-identified single-gender groupings for activities and discussions.

Also, our initial thought was to include texts, novels, essays, and short stories because we were teaching what would have been an 11th-grade pre-AP Literature course. After the first couple of weeks, though, we discovered that in-class reading of short pieces, rather than longer novels or dense scholarly articles, would work best. Ultimately, we found ourselves having to be reflexive and flexible about our lesson plans. Once we met students and engaged the class, we regularly debriefed class sessions and responded accordingly to adjust class plans week to week, and sometimes day to day. We also amended our weekly class plans to include interactive ways to engage current events, including the presidential campaign, after discovering students had a desire to discuss police brutality, the bigotry of the Trump campaign, and other events possibly impacting their lives.

As we engaged the curricular material, students seemed to appreciate reading pieces written by relatively local Puerto Rican youth. In particular, after reading "Ballin'" by Shabazz Napier, students grappled with racial identity. One student mentioned that he didn't want to just say he is Black and Puerto Rican because there was more to it, but he was struggling to explain. This same student shared that he doesn't speak Spanish and has never been to Puerto Rico. Shabazz's story connected with him because he has also been looked down on. The readings on identity raised important questions about how the students perceive themselves, but also prompted reflection about our subjectivities and identity as non–Spanish speaking Black women scholars from African and Caribbean descent teaching students about Puerto Rican history/colonialism. For example, we found ourselves navigating the "n" word during the school year because so many of the male students, in particular, were using the term to refer to one another. Unfamiliar with the wide spread use of the "n" word among Puerto Rican students, we attempted to engage in dialogue about the historical and contemporary perspectives of whether the word should be a part of everyday lexicon considering its roots in institutional racism and the U.S. enslavement of Black people. Admittedly, we felt vulnerable sharing our discomfort with and reluctance to allow the use of the word, particularly since most of the students had not engaged in an exploration of their Boricua or African descendant identities prior to our class (and therefore many viewed themselves as "white" Puerto Ricans).

Students, however, expressed appreciation for having access to this type of social justice curriculum and discussed how they didn't talk about such issues otherwise. For example, one of our male students explained that his sister was not teaching his niece Spanish because she wanted her daughter to "grow up white." Pushing back, we asked him where he thought his sister's decision came from. At first the student quipped, "because she's stupid." Digging deeper, we prompted the student to consider where the source of an idea not to teach someone her own language might stem. Another student joined in the conversation, replying, "the government." We acknowledged that this response was indeed plausible, as historically schools have endorsed English-only policies and admonished bilingual parents for speaking to their children in any language other than English. These Puerto Rican students were able to think critically about the affordances of white privilege, such as speaking English, particularly as they were attending the underperforming and underenrolled CTE high school with few white students compared to the higher performing high school in their district with more white students and fewer Puerto Rican students.

Regarding the scheduled guest speakers, we invited people of color throughout the semester to visit the class. Looking back, we think this diverse group worked to illustrate how people of color are collectively impacted by systemic oppression and may work in solidarity to resist. For example, we invited a Filipino critical education scholar from the University of San Francisco who happened to be speaking at a nearby university to emphasize the consequences of colonialism and the proliferation of the prison system. Sharing his own experience with both colonialism and imprisonment as a person of Asian descent helped students understand how institutional racism impacts all people of color, including Asians, Latinx, and Blacks. Another highlight of the school year was a field trip to Harvard University. We registered the students to participate in a one-day conference on the school-to-prison pipeline. Additionally, we connected with the Nasir Jones Hiphop Fellowship scholar for a tour of the Harvard University Hip Hop Archives. During the tour of the archives, we learned that many of the students listened to hip hop and rap music, as well as wrote lyrics and rap. Thinking back to our class conversations on race, identity, and diaspora, we wondered if students viewed hip hop as a part of their own Puerto Rican youth culture *and* heritage, considering its roots in the South Bronx of New York, where the founders of hip hop were African American, Afro Latinx, and Afro Caribbean youth. This complicated our perceptions of how our students identified or felt connected with Black youth culture, histories, and experiences.

Finally, the last module of the course focused on defining and enacting youth participatory action research (YPAR). As a class, we began by answering the question: What is YPAR? Once we had a collective understanding of YPAR as an emancipatory research method and pedagogical approach, we started to consider concrete problems in the school, asking students to consider how to investigate (tools to answer questions) and how to create change or engage in action, which meant building research skills and learning how to conduct research, collect data, analyze data, and write about their findings. Part of this process included talking about inequities in their college preparation and attendance postgraduation, as well as about employment rates based on level of education and incarceration rates among students of Color, specifically Latinx students—all of which were connected to overarching racial issues covered in the class. This curricular plan took place in the context of a CTE high school, one of two high schools in a school district declared "chronically underperforming" by the state's commissioner of education. The poor attitudes and beliefs about the school trickled down to the students, who often articulated a negative opinion about the school climate and culture. Most students described themselves as passing through to graduation with little school pride.

Ultimately, we found that one of the more critical outcomes of the class was the opportunity for students to experience how classroom spaces could be democratic and participatory. One student, Dan (pseudonym), shared during an interview that he thought "this class [was] more . . . like a really interactive class. When I look at this class I don't really think of it as English class, I think of it as how to better your life." Dan elaborated why the class was different from his other classes. According to him, in

> most of [his] classes, teachers will just slap assignments on our desk and be like, "Go talk about it for 5 minutes." Write some notes on the board and then it's done. Here, we go on field trips. Here, we have little interventions where we talk to each other and all that. In our other classes it's not really anything like that.

Similarly, Laura (pseudonym), another student in the class, shared that she wanted to know about everything that's happening in the world. "That's exactly what we're doing. We're learning about everything interesting in the world, in our environment, where we're at, our society, everything. It's more interesting for me to know what's going on in this school, in this world, and how others are thinking about it."

Her sentiments were at the heart and soul of what our social justice curriculum was meant to accomplish. Despite the many adjustments to lesson plans, all of us—students and teachers—were changed by the space we co-constructed, and not because we met every curricular goal or won the affections of each student, but rather because we demonstrated that another way is possible. We can develop and enact a critical education that is student centered and liberatory, and where students ultimately gain the skills and acquire the dispositions needed to succeed beyond the classroom.

## When Theory Meets Praxis: Lessons Learned

The experiences we describe in this chapter demonstrate the synergies and tensions we felt in working with Hillside Tech teachers and administrators as well as in developing and enacting the curriculum that guided the *Our Literate Lives Matter* course. These synergies and tensions are directly connected to the relationship between how we entered the school space (theory informed) and what we actually experienced and enacted (praxis). As educators and scholars, we engage in social justice work as a means of moving theory into praxis (Adams, 2016; Freire, 1970). Therefore, our reflections in this chapter are meant not only to share our lived experiences, but also to provide concrete examples of our progress and struggles that others might consider as they engage in social justice education work. As we reflect on how EFE and DDM informed our project at Hillside Tech, we have three major lessons to share.

The first lesson is that while theory informed our practice at Hillside Tech, it also complicated our practice. EFE and DDM demonstrate the promise, possibility, and potential of social justice education at Hillside Tech, but they also illuminate the pitfalls. We constantly felt the tensions between being guided by these theories and the limitations that we faced within an educational space that had its own mission, vision, and guiding principles that were at times in conflict with these theories or did not acknowledge their value. In our praxis, theory made us feel what we call "scholar's guilt" when we did not achieve all of the goals we set out to accomplish. Although in the long run we experienced a number of successes with the Hillside Tech project, it was not without making some compromises that seemed in the short term to run counter to our theoretical ideals. At the same time, EFE and DDM gave us what we call "theoretical accountability" in that they were always present in guiding our worldviews and gave us a foundation with which to ground ourselves as educators. Throughout our time at Hillside Tech, we consistently returned to the texts and words of critical scholars in making decisions about how to work with students and teachers or in how to build the course curriculum. Thus, using theory to guide our work was not merely an intellectual exercise. Instead, we recognize that it was an inherent part of our pedagogical and reflexive praxis as Black women social justice educators.

The second major lesson to share is that social justice education is not, and should not, be viewed as static. It should be responsive, multifaceted, and flexible to meet the needs of the educational context and community. For example, as Black women working with predominantly Puerto Rican youth, we became learners of Puerto Rican culture, history, and diaspora in order to develop a curriculum that was culturally sustaining for our students. This required us to step outside of the comfort zone of our own racial-ethnic identities as well as find ways to connect ourselves with the curriculum. Yet, equally important, we sought to be responsive by understanding how our students perceived Puerto Rican culture, history, and diaspora as well as where they positioned themselves within these contexts. We had to move beyond our assumptions about what they might know and value in order to engage authentically and support a participatory and evolving classroom climate. This did not go without challenges from the students and high school staff, who were accustomed to a more predetermined curriculum. However, the use of a youth participatory action research framework provided us with the scaffolding to prioritize a social justice and humanizing orientation in our work (Irizarry & Brown, 2014).

The third lesson gained from our experience was remembering to embrace our identities and positionality throughout the process. Being Black women, nonfluent Spanish-speaking scholars complicated our working with primarily Puerto Rican, mostly bi- or multilingual youth at Hillside Tech. Having made some key decisions on how we would approach working with our students, we entered the context assuming students would embrace a sense of Black and Brown solidarity and/or understanding of our commonality in being members of oppressed communities. However, unique to our students was their situatedness in a predominantly Puerto Rican enclave where many might have felt some quasi-form of "protection" from feeling "othered" in their school, community, and/or society writ large. Conversely, our own personal educational experiences include narratives of being one of few students of color in predominantly white institutions where we were (and continue to be) acutely aware of our "otherness." We used this point of departure as a teachable moment finding ways to interact authentically and enact a culturally sustaining pedagogy for our Latinx students. As our reflections demonstrate, this caused us to consistently reflect on how our positionalities impacted how we entered into the project and how we engaged within the Hillside Tech community as educators. While theory could help to guide our work, in order to practice responsive praxis, we had to also depend on our instincts, lessons learned from previous experiences, and our growing knowledge of the Hillside Tech educational space. Thus, this experience not only helped us to better understand the connection between theory and praxis as a form of social justice education, but also the critical interplay of identity and positionality (ours, students, high school staff) within this process.

## References

Adams, M. (2016). Pedagogical foundations for social justice education. In M. Adams & L. Bell (Eds.), *Teaching for diversity and social justice* (3rd ed.) (pp. 27–54). New York: Routledge.

Carspecken, P. (1996). *Critical ethnography in educational research: A theoretical and practical guide.* New York: Routledge.

Christensen, L. (2000). *Reading, writing, and rising up: Teaching about social justice and the power of the written word.* Milwaukee, WI: Rethinking Schools.

Dillard, C. B. (2000). The substance of things hoped for, the evidence of things not seen: Examining an endarkened feminist epistemology in educational research and leadership. *The International Journal of Qualitative Studies in Education, 13,* 661–681.

Dillard, C. B. (2003). Cut to heal, not to bleed: A response to Handel Wright's "an endarkened feminist epistemology"? Identity, difference and the politics of representation in educational research. *Qualitative Studies in Education, 16*(2), 227–232.

Dillard, C. B. (2006). *On spiritual strivings: Transforming an African-American woman's academic life.* Albany: State University of New York Press.

Freire, P. (1970). *Pedagogy of the oppressed.* New York: Continuum.

Freire, P. (1985). *The politics of education: Culture, power, and liberation.* South Hadley, MA: Bergin.

Gaunt, K. (2006). *The games Black girls play: Learning the ropes, from double-dutch to hip hop.* Albany: State University of New York Press.

Green, K. L. (2014). Toward a double dutch methodology: Playing with the practice of participant observer. In D. Paris & M. T. Winn (Eds.) *Humanizing research: Decolonizing qualitative inquiry with youth and their communities.* California: Sage.

Hill Collins, P. (1990). *Black feminist thought.* London: Harper Collins.

hooks, b. (1989). *Talking back: Thinking feminist, thinking Black.* Boston: South End Press.

Irizarry, J. G. (2011). *Latinization of U.S. schools: Teaching and learning in shifting cultural contexts.* Boulder, CO: Paradigm.

Irizarry, J. G., & Brown, T. M. (2014). Humanizing research in dehumanizing spaces: The challenges and opportunities of conducting participatory action research with youth in schools (pp. 63–80). In D. Paris & M. T. Winn (Eds.) *Humanizing research: Decolonizing qualitative inquiry with youth and communities.* Thousand Oaks, CA: Sage.

Kelley, R. D. G. (1997). *Yo' mama's disfunktional! Fighting the culture wars in urban America.* Boston: Beacon Press.

Kinloch, V., & San Pedro, T. (2014). The space between listening and story-ing: Foundations for projects in humanization (PiH). In D. Paris & M. T. Winn (Eds.), *Humanizing research: Decolonizing qualitative inquiry with youth and communities.* Thousand Oaks, CA: Sage.

Ladson-Billings, G. (2007). Pushing past the achievement gap: An essay on the language of deficit. *The Journal of Negro Education, 76*(3), 316–323.

Ladson-Billings, G. (2014). Culturally relevant pedagogy 2.0. *Harvard Educational Review, 84*(1), 74–84.

Lei, J. L. (2003). (Un)necessary toughness?: Those "loud Black girls" and those "quiet Asian boys." *Anthropology and Education Quarterly, 34*(2), 158–181.

Madison, D. S. (2005). *Critical ethnography: Methods, ethics, and performance.* Thousand Oaks, CA: Sage Publications.

Okpalaoka, C. L., & Dillard, C. B. (2012). (Im)migrations, relations, and identities of African peoples: Toward an endarkened transnational feminist praxis in education. *Educational Foundations, 26*(1–2), 121–142.

Padilla, A. M. (1994). Ethnic minority scholars, research, and mentoring: Current and future issues. *Educational Researcher, 23*(4), 24–27.

Paris, D. (2012). Culturally sustaining pedagogy: A needed change in stance, terminology, and practice. *Educational Researcher, 41*(3), 93–97.

Paris, D., & Alim, S. (2017). *Culturally sustaining pedagogies: Teaching and learning for justice in a changing world.* New York: Teachers College Press.

Winn, M. (2011). *Girl time: Literacy, justice, and the school-to-prison pipeline.* New York: Teachers College Press.

Chapter 19

# Scholarly Personal Narrative of an Inaugural Chief Diversity Officer

*A Primer for Municipality Leaders*

Malika Carter

Part I

*Introduction and Statement of Problem*

The purpose of this scholarly personal narrative (SPN) was to assess how a singular professional has experienced the inaugural role of municipal-based Chief Diversity Officer (CDO) for the City of Worcester, Massachusetts, the impact of that individual's social identities on the municipal-based CDO experience, and to examine how the role maneuvers while integrating diversity functions cross-agency, as related to the mastery and leadership skills critical for a CDO to perform effectively.

As CEO of Passion4Pivot, a social justice consulting firm and the first-ever Chief Diversity Officer for the City of Worcester, Massachusetts, I seek, and have always sought, "greater self- and/or professional understanding" (Nash & Bradley, 2011, 7). SPN was an attractive methodology because it helped me to "connect the personal and professional, the analytical and the emotional, and most important, to show the relevance of these connections to other selves" (57). From SPN, as explained by Nash and Bradley (2011), "we know that every life is a story, and every story has the potential to teach" (55). SPN "puts the self of the scholar front and center" (Nash, 2004, 18) and is always profoundly personal and unique to some degree, never replicated in exactly the same forms by anyone else" (55). Heidelberger and Uecker (2009) explain Nash's (2004) 10 guidelines for a successful SPN:

> (1) Establish clear constructs, hooks, or questions; (2) Move from the particular, to the general, and back again . . . often; (3) Try to draw larger implications from your personal stories; (4) Draw from your vast store of formal background knowledge; (5)Always try to tell a good story; (6) Show some passion; (7) Tell your story in an open-ended way; (8) Remember that writing is both a craft and an art; (9) Use citations whenever appropriate; (10) Love and respect eloquent (i.e., clear) language. (2)

I employ the methodology of SPN to construct meaning from narrative and personal story. SPN permits the writer to occupy both researcher and subject. Robert Nash (2004) wrote: "SPN is about giving yourself permission to express your own voice in your own language; your own take on your own story in your own inimitable manner" (24).

Due to federal acts that operationalize mandates, institutions that two generations ago were insular and explicitly protective of sociopolitical affiliation and dominant identities now employ equity workers to outfit industries, government agencies, and institutions with equitable policies and access procedures under threat of federal monetary penalties. Although bound by federal-level mandates, few municipalities have established executive roles tasked solely with institutional-level diversity and inclusion.

More than any other time in history, people with perceived and actual underrepresented identities (i.e., low socioeconomic status, gender and racial minorities) are recognized as contenders holding generational education, wealth, and intimate access to the same institutions that have denied and mistreated them. Historically, and in contemporary viewpoints, despite institutional champions, underrepresented groups such as those groomed from low social and economic environs, women, people of color, and other underrepresented groups have continually faced various boundaries that impede unbiased access into arenas such as government, business, health care, and education.

Although many U.S. cities house rich diversity largely acknowledged as a staple in conducting business, and despite the increased emphasis placed on workforce diversity, in my experience, the philosophy of diversity and its alignment with agency leadership responsible for arranging that philosophy throughout municipal departments is not steadfastly integrated into practice. In addition, empirical literature addressing municipal-based authority on issues of diversity is limited. In an era of municipal-based racial tensions and civil servant scrutiny (including police), alignment between philosophy of diversity in civic life and commitment to professionalizing the work of diversity agency-wide is paramount. A step in making such alignments includes determining the influence and functions of municipal-based diversity administrators.

*Problem of Practice*

Nixon (2013) in her dissertation entitled *Women of Color Chief Diversity Officers: Their Positionality and Agency in Higher Education Institutions* posits: "As yet unexamined in CDO literature are questions regarding how CDOs experience their roles, the impact of social identities on their experiences, and how they exercise agency in their work to integrate diversity functions cross-institutionally" (7). While Nixon (2013) centers these aspects for CDOs who labor in postsecondary education, the problem of practice addressed by this SPN was the lack of alignment between experiences, agency, and the understudied role of the municipal CDO. As a partner to every city department in advancing the municipalities' mission, the CDO is responsible for agency-wide diversity and inclusion. "Where others work on issues of diversity as a matter of second or third priority, chief diversity officers engage matters of diversity as a matter of first priority" (Williams & Wade-Golden, 2006, 1).

*Problem of Research*

The problem of research addressed herein was the lack of empirical literature addressing the experience and influence of municipal-based CDOs. Literature on the impact of CDOs on practice is limited (Nixon, 2013; Williams & Wade-Golden, 2006). As of this writing, no study has addressed the experience or influence of municipal-based CDOs. In addition, the body of knowledge addressing CDOs is primarily composed of the literature of postsecondary education or based exclusively on anecdotal evidence. No studies tangentially legitimize first-hand accounts or address factors that influence the municipal-based CDO experience or the impact of these professionals.

*Project Goals and Guiding Questions*

To investigate how I experience my roles, the impact of my social identities on my experiences, and how I exercise agency as a municipal-based CDO, this SPN seeks to cull from a framework posited by scholars Williams and Wade-Golden (2006) that characterizes the work of CDOs. Using relatable characteristics posited by these researchers to broadly define the CDO role, I have worked to fill a literature gap while simultaneously situating my understudied experience as an inaugural municipal-based CDO. Deriving from research questions that Nixon (2013) posed in dissertation work examining women of color CDOs, my guiding questions were these:

1. How do I as a woman of color CDO experience my identities as a woman and as a person of color? How do these experiences influence my work as a diversity and inclusion thought leader?

2. How am I positioned as a CDO? As a woman of color, how do I navigate a complex municipal context to create diversity and inclusion change? How do I shift my institutional position to maximize my influence?

This SPN applies three key subquestions across the main research questions and my lived experience: (1) How do I know what I know? (2) Where and/or who did it come from? (3) Who does it serve? (M. Mikulack, personal communication, February 2014). University of North Dakota anthropologist Dr. Marcia Mikulack asked these questions of me during a conversation on balancing professional and personal integrity.

*Importance of the Study*

In light of the dearth of empirical research on the institutional role of municipal-based CDOs or their institutional impact, this SPN provides information about an inaugural municipal-based CDO experience from a personal account. Informing the professional development of those who aspire to serve as senior-level diversity administrators for a city, this study provides authentic perspective about the training and development needed for municipal-based CDOs. Municipalities can use this SPN to inform how a CDO position will be crafted. The analysis of my SPN will result in a synthesis of practices common to the role of municipal CDO, as well as cautions, to be shared with institutional planners and other individuals interested in a professional depiction for municipalities to consider in developing or modifying administrative roles that care take diversity.

*Definition of Terms*

The following terms were defined operationally for the purposes of this study:

*Chief Diversity Officer:* Institutional thought leader related to matters of
 diversity, inclusion, equity, and equality.

*Effectiveness:* "The extent to which institutions meet their stated mission, goals, and objectives" (Dugan & Hernon, 2002, 376)

*Stakeholder:* "Any person, group, or organization that can place a claim on an organization's attention, resources, or output, or is affected by that output" (Herman & Associates, 2005, 176).

*Strategic Planning:* "A disciplined effort to produce fundamental decisions and actions that shape and guide what an organization is, what it does, and why it does it" (Bryson, 1995, 4–5)

## Part II

The question "Is it fair?" pervades my intellectual thought, research agendas, and my lived experience. My professional passion for justice within institutions became pronounced as I earned a Higher Education and Student Affairs Administration master's degree and secured a postsecondary education position in multicultural student services. It was then that I began to see that I had always taken opportunity to become instrumental in institutional fairness and accountability as complemented by my personal and professional roles.

With professional and scholarly trajectories across four academic degrees, and many professions—from working with people with disabilities; witnessing increasing numbers unjustly incarcerated as a stenographer in the legal field; experiencing personal, professional, residential and environmental discrimination as a middle school teacher in K–12; dabbling in real estate; working in higher education; owning a business; and working as a municipal public servant, I have witnessed bias throughout my institutional affiliations. Consequently, the definition of integrity as provided by the author Stephen Carter (1996) is one that I have adopted as my definition of leadership. In his book *Integrity*, Carter uncovered steps to define the concept. He articulates that integrity "demands a difficult process of discerning one's deepest understanding of right and wrong, and then further requires action consistent with what one has learned" (Carter, 1996, 10), as well as "saying publicly that we are doing what we think is right, even when others disagree" (11). To me, this is largely the work of a CDO.

Leveraging the knowledge that Williams and Wade-Golden (2006) garnered during a national study of CDO positions, the following sections apply what they identified as the "main characteristics, and the key knowledge, skills, and abilities that institutions should seek when searching for a new [CDO] officer" (Williams & Wade-Golden, 2006, 1). After a brief description of the setting, the sections with accompanying vignettes and relationship to research questions were organized into a few (not all) of the sections highlighted by Williams and Wade-Golden: (a) a functional approach; (b) collaboration & political savvy; (c) leading through status and influence; and (d) understanding of the culture.

*Description of Setting*

The inaugural role of CDO for the City of Worcester, Massachusetts, began in February 2016. The primary goal of the role is to diversify the city workforce and enhance the employee experience in matters of diversity and inclusion. The CDO role, as situated within Worcester city government, is located in the department of Human Resources with no staffing or budget, reporting to the Assistant Director of the department. In turn, the Assistant Director reports to the Director (housed in the City Manager's office), and the Director to the City Manager, who is the administrative lead of the city accountable to the city council. Human Resources, staffed by a management team of seven full-time professionals (diversity, training, employment law, worker's compensation, benefits, employment, and assistant director) has an array of front-line customer service, interns, and other process-based professionals.

*Approaching Professional Function with Layered Consciousness*

Layered consciousness for an inaugural municipal CDO is like juggling—including fitting one's own position into a rigid preexisting structure, undertaking one's professional charge amid change resistance, and balancing that with the demand for outcomes within a sociopolitical reality that counters the role's existence and subsequent work.

CDOs have responsibility for guiding efforts to conceptualize, define, assess, nurture, and cultivate diversity as an institutional and educational resource. Although duties may include affirmative action/equal employment opportunity, or the constituent needs of minorities, women, and other bounded social identity groups, CDOs define their mission as providing point and coordinating leadership for diversity issues institution-wide. (Williams & Wade-Golden, 2006, 13)

**Vignette 1.** 6:45 a.m. of the first day of work, I enter a coffee shop across the street from city hall (where Human Resources is housed) and longingly view the building. Excited for a start time of 8 a.m., I enter at 7:45 a.m. to a dim municipal building hallway with no activity. "Is it a holiday?" I muse. "Have I arrived on the wrong day?" Full of first-day anxiety heightened by the darkened empty hallway, I stand under the Human Resources moniker and notice a job board that occupies an opposing wall. As I approach and examine the board, I notice that each of the jobs posted have different statements related to equal opportunity and/or affirmative action, ranging from "The City of Worcester is an AA/EEO employer," ". . . Equal Opportunity Employer," "The City of Worcester is an Affirmative Action/Equal Employment Opportunity" employer, and other configurations.

*How do I know what I know?* Initial first-day impressions were that (1) no one had taken the opportunity to tell me the workday began at 8:30 a.m., and (2) there exists public disjointed language to describe affirmative action and equal opportunity—functions central to my role as CDO. Federal guidelines exist that have established equal opportunity and affirmative action language for public use.

*Where and/or whom did it come from?* Throughout history, laws, policies, and practices have been created and perpetrated by and within institutions to impede successful entry by and matriculation of various marginalized groups. Consequently, historical benefits thereof are bestowed to those who interpret, navigate, and endure processes relegated by those institutions. Government, like original guilds, by design regulates industry-specific knowledge and preserves systems of domination and subordination through bureaucracy, creating oppressed and oppressor. This history is inextricably related to the functions of Western government and other institutions that control wealth and access to information, goods, and services. By federal mandate, modern government strives to safeguard prospective and current employees from employment-based discrimination, but many narratives, procedures, and policies within government continue to reify the "meta" imagination of who should be included, protected, and celebrated.

*Whom does it serve?* This initial experience furnished by my employer framed much of the work I would do in the coming months to streamline clear expectations and information to prospective job applicants, employees, city staff, and administrators in addition to creating outward-facing uniformity of official narrative, policies, and practices.

*Collaboration and Political Savvy*

Devoid of a budget or staff, I have needed to collaborate, praise publicly, and humbly criticize privately while holding minoritized identities of race and gender. These identities alone challenge the convention of the environment, rendering my behaviors (decision making) and language hypervisible across the agency, be it in print via an agency-wide memo or in person.

Like comparable roles in other administrative areas, such as the "chief financial officer" or "chief technology officer," the work of the chief diversity officer does not fit into a traditional administrative box . . . the role of chief diversity officer spans the boundaries of the institution as officers and their units collaborate . . . to enhance diversity up, down, and across the institution. (Williams & Wade-Golden, 2006, 3)

*Vignette 2.* As an African American woman who has worked mainly inside predominantly white/male environs, I realize that the complexity of my experience can rarely be voiced and named without social and professional consequence. This is a position that can be difficult to explain to people whose identities are normalized in predominately white/male spaces or who have institutional power by virtue of normalized visible identity. It can also be risky to authentically collaborate in full disclosure because of possible suspicion, resource removal, or resources withheld.

Showing up as the first CDO, and/or showing up as a female and Brown challenges the institution to examine previously held values, beliefs, and behaviors. Presence of identity, plus my rare professional experiences, dictate that spaces previously not occupied by the combo of my archetype and authority will be confronted with ideas that many may be flustered to consider (e.g., establishing performance reviews for employees citywide, objective employment screening instruments, etc.). Just as I had to enter, and with a level of difficulty learn and apply the concepts held true by colleagues of dominant identities, I can understand how dominant-identified institutional gatekeepers feel unaccustomed to shoulder-partnering with and being collegially responsible to people with subordinate identities. By virtue of position, I am afforded a level of trust and latitude, and must be acknowledged to move the institution forward.

*How do I know what I know?* Having been institutionally socialized, I know that institutions such as government that control generational power, wealth, and access were not built for underrepresented or historically marginalized populations. Until the hire of the CDO, many structures had gone unchecked, impeding true equity. Therefore, the onus fell to the CDO to design easily adoptable language and procedures through collaboration in order to successfully correct for past disparity creation. Through political savvy, I shoulder-partnered to implement internal networks of equity that informed agency practice.

*Where and/or whom did it come from?* As the first position of its type, expectations can often be unclear for how the CDO's work is to align with and influence departments. The lack of alignment presents a challenge to a diversity practitioner who is increasingly called to demonstrate the impact and effectiveness of my work to internal and external stakeholders. More important, the lack of alignment also challenges me in attempts to legitimize efforts. As a consequence, disconnect arises between what is required and expected—and what is being done in practice. Intentionally and unintentionally implicit and explicit bias widens disconnect. My experience as a gender and racial minority has conferred upon me a cumulative result born of a set of interrelated experiences sustained over an extended period of time that render me knowledgeable about how institutions arrange contributors and the value of their collaboration in keeping with their dominant and subordinate social identities.

*Whom does it serve?* Differing realities and segregated specialty work create isolated activities and misaligned priorities that may benefit one functional area of a municipality, but not the city as a whole. Too often, my work is regulated, restricted, and isolated to areas that pose the least threat to systems and perpetrators of bias. I combat the restriction and isolation through the collective impact of partners and allies during face-to-face engagement that builds formal and informal education, shared institutional history of resource scarcity, and information sharing. Further, much of my work is not viewed as deliberate, but rather as based on intuition and moral imperatives, which seems to appeal to the benevolence of fellow administrators in justifying the role's existence. In my experience, institutional collaboration and mutuality is sharing power and information among those who control agency fate. The generational compound interest of poverty, unequal distribution of wealth, and resultant residential segregation has resulted in women and people of color not participating in postsecondary education at the same rates as their white/male counterparts. Therefore, I, as a gender and racial minority, recognize that I, and those like me, will not become agency decision makers at the same rate. Consequently, because many of my colleagues lack a similar/same identity and lived experience to myself, I must transform parts of my identity that are recognizable to the majority identity so that I am able to be in a position to collaborate. Transformation is a cost that I pay to posture my political savvy so that my professional efforts may succeed.

*Leading through Status and Influence*

As CDO, I heavily appeal to the morality of institutional and community leaders to accomplish the agenda of equity, diversity, and inclusion. Individuals whom I approach control access to institutional wealth and related activities.

Attempts at aligning with persons of influence do not come without sacrifice, explanation, and fear. When alignment is visible, power brokers often inquire why or how I choose to be aligned to leaders with vast resources. I can only assume that this is because they have traditionally benefitted from those resources and are concerned with having their resources reduced.

CDOs "generally have no formal authority to command, reward, or punish individuals outside of their formal span of control and leadership. As a result, their source of 'power' is often grounded in status, persuasion, and symbols" (Williams & Wade-Golden, 2006, 3). Location and formal administrative hierarchy are other primary sources of power (3).

*Vignette 3.* "Dr. Carter, may I share something with you in confidence?" is a frequent query I hear from city employees, hiring managers, and sometimes community members and external agency leaders. Having heard this many times, I issued a memo first to city hiring managers, inviting each to discuss face to face the City Manager's diversity and inclusion agenda (equitable practices throughout the municipality), and second to all city employees. As I underwent this process with supervisory oversight, I experienced hyper-surveillance and paranoia, some leaders even asking why I wanted to meet with their subordinates.

*How do I know what I know?* Systemic community and institutional change occurs as people with power influence systems. I measure my impact by systemic changes that transpire in research agendas, policies, and practice. I know this works when I see improved institutional interaction with those it claims to serve. As a scholar and social justice professional called to connect historical truths about bias and understand its operation, it is important that I supplement my professional maneuvering with scholarly understanding of institutional, individual, and societal mechanics of bias.

*Where and/or whom did it come from?* Formal introductions by administration throughout the municipality are important to establish role legitimacy. Despite no formal introduction of the new CDO to city employees, and after the aforementioned memo was sent, I received employees' comments via telephone and email in effort to understand and/or challenge my source of power and realm of influence. "Whom do you report to?" and "I'm not sure if you can change [policy/procedure], but good luck" were frequent replies.

*Whom does it serve?* Changes in research agendas, policies, and practice are not by themselves sufficient to bring about philosophy alteration and improvement for disenfranchised people. Much depends on the nature of social relationships within institutions, between institution and community, in research-based partnerships, and the creation of shared purpose.

## Understanding of the Culture

"... should possess in-depth knowledge and experience regarding the culture..." (Williams & Wade-Golden, 2006, 6)

In transitioning from a postsecondary environ to the municipal sector, it was surprisingly simple to see the similarities, which included, but were not limited to, systems of discipline and judicial matters, budget types and constraints, methods of project approval, and more. I was surprised to see antiquated processes and methods still used that slowed production and filched human time and professional talent. As per my primary responsibility to diversify the city's workforce, I needed to contend with outdated modes of operation that could easily translate to a less diverse workforce. I needed to understand the reasons for certain internal cultures in order to suggest changes.

*Vignette 4.* My second week of work, my supervisor shared with me that the City Manager, like me, had transitioned from higher education, and I thought, "the similarities between higher education and municipality work are uncanny." As in postsecondary environs, the population of the United States is and continues to become increasingly diverse, and the City of Worcester follows suit. No longer spoken of as an "urban" issue, cultural, racial, and religious diversity can be seen in major cities and rural communities alike. Affiliation with postsecondary and municipal environs afforded me first-hand knowledge of divisive agency practices. To accomplish a larger equity agenda tasked to me by the City Manager, as I do as a consultant with Passion4Pivot LLC, I must simultaneously avoid political minefields while providing the agency with the tools and training needed to identify and address inhibiting institutional practices and policies.

*How do I know what I know?* Regardless of institutional affiliation, the pattern remains. Systemic and institutional bias are the overt and covert dynamic expressions of power and privilege manifested through institutional policies, structures, and patterns of behavior that result in the advantaging and disadvantaging of groups of people based on skin color, ethnicity, and physical and other characteristics. Because it is insidious and longstanding, systemic and institutional racism as a single shade of bias among many (sexism, homophobia, misogyny, etc.) is often ignored or thought to be impossible to eliminate. While segregated specialties differ, each partnership can support the process of deliberate organizing for systemic institutional change and to build the municipal capacity needed to reach agency-wide, anti-biased identity. Regardless of the institution that I have aligned myself with, this knowledge has served to scaffold my understanding of culture.

*Where and/or whom did it come from?* If I fail to stimulate discussion and debate of the merit of alternative choices, organizational efficiency is slowed, and leads to lowered productivity, work satisfaction, and weakened organizational achievement. Understanding the culture often limits my imagined possibilities for institutional improvement. This happens because I begin to justify the culture, like those already entrenched in the culture. Such justification moves me away from the objective place that can be easily seen when first witnessing institutional workings. However, I have learned that even when understanding of culture is closely entrenched, enthusiasm toward an adopted concept of improvement can transcend allegiance to the way things have always been done.

*Whom does it serve?* When understanding is clear, the participation becomes genuine and others buy in a lot easier. Then, we can get to the business of serving the municipality.

## References

Bryson, J. M. (1995). *Strategic planning for nonprofit organizations* (Revised edition). San Francisco: Jossey-Bass.

Carter, S. L. (1996). *Integrity.* New York: Basic Books.

Dugan, R. E., & Hernon, P. (2002). Outcomes assessment: Not synonymous with inputs and outputs. *Journal of Academic Librarianship, 28*(6), 376–383.

Heidelberger, C. A., & Uecker T. W. (2009). *Scholarly personal narrative as information systems research methodology.* Midwest Association for Information Systems.

Herman, R. D., & Associates (2005). *The Jossey-Bass handbook of non-profit leadership and management.* 2nd ed. San Francisco: Jossey-Bass.

Nash, R. J. (2004). *Liberating scholarly writing: The power of personal narrative.* New York: Teachers College Press.

Nash, R. J., & Bradley D. L. (2011). *Me-Search and re-search: A guide for writing scholarly personal narrative.* Charlotte, NC: Information Age Publishing.

Nixon, M. L. (2013). *Women of color chief diversity officers: Their positionality and agency in higher education institutions* (Doctoral dissertation). Retrieved from search.proquest.com/pqdt/docview/1428435516/previewPDF/142AEF02402460BEE70/4?accountid=14537

Williams, D. A., & Wade-Golden, K. C. (2006, April 18). What is a Chief Diversity Officer? *Inside HigherEd.* Retrieved from insidehighered.com/workplace/2006/04/18/williams

# Part V

## AFTER WORDS

Chapter 20

# The Dialectic of Radical Black Feminism

Keeanga-Yamahatta Taylor

Association of Black Women Historians (ABWH), Luncheon Keynote Address Saturday, September 30, 2017, at the Association for the Study of African American Life and History (ASALH) Annual Meeting, Cincinnati, Ohio, Regency Hotel

For anyone who thought that Trump's dalliance with white supremacists throughout his campaign and certainly in his reaction to the white rampage in Charlottesville was just impolitic behavior or the impetuousness of an unhinged elected official, you would do well to think again.

The actions of Trump over the fall of 2017 were the cynical actions of a calculating billionaire politician. Trump uses race as a bludgeon not only to distract from the stasis of the Republican-led Congress but also to create scapegoats to explain away the economic hardship and social tumult in the lives of ordinary people in this country. The message is blunt.

According to Trump and his acolytes in the Republican Party, it's not the system that produces hardship and economic anxiety—it's Black men and women who disrespect our heritage and our country (and the "our" almost never includes *you*); it's Mexican immigrants who have stolen your livelihood; and it's Muslims who want to destroy your way of life. In the aftermath of a catastrophic hurricane in the Caribbean, it was "lazy" Puerto Ricans who "want[ed] everyone to do everything for them" in the efforts to rebuild the island.

For Trump, it's not so much the "art of the deal" that is important—it is the art of racist demagoguery that he sees as crucial to his governing strategy. Not only is the Trump rhetoric maddening, it is also dangerous. As white supremacists take comfort in having one of their own in the White

House, Trump has emboldened racists of all stripes to physically and verbally abuse people of color across the country. Trump's racist menace has not only posed a threat to those he insults, but it is used to shield from the public the dangerous actions taken by Trump administration officials and the Congress that will continue to reverberate throughout our society long after the Trump menace is gone.

Consider Scott Pruitt, head of the EPA, who is systematically removing environmental protections that will have a disproportionate impact on Black and Brown communities suffering from lead poisoning, water pollution, and asthma produced by poor air quality in the communities where they live. Half of all Latinos live in communities designated as having "poor air quality," as just one example. Or consider Betsy DeVos, the Secretary of the Department of Education, who is working to systematically dismantle public education while simultaneously profiting from the promotion of unregulated charter school systems. Across Trump's cabinet are purposefully incompetent directors who have been deputized to unravel and mismanage the functions of the administrative state.

But this is not only about Trump, as much as that would comfort some of us to say. The watered-down, so-called "resistance" of the Democratic Party would have us believe that our goal should be to simply get things back to pre-Trump "normal."

Well, we would do good to remember that the old "normal" is what produced the social eruption of Black Lives Matter. The old "normal" is what led to the longest period of anti-racist organizing since the last moment of Black insurgency in the 1960s and 1970s. Black Lives Matter was not just about police abuse and violence, it was an expression of the visceral rage of a generation of Black millennials who came of age during an era of endless war and occupation, the crash of the housing market, mass incarceration, and a political ethos that blamed African Americans for the disproportionate rates of poverty and unemployment while systematically dismantling public institutions intended to mitigate those hardships in the first place.

Of course, that hardship existed long before Barack Obama assumed the presidency in 2008, but millions of young African Americans expected his presidency to offer an alternative to the status quo. While some self-anointed Black leaders like to describe these desires as ordinary Black people wanting Barack Obama to perform miracles, what people actually wanted was substantive change as opposed to hollow symbolism. There is no other way to explain the drop in Black participation in this past election except as disappointment with the persistence of inequality and with the disbelief that there is a solution to that persistence within the system itself.

It does not mean that African Americans are all raving radicals now, but it does not take raving radicalism to question whether Black people will ever be free in this deeply racist and unjust country. This political malaise is not conjecture—it is borne out in the numbers. After historic turnouts in the 2008 and 2012 elections, Black voter turnout for the 2016 presidential election declined. In fact, it was the first time in in 20 years that Black turnout fell in a presidential election, falling from a high of 66% in 2012 to 59% in the 2016 election.

A popular meme produced in the aftermath of the 2016 presidential election showed that 94% of Black women voters cast their ballot for Hillary Clinton for president. The meme was true but did not capture the larger dynamic that was unfolding during the election: 64% of Black women participated in the election, which was a decrease from the 70% who had voted in 2012. Of course, 64 is still a relatively high number, but what did the decline in overall voter participation represent? A recent poll shed some light. A 2017 "Power of the Sister Vote" and *Essence* magazine poll cited an 11% drop in support for the Democratic Party among Black women. The poll also expressed that the percentage of Black women who felt that the Democratic Party did not support them had jumped from 13% to 21% between 2016 and 2017.

This dilemma created by the persisting bigotry of the Republican Party and the perpetual ineffectiveness of the Democratic Party has left most ordinary people, but particularly young Black people, posing not only the question, "What is to be Done?" but more important, "How do we get free?"

This, of course, is not a new question for African Americans. The question has been asked repeatedly at each juncture where the question of Black liberation has been posed most sharply: at the end of the Civil War, the end of Reconstruction, the onset of the Great Migration, the Civil Rights Movement, the period of Black rebellion, and now in the aftermath of the Black president and the reconstitution of white supremacy embodied in the seat of the U.S. presidency. It is in a political moment such as the one we are living through that it is necessary to draw on the history and politics of previous movements in order to strategize the needs of our contemporary struggle. But we cannot limit our conversations to only strategy and tactics; we must also imagine what freedom would look like as well.

This year marks the 40th anniversary of the Combahee River Collective's publication of a statement that provided a radical Black feminist analysis on the problems confronting Black people and Black women in particular, and the type of struggle that would be necessary for Black people, and all oppressed people, to achieve freedom.

The Combahee River Collective was an organization of radical Black feminists who took their name from a raid organized and led by Harriet Tubman on the Combahee River in South Carolina in 1853. That raid freed 753 slaves from bondage. This was the point of departure for the Combahee Collective: Freedom is not doctrine but a constant struggle, and thus requires a plan of what they described as "revolutionary action."

The group formed in 1974 as a left-wing break from the National Black Feminist Organization, which itself had formed as an alternative to white feminist organizations that the NBFO believed did not take the struggle against racism seriously.

Politically, the Combahee Collective built on a longstanding analysis of Black women's oppression as the product of both gender and racial discrimination that when combined created an entirely new dimension of oppression and exploitation. In other words, it was impossible to measure the experiences of Black women through the lens of race or gender; instead, each of those social categories compounded each other, and when intersected with class or sexual orientation, those experiences were compounded again. The sum total of those experiences was greater oppression and economic exploitation in the lives of Black women.

This analysis led the Combahee Collective to then theorize how identity created the means for political action, which led to the conceptual breakthrough of "identity politics." Of course, identity politics has been bastardized into a term denuded of most of its original meaning. "Identity politics" described the means through which Black and Brown people became politicized. Black women were coming to radical conclusions about the world based on their position in it. So the phrase "the personal is political" was not about retreating into an apolitical internal world, as it came to be understood much later. No, for Black women, it was a description of how their personal experiences with racism, sexism, sexual assault, low-income, substandard housing, the humiliations experienced at the welfare office, forced sterilization, and the inaccessibility of abortion and reproductive health care crystalized their potential as radical subjects.

"Identity politics" was the way that these daily indignities experienced by Black women became the basis of their political activism. It was not abstract. It was common sense that Black women were becoming politically active, not for reasons of doctrine but because of their lived experiences. This is why Black feminists were at the forefront of the struggles for abortion rights, campaigns against sterilization, and activism against domestic violence. It also explained why Black women played an outsized, if underreported, role in all of the various iterations of movements and campaigns that have offered the promise of a better life and a brighter future for all Black people. This is not because Black women had a predisposition toward activism, but because the unvarnished experiences of Black women in the United States led them to question the basic tenets of American exceptionalism.

This has been our history. But the Combahee Collective also came into existence at the height of the development of the New Left. Indeed, Barbara Smith had cut her teeth in the anti-war and student movement of the late 1960s. Demita Frazier, who also authored the Combahee statement, had been active in the Black Panther Party. They came to feminist politics as anti-capitalists and recognized that Black women's oppression could not be resolved within the confines of American capitalism. But they also recognized there could be no genuine socialist revolution that did not recognize the oppression experienced by Black women and that did not have a political plan of action on how to combat that oppression.

To this end, the Combahee Collective Statement was not just a document for radical Black feminists—it was an important document for the revolutionary Left as a political perspective or plan of action for the movement of the 1970s. It included areas of work that radicals could involve themselves in as a way to relate to the struggles of Black women while also raising the level of political education concerning the conditions that constrained the lives of Black women. Perhaps most important as we elaborate on this concept of "political imagination," the Combahee statement recognized that to actually end Black women's oppression, we needed to consider the possibility of ending capitalism. And it was here that they unlocked the dialectic at the heart of their manifesto. Orienting on the most oppressed in a society—in the United States, that meant Black women—exposed the injustice of the entire system. This is why the Combahee Collective insisted, "If Black women were free, it would mean that everyone else would have to be free since our freedom would necessitate the destruction of all systems of oppression." The liberation of Black women is the genesis for human liberation.

Indeed, this is also a critical intervention made by the Collective. "Black feminism," "identity politics," and "the personal is political" are all terms and units of analyses that have been misconstrued as demands for separation and exclusion. But the concept of solidarity—in all its complexity and difficulty—was at the heart of their politics. They called it coalition building and recognized its necessity in building movements beyond those who were directly affected. This was not easy, but it was necessary if we were going to organize struggles that we actually won.

These are all critical lessons in the struggles we face today. After 40 years, these are analyses that are important not only in understanding the conditions that shape the life and experiences of the majority of African Americans; most importantly, the politics of the Combahee Collective are the politics that are necessary to actually win the struggle for Black liberation and freedom.

What does that mean? It means recognizing the significance of the recent campaigns to highlight Black women's oppression and struggles. When feminists insist on "centering" the experiences of Black women, it is not a cry for attention; it is because by doing so, the depths of oppression and exploitation in American society are laid bare for all to see. When we tell the truth about the experiences of Black women, we tell the truth about the United States. And in doing so, it reveals the same conclusion that the women of Combahee came to: that Black women will never be free within capitalism. It is a system dependent on racism, gender and sexual oppression, and sexism. We live in a country where these oppressions are so tightly wound into its marrow that there has never been a single moment in its entire history when freedom from this injustice and oppression existed.

There has never been a golden age for African Americans in the United States, nor a golden age for Black women or Brown women; there has never been a golden age for Black lesbians in the United States. And so to expect one now is to be in deep denial about the ways that inequality, racism, and oppression are structured into the very system itself. This was as true 40 years ago as it is today.

Black people have been repeatedly told, at least for the last 50 years, that "Black faces in high places" was evidence of our achievements. It was held out as hope for the future. But the gains of the few have been illusory. And even those who have gained more than most other African Americans know that those gains are always tenuous, sometimes fleeting, and never secure. One need only look at how the housing crisis wiped out the wealth of Black communities. The accomplishments of a small layer of Black elites, including those of the political class, should never be confused with all Black people enjoying that level of wealth, access, political power, and influence.

Indeed, perhaps the most salient distinction between today and 40 years ago when the Collective statement was published has been the growth of the class divide among African Americans. That division is noteworthy because it influences politics and the direction of our movement. It could be seen on the streets of Ferguson. I write in my book *From #BlackLivesMatter to Black Liberation* how Black congressmen were coming to Ferguson pleading with young people to get off the streets and register to vote. It was as if they were telling those young people to turn their power over to the elected officials by getting off the streets and entrusting them to solve this tangle of racism, police abuse, violence, and murder.

Unfortunately, what they failed to understand was that young Black people had voted like they never voted before *to put Obama in office*. And in their experience, not much had changed except the brazenness of police violence and murder. In fact, in 2008 and 2012 they had entrusted their future to the political class by voting in unprecedented numbers. It was not just that Obama failed to deliver on those hopes, he also preserved and legitimized the public space to chastise Black people. This included blaming Black inequality on the very people suffering from that inequality. From Cousin Pookie, to feeding kids Popeye's fried chicken, to watching Sports Center, there was no stereotype from which Obama spared African Americans. The rise of the Black Lives Matter (BLM) Movement was a rejection of these kinds of mean-spirited respectability politics and the pathetic tradition in American politics of currying the favor of middle-class voters of all races on the basis of insulting poor and working-class Black people. In that sense, BLM is a part of the tradition of Combahee. That it is led by ordinary Black women from Ferguson and other queer Black women exemplifies this.

But if we are going to fundamentally challenge and politically confront the white supremacist menace of Donald Trump, we must continue to engage with the legacy of the Combahee. We must build on what the Black Lives Matter Movement has begun. And in doing so, we cannot restrict our thinking to what happens in the next election or the election after that. If we are thinking only in those terms, we are almost certainly never thinking of "how we get free" or what would Black liberation look like? And to imagine that world, we don't need the nostalgia of Combahee—we need their politics. They called for revolutionary action to defeat capitalism. They called for a socialist reorganization of our society. They understood that solidarity and coalition building were the way forward. And they believed that the liberation of Black women could free the world. These remain the tasks of the current moment.

Chapter 21

# For Black Women Who Educate for Social Justice and Put Their Time, Lives, and Spirits on the Line

RHONDA Y. WILLIAMS

### Coda as Preface

*Individuals, collectives, and struggles for liberation are never finished, but always in/a process—of cyclical (self-)discovery, imagination, awareness, fatigue, splendor, assault, recuperation, invention, maturation, death, rebirth, change, awe, and continuation. This is not your ordinary essay. It is prose playing & searching for freedom & echoing historical and contemporary scenes to bear witness to the messages, stories, poetics, people, politics, activism, and scholarly journeys that expose the tragic everydayness of inequality, that lay bare the entrenched regimes of injustice, that call up the ancestors and call on us, in the words of Audre Lorde, to "look clearly and closely at the genuine particulars (conditions) of his or her life and decide where action and energy is needed and where it can be effective."[1] In this process, may we also find deliverance, inspiration, wellness, joy, love, & people—including us—who love us.[2]*

### Intro: Three Words

*Truth-Telling.*
*Empathy.*
*Self-Care.*

Figuring out what else to say beyond these *Three Words* proved [pause] challenging, initially. It is why I wrote this and the preceding sentence. Then [pause] having written these *Three Words, and* these two sentences, & with nothing else flowing . . . (*You know, sometimes, we just need to put a period, or [. . .], at the end of our sentences and get out of the way*) . . . I turned to the universe for guidance. Period.

Calm & pauses opened up a universe of [  ]
Space to muse, to feel, to question
What
to say, or
Echo.

(*I do a lot of echoing, echoing, echoing these days.*)

And, there, in the [pauses], [ . . . s ] & [   ]s, Black women who *are* the blank[3]—not as in *lack*, but as in STILLNESS in/the/gap—their voices, Black women's voices invited me to dig deep & ponder the ponderous work of these *Three Words* . . .

*Truth-Telling.*
*Empathy.*
*Self-Care.*

Whoosh—*flow*—always in/a process—*words*—playing together—*Prose-Play* . . . for . . . Black Women __ Who __ Educate . . . for . . . Social Justice & Put Their Time, Lives, and Spirits on the Line.[4]

## I: Truth-Telling

*Echo, echo, echo*
Reverberate, Vibrate, Reflect
Reflect, Bounce, Recoil
Repeat

*Repeat*
Wincing Past

*Silence*
From whence this Wincing Past not past, but
Present.

*In Stillness*
Witness the Present still wincing presently, but
Future?

Reverberate, Vibrate, Reflect
Reflect, Bounce, Recoil
Repeat

*Summon—*
*Three Words.*

*Echo, echo, echo*

～

In the history of the United States, there has never been a moment when Black women did not expose inequalities or fight for social justice. Indeed, Black women have defied horrifying earthly circumstances in familiar and maybe not always recognized ways: **from** carrying, invoking, and creating traditions; **to** theorizing double jeopardies, multiple jeopardies, triple exploitation & triple jeopardies, interlocking oppressions, metalanguages, and intersectionalities; **to** testifyin', offering solace, and imparting wisdom; **to** conjuring sundry challenges to sundry oppressions. *Echo.* Black women have conceived a universe of familiar and maybe not always recognized ways to bring to light, keep in the light, alllll *that* ig-nor-ance that ro-bust-ly grows in the dark.[5] These Black women, they all be social justice educators, and **we** be sharing they stories, and weaving **we** new stories (yet) to be told, as **we** too be S.J.E.s. Not so easy.

*Snap. 3x.*

*Snapshots.*

**Calling** *the ancestors . . .*[6]

Black women liberated themselves and others from the clutches of enslavers by hiding in attics, writing anti-slave narratives, walking and running away, crossing Combahee Rivers, and guiding by way of the North Star and liberation drums. **Calling**: *Harriet Jacobs, Ona Judge, Harriet Tubman . . .*[7]

They lectured to promiscuous and hostile audiences. **Calling**: *Maria W. Stewart, Sojourner Truth . . .*[8]

They exposed lynching, unraveled threadbare lies, and demanded reparations for a sundry . . . echo . . . of whats. **Calling**: *Ida B. Wells, Billie Holiday, Callie House, Audley "Queen Mother" Moore . . .*[9]

They started schools and clubs and penned foundational scholarly essays on Black women's rights. **Calling**: *Mary McLeod Bethune, Mary Church Terrell, Anna Julia Cooper . . .*[10]

They stood up, and sat down. They walked instead of riding. They protested for education, housing, jobs, income, self-determination, dignity, respect. They pushed for civil rights, voting rights, economic rights, tenants' rights, welfare rights, right-to-be-all-of-me rights, human rights. They advocated for truth, commissioning truth. **Calling**: *Diane Nash, Rosa Parks, Septima Clark, Pauli Murray, Ella Baker, Addie Wyatt, Flo Kennedy, Shirley Chisholm, Ericka Huggins, Combahee River (echo, echo, echo) Collective, Shirley Wise & Goldie Baker, Johnnie Tillmon, Marsha P. Johnson, Mary Frances Berry . . .*[11]

They experienced, they navigated, they confronted . . . the intricacies, the ugliness, the discriminatory practices . . . of . . . the . . . lock up. **Calling**: *Fannie Lou Hamer, Mae Mallory, Angela Y. Davis, Ericka Huggins (echo, echo, echo), Assata Shakur . . .*[12] **Calling, calling, calling**: *Name, name, name; name, name, name; name, name, name . . . name . . . name . . . names . . .*[13]

They warn us about & imagine the power of suchness. **Calling**: *Toni Cade Bambara, Octavia Butler, N. K. Jemisin . . .*[14]

Clearly, Black women adopt, adapt, and create various modes and genres of truth-telling across time and space. They educate through consciously and courageously BEing, theorizing, researching, teaching, writing, producing art and literature, activating activism, and fashioning institutional spaces for the work of social justice to seed and grow. And they do this in times and spaces where Black women's presence and voices are often scarce, hidden, obfuscated, ignored . . . & sometimes heard. The academy is one small corner of this broader space—one that Black women have used to ignite greater understanding of the difficulties, potentialities, and realities of greater interconnectedness and liberation.[15] From the streets to the academy, Black women have educated and written the past and present lessons of social justice.

*Echo, echo, echo . . .*

*Silence*
From whence this Wincing Past not past, but
Present.

∽

**. . . LISTEN. Coretta Scott King. May 1968. Mother's Day. March of Welfare Recipients, DC:** "[It is] not an easy way, particularly in this day when violence is almost fashionable, and in this society, where violence against poor people and minority groups is routine. I must remind you that starving a child is violence. Suppressing a culture is violence. Neglecting school children is violence. Punishing a mother and her family is violence. . . . Ignoring medical needs is violence. Contempt for poverty is violence. Even the lack of will power to help humanity is a sick and sinister form of violence."[16]

∽

*Echo, echo, echo*

*In Stillness*
Witness the Present still wincing presently, but
Future?

∽

These 21st-century echoes of 1968 reveal not only the evidence of things done, but also those things still being done. No doubt. It is imperative to fashion and support relevant and emancipatory spaces. For in these kinds of spaces, educators take seriously the imperative of critical analysis, truth-telling, imagining different societies, and creating better worlds.

## II: Empathy

*They* tell the truth. And, sometimes, *they* truth-telling be embodied empathy. But, other times, *they* just . . . be . . . too exhausted, or amazed, or something . . .

Empathy shall not be passive. Shall not be simply a noun—a *thing* to be claimed or possessed.[17] Nor shall it only be commiseration. Empathy is creation, action, process.[18] Aspiration. Art. Awareness. Bodies in motion, flowing, improvising, voguing.

Empathy emerges as people deeply study and evaluate their worldviews with the goals of transforming internal dogmatism, analyzing inequality and power, exchanging know-how, and advancing social change that seeks to resist commonplace and systemic violence and promote clarity and human well-being.

Say, what's the *word, word, word*?

## III: Self-Care

*i: Social Justice Work*

Energy expended out there
&
in here.
Labor with the fruits of
Pain
&
Joy.
Will you breathe with me?

*Interlude*

> *Play Song (6 minutes 19 seconds)*
> *Lalah Hathaway, "Little Girl/Breathe"*[19]

*ii: Disarming*[20]

**Setting**: *Any day, sunny, snowy, rainy, but every day with thunderstorms in her head. Playing in the background is Nina Simone's "I Wish I Knew How It Would Feel to Be Free."*

My Dear Sister Sonia:

I was re-reading the notes I jotted down to introduce you at the Social Justice Institute's biennial Think Tank "Educating for Struggle: In the Academy, Schools, Prisons & Streets" in November 2013.[21] I scribbled: "Grenades are not free," from your poem "Reflections After the June 12th March for Disarmament," in *Homegirls and Handgrenades*.[22]

The entire poem, even as I re-read it now, I shake my head yes, yes, yes. FOR IN YOUR WORDS exposing the sordid history of the United States' love affairs with profit and power—from slavery to nuclear threat and nuclear minds—I find a safe space to disarm for a moment from the justice battlefield. I find . . . a moment . . . to sit, sit, sit, AND stay just a little while, knowing that no-one here in this vocalized space will spit out passive aggressive ballistics, OR excessive bluster projectiles, OR toss around the living word "activist" as if it were an epithet—**NOT here** . . .

I especially find sanity in the following stanza that echoes, echoes, echoes in my head . . . "I have come to you tonite because there are inhumanitarians in the world. they are not new. they are old. they go back into history."

As a historian, I sure enough smiled at that. Indeed, the inhumanitarians do go back into history. And they occupy our present, some with unapologetic white supremacist, sexist, ethnocentric, classist, imperialist venom. And we must challenge them, mustn't we, as scholars and activists, as weavers of the word in poems and monographs and marching chants? No justice, no . . . !

Though, it behooves us to remember, too, don't you think, Sister Sonia, that prejudice and oppressive tendencies come in lots of packages—implicit, mild-mannered, even sugar-rimmed liberal packages. I know YOU know all this, but your reflections got me thinking, thinking, thinking . . . as I am writing, writing, writing.

This persistence of injustice is unfortunately and fortunately so staggeringly clear to me **as a professor of history** who teaches *and* tries to **EMBODY** some of what she teaches . . .[23] **As a Black woman** who tries to teach her students in "City As Classroom"[24]—taught off-campus at a community home featuring rigorous readings, the voices of community partners, and a social change activism project—tries to teach her students that the world ain't the bubble of academe . . . but you can use academe to learn more about AND WORK to change the world. Right?

The persistence of injustice and our need to challenge it is so clear to me, **as someone** who lives her life with history on her mind . . . and the everyday of . . . EVERY . . . day . . . whistling in her ear . . . **As someone** . . . who . . . dares to struggle to "not give the earth up to" non-humanistic dreamers . . .

This kind of struggle costs ya.

But Sister Sonia, I KNOW you KNOW this already, because you taught at San Francisco State in the late 1960s, because you taught pioneering courses on Black women's literature. I KNOW you KNOW because you organized with CORE and helped usher in the Black Power & Black Arts movements, because you not only **urged** Black unity, but also **worked** toward it. Because you alchemized and word-smithed Black pain & Black promise & the words of the street into candid verses. Because you ventured out to those streets/sidewalks/schools/stepladder-corners/stores in cities across the nation.

So, I know you—a scholar, poet, author, activist, truth-teller—know that struggle costs ya . . . time, energy, and your blinders and comfort, and . . . oftentimes . . . you know, I get oh so angry and . . . sometimes . . . I get oh so weary . . .

But, don't worry, I will try to hang on to the world as it spins around, like Donny Hathaway said, and keep my stride. And as I stride, I will carry your words and your reflections and your encouraging inscription penned in my copy of *Homegirls and Handgrenades*: "To Sister Rhonda, Please continue to do your most important work, my dear Sister. Please continue to walk your intellect and beauty and love across this country! In love/struggle/peace, Sonia Sanchez." *Signed November 15, 2013.*

*iii: Weight*

My Dear Sister . . . Toni Cade Bambara . . . *The Salt Eaters* . . . Echoes.

First thing, on first page, the first line . . . first things first . . .
*"Are you sure, sweetheart, that you want to be well?"*

Echo . . . *(Page 5): "A lot of weight when you're well . . ."*

Echo, echo . . . *(Page 10): "Just so's you're sure, sweetheart, and ready to be healed, cause wholeness is no trifling matter. A lot of weight when you're well."*

*iv: Well*

So this brings me back to finding inspiration, to finding deliverance, to finding and gently holding joy and happiness and love in the midst of engaging in purposeful social justice work, however we find ourselves educating, wherever we find ourselves as educators. This work cannot only test our tempers, indeed make us question the realness of reality, but also test our physical health and overall wellness. And . . . *echo, echo, echo* . . . we already know that there's "a lot of weight when you're well."

Carrying this weight requires that we honor physical and intuitive calls for self-care. Self-care must become as critical a part of social justice education, theory and praxis, as recognizing, articulating, and challenging the oppressive -isms that render inequality and limit our human potential. Understood in this way, self-care does not have to feed egocentrism and is not a priori selfish. But, we must be careful not to "weaponize" self-care, thereby allowing it to become an excuse for not engaging in purposeful and conscious work for change—whatever that looks like. Period.

## Outro: No Final Words

*Head steady, eyes lowered and closed. In/out. Repeat with the breath: no fear, no fear, no fear. Half-smile. Head steady, eyes raised, and open. Imagine, Aspire & Live: Solidity, Justice & Dignity. Full smile. Stand up. No final words. Bow. Silently, put on the chucks. And. To the rhythm, to the beat, to the groove . . . Be . . . Do . . . & . . . Dance*

## Notes

1. Audre Lorde (1984). "Learning from the 60s," *Sister Outsider: Essays & Speeches* (Freedom, CA: The Crossing Press), 141.

2. bell hooks (1994), *Teaching to Transgress: Education as the Practice of Freedom* (New York: Routledge); Alice Walker (2006), *We Are the Ones We Have Been Waiting For: Inner Light in a Time of Darkness* (New Press). Also see Thich Nhat Hanh (1993), *Love in Action: Writings on Nonviolent Social Change* (Parallax Press): Zenju Earthlyn Manuel (2015), *The Way of Tenderness: Awakening through Race, Sexuality, and Gender* (Somerville, MA: Wisdom Publications).

3. In "Revolutionary Hope," a dialogue between Audre Lorde and James Baldwin published in *Essence* in 1984, in which they discussed the exclusionary "American Dream," the normality of loathing, and the pervasiveness of oppression, Lorde spoke thusly: "Even worse than the nightmare is the blank. And Black women are the blank. I don't want to break all this down, then have to stop at the wall of

male/female division. When we admit and deal with difference; when we deal with the deep bitterness; when we deal with the horror of even our different nightmares; when we turn them and look at them, it's like looking at death: hard but possible. If you look at it directly without embracing it, then there is much less that you can ever be made to fear." See mocada-museum.tumblr.com/post/73421979421/revolutionary-hope-a-conversation-between-james

4. Honor the stylistic naming energy of Ntozake Shange, *For Colored Girls Who Considered Suicide/When the Rainbow Is Enuf*. Reprint Edition (Scribners, 1997).

5. For essays by Frances Beal on "double jeopardy," Deborah K. King on "multiple jeopardy," and the Combahee River Collective on "interlocking oppressions," see *Words of Fire: An Anthology of African-American Feminist Thought*, edited by Beverly Guy-Sheftall (New York: The New Press, 1995). On the Combahee River Collective, also see *How We Get Free: Black Feminism and the Combahee River Collective*, edited by Keeanga-Yamahtta Taylor (Chicago: Haymarket Books, 2017). On triple exploitation and/or triple jeopardy, see Ashley D. Farmer (2017), *Remaking Black Power: How Black Women Transformed an Era* (Chapel Hill: University of North Carolina Press), Chapter 5; Erik S. McDuffie (2011), *Sojourning for Freedom: Black Women, American Communism, and the Making of Black Left Feminism* (Durham, NC: Duke University Press), 112; Rhonda Y. Williams (2015), *Concrete Demands: The Search for Black Power in the 20th Century* (New York: Routledge), 32. On "intersectionality," see Kimberlé Crenshaw (1991, July), "Mapping the Margins: Intersectionality, Identity Politics, and Violence against Women of Color," *Stanford Law Review*, *43*(6), 1241–1299. On the "metalanguage of race," see Evelyn Brooks Higginbotham (1992, Winter) "African-American Women's History and the Metalanguage of Race," *Signs*, *17*(2), 251–274.

6. There is absolutely no way that I can "call" by name all the ancestors. At different times, I call different names—sometimes woefully, but always thankfully, because there are so many Black women, known and unknown, who have struggled for a better world. Feel free to echo your own as you read. Honor the poetics naming energy of Sonia Sanchez. See Sister Sonia's keynote address, "Social Justice Institute Think Tank 2013 Day 1 Keynote," at case.edu/socialjustice/events/media

7. Harriet Jacobs (2001), *Incidents in the Life of a Slave Girl*, edited by Nellie Y. McKay and Frances Smith Foster (New York: W.W. Norton); Erica Dunbar Armstrong (2017), *Never Caught: The Washingtons' Relentless Pursuit of Their Runaway Slave, Ona Judge* (New York: Atria Books). There are several biographies of Harriet Tubman.

8. The phrase "promiscuous audiences" often referred to audiences mixed by race and gender. For biographical information and speeches by Maria W. Stewart, see BlackPast.org and www.Blackpast.org/aah/stewart-maria-miller-1803-1879. On Sojourner Truth, see *Narrative of Sojourner Truth* (Penguin Books, 1998); Nell Irvin Painter (1996), *Sojourner Truth: A Life, A Symbol* (New York: W.W. Norton).

9. Ida B. Wells (1996), *Southern Horrors and Other Writings*, edited by Jacqueline Jones Royster (Boston: Bedford/St. Martins); Paula Giddings (2008), *Ida: A Sword Among Lions: Ida B. Wells and the Campaign Against Lynching* (New York: HarperCollins); Mary F. Berry (2005), *My Face Is Black Is True: Callie House and the Struggle for Ex-Slave Reparations* (New York: Knopf); Ayesha Bell Hardaway (2015),

"The Breach of the Common Law Trust Relationship between the United States and African Americans—A Substantive Right to Reparations," *New York University Review of Law & Social Change,* 39(4), 525. On Audley "Queen Mother" Moore, see, for instance, Erik S. McDuffie and Komozi Woodard (2013), " 'If you're in a country that's progressive, the woman is progressive': Black women radicals and the making of the politics and legacy of Malcolm X," *Biography—An Interdisciplinary Quarterly,* 36(3), 507–539. Also see Williams, *Concrete Demands.*

10. Brittney C. Cooper (2017), *Beyond Respectability: The Intellectual Thought of Race Women* (Urbana: University of Illinois Press); Paula Giddings (1984), *When and Where I Enter: The Impact of Black Women on Race and Sex in America* (New York: Bantam Books).

11. *Hands on the Freedom Plow: Personal Accounts by Women in SNCC,* edited by Faith S. Holsaert, Martha Prescod Norman Noona, Judy Richardson, Betty Garman Robinson, Jean Smith Young, Dorothy M. Zellner (Urbana: University of Illinois Press, 2012); *The Montgomery Bus Boycott and the Women Who Started It: The Memoir of Jo Ann Gibson Robinson,* edited by David J. Garrow (Knoxville: University of Tennessee Press, 1987); *Chisholm '72: Unbought & Unbossed,* DVD Documentary, Director Shola Lynch, 2005; Mary Frances Berry (2009), *And Justice For All: The United States Commission on Civil Rights and the Continuing Struggle for Freedom in America* (New York: Knopf); David Halberstam (1999), *The Children* (New York: Fawcett Books); Marcia Walker-McWilliams (2016), *Reverend Addie Wyatt: Faith and the Fight for Labor, Gender, and Racial Equality* (Urbana: University of Illinois Press); Ericka Huggins and Angela D. LeBlanc-Ernest (2009), "Revolutionary Women, Revolutionary Education: The Black Panther Party's Oakland Community School," in *Want to Start a Revolution?: Radical Women in the Black Freedom Struggle,* edited by Dayo F. Gore, Jeanne Theoharis, and Komozi Woodard (New York: New York University Press), 161–184; Pauli Murray (1956/1998), *Proud Shoes: The Story of an American Family* (Boston: Beacon Press); Premilla Nadasen (2004), *Welfare Warriors: The Welfare Rights Movement in the United States* (New York: Routledge); Sherie Randolph (2015) *Florynce "Flo" Kennedy: The Life of a Black Feminist Radical* (Chapel Hill: University of North Carolina Press); Barbara Ransby (2003), *Ella Baker & the Black Freedom Movement: A Radical Democratic Vision* (Chapel Hill: University of North Carolina Press); Rosalind Rosenberg (2017), *Jane Crow: The Life of Pauli Murray* (New York: Oxford University Press); Jeanne Theoharis (2015), *The Rebellious Life of Mrs. Rosa Parks* (Boston: Beacon Press); Rhonda Y. Williams (2004), *The Politics of Public Housing: Black Women's Struggles Against Urban Inequality* (New York: Oxford University Press). For information on Marsha P. Johnson see "The Death and Life of Marsha P. Johnson," Netflix Original Documentary, Director David France, 2017. (It should be noted that after the release of this documentary, there was immediate public debate regarding who had the original idea for a film on Marsha P. Johnson, a Black gay liberation activist, transvestite, and drag queen. In particular, the transgender woman of color filmmaker Reina Gossett raised an alarm, given her work on a documentary titled "Happy Birthday Marsha!" Readers can explore the media reports for themselves.)

12. Angela Y. Davis (1974/1988), *An Autobiography* (New York: International Publishers); Ashley Farmer (2016, June 2), "Mae Mallory: Forgotten Black Power Intellectual," *Black Perspectives*, AAIHS; Chana Kai Lee (1999), *For Freedom's Sake: The Life of Fannie Lou Hamer* (Urbana: University of Illinois Press); Assata Shakur (1987), *Assata: An Autobiography* (Westport, CT: Lawrence Hill). On Ericka Huggins, see "Ericka Huggins: The Official Website," www.erickahuggins.com. Also see Robyn C. Spencer (2016), *The Revolution Has Come: Black Power, Gender, and the Black Panther Party in Oakland* (Durham, NC: Duke University Press).

13. "Name, name, name . . ." is an opportunity for those reading/listening to call out names, and to recognize and honor all those sisters who have been fighting for better—more humane and fair conditions—on the inside and outside of the (literal and figurative) "lock up." Many of their names we will not know because they were not always deemed worthy of attention, concern, or care. For a sampling of scholarly works on race, gender, Black women, criminalization, and the carceral state, in particular, see Talitha L. LeFLouria (2016), *Chained in Silence: Black Women and Convict Labor in the New South* (Chapel Hill: University of North Carolina Press); Kali N. Gross (2006), *Colored Amazons: Crime, Violence, and Black Women in the City of Brotherly Love, 1880–1910* (Durham: Duke University Press); Sarah Haley (2016), *No Mercy Here: Gender, Punishment, and the Making of Jim Crow Modernity* (Chapel Hill: University of North Carolina Press); LaShawn Harris (2016), *Sex Workers, Psychics, and Numbers Runners: Black Women in New York City's Underground Economy* (Urbana: University of Illinois Press); Cheryl D. Hicks (2010), *Talk with You Like a Woman: African American Women, Justice, and Reform in New York, 1890–1935* (Chapel Hill: University of North Carolina Press); Monique W. Morris (2016), *Pushout: The Criminalization of Black Girls in School* (New York: The New Press). Also, for examples of contemporary policy work and struggles that were initiated by Black women, have Black women in leadership, and/or that take seriously interlocking oppressions, see African American Policy Forum (AAPF), www.aapf.org; Black Lives Matter, Blacklivesmatter.com; The Movement for Black Lives, policy.m4bl.org; Black Youth Project 100, byp100.org.

14. Toni Cade Bambara (1992), *The Salt Eaters*, Reissue Edition (New York: Vintage); *Savoring the Salt: The Legacy of Toni Cade Bambara*, edited by Linda Jacob Holmes and Cheryl A. Wall (Philadelphia: Temple University Press, 2007); Octavia Butler, including *Kindred* (Boston: Beacon Press, 2004), *Lilith's Brood* (Grand Central Publishing, 2000), *Parable of the Sower* (New York: Warner Books, 1993); N. K. Jemisin (2015), *The Fifth Season (The Broken Earth)* (Orbit). Also see adrienne maree brown (2017), *Emergent Strategy: Shaping Change, Changing Worlds* (AK Press).

15. The establishment of Black Women's Studies is a foundational example of this. See *All the Women are White, All the Blacks are Men, But Some of Us Are Brave: Black Women's Studies*, edited by Gloria T. Hull, Patricia Bell Scott, and Barbara Smith (New York: The Feminist Press, 1982); *Still Brave: The Evolution of Black Women's Studies*, edited by Stanlie M. James, Frances Smith Foster, & Beverly Guy-Sheftall (New York: The Feminist Press, 2009). More recently in the academy, Black women scholar-activists or community-engaged researchers have founded and directed efforts to create organizational and/or institutionalized spaces for social justice education and

activism. Examples include Cathy J. Cohen, principle investigator for the Black Youth Project (BYP), Blackyouthproject.com; Barbara Ransby, who directs the Social Justice Initiative at University of Illinois Chicago, sji.webhost.uic.edu; Rhonda Y. Williams, who founded the Social Justice Institute at Case Western Reserve University and served as its inaugural director, case.edu/socialjustice/; Mia Henry and Lisa Brock, who serve as the executive director and academic director, respectively, of the Arcus Center for Social Justice Leadership at Kalamazoo College, reason.kzoo.edu/csjl/; Kimberlé Crenshaw, who is co-founder and executive director of AAPF; Elaine Richardson, founder, Hip-Hop Literacies Conference, www.hiphopliteracies.com; Bettina Love, founder, Hip Hop Civics Curriculum GET FREE, www.bettinalove.com.

16. *Welfare & the Poor*, edited by Lester A. Sobel (New York: Facts on File, 1977), 28–29. See also Coretta Scott King (2017), *My Life, My Love, My Legacy* (New York: Henry Holt).

17. "Passive empathy," a term used by Megan Boler, is defined as "a safe and simplistic identification with less privileged others that does not require that we question our own position or challenge our own worldview." See Diane J. Goodman (2011), Introduction, *Promoting Diversity and Social Justice: Educating People from Privileged Groups* (New York: Routledge), x.

18. Educator, poet, playwright, and artist-scholar Mary E. Weems writes: "The arts are a powerful way to counter apathy and encourage empathy." See Mary E. Weems (2013), "One Love: Empathy and the Imagination-Intellect," in *Writings of Healing and Resistance: Empathy and the Imagination-Intellect*, edited by Mary E. Weems (New York: Peter Lang), 2.

19. Lalah Hathaway (2015), *LIVE*, 8th Floor Productions/eOne. I also highly suggest Tracks 8 and 12, "This is Your Life" and "Mirror," respectively. The whole album is great.

20. A version of this "Letter to My Dear Sister Sonia" was initially presented as part of a keynote lecture titled "From the Streets to the Academy: Struggle Costs Ya . . . in Ten Parts," presented at the Women in the Historical Profession Luncheon, at the Annual Conference of the Organization of American Historians, April 8, 2016.

21. I also would like to note that Maytha Alhassen shared the stage as opening keynote lecturer alongside Sister Sonia Sanchez for the biennial SJI Think Tank held in 2013 in Cleveland, Ohio. My continued thanks to Bakari Kitwana, who connected SJI to both Sister Sonia and Maytha. For the keynote lectures, see "Social Justice Institute Think Tank 2013 Day 1 Keynote," case.edu/socialjustice/events/media

22. Sonia Sanchez (2007), *Homegirls and Handgrenades* (Buffalo, N.Y.: White Pine Press, 1984).

23. In her chapter on Paulo Freire in *Teaching to Transgress*, bell hooks has a playful dialogue with herself, Gloria Watkins (GW). And bell hooks says to GW: "It always astounds me when progressive people act as though it is somehow a naïve moral position to believe that our lives must be a living example of our politics," bell hooks, 48.

24. I piloted my "City as Classroom" course, which I developed with a UCITE grant at CWRU, in 2000. (UCITE stands for University Center for Innovation in

Teaching and Education.) The course philosophy, which is informed pedagogically by hooks and Freire, reads this way in my syllabus: "In the tradition of critical pedagogy, education and learning should be 'relevant and emancipatory' and based upon a humanist agenda. It is my belief that the practice of history should be part of a broader liberation project—one that arms students and scholars with the necessary analytical tools and information to combat social, cultural, and political myths and to address historical and contemporary issues."

# Concluding Thoughts

*Black Women Educators, Healing History, and Developing a Sustainable Social Justice Practice*

Andrea D. Domingue and Stephanie Y. Evans

This collection is a continuation of discussions about liberation that have been held for several generations. Love and Jiggetts brilliantly describe Black women's work in terms of jumping double-dutch between racism and sexism. As such, our concluding words are not a closing statement, but rather a series of reflections to keep in mind as we move forward with our work.

As Tania Mitchell opened the book with a challenge to more mindfully theorize SJE, Andrea and Stephanie bring the book to a close by pointing the way to more informed practice. Dre's letter addresses the frustrations of challenges found in the education profession and offers encouragement to those in the struggle. Stephanie's closing reminds social justice workers to draw on guides from the past to show how to manage stress, conflict, and crisis but still make the struggle for justice sustainable.

## A Letter from Andrea: To Sisters in Social Justice Education

Social justice is a framework that continues to dominate contemporary educational discourses, particularly as educators must navigate ever-evolving social issues within the United States and global contexts (Wong, 2016). When I began my work as a scholar-practitioner almost 15 years ago, the conversations within the field of student affairs centered on diversity or the acknowledgment and appreciation of social difference (Landreman & MacDonald-Dennis, 2013). As a new professional, I remember being encouraged to pay considerable attention to helping campus members define terminology, encouraging learners to reconsider how they may have treated those different from themselves and, lastly, to take on the role of ally by providing a safe space for those of marginalized social identities to find refuge when faced with prejudice or discrimination. While there were some conversations about advocating for institutional changes to better foster inclusion and retention of marginalized social identity groups on campus, little attention was paid to systemic and historical power dynamics, and oppression was approached as a single-issue effort (Adams, 2013).

Frustrated with the limitations of a diversity framework, social justice education emerged during the early 2000s as a hot topic and desired practice within student affairs (Landreman & MacDonald-Dennis, 2013). With core principles in the analysis of systemic and relational power dynamics between social identity groups, work on campuses moved beyond awareness of difference and inclusion toward equity and changes to institutional structures, policies, and resources. Social justice education was often delegated to and driven by professionals who held specialized roles on campus focusing on race, gender, sexuality, nationality, religion/spirituality, and ability (Wong, 2016). Often, these professionals worked as one-person offices with high student needs, limited institutional support, and lack of guidance on how to make to make sustainable campus changes.

Student affairs social justice educators during this time relied on two strategies to survive and ultimately thrive through these initial institutional challenges. First, professionals created networks with peers doing similar work regionally and nationally for support. As the number of these professional roles and establishment of offices increased, ACPA College Student Educators International, one of the largest and longest running student affairs professional organizations, created an affinity group for these professionals titled the Commission for Social Justice Educators (K.E. Edwards, personal communication, March 27, 2017). Second, student affairs educators anchored their work on social justice education pedagogy and facilitation. As a means for advocating the significance of identity-based centers and social justice campus efforts, student affairs practitioners needed to develop workshops and trainings as strategic interventions. While many higher education graduate programs may include a diversity course, these practitioners often enter the field of student affairs with little to no skills in pedagogy and facilitation. The pivotal texts, *Teachings for Diversity and Social Justice* and *Readings for Diversity and Social Justice*, and their subsequent editions served as guides for how to develop social justice programs with attention to behavior change and strategies to de-escalate conflict and resistance (Adams, 2013; Landreman & MacDonald-Dennis, 2013).

During this time, I worked at New York University (NYU)'s Office of Lesbian, Gay, Bisexual and Transgender (LGBT) Student Services. Coming from my undergraduate experience as a student activist fighting for recognition, I remember how exciting it was to work in an office with a dedicated space, several staff members, and resources dedicated to the support of students across sexuality and gender identities. While I was in a privileged professional position, I also faced isolation and marginalization as one of the few Black queer women doing social justice work. I also struggled with the field's lack of attention to intersectionality within practices and observed students with multiple targeted social identities struggle to be their full selves on campus.

After several complicated years of passion, and yet frustration, working in student affairs, I realized I needed a stronger social justice pedagogical foundation to approach my work. In 2008, I left my position at NYU to begin the Social Justice Education doctoral program at the University of Massachusetts Amherst (UMass), the program where many of the editors of *Teaching for Diversity and Social Justice* and *Readings for Diversity and Social Justice* served as faculty. This program provided Black women educator role models and mentors as I learned critical pedagogy, historical constructions of oppression theory, and the relationship between social identity and college student development theory. While in this program I also began my leadership tenure with ACPA's Commission for Social Justice Educators first as a directorate body member and ultimately serving as Chair. This group served as my professional home where I created a community of colleagues that either shared my experience as a Black queer educator and/or understood the challenges of doing social justice work on college campuses.

During my time at UMass and as Commission Chair for ACPA, I had the opportunity to witness and participate in the evolution of social justice education nationally and its impact on student affairs practice. First, the election of Barack Obama as President of the United States in 2008 generated critical discourse on race across the country. Specifically, questions were raised on whether the United States was now, in fact, post-racial, and generally how much progress, if any, had the country in fact achieved in terms of social equity? As a then doctoral student who taught college courses and advised student groups, I found myself engaging with these questions regularly.

I remember my pedagogy focusing on defining microaggressions, challenging colorblind ideology, and trying to convince my students that the election of a Black president did not negate the existence of contemporary racism. My identity as a Black queer woman was consistently salient, and the labor of addressing racism (in addition to other systems of oppression) was deeply felt and taxing. Endless examples dominated the news cycle to demonstrate systematic oppression, such as racial violence, police brutality, and a resurgence of oppressive immigration laws. Critical of the popular ally as an identity approach to social change, I provided my students skills and knowledge to take direct and immediate social action within campus communities. While I had many successes in the classroom and started to see positive societal and campus shifts, nothing could have prepared me for the current U.S. sociopolitical climate.

In what some are describing as a conservative backlash, numerous events before and after the most recent U.S. presidential election have fostered an increasingly oppressive and hostile landscape. While systematic and cultural oppression are not new topics of discourse, what is noteworthy is the explicitness of how political leaders and the general public are in targeting marginalized communities. College campuses more than ever are racially divided, have increased student unrest, and are well-desired sites of White supremacist leaders to challenge free speech parameters. I also observe institutional leaders are struggling to respond to tensions and conflict among students, faculty, staff, and community and more than ever turn to social justice education as a solution.

As an assistant dean of students who focuses on diversity and inclusion, my daily work centers on navigating what feels like an uncharted territory of institutional and societal racism. The rapid pace of attacks on marginalized communities combined with discoveries that many of my past successful interventions have lost their impact sometimes leaves me feeling hopeless at times. This was particularly the case as I faced challenges implementing programs and dialogue efforts on my campus after multiple race-related protests. Retention challenges persist among faculty, staff, and student of color, resulting in Black women who continue to be underrepresented and undersupported in higher education. For those campus members that do persist, I now witness intragroup conflicts, particularly among students of color, where individuals are evaluated not only on how "woke" they are in terms of racial justice. For some students, they believe, counter to what Audre Lorde argues, there is in fact a hierarchy of oppression, and those who challenge their standpoint run the risk of public shaming and alienation from community (Bodenner, 2017).

Despite institutional commitments to anti-racism and claims of White allyship among colleagues, I am constantly navigating the archetypes so often ascribed to Black women: (1) viewed as difficult (or confrontational) if I am too outspoken or direct, (2) expected to serve as a caretaker for multiple campus constituencies, and (3) assumed to be self-sacrificing (or strong) where I forfeit my own needs for the greater good of the institution (Domingue, 2015; Harris-Perry, 2011). Recently, a new archetype has been often ascribed to me: racism problem solver. Primarily through my work as a consultant, I acquired the nickname Olivia Pope, a homage to the popular character on the television series *Scandal*. Like the character, I am often asked to fix the racism problem on campuses after major moments of conflict. While I do find this descriptor fitting and even humorous at times, the weight of these stereotypes combined with the complexity of oppression dynamics makes it difficult to stay committed to social change work in higher education.

While I'm weary, I'm not defeated. *Black Women in Social Justice Education: Lessons and Legacies* is an incredibly timely book that continues in the historical tradition of Black women as visionaries and groundbreaking educational leaders. This text serves as a contemporary kitchen table where authors have come together to find connection and nourishment as they share resistance strategies with the hopes of helping Black women educators and their accomplices better navigate oppression and move toward liberation. The authors provide insights and valuable contributions to the discourse of contemporary social justice education at a time when attempts to silence, dismiss, and co-opt Black womanhood are increasingly pervasive (Harris-Perry, 2011).

Jiggetts and Love explain the challenges we face in their chapter, "Black Women Rising: Jumping Double-Dutch with a Liberatory Consciousness," and Mwangi and Green operationalize our response to those challenges in Chapter 18, "Reflections on Moving Theory to Practice." Black women educators have learned to develop and maintain a liberatory consciousness, and then put it to work. We must center liberation and hope despite the challenges, not only for the greater benefit of the spaces we work in but also for our own self-preservation. Another important contribution is the discussion by both Alston and Taylor as they encourage Black women to approach leadership authentically by embracing multiple social identities and locations. While authentic leadership serves some Black women educators well, Lenzy's chapter highlights the challenges other may encounter due to some educational and activist spaces having a lack of intersectionality. Building on this insight, Howard's "The Reproduction of the Anti-Black Misogynist Apparatus in U.S. and Latin American Pop Culture" cautions readers not to hold onto monolithic assumptions about Black women's experiences and argues the necessity of more attention to their diverse social locations and offers transnationalist analyses on systemic oppression. Last, in the context of pedagogy and facilitation, Brown and Brooks remind educators of the importance of reflection and experimentation when engaging with our practice. We must be dynamic and adjust our approach and content to our audiences for optimal shifts in perspectives and social action.

These contributions offer key considerations for next steps in theory and practice for social justice education. While the challenges within the United States generally and educational institutions specifically will continue to surface, what is certain is that Black women educators have always and will continue to provide a pathway to liberation and strategies toward social change. In conclusion, I want to offer some reflections directed specifically to Black women educators reading this book. Inspired by the Crunk Feminist Collective, here is a love letter that I hope inspires a resiliency and sustainability when the labor of social justice education feels trying:

Dear Sis,

The world might feel heavy on your shoulders right now. Your to-do-list is long and as soon as your move through one challenge, several more surface. It's hard to separate the differences between feeling physically and emotionally tired. You are angry and frustrated. You might even feel like giving up. If no one has told you this, let me be the one to tell you that you are allowed to feel all these feelings. You aren't alone in these feelings. I see you and I can relate to your struggles.

You will survive this, in fact you will thrive. But before you do, take some time for yourself. Rest. Find a way on your own terms to rejuvenate before moving forward. Set boundaries. It's okay to say no. Ask for help. Especially from social justice allies. Take a step back in the work and let others step-up. Seek out support. Create a community of care for yourself.

Lastly, you were born from a collective history of Black women's struggle but remember you are their legacy of resiliency and hope.

Love,

Dre

## Dr. Evans, Heal Thyself: Healing History for Sustainable Struggle

I have found that history, particularly intellectual history, can be a source of healing. My motivation for initiating this project was similar to the reasons I have begun all of my writing projects: I am seeking answers from my Ancestors, elders, and colleagues on how best to survive as a Black woman in this world. The answers I have found along the way to publishing books and articles about Black women's life writing have been satisfying and helpful. These projects have also produced more questions about the nature, values, and strategies of Black women's survival. In the face of the social justice work that is imperative for our basic functionality in the world, freedom is daunting. Given what we have come up against, as Nannie Helen Burroughs indicated, "we specialize in the wholly impossible." Black women's inner peace seems illusive, but the more I read memoirs by Black women in history, the more I know that health and wellness are, in fact, possible.

*Black Women and Social Justice Education: Legacy and Lessons (BW & SJE)*, originated from a moment of clarity about the imperative to codify how we can best teach liberation. This collection is grounded in a long tradition of scholar-activists who seek to survive hostilities of the world and, at the same time, transform the world into a more sustaining and sustainable environment. In short, we are working to resist oppression, create our best selves, and contribute to a more habitable and humane world. And, though we sometimes struggle and often fail, this collection proves we remain committed to that goal.

In *Shining Tread of Hope: The History of Black Women in America*, Darlene Clark Hine summed up the overarching meaning of Black women's history by pointing out that, above all, we are survivors. Her concluding remarks in the two final chapters, "The Caged Bird Sings" and "A New Era for Black Women," marveled at Black women's ability to survive and confirmed our ability to teach values and survival skills useful for others in hostile environments to do the same (Hine, 1998). A survey of African American women's collective writing underscores Hines's point. Several foundational anthologies reiterate Black women's efficacy and the deftness with which we have survived personal, cultural, and structural violence. As Hine indicates, Black women's writing also warns against the conclusion that Black women are particularly "strong," a stance that dehumanizes Black women by not recognizing our vulnerability and the need not to be placed in situations that are disproportionately oppressive. Essentially, we have and can survive inequities, but we should not be required to. Hine anticipated important work on survival by both Alexis Pauline Gumbs and Bettina Love.

An investigation of African women's experiences in world history demonstrates this pattern of survival is global. Black women' traditions of survival are reflected in writings from early collections such as Toni Cade Bambara's *The Black Woman* and the seminal Black women's studies text *All the Women are White, All the Blacks are Men, But Some of Us are Brave* (1982) to Beverly Guy-Sheftall's expansive anthology of Black women's writing *Words of Fire*. Guy-Sheftall's introductory epigraph was actually an excerpt from Kesho Yvonne Scott's book, *The Habit of Surviving*. Scott's book title indicates the author's main point: Black women must survive, but we must also move beyond basic actions of minimal preservation toward liberation and, ultimately, joy.

Thus, Black women's task is not only to survive, but to survive well. Ours is the quest of sustainable struggle. This collection by Black women educators explores the terrain of those who have built their life's work on improving the quality of life for themselves and others. Dre's comments above echo the frustration of many in this book that the task is sometimes overwhelming in that we want to fulfill our purpose to work for social justice but want to do so in a way that does not require martyrdom. With all respect to the generations of ancestors and elders who sacrificed themselves for our opportunity to live, we are frantically trying to make a way for future generations that does not necessitate paving the path with our broken bodies and murdered spirits. This is a challenge because we must fight structural violence, but as the #MeToo campaign and the Center for Disease Control (CDC) statistics reveal, we have to fight for our lives in our households and communities at the same time that we fight larger social, political, and institutional racism, sexism, and classism. Wellness: This is Black women's work. As we fight for a better world, we cannot escape the unfortunate need to fight for our own basic existence. Elders are instructive and offer guidance through narratives of historical wellness.

Editors of the foundational book on Black women's studies, *But Some of Us are Brave*, coined the term "creative survival" as a description of the ways in which we sustain ourselves. In a section bearing this title, editors introduce four chapters that discuss the goal to "preserve mind, body, and spirit." The chapters cover topics of health, education, theology, and music. These themes frame, guide, and permeate the work I have done on Black women's intellectual history. Over the past 2 decades, my books and digital humanities projects have all engaged these topics:

- Health: *Black Women's Mental Health: Balancing Strength and Vulnerability* (2017).

- Education: *Black Women in the Ivory Tower, 1850–1954: An Intellectual History* (2007) and *Black Passports: Travel Memoirs as a Tool for Youth Empowerment* (2014).

- Spirituality: "BlackWomensSelfCare.net" (2017, website)

- Music: *Breathing Life into Myself: Five Traditions of Black Women's Self-Care* (Lever Press, 2019)

In addition to these books, *BW & SJE* is an extension of my first co-edited volume, *African Americans and Community Engagement in Higher Education (AACE): Community Service, Service-Learning, and Community-Based Research* (SUNY, 2010). Two of the *AACE* co-editors, Colette Taylor and Michelle Dunlap, also contributed chapters to *BW & SJE*, signaling the maintenance of connection of Black women educators reminiscent of past networks. We are not only surviving, we are surviving together.

So, what does sustainable struggle look like? As Layli Maparyan notes in *Womanist Idea*, first you change yourself, and then you change the world. To that end, we must acknowledge that sustainable struggle requires a vision of self-determination that is both individual and collective; one without the other is not sustainable.

To understand individual self-determination, we must look to Byllye Avery, the founding mother of the modern movement for Black women's health. Avery spearheaded the Black Women's Health Project in 1981 and hosted a conference at Spelman, which spawned local organizations in Atlanta (Center for Black Women's Wellness-CBWW) and national organizations (Black Women's Health Imperative-BWHI). The Black Women's Health Imperative has published several important works on health and wellness, particularly, *Health First! The Black Woman's Wellness Guide* (2012) and *IndexUS: What Healthy Black Women Can Teach Us about Health* (2016).

*Health First!* is a full-length book treatment of the top 10 health risks and means of self-care for each age group. Similarly, *IndexUs* reports comprehensive findings from an extensive survey of Boston University's 20-year data collection of almost 60,000 Black women. Of those surveyed, 38,706 self-reported good or excellent health, so while BWHI is fighting against health disparities, they are also focusing on healthy populations of Black women to find out how we get it right. Avery herself defines health as self-love, self-respect, and self-care; this is vital to understanding how we can survive without sacrificing quality or longevity of life. As founder and inaugural director of a center for social justice at Tier I Research University, Rhonda Williams's work exemplifies this imperative to understand the "long game" and treat justice work as a marathon, not a sprint. If we burn out in our work, we will lessen our potential impact. We also deserve to recognize our own humanity and show ourselves compassion.

Self-determination as a collective act mirrors individual processes: to survive, Black women collectively must love, respect, and care for one another. Traditions of collective sustainable struggle can easily be seen in activist writing groups, from the Combahee River Collective and *But Some of Us are Brave* editors to national professional organizations such as the Association of Black Women Historians (ABWH) and National Women's Studies Association (NWSA). Both ABWH and NWSA invited Keeanga-Yamata Taylor as keynote speakers to their 2017 events in Cincinnati, Ohio (ABWH), and Baltimore, Maryland (NWSA). Each organization was keenly aware of Keenga's work, *From #BlackLivesMatter to Black Liberation* (2016) and her work interviewing founders of the Combahee River Collective for the book *How We Get*

*Free* (2017). After speaking out against policies and practices of the 45th U.S. president, Taylor was viciously attacked and threatened. Her invited talks at AWBH and NWSA signaled a collective understanding of the need to appreciate, support, encourage, and intellectually care for someone at the forefront of our struggle. Yet, her work represents just one of a truly impressive collection of Black women in higher education committed to collective and collaborative liberation.

Liberatory networks are present in all levels of education and Black women caucuses in professions around the country. These are key sites of resistance, but also locales to reinforce the need—and right—of us to take the world off our shoulders and take time for our own joy and growth. Further, networks of Black women originate and extend far beyond educational institutions. In my own work, I have been involved with critical partnerships that include therapists in anti-sex-trafficking organizations such as youthSpark (Dr. Sharnell Myles) and activists at the forefront of the #MuteRKelly movement (Kenyette Tisha Barnes). Dr. Myles and I have worked together on several projects that involve mentoring girls who are survivors of several types of sexual violence. We co-edited a book of poems by survivors *Purple Sparks* (2016) as a fundraiser for youthSpark Voices programs. I met Kenyette, a professional lobbyist for social justice, through Sharnell, and when I coined the term #muterkelly in a social media post, Kenyette put boots on the ground and incorporated the hashtag into her long-term activism against sexual violence in the lives of Black girls and women. Ideas matter, but ideas without action are futile. Black women's social justice education has always been grounded in networks beyond formal educational institutions.

Black women's survival has always been, and will continue to be, a struggle. When we have the courage and audacity to love, respect, and care for ourselves as individuals and as a group, we embody Anna Julia Cooper's notions of regeneration—looking back for wisdom, looking inward for strength, and looking forward for hope. Black women's survival means we claim our right to grow. Black women's sustainable struggle means we cultivate regeneration of mind, body, and spirit in ourselves and others.

Sustainable struggle for human rights are the values Black women's social justice education imparts. Black women's intellectual history is filled with lessons on survival through love, respect, and care for life. With direction from Black women writers such as Toni Morrison, we examine, evaluate, posit, and reinforce the individual and collective struggle for the right to grow.

Our quest for social justice is grounded in claims of self-love, self-respect, and self-care. We state our desire for inner peace even as we demand human rights. The preface to this book clearly defines the need for awareness, analysis, action, and accountability in our quest for individual and collective struggle freedom. While struggle is necessary, suffering is not. So, we bring joy, creativity, health, and wellness to the struggle. As the regenerative and powerful Miriam Makeba sang about movements for social justice in Mozambique, Nigeria, and South Africa, *A Luta Continua*—the struggle continues.

## References

Adams, M. (2013). Conceptual frameworks: Introduction. In M. Adams, W. J. Blumenfeld, C. Castaneda, H. W. Hackman, M. L. Peters, & X. Zúñiga (Eds.), *Readings for diversity and social justice* (3rd ed.) (pp. 1–5). New York: Routledge

Bodenner, C. (2017, Nov. 2). The surprising revolt at the most liberal college in the country. *The Atlantic*. Retrieved from www.theatlantic.com/education/archive/2017/11/the-surprising-revolt-at-reed/544682

Domingue, A. D. (2015, Sept.). "We our leaders are just we ourself": Black women college student leaders' experiences with oppression and sources of nourishment at predominantly White college campus. *Equity & Excellence in Education*, 48(3), 454–472.

Harris-Perry, M. V. (2011). *Sister citizen: Shame, stereotypes and Black women in America*. New Haven, CT: Yale University Press

Hine, D. (1989). *A shining thread of hope: The history of Black women in America*. New York: Broadway Books.

Landreman, L. M., & MacDonald-Dennis, C. (2013). The evolution of social justice education and facilitation. In L. M. Landreman (Ed.), *The art of effective facilitation: Reflections from social justice educators* (pp. 231–252). Sterling, VA: Stylus.

Wong, K. (2016). Building capacity for inclusion by working across differences: An institutional and societal imperative. *Diversity & Democracy*, 19(2). Retrieved from www.aacu.org/diversitydemocracy/2016/spring/wonglau

# Contributors

## Editors

**Andrea D. Domingue** is a 14-year veteran in the field of Student Affairs and Social Justice Education. Dr. Domingue currently holds the position of Assistant Dean of Students for Diversity and Inclusion at Davidson College. Prior to this role, she taught and worked as consultant on leadership, social justice education, intergroup dialogue, and anti-racism initiatives in both academia and in the nonprofit world. Domingue is a recognized leader in higher education professional associations and currently serves on the Leadership Assembly as Coordinator for Commissions for ACPA International.

**Stephanie Y. Evans** is Professor and Chair of the Department of African American Studies, Africana Women's Studies, and History (AWH) at Clark Atlanta University. She has authored two books—*Black Passports: Travel Memoirs as a Tool for Youth Empowerment* and *Black Women in the Ivory Tower, 1850–1954: An Intellectual History*—and co-edited *Black Women's Mental Health: Balancing Strength and Vulnerability* and *African Americans and Community Engagement in Higher Education*. She earned a PhD in Afro-American Studies and a graduate certificate in Advanced Feminist Studies from the University of Massachusetts-Amherst.

**Tania D. Mitchell** is Associate Professor of Higher Education in the Department of Organizational Leadership, Policy, and Development at University of Minnesota's College of Education and Human Development. Her teaching and research focuses on service learning as a critical pedagogy to explore civic identity, social justice, student learning and development, race and racism, and community practice. She is the former Associate Director of Stanford University's Center for Comparative Studies in Race and Ethnicity, and has taught at Mills College, California State University-Monterey Bay, and University of Massachusetts-Amherst. She is editor of three volumes: *Civic Engagement and Community Service at Research Universities: Engaging Undergraduates for Social Justice, Social Change, and Responsible Citizenship*, *Cambridge Handbook of Service Learning and Community Engagement*, and *Educating for Citizenship and Social Justice: Practices for Community Engagement at Research Universities*.

## Authors

**Sarah Abdelaziz** is an adjust professor at Georgia State and Auburn Universities. They recently graduated with an MA in Women, Gender, and Sexuality studies from Georgia State University, and received a BA in Philosophy. Sarah has studied and written about the contestation of respectability politics and the ratchet in Atlanta through the lens of Freaknik and the Black Lives Matter movement. They are additionally interested in ecological change and its bearings on Black, Brown, and native feminisms. Sarah is an aspiring PhD candidate and a lifelong organizer who hopes to realize the role of "scholar activist."

**Judy A. Alston** is Professor in the Department of Doctoral Studies and Advanced Programs at Ashland University. She is author of *Multi-leadership in Urban Schools* and co-author of the textbook, *School Leadership and Administration: Important Concepts, Case Studies, & Simulations* and *Herstories: Leading with the Lessons of the Lives of Black Women Activists*. She earned her PhD from Penn State University. She holds two MEd degrees from the University of South Carolina and a MDiv from Methodist Theological School in Ohio.

**Penney Jade Beaubrun** is a Connecticut College graduate in Human Development and a selected scholar in the Toor Cummings Center for International Studies and the Liberal Arts (CISLA). She enrolled in a Fellowship at Merrimack College where she obtained a Master's Degree in Education with a concentration on Community Engagement. She served as the Holleran Center Assistant Director for Alumni Development and Publications for 3 years at Connecticut College. She currently is the Assistant Director for Alumni and Parent Relations at Wesleyan University where she works closely with the Professional and Affinity Networks.

**Robin Brooks** is Assistant Professor of Africana Studies at the University of Pittsburgh. Her research and teaching interests include 20th- and 21st-century literature, particularly African American, Caribbean, African, and American multiethnic literatures, as well as feminist theories and postcolonial studies.

She holds a PhD in English from the University of Florida, an MA in Afro American Studies from the University of Wisconsin-Madison, and a BA in English from Florida State University. Before joining her current institution, she was a Diversity Postdoctoral Fellow at the University of San Diego and a Provost's Postdoctoral Scholar at the University of South Florida.

**Keffrelyn D. Brown** is Associate Professor of Cultural Studies in Education in the Department of Curriculum and Instruction at University of Texas at Austin. She is also an Elizabeth Glenadine Gibb Teaching Fellow and faculty in the Department of African and African Diaspora Studies, the Warfield Center for African and African American Studies, and the Center for Women and Gender Studies. Her research and teaching focus includes sociocultural knowledge of race and critical multicultural teacher education. Keffrelyn has published extensively; her most recent book is *After the "At-Risk" Label: Reorienting Risk in Educational Policy and Practice* (Teachers College Press). In 2017 she received the Division K Mid-career Award from the American Education Research Association (AERA).

**Christina "Mobile" Burrell** earned a Master of Social Work degree from Boston College in addition to a Bachelor of Arts in Human Development & Psychology from Connecticut College. She is a highly skilled group facilitator in a number of topic areas, including Black and Brown families, LGBTQ+ folks, youth impacted by the foster care system, and individuals of all ages living with mental disabilities. Christina earned a Certificate in Community Leadership and Social Change from the Jonathan M. Tisch College of Civic Life at Tufts University through the Institute for Nonprofit Practice.

**Malika Carter** serves as CEO of Passion4Pivot, a social justice consulting firm. In addition to her roles in consulting, she has served in higher education as a Student Affairs professional and in municipal government as Chief Diversity Officer (CDO) for the City of Worcester, Massachusetts. Currently, she serves as CDO for SUNY College of Environmental Science and Forestry in Syracuse, New York. She earned her PhD in Institutional Analysis from North Dakota State University and an MEd in Higher Education from the University of Vermont.

**Michelle Dunlap** is Professor of Human Development at Connecticut College. She is author or co-editor of four books, including *African Americans and Community Engagement in Higher Education*. She has authored journal articles and book chapters on the topics of cultural competency and community engagement; service-learning and diversity; and racial identity and adolescent development. She has consulted for universities and other educational institutions, social service and community agencies, and corporations. She is completing a manuscript for her fifth book, with the working title, *Shopping While Black: Minority Experiences in Consumer Marketplaces*.

**Dominique Garrett-Scott** is currently pursuing a PhD in Sociology at the University of Texas at Austin. Her research, published in the *Ronald E. McNair Scholar Journal*, focuses on Black food servers, performance, and emotional labor. Her works illuminates the invisible uncompensated labor of Black workers in the food service industry, which leaves them at an economic disadvantage. In 2017, she received a BA in Sociology from the University of Mississippi. During her time at UM, she served in many capacities as a student organizer, including Mississippi Regional Organizer for United Students Against Sweatshops and president of Students Against Social Injustice.

**Shennette Garrett-Scott** is Assistant Professor of History and African American Studies at the University of Mississippi. She completed her PhD in American History at the University of Texas at Austin in 2011. Her research interests and writing focus on race, gender, and business from the late nineteenth to early twentieth century. Her book *Let Us Have A Bank: The St. Luke Bank, Race, and Gender in U.S. Finance, 1850s–1930s* is forthcoming from Columbia University Press in its History of Capitalism Series.

**Chrystal A. George Mwangi** is Assistant Professor of Higher Education in the Department of Educational Policy, Research, and Administration at the University of Massachusetts Amherst. Her scholarship centers on college access and success for minoritized populations as well as African and African Diaspora populations in higher education. She has published in journals including *Review of Higher Education, Teachers College Record*, and *Journal of Diversity in Higher Education*. Prior to her faculty appointment, Dr. George Mwangi worked as a college administrator. She received her PhD in Higher Education Administration at the University of Maryland, College Park.

**Keisha L. Green** is Assistant Professor of Department of Teacher Education and Curriculum Studies at University of Massachusetts-Amherst. Her scholarly interests are English Education, youth literacy practices, critical literacy, and critical pedagogy. She has published in journals including *Equity & Excellence in Education, Race, Ethnicity, and Education*, and *Educational Forum*. She has authored chapters in edited volumes including *Humanizing Research: Decolonizing Qualitative Inquiry with Youth and Communities* and *Youth Voices, Public Spaces, and Civic Engagement*. Prior to her faculty appointment, Dr. Green was a Presidential Postdoctoral Fellow at Rutgers University. She earned her PhD in Educational Studies from Emory University.

**Natasha Howard** earned a PhD in Educational Thought and Sociocultural Studies from the University of New Mexico. She holds an MA in Latin American Studies focusing on the Black experience in Latin America. Dr. Howard's research centers on unveiling the structure of anti-Black racism and the production of anti-Black racial discourses in the Americas. She is an interdisciplinary scholar drawing on ethnic studies, Black feminist thought, and sociology. Her graduate work explored the subtle (re)production of anti-Black ideology in critical discourses on race.

**Valerie Jiggetts** is a facilitator and social justice educator focused on racial healing and liberation for all people. Her BA in sociology from Spelman College and MEd in Social Justice Education from the University of Massachusetts-Amherst provide the foundation for her work and research on counteracting the multigenerational impacts of internalized racism on individuals and communities. She is an academic and career coach, and consultant with youth-serving institutions, public health, and educational organizations. She has worked with Public Allies and the Obama Foundation and is a W.K. Kellogg Racial Equity and Healing Fellow.

**Cherjanét D. Lenzy** is a PhD candidate in Higher Education and Student Affairs Leadership at the University of Northern Colorado. Her research interests include intersectionality of Black women, activism, and social justice advocacy in higher education. Prior to pursuing her PhD, she worked in Student Affairs for 10 years, mainly in the areas of diversity, social justice, and inclusion. Lenzy received her MEd in College Student Affairs Leadership from Grand Valley State University and a BA in Mass Communication from Wright State University.

**Jaymee Lewis-Flenaugh** is Resident Director at Miami University in Ohio. She is currently pursuing her doctorate in Student Affairs in Higher Education, researching social justice leadership within residential education organizations. Jaymee serves as a NASPA IV-East Knowledge Community Coordinator on the Region Executive Board, where she oversees the development and initiatives of 33 special interest/affinity groups. Additionally, Jaymee role-models the audacious leadership of young, African American practitioners within Student Affairs. She received her Master of Science in College Student Personnel from Western Illinois University and her BA in African/Black Diaspora Studies and English from DePaul University.

**Barbara J. Love** is Professor Emeritus of Social Justice Education at the University of Massachusetts-Amherst. Her research focuses on personal, organizational, and societal transformation and strategies for liberation. Her publications appear in journals, books, anthologies, and magazines. Her work on Developing a Liberatory Consciousness provides individuals and organizations with a framework for strategizing the transformation to socially just and equitable policies and practices. Dr. Love directs the Black Liberation and Community Development Project of the International Re-evaluation Counseling Communities.

**Bettina L. Love** is Associate Professor of Educational Theory and Practice at the University of Georgia. Her research focuses on urban youth negotiate Hip Hop music and culture to form social, cultural, and political identities to create new and sustaining ways of thinking about urban education and intersectional social justice. Her research also focuses on how teachers, schools, parents, and communities build communal, civically engaged, anti-racist, anti-homophobic, and anti-sexist educational, equitable classrooms. In 2016, Dr. Love was named the Nasir Jones Hiphop Fellow at the Hutchins Center for African and African American Research at Harvard University. She is the creator of the Hip Hop civics curriculum GET FREE.

**Layli Maparyan** is the Katherine Stone Kaufmann '67 Executive Director of the Wellesley Centers for Women and Professor of Africana Studies at Wellesley College. She is the author or editor of two books on womanism: *The Womanist Reader* (2006) and *The Womanist Idea* (2012), with a third, *Womanism Rising*, in production. A developmental psychologist by training, her interests range from identity to spirituality to social justice and earth justice and are informed by her Baha'i upbringing as well as her lifelong study of world religions, wisdom traditions, and metaphysical thought systems.

**Brenda L. H. Marina** is a retired higher education leadership educator. Dr. Marina has served as an associate dean at Baltimore City Community College, an associate professor at Georgia Southern University, and an assistant dean at the University of Akron. Dr. Marina has published book chapters related to identity development for female students of color, religiosity, and spirituality in leadership programs as well as on managing diversity in workplaces and society. She has published journal articles on cultural competence and the glass ceiling. Her most recent published books are *Beyond Retention: Cultivating Spaces of Equity, Justice, and Fairness for Women of Color in U.S. Higher Education* and *Mentoring Away the Glass Ceiling in Academe: A Cultured*

*Critique*. Her scholarship continues to explore women in leadership, mentoring for leadership, multicultural competence in higher education, and global education issues from a womanist perspective.

**Katie McCabe** is the co-author, with lawyer and minister Dovey Roundtree, of *Justice Older than the Law*, which received the 2009 Letitia Woods Brown Memorial Book Prize from the Association of Black Women Historians. Her National Magazine Award–winning *Washingtonian* article on black cardiac surgery pioneer Vivien Thomas, "Like Something the Lord Made," formed the basis for the 2004 Emmy and 2005 Peabody Award–winning HBO film *Something the Lord Made*. The American Film Institute called the film "a revelation . . . a bittersweet story that is an important tool for America as it continues to search for a public vocabulary to discuss issues of race."

**Maia Niguel Moore** is Assistant Professor in the Counseling program at Missouri State University. Dr. Moore is passionate about training multiculturally conscious counselors on how to use culturally relevant interventions with clients. She is also passionate about exploring issues related to race, power, privilege, and implicit bias in the classroom and in predominately Black, high-crime communities. She now serves on the Diversity and Human Rights committee for the Association for Specialists in Group Work. Additionally, Dr. Moore was recently invited into the Association of Multicultural Counseling and Development's Mentee Program as a new professional.

**Sharee L. Myricks** is Assistant Director of the Passport Office: Indiana University Purdue University Indianapolis & Ivy Tech Coordinated Programs. She completed her MEd at Texas A&M University within the Student Affairs Administration in Higher Education program. In addition to 7 years of regional and national involvement with the NASPA New Professionals and Graduate Student (NPGS) Knowledge Community, she was elected as the 2016–2018 national Co-Chair. In 2017, Sharee was recognized by NASPA IV East with the Indiana Outstanding Mid-Level Professional Award.

**Ashley Robertson Preston** is a curator and museum director for the Mary McLeod Bethune Foundation-National Historic Landmark at Bethune-Cookman University, where she is also an assistant professor. Dr. Preston graduated from Howard University in 2013 with a PhD in African Diaspora History. She also holds a BA in Business Administration from Bowie State University and an MA in African American Studies from Temple University. She is the author of three books, including *Mary McLeod Bethune in Florida: Bringing Social Justice to the Sunshine State*.

**Michele Smith** is Assistant Professor in the Counseling, Leadership, and Special Education Department and serves as the Assistant Vice President for Student Affairs at Missouri State University. Her research explores mentoring undergraduate and graduate students and new faculty with a focus on women faculty of color, women in leadership, and issues of race and gender in athletics. She currently teaches and advises students in the Student Affairs in Higher Education Master's program and uses her unique background and perspective to investigate historical and current issues in higher education and how these issues impact faculty and students.

**Colette M. Taylor** is Associate Professor of Educational Leaders in the Department of Leadership and Professional Studies Department at Seattle University's College of Education. She spent 14 years as higher education professional at various institutions prior to becoming a faculty member at Texas Tech University in 2008. She has co-edited *African Americans and Community Engagement in Higher Education* (SUNY, 2009). She earned her EdD in Educational Leadership, Policy, and Foundations from the University of Florida.

**Keeanga-Yamahtta Taylor** is Assistant Professor of African American Studies at Princeton University. Taylor is author of the award-winning *From #BlackLivesMatter to Black Liberation* (2016). She has also recently published *How We Get Free: Black Feminism and the Combahee River Collective*. Her forthcoming book is titled *Race for Profit: Black Housing and the Urban Crisis of the 1970s*. Taylor's writing looks at Black politics, Black social movements, and Black radicalism, in addition to public policy and racial inequality. Her writing has been published in the *New York Times, Los Angeles Times, Boston Review,* and *The Guardian*, among others.

**Eboni N. Turnbow** is Assistant Director of the Office for Student Engagement at University of Michigan-Dearborn. Currently, she is a sociology doctoral candidate studying gender and work in higher education at Wayne State University. She serves as the Women in Student Affairs (WISA) Knowledge Community Representative for the National Association of Student Personnel Administrators (NASPA) Region IV-E. In 2014, Eboni was recognized with the Outstanding New Professional Award by NASPA IV-E and the NACA C. Shaw Smith New Professional of the Year Award in 2016.

**Lydia Washington** is Director of Student Engagement and Leadership and Associate Director of Student Activities and Involvement at the University of Massachusetts-Amherst (UMass). She has served in several leadership roles with the National Association for Campus Activities (NACA), American

College Personnel Association (ACPA), and National Association of Student Personnel Administrators (NASPA). She earned her BA from the University of Florida and Masters of Education in Higher Education from the University of Massachusetts. She is currently working on her Educational Specialist Degree in Social Justice Education at UMass.

**Rhonda Y. Williams** is Professor and the inaugural John L. Seigenthaler Chair in American History at Vanderbilt University. A scholar-activist, she founded and served as the inaugural director of both the Social Justice Institute at Case Western Reserve University and the Postdoctoral Fellowship in African American Studies at CWRU. The author of *Concrete Demands: The Search for Black Power in the 20th Century* and *The Politics of Public Housing: Black Women's Struggles against Urban Inequality*, Dr. Williams also co-edits the *Justice, Power, and Politics* book series at University of North Carolina Press. She is a Baltimore native.

# Index

13$^{th}$ (Ava DuVernay documentary), 214, 216

Academe, 75, 76, 80-82, 88, 89, 246, 247, 249, 254, 256, 333, 358
   academia, 46, 57-59, 68, 76, 85, 92, 179, 184, 187, 198, 199, 205, 212, 245, 250-254, 256, 257, 353
   *See also* higher education; ivory tower
Activism, 5, 6, 9, 16, 17, 18, 40, 44, 116, 118, 123, 136, 139, 140, 184, 322, 323, 327, 330, 333, 339, 350, 357
   race-based, vii, 17, 261-274
   scholar-activism, 1, 18
   student activism, vi, 16, 141, 156-163
Addams, Maurianne, ix, 2, 76, 89, 193, 195
Advancement, 4, 5, 57, 59, 71, 107, 108, 168, 253
   career advancement, 55, 56, 61, 62, 204
Advocacy, 142, 203, 220, 227, 357
*African Americans and Community Engagement in Higher Education*, 20, 179, 216, 348, 353, 355, 360
African Methodist Episcopal (AME) Church, 121, 132, 147
   African Methodist Episcopal Zion (AMEZ) Church, 126
   Emanuel African Methodist Episcopal Church, 147
Ageism, v, 14, 55-66, 248, 253, 255, 347

*All the Women are White, All the Blacks Are Men, but Some of Us Are Brave: Black Women's Studies)*, ix, 256, 338, 348, 349
Ancestors (calling the), ix, 51, 183, 327, 329, 348
Anti-Black misogyny, 15, 91-92, 96, 99-100
   Moya Bailey 15, 100
   *See also* misogynoir, 15, 100
Anti-racism, 344, 353
Applied research (applied learning), 1, 4
Asian Americans, xii, 57, 89, 106, 186, 211, 223, 246, 248, 274, 298, 302
Association of Black Women Historians (ABWH), 319, 349, 359
Authenticity (authentic), vii, 2, 7, 8, 10-13, 16, 17, 68, 71, 72, 74, 94, 204, 208, 219-230, 283, 301, 312, 345
Autobiography *View under* memoir
Autoethnography, 248, 255
Audio, 186, 192

Baker, Ella, x, 5, 6, 37, 38, 40, 161, 330, 337
Bethune, Mary McLeod, vi, 4, 7, 8, 15, 105-119, 138, 330, 359
   *Aframerican Women's Journal*, 110
   Bethune-Cookman College, 106, 113, 359

Bethune, Mary McLeod *(continued)*
  as mentor to Dovey Johnson
    Roundtree, 127
  National Council of Negro Women
    (NCNW), 108–111, 117
  National Youth Administration
    (NYA), 114, 118
  United Negro College Fund, 114
Bisexual, 28, 203, 343
  *See also* sexuality
Black feminism, viii, 56, 63, 99, 100,
  160, 162, 319–325, 336, 360
Black feminist thought, vi, 15, 64, 74,
  75–89, 100, 101, 150, 160, 221,
  229, 255, 283, 286, 287, 357, 302
Black Girls Giving Circle (BWBGGC),
  213, 216
Black identity, 92, 267, 268, 269
  Black racial identity development, 207
Blackness, 46, 92, 101, 165, 166, 168,
  170, 172, 211, 265, 266, 267, 269
Black Lives Matter (#BlackLivesMatter),
  16, 38, 41, 161, 162, 168, 173, 178,
  189, 190, 196, 261, 263, 269, 273,
  274, 295, 320, 324, 325, 338, 349,
  354, 360
*Black Passports: Travel Memoirs as a
  Tool for Youth Empowerment*, 20,
  348, 353
Black Power 152, 161, 173, 179, 336,
  338, 361
  Black Power Movement, 143, 151,
    334
*Black Women in the Ivory Tower*, 1, 4,
  19, 20, 139, 140, 179, 348, 353
*Black Women's Mental Health*, 20, 348,
  253
Black women's studies, 13, 256, 338,
  347, 348
  Africana Women's Studies, 353
  National Women's Studies Association
    (NWSA), 349
  Women's studies, 11, 89, 229
Brown identity, 267

*Brown v. Board of Education*, 75, 128,
  130, 138, 140, 197
Burroughs, Nannie Helen, 1, 347

Cade (Bambara), Toni, 330, 334, 338,
  347
Capitalism, 173, 175, 323, 324, 325, 356
Care (ethic of), 35, 36
Career, xv, 12, 57, 60, 62, 65, 66, 95,
  106, 121, 132, 187, 219, 245, 246,
  248, 252, 253, 257, 278, 279, 285,
  293, 294, 295, 355, 357
  career advancement 55, 56, 59, 61
Challenges (Black women face), xii, 5,
  9, 16, 16, 49, 56, 58–60, 63, 76,
  79, 82–83, 85, 86, 89, 99, 132, 138,
  142, 144, 153, 179, 199, 202, 203,
  206, 210, 217, 220, 222, 223, 227,
  233–240, 247, 253, 264, 276, 283,
  284, 285, 289, 290, 292, 302, 312,
  329, 341, 341, 345
*Chicago Defender* 107, 111, 113, 114,
  117, 118, 119
Chief Diversity Officer, vii, 18, 305–316,
  355
Chisholm, Shirley, 37, 51, 330, 337
Civil rights, 3, 7, 10, 12, 37, 96, 101,
  128, 129, 136, 137, 162, 174, 330,
  337
  Civil Rights Act of 1964, 58
  Civil Rights Movement, 6, 9, 16, 96,
    127, 131, 132, 143, 151, 152, 155,
    160, 161, 183, 262, 263, 273, 274,
    321
Clark, Kenneth and Mamie (doll
  studies), 190, 197, 198, 213, 216
Clark, Septima Poinsette, 6, 7, 9, 330
Classroom activities, 185, 186–196, 237
Colorblind, 96, 202, 205, 207, 213, 217
  colorblind do-gooders, 202, 205, 206,
    207
  colorblind ideology, 16, 100, 207, 243
  colorblind racial ideology (racism),
    96

colorblindness, 81, 198, 202, 203, 206, 212, 216
Collaboration, ix, 4, 8, 121, 185, 202, 205, 209, 210, 212, 215, 234, 236, 238, 247, 292
Community-based research, 8, 179, 289, 348
Community service-learning, 6, 20, 179, 216, 348
Confederate flag, 16, 148, 154, 157, 161
Conflict, 24, 38, 57, 203, 204, 278, 279, 280, 282, 300, 341, 342, 344, 345
conflict resolution, 292
Coon, Allen, 149, 150, 154
Coppin, Fanny Jackson, 7, 8, 20, 37, 40, 124
Creative resistance, 7
Creative survival, 13, 348
Crenshaw, Kimberlé, 37, 40, 55, 56, 60, 64, 222, 225, 229, 248, 252, 255, 261, 262, 263, 264, 265, 272, 273, 336, 339
*See also* intersectionality
*Crooklyn*, 214, 216, 217
Collins, Patricia Hill, 14, 56, 64, 68, 69, 74, 83, 84, 85, 87, 88, 92, 94, 99, 101, 142, 143, 150, 160, 221, 222, 225, 229, 247, 248, 255, 283, 287, 302
*See also* care (ethic of), controlling images
Cooper, Anna Julia, 1, 3, 4, 5, 7, 8, 19, 37, 41, 122, 123, 136, 137, 138, 139, 330, 350
Cooper, Brittany, 337
Consciousness-raising, 5, 273
Controlling images, 86, 94
*See also* Patricia Hill Collins
Critical epistemology 1, 4
Crump, Ray, 15, 133, 134, 138
Culture, vii, 15, 17, 20, 26, 30, 44, 56, 60, 63, 71, 135, 140, 161, 172, 180, 183, 187, 188, 192, 199, 206, 208, 210, 217, 223, 230, 231, 237–244, 247, 248, 249, 252, 257, 267, 256, 269, 277, 286, 288, 294, 296, 299, 300, 301, 302, 310, 315, 316, 331, 358
Black culture, 82, 105, 173, 176, 177, 179, 224, 269
cultural capital, 242, 248, 249
cultural standpoint (cultural identity), 1, 286
dominant culture, 29, 69
organizational culture (institutional), 57, 59, 61, 226, 250, 253
pop culture (popular), vi, 79, 82, 91, 97–100, 217, 238, 345
youth culture, 289, 298
Curriculum, 2, 40, 41, 53, 122, 152, 179, 184, 211, 216, 217, 231, 235, 242, 255, 273, 274, 277, 293–289, 286, 293–301, 339, 355, 357, 358
Czarnecki, Kazimierz, xvii

Davis, Angela, 8, 9, 10, 12, 16, 91, 92, 101, 136, 221, 222, 330, 338
Decolonizing, xiv, 302, 356
Democracy (democratic), 1, 2, 5, 6, 12, 13, 16, 20, 23, 24, 25, 32, 37, 38, 39, 41, 98, 100, 101, 107, 109, 111, 137, 143, 144, 149, 160, 161, 166, 192, 221, 222, 243, 251, 295, 299, 351
Democratic Party, 320, 321
democratic praxis, 5, 6
Depersonalization, 84, 204
Discrimination, 28, 29, 36, 47, 55, 59, 60, 64, 65, 70, 78, 79, 82, 84, 98, 116, 144, 183, 186, 188, 207, 214, 215, 217, 222, 229, 264, 295, 309, 311, 322, 342
Diversity (diversities), 2, 3, 5, 14, 24, 39, 40, 41, 48, 65, 75, 78, 79, 87, 152, 156, 202, 203, 204, 205, 206, 212, 216, 220, 228, 229, 232, 243, 244, 257, 294, 339, 341, 342, 355, 356, 357, 358, 359

Diversity (diversities) *(continued)*
  diversity courses, 206, 342
  *See also* Chief Diversity Officer;
  inclusion, *Teaching for Diversity and Social Justice*
"Dixie" (song), 147, 154, 155, 160, 161
Documentaries, 93, 94, 95, 96, 101, 198, 213, 216, 217, 337
Do-gooders, vii, 16, 201–209
  good intentions, 81
  the well-intentioned, 203, 207, 209, 252
Dominance, 26, 27, 29, 30, 34, 35, 222
Double Dutch xi, xiii, xix, 1, 12, 14, 285, 286, 287, 288, 302, 341, 345
Double jeopardy, xi, 11, 60, 336
Du Bois, W. E. B., 3, 4, 19, 64, 72, 74, 118, 145, 273

Economic privilege, *View under* privilege
Echo (echoes), 327–331, 333–336, 348
  *Echo in My Soul*, 9
Educational access, 2, 4
Educational memoir, 7
Educational philosophy, 1, 4, 7, 13
Effectiveness, 226, 280, 309, 313, 321
Efficacy, 61, 251, 347
Elders, 18, 177, 346, 348
Empathy, 33, 34, 35, 36, 40, 220, 242, 275, 276, 277, 279, 280, 281, 282, 283, 284, 327, 328, 331, 332, 339
Empowerment *View under* power
Enactment, 71
Endarkened feminist epistemology 285, 286, 287, 302
Engagement, 5, 37, 64, 150, 179, 202, 206, 209, 212, 262, 272, 276, 281, 286, 287, 290, 313, 254
  civic engagement, 216, 354, 356
  community engagement, xi, 6, 20, 179, 203, 209, 210, 211, 214, 216, 289, 248, 353, 354, 355, 360
  dialectical engagement, 7, 18, 285
  student engagement, 235, 360

English education, 293, 356
English language arts (ELA), 286, 294, 295
Equity (equitable) xiii, xiv, xv, 3, 5, 39
Escalation model, 148
Ethnicity, 1, 5, 26, 55, 59, 65, 101, 147, 160, 199, 219, 222, 229, 230, 242, 246, 269, 315, 353
  *See also* race
Exploitation, 3, 31, 146, 322, 324, 329, 336
  *See also* inequality

Faculty, xiii, xv, 7, 9, 15, 18, 47, 58, 64, 65, 73, 75, 76–83, 87–89, 141, 142, 145, 148, 149, 151, 155, 159, 161, 205, 207, 210, 222, 223, 224, 233, 238, 240, 241, 243, 246, 247, 248, 250, 251, 256, 257, 279, 284, 285, 292, 293, 343, 344, 355, 356, 360
Federal Bureau of Investigation (FBI), 107, 154
Feminism (Feminists), xix, xx, 15, 37, 40, 41, 51, 55, 84, 85, 87, 88, 92, 178, 179, 247, 255, 256, 262, 265, 273, 274, 323, 324, 353, 354
  Crunk Feminist Collective, ix, 100, 346
  feminist epistemology, 142
  *See also* Black Feminist Thought; radical black feminism
Freedom, 9, 13, 15, 43, 47, 49, 74, 107, 112, 128, 135, 136, 137, 143, 162, 176, 179, 217, 227, 229, 321, 322, 323, 324, 327, 335–338, 347, 351
  Black freedom movement, 20, 41, 161, 337
  freedom riders, 129, 131, 134, 269
Freire (Paolo) xiii, xx, 9, 179, 185, 196, 198, 285, 290, 300, 302, 339, 340
  Pedagogy of the Oppressed xix, 9

Gay, 28, 203, 337, 343
  *See also* sexuality

Gender, xvii, 1, 3, 4, 5, 7, 9, 13, 19, 26, 30, 32, 33, 35, 37, 41, 52, 55–66, 69, 75, 76, 78, 83, 84, 88, 89, 91, 117, 122–124, 138, 139, 140, 147, 151, 159, 165, 173, 186, 198, 199, 203, 205, 207, 217, 219, 220, 223–225, 229, 234, 235, 236, 238, 242, 244, 246–248, 250, 252, 255, 256, 262, 269–274, 284, 286, 287, 291, 296, 297, 306, 311, 313, 322, 324, 335, 336, 338, 342, 354, 360
   Cisgender, 222
   gender privilege, 188, 222
   gender roles, 193, 263
   gender studies, 355
   *See also* transgender
Glass ceiling, 55, 56, 63, 66, 245, 246, 248, 249, 250, 251, 252, 254, 256, 257, 358
Gratuitous humiliation, 15, 96, 97, 99, 100
Guy-Sheftall, Beverly, 13, 14, 51, 247, 255, 336, 338, 347
   *Words of Fire*, 13, 65, 336, 347

Hair (politics of Black women's), 77, 87, 93–98, 166, 167, 174, 175, 184
Hamer, Fannie Lou, 37, 137, 330, 338
Harper, Frances E. W., 1
Healing, 3, 4, 46, 49, 105, 122, 123, 136, 276, 339
   healing history, viii, 135, 341, 346, 357
   *See also* mental health
Height, Dorothy, x, 37
High school, vii, 5, 18, 150, 188, 213, 238, 285–303
Higher education, 1, 2, 4, 5, 6, 7, 8, 9, 10, 14, 219, 245 higher education, vi, vii, xii, 5, 219, 245
   HBCUs (Historically Black Colleges and Universities), 114, 153
   PWIs (Predominantly White Institutions), 75, 153, 183, 188, 276, 279, 283
   *See also* academe

hooks, bell, xiii, xix, xx, 71, 74, 84, 85, 88, 92, 99, 101, 123, 124, 139, 165, 167, 175, 179, 188, 197, 198, 221, 222, 229, 262, 274, 287, 302, 335, 339, 340
Howard University, 359
   Houston, Charles Hamilton, 128
   School of Divinity, 132
   School of Law, 125, 128, 132
Human Rights, 3, 7, 41, 124, 135, 136, 137, 183, 186, 188, 194, 196, 198, 220, 330, 350, 359
   United Nations Declaration of Human Rights), 2, 19, 137

Identity (identities, identity formation), v, vi, xiv, 2, 5, 6, 10, 14, 17, 30, 31, 33, 42, 44, 58, 59, 86, 105, 122, 123, 127, 158, 174, 198, 203, 220, 221, 224, 225, 240, 246, 249, 261, 262, 270, 272, 279, 280, 283, 286, 287, 292, 294, 295, 301, 302, 312, 313, 315, 322, 358
   cultural identity, 4, 208, 223, 247
   identity development 16, 254, 256, 265–267, 276
   identity politics/politics of identity, 32, 67–74, 92, 101, 322, 323
   racial identity 18, 55, 62, 66, 136, 204, 297, 355
   racial identity development, 202, 204, 207–212, 216, 217
   self-identity, 251, 281
   social identity, 27, 184, 186, 222, 310, 342, 343, 344, 353
   *See also* intersectionality
Inclusion, xi, xii, xiii, 3, 6, 15, 93, 105–110, 117, 148, 157, 159, 217, 306, 307, 308, 310, 313, 314, 342, 351, 353, 357
   *See also* diversity
Inequality, 4, 24, 25–27, 30, 36, 39, 63, 65, 88, 116, 121, 145, 147, 150, 190, 222, 241, 248, 295, 320, 324, 325, 327, 332, 335, 337, 361

Inequality *(continued)*
   exploitation, 3, 31, 146, 322, 324, 329, 336
   gender inequality, 60, 66, 235
   injustice, 1, 4, 6, 7, 25, 26, 29–33, 36, 38, 44, 45, 47, 49, 50, 122, 142, 146, 156, 157, 170, 183, 185, 195, 197, 203, 212, 226, 296, 323, 324, 327, 333, 356
   racial inequality, 58, 101, 179, 197, 360
   racial oppression, 1, 61, 89, 92
Influence, 24, 44, 45, 49, 50, 66, 68, 78, 123, 127, 132, 145, 165, 169, 184, 224, 225, 246, 247, 264, 267, 269, 270, 288, 289, 294, 296, 307, 308, 310, 313–314, 324
   sociocultural influence, 233, 234, 241
Imperialism, 31, 194
Imposter syndrome, 79, 283
Intellectual history, 1, 4, 7, 8, 19, 40, 122, 124, 137, 140, 346, 348, 350, 353
Internalized racism, xvii, xviii, 64, 357
Interlocking systems, 84, 262
   *See also* inequality
Internet, 96, 149, 186, 192
Intersectionality, 16, 18, 37, 56, 63, 64, 221–225, 229, 248, 249, 255, 262, 264, 268, 273, 274, 336, 343, 345, 357
   intersectional identities, 263, 269
   "Mapping the Margins: Intersectionality, Identity Politics and Violence against Women of Color" Kimberlé Crenshaw, 40, 229, 255, 273, 336
   *See also* Crenshaw, Kimberlé
Interstate Commerce Act (Interstate Commerce Commission), 130, 138
Ivory tower, 1, 4, 19, 20, 76, 86, 139, 140, 179, 282, 348, 353
   *See also* academe; higher education
Invisibility Syndrome, 68, 74

Jackson, Mary, xvii, xix, xx
James, Joy, 9
Jim Crow, 96, 107, 116, 121, 127, 129, 130, 138, 139, 142, 160, 198, 338
   *See also* segregation, *Plessy v. Ferguson*
Jordan, Barbara, x, 37
Joy, 71, 166, 171, 285, 327, 332, 334, 347, 348, 350, 351
Justice League NYC, 149
*Justice Older than the Law*, 108, 118, 125, 126, 135, 137, 138, 140, 359

Kennedy, Florence, 330, 337
Kennedy, John F., 133
Kennedy, Robert F., 130, 131, 138
King, Rev. Martin Luther King, Jr., 125, 142, 161, 183
   Martin Luther King Jr. Complex, 152
Ku Klux Klan, 16, 127, 141, 149, 154

Lacks, Henrietta, 4
Latinx, 286, 294, 295, 298, 299, 301
   Latin American Black women (Afro-Latinas, *see also* Latinx), 99
   Puerto Rican youth, 297, 298, 300
Leadership, vi, x, xx, 5, 16, 18, 57, 59, 64, 67–73, 78, 110, 112, 117, 220–229, 251–255, 257, 262, 263, 268, 270, 274, 275, 277–283, 290, 292, 302, 305, 306, 309, 310, 314, 316, 338, 343, 345, 353, 354, 355, 358, 359, 360
   change agent, 69, 236
   masters' tools, 37, 67, 70, 71
   social justice leadership, 220, 221, 226, 339, 357
   soul work, 71, 72, 73, 74
   tempered radical, 69, 74
   Ubuntu, 48, 73
League of the South, 141, 149, 154
Learning, 5, 7, 16, 18, 20, 67, 147, 150, 184, 185, 186, 193, 195, 202, 206, 209, 213, 230, 232–239, 241, 243, 254, 255, 257, 274, 277, 279, 288,

289, 290, 292, 296, 299, 302, 303, 335, 340
applied learning, 4
higher learning, 70, 106
*See also* Community service-learning
Lesson planning (plans), 184, 186, 289, 295, 296, 297, 297
LGBTQ, 28, 355
*See also* sexuality
Liberation, xiii, xvi, xix, 18, 37, 40, 44, 49, 112, 117, 122, 149, 150, 173, 178, 179, 262, 273, 274, 302, 321, 323–325, 327, 329, 330, 337, 340, 341, 345, 346, 347, 349, 350, 357, 358, 360
liberation work, xvii, xviii, 115
Liberatory consciousness, v, xi, xiii, xiv, xv, xvi, xvii, xix, 14, 18, 114, 115, 116, 118, 122, 185, 186, 199, 345, 358
accountability xii, xiii, xvi, xvii, xviii, xix, 4, 14, 17, 52, 81, 300, 309, 350
action xiii, xvi, 5, 14, 17, 24, 25, 29, 30, 32, 40, 60–63, 83, 85, 87, 116, 122, 126, 131, 143, 147, 148, 186, 196, 203, 205, 232, 254, 273, 309, 322, 323, 327, 331, 335, 344, 345, 347, 350
allyship xiii, xvi, xvii, 14, 344
analysis xiii, xv, xvi, xviii, xix, 14, 17, 56, 65, 69, 84, 85, 123, 138, 139, 140, 160, 166, 185, 187, 193, 207, 222, 229, 236, 243, 248, 256, 283, 288, 308, 322, 331, 342, 350, 355
awareness xiii, xiv, xvi, xix, 5, 14, 17, 34, 37, 60, 115, 122, 124, 147, 184, 186, 208, 226, 227, 234, 239, 266, 288, 327, 331, 342, 350
Lorde, Audre, x, 37, 41, 51, 63, 65, 67, 74, 83, 84, 85, 89, 92, 101, 189, 222, 327, 335, 344
Lost Cause, 142, 159
Love, 2, 44, 45, 46, 49, 51, 52, 53, 66, 73, 96, 111, 125, 134, 136, 166, 167, 174–177, 179, 201, 209, 211, 217, 265, 266, 277, 280, 283, 306, 327, 333, 334, 335, 339, 346, 349, 350
Love, Barbara, v, xi–xx, 14, 17, 114, 122, 185, 358
*See also* Double Dutch; liberatory consciousness
Luxocracy, v, 14, 43–53

Macro-aggression, 202
Male privilege 89, 219, 222
Marginalization, 14, 31, 37, 55, 75, 220, 246, 247, 263, 343
Marino, Tysianna, 149, 151
Marshall, Thurgood, 128, 130
See also *Brown v. Board of Education*
Media, 16, 82, 99, 108, 118, 141, 149–152, 186–187, 190, 195, 207, 261, 263, 336, 339
multimedia, 212–215, 234, 237, 238
social media, 143, 149, 151, 154, 168, 183, 186, 191–192, 350
Memoir, 3, 7, 10–12, 20, 108, 121–124, 135–137, 162, 168, 244, 294, 337, 347, 348, 353
autobiography, 9, 10, 20, 91, 101, 123, 135, 139, 140, 236, 338
Mental health, 20, 61, 284, 348, 353
*See also* healing
Mentoring (mentorship), vii, ix, 16, 17, 76, 82, 121, 122, 245–257, 282, 303, 350, 358, 359, 360
formal mentoring, 246, 250–252
informal mentoring, 249, 250–252
peer mentoring, 247, 249, 250, 251, 257
Meyer, Mary Pinchot, 133–134, 139
Microaggression (micro-aggressive), 58, 61, 62, 169, 201, 217, 233, 343
Miller, David, 31, 32
Mindfulness, 17, 18, 62, 100, 227, 228, 230
Minorities, 55, 75, 136, 188, 199, 201–208, 212, 214, 216, 306, 310

Miseducation, 2
Misogynoir, *View under* Anti-Black misogyny
Moral existentialism 1, 4
Morrison, Toni, 100, 101, 137, 221, 251, 252, 256, 274
　teaching values in higher education (examine, evaluate, posit, reinforce), 13, 14, 142, 161, 247, 253, 256, 272, 350
Multicultural, 177, 210, 211, 213, 214, 215, 216, 217, 240, 294, 309, 344, 355, 359
　multicultural education, 41, 212, 231, 232, 238, 242, 243, 244
　multiculturalism, 41, 42, 230
Multiple identities, 58, 223, 227, 239, 261, 265, 268, 271, 272, 286
　*See also* intersectionality
Municipality leaders (city), vii, 18, 305–319
Murray, Pauli, 123, 128, 136, 139, 330, 337
#MuteRKelly, 350

NAACP (National Association for the Advancement of Colored People), 8, 127–131, 146–153, 156, 160, 162
　NAACP Legal Defense Fund, 128, 130
NASA, xvii, xix, xx
Native Americans, xii, 186, 188, 189, 194, 248, 249
Neutrality, 34, 35, 36, 106, 276
Newsome, Brittany "Bree," 149
Nielson, Ashley, 12
Noddings, Nel, 33, 35, 36, 41, 42
N-word, 206, 239

Okin, Susan Moller, 26, 29, 34, 35
Okoye, Chukwuebuka, 149, 150, 151
Oppression, xvii, xviii, xix, xix, 3, 4, 5, 7, 15, 17, 18, 29–32, 37–40, 47, 55–56, 58, 60, 63, 71, 77, 78, 82–85, 87, 89, 91, 99, 100, 115, 116, 121, 122, 135, 155, 156, 166, 178, 179, 186, 191, 193, 194, 196, 203, 207, 221, 224, 245, 262, 272, 278, 279, 287, 322, 335, 342, 344, 347, 351
　cultural imperialism, 31
　exploitation, 3, 31, 146, 322, 324, 329, 336
　five faces of oppression, 31
　gender oppression, 1, 83, 89, 225, 270
　interlocking oppressions, 1, 89, 329, 336, 338
　marginalization, 14, 31, 37, 55, 75, 220, 221, 246, 247, 263, 343
　powerlessness, xvi, 31
　systemic/systems of oppression, 295, 298, 323, 343, 345
　*See also* inequality; violence
Organizational mentoring relationships, 246
Outsider-within, 14, 56, 69, 74, 224, 255
　marginality, 69, 222

Parks, Rosa, 131, 162, 330, 337
Parrhesia, 72
Passion4Pivot, 305, 315, 355
Patriarchy, xix, 71, 92, 96, 188, 269, 270, 271
Participatory action research, 296, 302
　Youth participatory action research, 285, 286, 295, 298, 301
Peace, 3, 43, 46, 47, 49, 51, 53, 86, 122, 133, 136, 193, 217, 227, 334
　inner peace, 8, 137, 138, 347, 348, 350
　peace studies, 1, 136
　peaceful protest, 143
Pedagogy, vi, ix, 6, 16, 52, 152, 179, 239, 240, 243, 296, 301, 303, 342, 345
　critical pedagogy, x, 88, 238, 242, 295, 340, 343, 353, 356
　feminist pedagogy, 51

*Pedagogy of the Oppressed*, 9, 302
social justice pedagogy, 40, 41, 273
transformative pedagogy, 16, 183–199
See also teaching
Pictures, 115, 145, 149, 150, 151, 186, 189, 190, 192–194, 217
*Pittsburgh Courier*, 107, 119
People of the Global Majority (PGM), xii
People of Color (POC), xii, 77, 78, 81, 82, 125, 150, 168, 169–173, 181, 189, 191, 208, 217, 224, 239, 298, 306, 313, 320
Personal experience, 7, 56, 221, 227, 275, 322
*Plessy v. Ferguson* 15, 128, 194
See also Jim Crow; segregation
Politics, xix, xx, 6, 31, 37, 41, 42, 44, 45, 64, 88, 89, 91, 93, 95, 96, 100, 123, 136, 140, 160, 163, 172, 179, 197, 198, 203, 223, 224, 225, 230, 249, 274, 283, 302, 321, 323, 324, 327, 337, 339, 360, 361
Conservative, 2, 12, 73, 203, 344
identity politics, 32, 40, 92, 229, 255, 273, 322, 336
liberal, 1, 81, 202, 203, 204, 216, 333, 351
neoliberal, 175
political cartoons, 194
politics of deconstruction, 91, 92
politics of empowerment, 255
politics of identity vi, 67–74, 101
politics of respectability, 153, 161, 162, 325, 354
progressive, 1, 2, 3, 52, 62, 122, 142, 209, 214, 337, 339
radical, viii, 1, 7, 9, 12, 20, 40, 41, 48, 69, 74, 92, 118, 139, 140, 143, 146, 153, 161, 168, 171, 173, 179, 196, 198, 319–325, 337, 260
Popular culture View *under* culture
Porter, Dorothy, 109
Positionality, 16, 70, 184, 232, 234, 287, 288, 292, 301, 307, 316

Power, x, xii, 3, 6, 11, 15, 18, 26, 27, 38, 44, 45, 49, 51–53, 58, 68, 69, 72, 84, 85–87, 92, 99, 100, 101, 106, 124, 138, 140, 142, 145, 156, 167, 168, 169, 172, 174, 179, 189, 213, 216, 217, 225, 235, 240, 264, 312–316, 321, 324, 330–333
empowerment, 1, 5, 8, 20, 64, 74, 87, 88, 101, 105, 137, 139, 140, 160, 173, 209, 226, 228, 255, 275, 283, 348, 353, 227, 230, 278–279, 291, 295, 302, 339, 359
power dynamics, 60, 77, 86, 246, 264, 342
power relations, 173, 205, 223, 239, 287
powerlessness, xvi, 31
See also Black Power
Predominantly White institutions (PWIs), 70, 75, 153, 183, 188, 276, 279, 283, 301
See also Historically Black colleges and institutions
*Presumed Incompetent*, ix, 179, 184, 187, 198, 199
Professional development, 59, 61, 62, 63, 79, 86, 234, 247, 253, 290, 308
Privilege 3, 14, 16, 27, 34, 56, 75, 76, 78, 84, 85, 92, 165, 186, 188, 199, 204, 208, 216, 223, 232, 241, 270, 278, 315, 339, 343, 359
economic privilege, 5, 219, 222
male privilege, 89, 219, 222
white privilege, 77, 78, 81, 82, 85, 86, 87, 88, 89, 190, 198, 202, 206, 207, 210, 211, 212, 217, 255, 298
Praxis, ix, 3, 6, 23, 37, 38, 46, 147, 150, 229, 233, 240, 335
Black women's praxis, v, 23–42
democratic praxis, 5, 6
theory to praxis, vii, 18, 285–303
Puerto Rican youth/students, 18, 285, 287, 291, 297, 298, 300

Puerto Rican youth/students *(continued)*
  Puerto Rican history, literature, and culture, 294–296, 301, 319
  *See also* Latinx

Queer, 6, 20, 28, 38, 165, 168, 173, 178, 163, 263, 325, 343
  *See also* sexuality

Race, vii, 1, 2, 5, 6, 7, 8, 9, 10, 11, 19, 26, 30, 42, 76, 78, 79, 106, 109, 114, 117, 119, 123, 125, 133, 135, 147, 156, 162, 170, 175, 179, 186, 188, 190, 192, 196–199, 201–217, 220, 247, 248, 256, 295, 298, 311, 319, 336, 337, 343, 344, 353, 355, 356, 357, 359, 360
  critical race theory/studies, 89, 148, 160, 180, 239, 231–244
  human race, 43, 52, 81
  mixed race, 98
  race, class, and gender, xvii, 30, 32, 33, 37, 41, 55, 62–65, 69, 75, 83, 84, 88, 91, 92, 139, 140, 222, 223, 229, 286, 287, 322, 325, 338, 342
  race, gender, and justice, 7, 9, 122, 124, 202, 204, 207
  *Race: The Power of an Illusion*, 216, 217
  racial history, 201
  racial identity/development, 18, 55, 62, 66, 136, 202–217, 297, 355
  *Women, Race, and Class*, 101
  *See also* racism
Race-based activism, vii, 17, 261–274
Racism (racist), xii, xiii, xvii, xviii
  *See also* internalized racism; subtle racism
Radical Black feminism, viii, 319–327
Rawls, John, 26, 27, 30, 33, 39, 41
  difference principle, 27, 30
  justice as fairness, 33
  original position, 33, 34, 35
  veil of ignorance, 33, 34

*Readings for Diversity and Social Justice*, 19, 115, 118, 199, 245, 255, 342, 343, 351
Reciprocity, 68–70, 74, 288
  golden rule, 69–70
Reflexivity, 232, 288
Reframing, 210–211
Regeneration 3, 19, 123, 136, 139, 250
  social regeneration, 3, 4, 19, 122, 137
  regenerative education, 12, 20
  regenerative medicine, 4, 19
  regenerative power, vi, 15, 121, 138, 351
  regenerative writing, 4, 12
Representation, xii, 9, 30, 31, 79, 98, 99, 101, 109, 117, 122, 124, 136, 157, 158, 223, 234, 302
  and race in film/music, 94, 96, 99
  underrepresentation, 75
Resources, ix, x, xvi, 3, 4, 15, 77, 113, 114, 116, 117, 118, 137, 154, 184, 186, 202, 207, 209, 210, 254, 290, 291, 293, 309, 312, 314, 342
  human resources, 310, 311
  interpersonal resources, 210–216
  (re)distribution of material resources, 16, 23, 25–28, 30, 31, 33, 39, 40, 45, 58, 121, 112
  resources for classroom teaching, 186–195
Respect, 14, 24, 29, 30, 32, 34, 35, 36, 40, 44, 48, 50, 62, 71, 84, 86, 160, 161, 177, 203, 205, 220, 278, 330, 348, 349, 350
  disrespect, 143, 145, 319
  respectability *View under* politics
Responsibility, xvii, 4, 14, 23, 26, 27, 29, 30, 39, 49, 50, 70, 72–73, 82, 96, 100, 157, 175, 226, 232, 233, 250, 150, 270, 281, 287, 293, 310, 315
Rice, Condoleezza, 11, 12
Roundtree, Dovey Johnson, vi, 15, 108–109, 117, 118, 121–140, 359
  in AME Church ministry, 127, 132
  and anti-violence, 136

at Howard University School of Law, 125, 128, 132
and human rights, 124, 135–138
legal career, 124, 125, 128–138
mentorship by Mary McLeod Bethune, 108–109, 127, 138
military service, 127–130, 135, 138
and racism, 127
and religious faith, 125, 127
at Spelman College, 127
*See also* Women's Army Corps; Mary McLeod Bethune

Sanchez, Sonia, 334, 336, 339
#SayHerName, 196, 261, 263
Scholar-activism, 1, 18
Scholarly Personal Narrative (SPN), vii, 18, 305–316
Scott, Dominique, 142, 144–147
Self-
  self-awareness, 184, 226, 266
  self-care, 7, 43, 62, 72, 196, 327, 328, 332, 335, 349, 350
  self-love, 167, 175, 283, 349, 350
  self-respect, 26, 27, 28, 30, 87
Sexism, v, x, xii, xiii, xiv, 55, 56, 59–63, 66, 186, 192, 193, 221, 223, 242, 262–265, 271–272, 295, 315, 322, 324, 341, 348
  heterosexism, 19, 73, 118, 265
Sexuality, 91, 165, 199, 203, 235, 287, 335, 342, 343, 354
  bisexual, 28, 203, 343
  gay, 28, 203, 337, 343
  heterosexual, 2, 26, 187, 188, 203
  LBGTQ, 148
  lesbian, vi, 28, 42, 67–73, 101, 203, 324, 343
Simulacrum 220, 221
Slavery (enslavement), xiv, 5, 7, 88, 99, 135, 148, 155, 297, 333
Smith, Barbara, 51, 323, 338
Social change, ix, 6, 7, 16, 17, 51, 84, 142, 148, 223, 228, 229, 278, 286, 332, 333, 335, 337, 344, 345, 346, 354, 355
Social conceptions, vii, 17, 245–257
Social desirability, 207
Socialization, xvi, xvii, xix, 115, 116, 186, 193, 204, 221, 246, 247, 250, 256
Social justice (education) and curriculum, 296, 297, 299
  educators 2, 17, 50, 119, 121, 176, 178, 193, 198, 222–227, 250, 272, 273, 276, 281, 289, 300, 329, 342, 343, 351
  leadership, 220–223, 226, 339, 357
  recognition paradigm, 25, 29, 30, 31, 32, 34, 37, 38, 39, 40
  (re)distribution (distributive) paradigm, 25, 26, 27, 28, 29, 30, 31, 32, 33, 37, 38, 39, 40
  procedural paradigm, 25, 32, 33, 34, 35, 36, 37, 38, 39, 40
  sustainable practice, viii, 341
  theory, v, 14, 23–40, 121, 139
  values, v, 1, 13
Social justice education (SJE)
  degree program, University of Massachusetts-Amherst, ix, 3, 343, 354, 357, 358, 360, 361
Social media *View under* media
Social support, 246, 251
Sociocultural difference, 26, 27, 34, 35
Solange, vi, 15, 16, 105, 118, 165–178
Southern Christian Leadership Conference (SCLC), 143
Spelman College, ix, 11, 44, 127, 357
Spokesperson, 71, 205–206, 214
Stakeholder, 309, 313
Stereotypes, 58, 60, 61, 62, 68, 77–80, 84, 186, 188, 191, 193, 194, 197, 209, 213, 278, 251
Stewart, Maria, 1, 83, 329, 336
Storytelling, vii, 17, 18, 1, 95, 254, 255, 275–283
  life stories, 4, 122, 135, 136

Strategic Planning, 309, 316
Stratification, 24–27, 290
Status recognition, 34, 35, 36
Stress (stressors), 50, 77, 78, 79, 81, 89, 128, 150, 159, 204, 212, 219, 221, 224, 229, 280, 341
  anxiety, 283, 310, 319
  depression, 114, 127, 280, 281, 282, 283
Structural intersectionality 225
Structures of oppression, 60, 166
Struggle, xvii, xvii, 7, 15, 31, 32, 40, 58, 63, 84, 87, 91, 117, 121, 122, 123, 129, 136, 138, 139, 140, 144, 146, 147, 156, 160, 162, 168, 170, 172, 174, 187, 192, 198, 205, 212, 213, 221, 231–233, 237, 241, 268, 274, 277, 292, 293, 300, 321–324, 327, 332–334, 336–339, 341, 343, 346, 351, 361
  social justice struggle, 30, 227
  sustainable struggle, 136, 346–350
Students, 2, 14, 15, 16, 17, 18, 20, 42, 44, 47, 50, 51, 65, 70, 73, 80, 82–83, 87, 113, 114, 122, 124, 125, 128, 134, 179, 183–198, 201–228, 231–244, 246, 251, 256, 257, 276–284, 285–303, 333, 340, 343, 344, 353, 356, 358, 360
  student activism, vi, 16, 89, 99, 100, 141, 142, 141–163, 274
  students of color, 82, 148, 152, 156, 233, 238, 256, 257, 293, 299, 301, 34, 358
  student leaders, vii, 17, 142, 275–284, 351
Student Nonviolent Coordinating Committee (SNCC), 160, 337
Students Against Social Injustice (SASI), 146–148, 152, 155, 156, 159
Subordination, xvii, 17, 18, 19, 34, 35, 60, 85, 101, 191, 311

#TakeDowntheFlag, 142, 147, 150–155

Teaching social justice, vi, vii, 16, 17, 183–199, 219, 228
  teacher education, 17, 231, 232, 234, 235, 238, 240–244, 355, 356
  teaching philosophy, 185
  *See also* classroom activities; pedagogy
*Teaching for Diversity and Social Justice*, 2, 3, 19, 40, 60, 64, 178, 198, 245, 250, 252, 255, 273, 285, 300, 301, 343
TED talks, 187, 190
Theorizing, 14, 24, 25, 26, 29, 30, 35, 37, 39, 100, 222, 229, 329, 350
Theory to praxis, vii, 18, 285–303
Token, 75, 205
Tolerance, 158, 215, 216
*Toward an Intellectual History of Black Women*, 20, 122
Transformative 2, 9, 16, 45
  transformative pedagogy, vi, 183–199
Transgender, 28, 337, 343, 220, 257, 279, 283
  *See also* gender
Transnational oppression, 91
Trustworthiness 34, 35, 36
Truth, Sojourner, x, 5, 19, 37, 83, 112, 221, 329, 336
Truth-telling, 327, 328, 330, 331
Tubman, Harriet, x, 5, 111, 117, 135, 136, 139, 322, 329, 336
  S. S. Harriet Tubman, 112, 117, 118

Unconscious bias, xv
United Nations Declaration of Human Rights (*see also* human rights), 2, 3, 19
United Students Against Sweatshops (USAS), 142, 146, 356
Unite Here, 144, 146, 159
University of Massachusetts-Amherst, 3, 253, 354, 356, 358, 360
  *See also* Social Justice Education degree program

University of Mississippi, 16, 141, 142, 145, 147, 155, 156, 157, 159, 160, 161, 162, 356
University of Missouri Concerned Student 1950 Collective, 149
Urban education, 358

Video, 97, 98, 144, 151, 160, 161, 186, 187–191, 196, 197, 198, 217, 237, 238, 266
violence, 18, 31, 37, 47, 91, 97, 122, 131, 142, 144, 154, 175, 192, 199, 242, 264, 320, 324, 331, 332, 336, 338
  anti-violence, 136
  cultural, personal, and structural violence, ix, 347, 348
  domestic violence, 322
  police violence 189, 325, 263
  racial violence, 162, 265, 343
  sexual violence, 193, 197, 198, 350
  state violence, 38, 168, 170, 179
  violence against women of color, 40, 229, 255, 273

Walker, Alice, 53, 221, 335
Wellness, (to be well), 20, 89, 122, 123, 137, 327, 335, 347, 349, 351
Whiteness xiv, xvii, 2, 154, 161, 168, 170, 174, 177, 180, 207, 208, 211, 224, 244
  white fragility, 15, 75–89
  white liberals, 204
  white privilege *See under* privilege
  White Racial Identity Development, 207
White supremacy, xiv, xvii, xix, 6, 93, 95, 101, 145, 147, 168, 172, 174, 177, 266, 321
Womanism (womanist, womanist standpoint), 11, 13, 14, 43, 52, 53, 245, 359

*The Womanist Idea*, 11, 44, 52, 136, 139, 140, 256, 349, 358
*The Womanist Reader*, 52, 358
Women of color, 11, 16, 37, 40, 55, 66, 143, 179, 203, 229, 254, 255, 256, 263, 264, 265, 273, 274, 307, 308, 316, 336, 358
Women's Army Corps, 108, 110, 138, 140
  6888th Central Postal Directory Battalion, 110, 111
  Early, Charity Adams, 110
  *See also* Mary McLeod Bethune
Women's experiences, 15, 253, 262, 345, 347
Women's rights, 5, 9, 330
Women's Voices, 14, 18, 24, 61, 95, 328
Workplace, 45, 53–66, 146, 157, 246, 250, 316, 258

Yosso's Theory of Cultural Capital, 230
  aspirational capital, 249, 250
  linguistic capital, 249
  navigational capital, 249
  social capital, 249
Young, Iris Marion, 31, 32, 42
Youth, 45, 143, 144, 161, 196, 202, 207, 281, 302, 338, 355, 356, 357, 358
  *Black Passports: Travel Memoirs as a Tool for Youth Empowerment*, 20, 343, 348, 353
  Black Youth Project, 338, 339
  National Youth Administration, 106, 114, 118
  youth of color, 285, 288, 289
  youth participatory action research (YPAR), 285, 286, 295, 298, 301
youthSpark, 350

Zúñiga, Ximena, ix, 19, 118, 193, 198, 199, 255, 351